Y0-AAJ-953

REFERENCE SERVICES FOR UNDERGRADUATE STUDENTS:

Four Case Studies

by

Billy R. Wilkinson

The Scarecrow Press, Inc.
Metuchen, N.J. 1972

ISBN 0-8108-0464-6

Library of Congress Catalog Card Number 70-184963

For Ann

CONTENTS

ACKNOWLEDGMENTS

The aid and encouragement of the faculty of the Columbia University School of Library Service are gratefully acknowledged. They awarded me a Title II B Fellowship. This U. S. Office of Education grant under the Higher Education Act made possible full-time work on the doctorate.

Special thanks go to former Dean Jack Dalton, Professor Alice I. Bryan, and Professor Oliver L. Lilley. Professor Lilley served as principal advisor throughout the project. His intelligent guidance, patience, and kindness shall always be deeply appreciated.

I am grateful to Rolland C. Stewart, Associate Director, University of Michigan Libraries; Giles F. Shepherd, Jr., Associate Director, Cornell University Libraries; James F. Govan, Librarian, Swarthmore College; and Evan I. Farber, Librarian, Earlham College, for permission to study the reference services for undergraduate students at their institutions. Many librarians gave their complete cooperation and made possible the case studies. Thanks are extended to the fifty-one librarians who granted interviews. My lasting gratitude is also expressed for the outstanding assistance of Rose-Grace Faucher and Agnes N. Tysse at the University of Michigan; Ronald E. Rucker, Frances W. Lauman, Caroline T. Spicer, Barbara J. Brown, and Judith H. Bossert at Cornell University; James F. Govan and Howard W. Williams at Swarthmore College; and Evan I. Farber and James R. Kennedy at Earlham College.

The dissertation would never have been completed except for the devoted help of my wife, Ann M. Wilkinson. She assisted from beginning to end--planning the case studies, serving as monitor of reference activity during the research phase, and typing the many drafts. All doctoral students should be so blessed.

LIST OF TABLES

Table		Page

Table Page

LIST OF FIGURES

FOREWORD

It has been said of Americans that they rarely examine the mythology which enshrouds their cherished symbols. At a time when universities are under attack, charged with neglecting undergraduates, undergraduate libraries stand out symbolically as weapons for the defense. To emphasize how much is being done for undergraduates, the value of these libraries is usually presented in terms of their cost, square feet, seating capacity, collection and staff size, and total numbers of items circulated--the whole rhapsody of data so dear to the technological society. As a result, these libraries are overdescribed and understudied and their reality is concealed in their myth.

For me, the refreshing aspect of Dr. Wilkinson's book is that he seeks to identify the return on the investment rather than dwell on the investment itself. He asks what the effect is of your efforts on the attitudes of undergraduates; whether students now perceive undergraduate libraries and librarians as being more active participants in their intellectual growth. It is at this point that some will cry, foul, that it is not the purpose of undergraduate libraries to change student attitudes but to provide efficiently the fundamental supermarket library services for undergraduates: study space, reserve materials, and multiple copies of basic books. This argument is not consistent with the hope of many who have planned undergraduate libraries. They envisioned a library vital to undergraduates and undergraduate education; one which would be integrated into the student's community of learning and involved in helping him leave the university a capable self-learner. It was intended that undergraduate libraries increase contact between librarians and students, forge new links with classroom, and destroy the physical barriers which stand between library materials and students.

Assessing the impact of any institution on people is a difficult matter and the student of behavior always encounters the dilemma of selecting an appropriate method of investigation. However, a good place to observe and classify an undergraduate's attitude toward the library is at a point where he meets and interacts with staff--at the reference desk. The kinds of questions the student addresses to the reference librarian reveal more than his particular information need. The student also expresses his expectations in the form of inquiries which he feels will be understood by the librarian.

Do the types of questions students ask at the reference desk vary from one academic library to another? If so, why? Can librarians, by altering their approach, affect the service expectations of students? These important issues are the subject of Dr. Wilkinson's case studies of the reference services at four different institutions. I hope that as you read this book you will not see it as a critique of the dedicated work of many reference librarians, but as a vehicle to help us explore new possibilities.

John R. Haak
Assistant University Librarian
University of California at
San Diego

La Jolla,
October 29, 1971

Chapter 1

INTRODUCTION

> The great advantage we have when studying such animals [unidentified squirrels in zoo cage] is that we ourselves are not black-footed squirrels--a fact which forces us into an attitude of humility that is becoming to proper scientific investigation. How different things are, how depressingly different, when we attempt to study the human animal. Even for the zoologist, who is used to calling an animal an animal, it is difficult to avoid the arrogance of subjective involvement.
>
> Desmond Morris, The Naked Ape, A Zoologist's Study of the Human Animal (New York: McGraw-Hill, copyright 1967), p. 14. Used with permission of McGraw-Hill Book Company.

The first separately housed undergraduate library on an American university campus opened on January 3, 1949. Lamont Library was designed especially for the undergraduate students of Harvard College. Keyes D. Metcalf[1] and others[2] have documented the early planning, actual design, functions, and operations of Lamont Library. Even though university librarians[3] were keenly interested in this separate approach to library service for undergraduates, no university built a separate undergraduate library during the ensuing decade; the University of Minnesota did open its Freshman-Sophomore Library in January, 1952 in a classroom building. However, since 1958 when the University of Michigan Undergraduate Library was completed, many universities have taken this "Bunyanesque step."[4] Other universities are presently in various phases of planning or building separate undergraduate libraries.

The literature of librarianship contains many articles

which are descriptions of individual undergraduate libraries or philosophical essays concerning library services for undergraduate students. Recently, Braden[5] and Mills[6] have studied in some detail several undergraduate libraries. Kuhn[7] surveyed nineteen undergraduate libraries. Muller[8] and Orne[9] have also written on the undergraduate library. In her dissertation, Braden brought together the most substantial body of material in existence on undergraduate libraries--those at Harvard, Michigan, South Carolina, Cornell, Indiana, and Texas. Each of these libraries was visited and interviews with various staff members were conducted; documents and files relating to the undergraduate library were consulted. Because of the range of her study--from the architectural design and financing of the building through the gathering of the initial collections of books and other media to the host of services offered in the completed library--Braden could give only limited attention to the individual functions and services of undergraduate libraries.

With so many universities following the lead of Harvard in creating separate undergraduate libraries, there is need for studies of this phenomenon. Continuing the survey work of Braden, there should now be detailed studies of these post-World War II libraries for undergraduate students with a concentration upon the various functions or services provided, i.e., reserve books, audio-visual collections and services, open-stack book collections, reference collections and services, provision of "study hall" seating, and social or "student union" aspects. Discussion are at their most impressionistic and romantic when the subject is reference services provided for undergraduates or the actual use made of such services by students. Universities now contemplating separate undergraduate libraries need more than impressions as guidance in this vital area. For these reasons, this book concentrates on only one library service for undergraduate students: assistance at the reference desk. Background information on the parent institution and coverage of other aspects of the selected libraries, however, accompanies the studies of reference services in order to place them in their proper context.

John R. Haak's definition of an undergraduate library will be used:

> an undergraduate library is defined as follows: (1) a special library for undergraduate students; (2) located in a university or other institution

> supporting graduate work to a significant degree; (3) housed in either a separate building or in a self-contained section of a general building; (4) consisting of a collection designed to support and supplement the undergraduate curriculum, and a staff and services which promote the integration of the library into the undergraduate teaching program of the university.[10]

The definition of reference services, developed by the Committee on Reference Standards and Statistics, Reference Services Division, American Library Association, will also be used:

1. Reference services in a library should be recognized as a central responsibility of library administration, specifically organized to ensure the optimum use of the library's collections.

2. The distinguishing feature of reference services is in its relationship to the library's patrons. These services are of two essential types--direct and indirect.

3. Direct reference service consists of personal assistance provided to library patrons in pursuit of information. Direct reference service may take many forms, each of which may consist of a number of activities, of which only the most frequent and representative are cited below:

    a) Instruction in the use of the library and in the use of items in the library's collections. This service may range from demonstration of how to fill out a call slip to explanation of the use of catalogs, bibliographies, and reference works, to assistance in interpreting the contents of materials in the library's collections. The central feature of this instruction, irrespective of its level or its intensity, is to provide guidance and direction in the pursuit of information, rather than providing the information itself.

    b) Information Service. This service may range from answering an apparently simple question through recourse to an obvious reference source, to supplying information based on search in the

> collections of the library, combining competence in bibliothecal techniques with competence in the subject of inquiry... . The central feature of information service, irrespective of its level or its intensity, is to provide an end product in terms of information sought by the library's patron.

4. Indirect reference service comprises the preparation and development of catalogs, bibliographies, and all other reference aids which help in providing access to the library's collections and which extend the library's services through cooperation with other, or larger, or more specialized libraries. This recognizes the significant role of the technical or processing services of the library as indispensable to the reference function.[11]

The major purpose of this study is to identify and describe reference services for undergraduate students on university campuses, as contrasted with reference services for students in four-year liberal arts colleges. The use[12] made of professional reference staffs by undergraduate students is a first but limited area of investigation; more importantly, there is an analysis of the types of questions[13] asked by undergraduate students.

A series of questions best states the problem:

1. Have planners of separate undergraduate libraries correctly estimated the use[14] by undergraduate students of professional reference services in the separate building?

2. Have directors of separate undergraduate libraries and heads of undergraduate reference services succeeded or failed in stimulating use by undergraduate students of professional reference services?

3. Have librarians in four-year liberal arts colleges succeeded or failed in stimulating use by students of professional reference services?

4. In what respects do the types of questions asked by undergraduates at the reference desk of an undergraduate library differ from the types of questions asked by undergraduates at the reference desk in the main library of a four-year liberal arts college?

5. In what respects do the types of questions asked by undergraduates at the reference desk of an undergraduate library differ from the types of questions asked by undergraduates at the centralized reference desk in the main library at the same university?

6. Are the greater resources (particularly the union catalog of campus holdings) of the main library's reference department such strong magnets that the separate undergraduate library on the same campus will be unable to attract extensive use of its reference services and catalog?

For the purpose of this investigation, it is assumed:

1. that university libraries should serve students at all levels--from the freshman year to post-doctoral work;

2. that libraries should offer adequate reference services, but that each library should be economically operated;

3. that professional reference librarians should be performing services for which they were educated; and

4. that it is wasteful and bad planning to assign professional staff members to positions where they are not performing to their full capacities.

Hypotheses

Before the investigation was begun, it was hypothesized:

1. that separate undergraduate libraries have overestimated the use which will be made of professional reference services by undergraduate students;

2. that use of reference services in undergraduate libraries has decreased after the first years of operation;

3. that communications[15] between librarians in undergraduate libraries and the faculty concerning reference services for their students have been minimal when contrasted with communications between liberal arts college librarians and faculty members concerning available reference services for their students;

4. that no effective means of stimulating use of reference services (such as integrating bibliographical lectures or discussions by librarians with courses at the exact time students have need of such assistance) have been developed by reference librarians in separate undergraduate libraries (there having been only a reliance on brief and general orientation lectures or tours at the beginning of the students' freshman year);

5. that there is a difference in the types of questions asked by undergraduate students at reference desks of liberal arts college libraries and those asked by undergraduates at reference desks in undergraduate libraries on university campuses, and

> a) that the major difference is that a greater proportion of reference questions concerning bibliographical assistance at the library's catalog is asked of liberal arts college reference librarians than is asked of reference librarians in undergraduate libraries;

6. that there is also a difference in the types of questions asked by undergraduate students at the reference desk of a main university library and those asked by undergraduates at the reference desk of the undergraduate library on the same campus, and

> a) that the major difference is that a greater proportion of reference questions concerning bibliographical assistance is asked of librarians at the main university library reference desk than is asked of reference librarians in the undergraduate library on the same campus; and

7. that unassisted use by undergraduate students of the union catalog of campus holdings increases use of the main university library and decreases use of the undergraduate library on the same campus.

Methodology

Because of a desire to concentrate upon only a few representatives within the given universe (reference services for undergraduate students), the case study was chosen as the appropriate type of research design. The major characteristics of a case study are its detailed, developmental nature and its concentration upon one highly selective unit. The purpose of a case study is the investigation over a given period of time of an existing (or formerly existing) situation so that the causal factors which were or are in operation can be determined. Cases were selected where there has been time and opportunity for maximum occurrence of the phenomena under investigation. In other words, the best examples have been sought, not the average or mediocre.

Two university library systems were selected as cases. They demonstrate:

1. provision of professional reference services in an undergraduate library separate from and in addition to the reference services in the main university library;

2. availability of both of these reference services during many of the hours which the undergraduate library is open;

3. financial support for up-to-date maintenance of a reference collection of 3,000 or more volumes in the undergraduate library; and

4. documentation of the reference services in both the undergraduate and main libraries for a period of over five years.

It did not seem necessary to control such aspects of the libraries as geographical location; size of staff, budget, or student body served; or nature of the university (private or public).

The two university libraries selected as cases are those at the University of Michigan, Ann Arbor, Michigan, and Cornell University, Ithaca, New York. Their separate undergraduate libraries are: the University of Michigan Undergraduate Library and the Uris Library, Cornell University. The reference services in the main university libraries correspondingly are: the Reference Department, University of Michigan General Library and the Reference Department, John M. Olin Library, Cornell University.

As archetypes worthy of imitation by undergraduate libraries on university campuses, two four-year liberal arts college libraries were selected as cases. By comparing and contrasting the reference services of these college libraries with those of undergraduate libraries, it may be possible to describe a standard or model of achievement for the future development of reference services for undergraduate students--whether they are enrolled at a "multiversity,"[16] one of the "cluster colleges"[17] of a host university, or a "library-college."[18]

These liberal arts colleges differ from the universities in that the colleges have only one major library for both undergraduates and faculty while the universities have large research libraries in addition to their separate undergraduate libraries. However, in the present rapid development of networks of inter-library cooperation, it is not too far-fetched to say that the liberal arts college libraries already have large research collections as a back-up for their local collections.

These college libraries correspond to the previously chosen undergraduate libraries in:

1. availability of professional reference services during many of the hours which the college library is open;

2. financial support for up-to-date maintenance of 3,000 or more volumes in the reference collection;

3. holdings of 80,000 or more volumes in the college collections; and

4. documentation of reference services during the past five years.

Additional criteria for selection of the colleges were:

1. an enrollment of at least 1000 students;

2. a large majority of students working on bachelor's degrees in liberal arts;

3. accreditation by appropriate regional accrediting association; and

4. co-education for women and men students.

Such factors as geographical location or nature of the college (private or public) do not need to be controlled.

The two liberal arts college libraries chosen as cases are: the McCabe Library, Swarthmore College, Swarthmore, Pennsylvania and the Lilly Library, Earlham College, Richmond, Indiana.

Gathering the Data

The data gathering phase of the study was a three-month period during the Fall semester of the 1969/70 academic year. From September 29, 1969 until December 16, 1969, two visits each were made to the libraries of the University of Michigan, Cornell University, Swarthmore and Earlham Colleges.

Data were collected primarily by means of documentary analysis, using annual and special reports, articles written by staff members, formal and informal memoranda and correspondence, and other documents which were available in the files of the individual libraries. Interviews with fifty-one reference librarians and library administrators were conducted to complete the data and to corroborate and supplement the written records. A tape recorder was used for fifty of the interviews; one person did not wish its use.

Other bodies of data are the records of actual use by undergraduate students of the Michigan, Cornell, Swarthmore, and Earlham reference services. During two separate five-day periods of heavy use, all questions asked by undergraduates at the selected reference desks were monitored by the candidate or his wife, who is also a librarian. During the hours of 10 A.M.-12 Noon, 1-5 P.M., and 7-9 P.M., Monday through Thursday; and 10 A.M.-12 Noon and 1-5 P.M. on Friday, the monitor listened to all questions asked at the reference desk and recorded, on an individual card, each undergraduate student's question, as it was actually asked.

Swarthmore's reference services were usually available on weekdays from 8:30 A.M.-12 Noon and 1-4:30 P.M. with no evening hours. The Reference Librarian attends a meeting on Friday morning. Therefore, the survey times at Swarthmore were adjusted to 9:30 A.M.-12 Noon and 1-4:30 P.M., Monday-Thursday, and 1-4:30 P.M. Friday.

Only professional staff members were on duty during the hours of the survey, with the exception of the Undergraduate Library of the University of Michigan. During six hours of the first week and eight hours of the second week, a Work-Study Scholar (a staff member currently enrolled in the University's School of Library Science) was one of two persons at the reference desks. A professional staff member was always with the Work-Study Scholar during the survey hours. Friday nights from 7-9 P.M. and Saturdays and Sundays were excluded from the study because of the decreased reference activity at these times.

Two separate periods of five days each were selected in order to sample the reference activity at different times during the same semester at the college or university. For the University of Michigan, the sixth week (October 6-10, 1969) and the eleventh week (November 10-14, 1969) of the Fall term were chosen. This term and its examination period ended on December 20, 1969. The University of Michigan has an academic calendar of three terms plus a summer half-term. The eighth week (November 3-7, 1969) and the thirteenth week (December 8-12, 1969) of the Fall semester comprised the sampling periods at Cornell University. All class meetings were completed at Cornell by December 20, 1969, but the examination period was not until January 12-20, 1970. Cornell has two semesters and a summer session. At both Michigan and Cornell, the activity at the reference desk in the undergraduate library was recorded by one monitor while the other monitor was recording during the same hours the questions asked by undergraduate students at the reference desk of the main university library.

At Swarthmore, the fifth week (October 20-24, 1969) and the eleventh week (December 1-5, 1969) of the Fall semester were used. The Fall semester did not end until January 30, 1970. Swarthmore has a two-semester academic year; there is no summer session. At Earlham, the fourth week (October 13-17, 1969) and the ninth week (November 17-21, 1969) of Term I were chosen. The term ended on December 3, 1969. Earlham operates on a three-term year with no summer school. The first three weeks and the last week of the term were purposely excluded as possible times to monitor the reference activity because of the atypical nature of these weeks.

At the reference desks in the University of Michigan Undergraduate Library and the Uris Library, all persons asking questions were assumed to be undergraduates, except in a very few instances when the questioner was obviously a faculty member, graduate student, or staff member.

Studies[19] at Cornell have shown that 91-93% of the questions asked at the Uris Library reference desk were asked by undergraduate students. Therefore, the monitor did not ask the questioner his academic status. The few apparent instances of faculty, graduate students, and staff members using these two reference desks were simply excluded from the data. However, the questions by undergraduates were distinguished from those of all other patrons at the reference desks of Swarthmore and Earlham libraries and in the main university libraries of Michigan and Cornell. At the conclusion of the question-answer dialogue between the patron and the reference librarian, the monitor asked each person his academic status. Only questions asked by the institutions' own undergraduates are included.

Telephone questions from undergraduates are included for all libraries except the University of Michigan, which has a policy of no telephone service for students.

The monitor attempted to be as unobtrusive as possible in order not to create an artificial situation, hinder anyone from approaching the reference desk, or antagonize patrons. It is believed that this attempt was successful. After the data gathering had been completed, the head of one reference department wrote: "Before you came we were a little concerned about the kind of reaction you might get to your questions from some of our clientele, but your approach was low-keyed and disarming, and--judging from what I was able to observe--there was little or no resentment."[20]

Definitions and sub-categories of questions were developed in advance of the actual field work. They were based on the United States of America Standards Institute's definition of a "reference question" as "any request for information or aid which requires the use of one or more sources to determine the answer, or which utilizes the professional judgment of the librarian."[21] However, elaborations were made and a time element was added to the definitions. It is recognized that the length of time which an individual question requires to be answered may be a factor of inexperience on the part of the reference librarian attempting the solution or of inadequacies of the collection. Nevertheless, the time spent on each question does somewhat indicate the superficiality or thoroughness of service and provides an estimate of the number of reference contacts during a certain time period.

For this study the definitions of major types of questions are:

1. Information question: requires brief directional answer from reference librarian who uses no library resources;

2. Reference question: requires use of one or more library resources and less than thirty minutes in obtaining answer;

3. Search question: requires use of several library resources and over thirty minutes but less than one hour in obtaining answer;

4. Problem question: requires use of several resources and more than one hour in obtaining answer.

In order to explore more fully the type of substantive question most frequently asked by undergraduate students, reference questions (No. 2 above) are sub-divided into the following categories:

R-1. Bibliographical assistance with the library's own catalogs and holdings;

R-2. Bibliographical assistance with the holdings of other campus libraries;

R-3. Bibliographical verification of material not on the campus;

R-4. Retrieval of factual, non-bibliographical information from any source;

R-5. Counseling of students in a reader's advisory capacity (reading guidance);

R-6. Informal personal instruction in use of library or any of its resources;

R-7. Miscellaneous questions not covered by the preceding six categories

In order to clarify further the definition of R-6 reference questions, it should be noted that some personal instruction takes place in almost all encounters between librarians and inquirers at a reference desk. The simple act of going to a particular reference source may teach the student that he might go there himself in the future when he has a similar question. However, questions were placed in the R-6 category only when more than this simple act was performed by the librarian. The R-6 questions are those instances in which the librarian overtly gave instruction to the student, spending at least some measurable amount of time in the process.

In the sections entitled "Samples of Questions" in the chapters on Michigan, Cornell, Swarthmore, and Earlham, when "information question," "reference question," "search question" or "problem question" appears in the text, the phrase refers to one of the definitions noted above. When "question" or "questions" is used, all four types of questions are meant.

A final procedure for collecting data was the interviewing of undergraduate students using the union catalog of holdings of all campus libraries at the University of Michigan and Cornell University. The fifth week (September 29-October 3, 1969) of the Fall term was chosen at the General Library of the University of Michigan. At Cornell University's John M. Olin Library, the seventh week (October 27-31, 1969) of the Fall semester was selected. The hours of each week's study were 10 A.M.-12 Noon, 1-5 P.M., and 7-9 P.M., Monday through Thursday; 10 A.M.-12 Noon and 1-5 P.M. on Friday.

All persons[22] using the union catalog at these times were asked their academic status at the university. If the user said he was an undergraduate, he was then asked if he would answer ten questions concerning his use of the union catalog and the undergraduate library's catalog. Non-undergraduate users were asked no questions; a tally was kept of their number in the various categories of academic status. Library staff members using the union catalog were totally excluded from the tally.

Analysis of the Data

Specifically, the first hypothesis (over-estimation of use of reference services in separate undergraduate libraries) was tested by an examination of the early written programs and plans for staffing the University of Michigan Undergraduate Library and the Uris Library at Cornell. Interviews with the directors of the two university libraries and with the first librarians of the undergraduate libraries supplemented the documentary data.

Hypothesis 2 (decreasing use of reference services in the undergraduate library after the first years of operation) was examined in conjunction with the monthly and yearly reports over an eleven-year period in the case of the University of Michigan and over a seven-year history for the Uris Library.

Hypothesis 3 (communications with faculty by librarians in both undergraduate and liberal arts college libraries) was tested by interviewing librarians in both the undergraduate and liberal arts college libraries. Extant written communications (as defined previously in this chapter) were collected and reviewed.

Extensive questioning in the interviews with librarians in the undergraduate and college libraries was the tool used to test hypothesis 4 (integrated bibliographical lectures at time of need versus freshmen orientation lectures or tours). Documentary evidence (complete scripts, outlines, or notes of lectures) was also examined in connection with this hypothesis.

Hypotheses 5, 5a, 6, and 6a (the differences in the types of questions asked by undergraduates) were tested in the following way: the investigator defined, categorized, and monitored all reference questions asked during two separate five-day periods at each of the selected reference desks. Individual reference librarians with their varying skills, backgrounds, experience, and interpretations of reference questions were not called upon for this stratification of data. A monitor, instead, performed the task. Therefore, evidential data consisting of all the questions asked by undergraduate students at six different reference desks were collected for the two time periods previously noted.

In order to gather and analyze data for testing hypothesis 7 (unassisted use by undergraduates of union catalogs in main university libraries), interviews of all undergraduate users during a five-day period were conducted in the General Library, University of Michigan, and the John M. Olin Library, Cornell University.

Limitations of the Study

The reader is forewarned of the following limitations of the study:

Questions are asked in various areas of a library of both professional and non-professional staff. An example of this is the staff member working at the library's public catalog who is asked both simple and difficult questions about how to use the catalog or for an interpretation of information on a card in the catalog. No attempt has been made to study all questions asked by undergraduate students in a library. Only those questions asked at the library's reference desk when a professional staff member was on duty are included. The exclusion of questions asked at other places in the library does not mean that they are insignificant. Only a logistical problem of recording them accurately precluded them as data.

Both Swarthmore and Earlham Colleges have separate science libraries where reference services are available in addition to the reference assistance in the main college libraries. These science libraries are briefly described, but there is no analysis of the reference questions asked in the science libraries. In a similar manner, there are numerous special libraries on the Michigan and Cornell campuses where undergraduate students receive reference assistance. This study, however, is limited to the reference services in the undergraduate and the main university libraries.

In sections dealing with the actual questions asked by undergraduate students, each question was recorded as asked, not as might be finally negotiated by a student-librarian dialogue.

No attempt was made to evaluate the sources used by the librarian in answering the question. Nor was there any attempt to find out the degree of satisfaction of the student with the answer. These were outside the scope of the study.

The final limitation is inherent in the research method selected--the case study. Only four cases are described. This gain in depth naturally sacrifices breadth. It is, therefore, not possible to generalize the findings into theories applicable to the reference services for undergraduate students in other college and university libraries. However, in time, with the accumulation of additional cases, the theorizing may begin with a more solid foundation than is possible at present.

Notes

1. Keyes D. Metcalf, "The Lamont Library, Part II: Function," *Harvard Library Bulletin*, III (Winter, 1949), 12-30.

2. Morrison C. Haviland, "The Reference Function of the Lamont Library," *Harvard Library Bulletin*, III (Spring, 1949), 297-99.
   Philip J. McNiff, "The Charging System of the Lamont Library," *Harvard Library Bulletin*, III (Autumn, 1949), 438-40.
   ________ and Edwin E. Williams, "Lamont Library: the First Years," *Harvard Library Bulletin*, IV (Spring, 1950), 203-12.
   Richard O. Pautzsch, "The Classification Scheme for the Lamont Library," *Harvard Library Bulletin*, IV (Winter, 1950), 126-27.
   Henry R. Shepley, "The Lamont Library, Part I: Design," *Harvard Library Bulletin*, III (Winter, 1949), 5-11.
   Edwin E. Williams, "The Selection of Books for Lamont," *Harvard Library Bulletin*, III (Autumn, 1949), 386-94.

3. "Library Service to Undergraduates: a Symposium," *College and Research Libraries*, XIV (July, 1953), 266-75. Contains articles by Arthur M. McAnally, Stanley E. Gwynn, Philip J. McNiff, William S. Dix, and Wyman S. Parker.

4. Jerrold Orne, "The Place of the Library in the Evaluation of Graduate Work," *College and Research Libraries*, XXX (January, 1969), 27.

5. Irene A. Braden, "The Separately Housed Undergraduate Library," *College and Research Libraries*, XXIX (July, 1968), 281-84.
   ________, *The Undergraduate Library* ("ACRL Monographs," No. 31; Chicago: American Library Association, 1970).
   ________, "The Undergraduate Library on the University Campus (unpublished Ph. D. dissertation, Dept. of Library Science, University of Michigan, 1967).

6. Elizabeth Mills, "The Separate Undergraduate Library," College and Research Libraries, XXIX (March, 1968), 144-56.

7. Warren B. Kuhn, "Undergraduate Libraries in a University," Library Trends, XVIII (October, 1969), 188-209.

8. Robert H. Muller, "The Undergraduate Library Trend at Large Universities" in Advances in Librarianship, ed. by Melvin J. Voigt (New York: Academic Press, 1970), I, 113-32.

9. Jerrold Orne, "The Undergraduate Library," Library Journal, LXXXXV (June 15, 1970), 2230-33.

10. John R. Haak, "Goal Determination and the Undergraduate Library," (paper presented at the Institute on Training for Service in Undergraduate Libraries, University of California, San Diego, August 17-21, 1970), p. 1.

11. Louis Shores, "The Measure of Reference," Southeastern Librarian, XI (Winter, 1961), 299-300.

12. "Use" is defined as the number of questions asked by undergraduate students at a reference desk where a professional is on duty.

13. The "types of questions" are defined as:
    1. Information question: requires brief directional answer from reference librarian who uses no library resources;
    2. Reference question: requires use of one or more library resources and less than thirty minutes in obtaining answer;
    3. Search question: requires use of several library resources and over thirty minutes but less than one hour in obtaining answer;
    4. Problem question: requires use of several library resources and more than one hour in obtaining answer.
    Reference questions (No. 2 above) are sub-divided into seven categories which are defined later in Chapter 1.

14. "Use" is defined as the number of questions asked by undergraduate students at a reference desk where a professional is on duty.

15. "Communications" are defined as: conferences with chairmen of departments and with individual faculty members; informal discussions between librarians and faculty in any academic or social situation; orientation sessions given by librarians for new faculty; brochures, letters, memoranda, or other written material sent to faculty by librarians; and other similar methods.

16. Clark Kerr, The Uses of the University (Cambridge: Harvard University Press, 1964), pp. 9-28.

17. H. R. Kells and C. T. Stewart, "Summary of the Working Sessions; Conference on the Cluster College Concept," Journal of Higher Education, XXXVIII (October, 1967), 359-63.

18. Robert T. Jordan, "The 'Library-College,' a Merging of Library and Classroom," Libraries and the College Climate of Learning, ed. Dan Bergen and E. D. Duryea (Syracuse: Program in Higher Education of the School of Education and the School of Library Science, Syracuse University, 1964), 51-60.

19. Cornell University. Library. "Library Use Survey," May 17-20, 1965 and January 10-13, 1967. (In the files of the John M. Olin Library.)

20. Letter from Agnes N. Tysse, Head, Reference Department, University of Michigan General Library, to Billy R. Wilkinson, November 18, 1969.

21. United States of America Standards Institute. Sectional Committee Z39 on Standardization in the Field of Library Work and Documentation. U. S. A. Standard for Library Statistics (New York: United States of America Standards Institute, 1969), p. 17.

22. One interviewer was able to ask all persons using the union catalog his academic status and then had sufficient time to interview all undergraduate users. In the planning stage, only a sampling of the users was

thought possible. However, a test run of the procedure at the University of Michigan union catalog proved that a sampling device was unnecessary.

Chapter 2

THE PHENOMENON OF THE SEPARATE UNDERGRADUATE LIBRARY

> I am confident that this new Lamont Library will have a great influence on American education.
>
> Harvie Branscomb, "The Future of Libraries in Academic Institutions, Part III." Harvard Library Bulletin, III (Autumn, 1949), p. 339.

Early History

Before concentrating on the past twenty years when the major development of undergraduate libraries occurred, the historical precedents of library services for undergraduate students in colleges and universities should be briefly noted.

Wagman[1] has traced the idea of a separate undergraduate library back to the early years of the seventeenth century in England. Sir Thomas Bodley made his famous proposal in February, 1598 to Oxford University to restore the library. For the next fifteen years, Bodley made the Oxford library the "one passion"[2] of his life. Even before the opening of the library in 1602, he had hired Thomas James as his librarian to assist in this passion. It was as first Keeper of the Library that James recommended in 1608 the establishment of an undergraduate library to serve the younger students at Oxford. Bodley, however, refused to approve the idea, writing to James:

> Your deuise for a Librarie for the yonguer sort, will have many great exceptions, & one of special force, that there must be an other keeper ordeined for that place. And where you mention the yonguer sort, I knowe what bookes should be brought for

> them, but the elder aswell [as] the yonguer, may have often occasion to looke vpon them: and if there were any suche, they can not require so great a rowme. In effect, to my understanding there is muche to be saide against it, as vndoubtedly your self will readily finde, vpon further consideration.[3]

There was so "muche to be saide against it" that little was done for Oxford undergraduates for the next 150 years. Finally, in 1856, the statutes of the Bodleian Library were changed to allow undergraduates as well as graduate students to study in the library.[4] The Radcliffe Camera was the reading room in which the undergraduates might read if they presented a written note from their tutors and wore their gowns. Only fifty seats were available for all readers. The number of undergraduates admitted to the Camera in the 1860's averaged only eighty per year.[5] But by 1872 the graduates complained that they were being inconvenienced by the undergraduates.

With the appointment of Edward Williams Byron Nicholson as Librarian of the Bodleian in 1882, a librarian with more sympathy for the needs of undergraduates took charge of the Radcliffe Camera. He wanted many more books on open shelves: a select collection for undergraduates, a reference library for researchers, and a periodical reading room. Nicholson immediately selected some 6,000 volumes as a students' library and placed them on open shelves in the Camera. This was, however, a short-lived period of open access. In 1894 he was forced to lock up the collection because of book losses.[6]

American Colonial Colleges

On the American scene, nine colleges have had a continuous history from before the revolutionary war with Great Britain. Harvard, established in 1636, is the oldest American college. A grant of four hundred pounds from the Massachusetts General Court was the initial gift in 1636. Two years later, the "Rev. John Harvard, of Charlestown, gave by his will the sume of £779. 17. 2 in money, and more than three hundred volumes of books."[7] Thus was begun the first college library in this country. Shores[8] has chronicled the early history of Harvard College Library and the libraries of William and Mary, Yale, Princeton, Columbia, Pennsylvania, Brown, Rutgers, and Dartmouth. The various rules, regulations, and codes of these libraries clearly reveal that the undergraduate student was not a pampered library patron. Libraries existed primarily for the faculty. The early college libraries also had very small collections. Harvard, the largest, had only 13,000 volumes before 1800; Rutgers, the smallest, had a few hundred volumes. The other seven colonial college libraries had holdings ranging from 1,000 to 4,000 volumes.[9]

There were two responses to this inadequate service for undergraduate students: the segregation of books into a separate library for students and the founding of society libraries by the students themselves.

As early as 1765, the separation of books considered most suitable for use by students was required by the laws of Harvard College Library.[10] "There shall be a part of the Library kept distinct from the rest as a smaller Library for the more common use of the College."[11] This was not very effective because Harvard librarians, throughout the succeeding years, continued to recommend the same measure as a way to serve undergraduates.

In reaction to the restrictive nature of the regulations of use and the small number of volumes available to them, students began to found society libraries. For example, Yale College students Timothy Dwight, Nathan Hale, and James Hillhouse began the Linonia Society Library in 1769; the Brothers in Unity Library was begun later.[12] Both of these student society libraries were housed in separate wings of the college library building. In later years, they were combined in a browsing room of Yale's Sterling Library.

Harvard College

The society libraries, however, were not the magic answer to the library problems of undergraduate students. Harvard students, who were provided with a small collection in the anteroom of the College Library in Gore Hall and also had their own society libraries, drew up in 1857-58 a proposal calling for an undergraduate library in a separate building which would be free from the restrictions of the College Library.[13] These nineteenth century students, using the tactics of twentieth century students, condemned the "utter inadequacy of the College library to meet the wants of undergraduates in their last two years."[14] Their own society libraries were also found lacking: "The Society libraries, intended to supply a want which the College library cannot, are in this College few and confined either to a half or to a small minority of the upper classes."[15]

Again in the same year, students petitioned

> that the lower story of Holden Chapel, when no longer needed for its present use, be granted to the Senior Class, as a Reading Room, Club Room, and Undergraduate Library, to be open in regular course to every member of the two upper classes.[16]

A faculty committee to investigate the situation was appointed. The committee succeeded in getting the faculty and the Harvard Corporation to approve some extension of hours and greater accessibility of current periodicals.[17] Protests by the undergraduates simmered down for several years.

Then, in 1870, the students petitioned again. This time they were promised the lower floor of Massachusetts Hall if the students themselves would come forward with sufficient money for the support of the reading room. In 1872 the students organized a Reading Room Association, raised enough money to furnish the room, pay a student attendant, and subscribe to several periodicals and newspapers.[18] The quarters in Massachusetts Hall were officially granted, but the Reading Room Association was short-lived.

A professor of history and a new librarian of Harvard College Library finally combined to give the students better library service. In 1875, Professor Henry B. Adams, who as a student had signed the student petition of 1857-58, petitioned the Harvard Corporation for reading space for his students in the College Library.[19] President Charles W. Eliot backed Adams and the Library was soon cleared of showcases and other fixtures and given over to more accommodations for readers. Then, Justin Winsor, who had been head of the Boston Public Library, was appointed Librarian of Harvard in 1877. Winsor began a reserve book system, extended the hours of opening, and by 1880 admitted students to the stacks for limited periods of time.[20]

The Columbia College Study

Another prominent ancestor of the separate undergraduate library on American university campuses was the Columbia College Study established in Hamilton Hall in 1907. It became the Columbia College Library in 1934, moving into its present quarters in the Butler Library. "Columbia was the first American university to provide special library facilities for its undergraduates (1907)."[21] To borrow a phrase from the musical Guys and Dolls, the Columbia College Library is the "oldest, established, permanent, floating" undergraduate library on the campus of an American university.

James H. Canfield, Librarian of Columbia, 1899-1909, stated the case for a library for Columbia College students in his 1905 annual report:

> There is again a demand for the establishment of departmental libraries in that building [Hamilton Hall] for the convenience of officers and students. The distance from the Library building, and all the other usual arguments, are being put forth in favor of this demand.
>
> I beg leave to suggest that a proper treatment of this subject will involve the use of one of the large rooms at either end of the building, say, on the second floor, as a reference library for Columbia College. In this may be placed the books now in the undergraduate Historical Reading-Room, and any other books available for undergraduate work--either by duplication or by temporary withdrawal from the main Library. By a system similar to that which enables us to place on special reserve the texts referred to by instructors, this collection could be kept fresh from term to term and from year to year, and would exactly meet the daily demands of both officers and students. A thoroughly trained and expert custodian should have charge of this room, with at least one page, and with local telephone connections with each department. It is not too much to say that the service thus made possible would surpass in convenience and satisfaction any service which could possibly be rendered by and through the departments themselves, with smaller collections in each department: and would be free from the objections to

> this latter plan, upon the score of extraordinary expense in duplication, or in care, and from the inevitable delay and annoyance caused by the necessary overlapping and interlacing of the interest of departments.[22]

Only two years later, Canfield happily reported:

> The establishment of the College Study--undoubtedly the best lighted, best ventilated, and most commodious reading room on the campus--is an excellent illustration of our desire to help undergraduates to help themselves, our constant effort to develop in the student self-reliance in the selection and use of books. It also enables us to test a theory which is not new, but which thus far has never been put into actual practice. That is, that a collection of not to exceed 6, 000 volumes, carefully selected and kept fresh and up-to-date in every sense of the word, is sufficient to meet all ordinary demands of the undergraduates of the average college. This has been given just a half year's trial, and the result is entirely satisfactory. In a certain sense this is a branch library. From another standpoint it is an undergraduate seminar. Books are classified and shelved according to subjects of instruction and are held for reference only. The open-shelf system prevails, except as to something less than a thousand volumes, which are in such constant demand that the special reserve scheme seems necessary there. It has been our good fortune to have Mr. [C. Alexander] Nelson, the head reference librarian of the University, as the administrator of this new undertaking, in which his wide and varied library experience has been of great value. The use of this collection has increased steadily since its opening day, averaging nearly 1, 100 readers each week; and from officers and students alike come words of commendation and satisfaction. Many of the books have been purchased expressly for the College Study, but a large number are loans from the main Library, returnable to the Library, when the course of instruction changes. Undergraduates are not forbidden to use the main Library; but this special collection fitting so admirably their daily work, in the building in which their classes and lectures are held, proves far

> more convenient and far more attractive than the Library itself. We have every reason to be satisfied with this experiment.[23]

Upon reading Canfield's praises of the Columbia College Study in 1907, the present day undergraduate libraries do not seem so pioneering. At this early date Columbia had already established an undergraduate library in a classroom building, appointed a librarian of the College Study who seemed attuned to the needs of students, and gathered a collection of books based directly on the curriculum which were freely accessible to the students. However, it should be remembered that the library was only one study room with a very small, non-circulating collection.

Harvard in the Twentieth Century

To return to Harvard and its early twentieth century developments, the year 1915 stands as the high point. In 1915 a Reference Librarian was appointed to assist students and faculty in their use of the library; a handbook, Notes on the Use of the Harvard College Library, was published; and the new Widener Library was dedicated.[24] Complaints, however, continued about the library services for undergraduate students.

A. Lawrence Lowell, who became President of Harvard in 1909, wished to strengthen undergraduate education as against the emphasis on the graduate and professional schools under President Eliot (1869-1909).[25] Lowell's dream finally became a reality in 1930 when Lowell House and Dunster House opened. Five other Houses followed a year later. This residential plan for undergraduates sought to bring together students and faculty as part of the tutorial system of instruction begun in 1926.[26] Each House had its own library, ranging in size from six to ten thousand volumes. These libraries were administered by the students and tutors, who were directly responsible to the House Master, not to the Director of the University Library. By 1948 the holdings of each library averaged twelve thousand volumes. Harvard undergraduates thus "enjoyed the use of intimate library service in their House libraries with a minimum of cost and a minimum of formality."[27]

Metcalf has summarized the library facilities available for undergraduates from 1932 until the opening of the

Lamont Library in 1949 as:

> 1. Those in the Harry Elkins Widener Memorial Library, which house the larger part of the central collection of the Harvard University Library which is called the Harvard College Library.
> 2. The reserved book reading rooms and collections that represent primarily an overflow from Widener, and are found in Boylston Hall and in the Union.
> 3. The House Libraries.
> 4. Other libraries, special and departmental, throughout the university which provide a greater or lesser amount of service to the undergraduate students.[28]

But he also stated that:

> A student at Amherst, Williams, Dartmouth, Bowdoin, Oberlin, or one of the better women's colleges has at his or her disposal a much larger and better collection of books than has the Harvard undergraduate. The House Libraries with 10, 000 to 12, 000 volumes each, and the Union Library with 18, 000, are the largest general collections completely available to the undergraduate student, and this in spite of the large number of different facilities described earlier in this statement, and in spite of the fact that the students use freely the main reading room in the Widener building, which itself contains in its chief stack area 2, 000, 000 volumes and pamphlets. This central collection is so large that it cannot be opened to the undergraduate except under very special circumstances, and as a result there is no large general collection freely accessible to the undergraduate at Harvard--no collection which will include a large share of the volumes that the student will need in any of his work or in the general reading which is desirable for him to do when in college.[29]

Undergraduate Quarters within University Libraries

During the first half of the twentieth century, other university libraries began to set aside reading rooms, special collections, and reserve books for their undergraduate students. Often these undergraduate quarters were within the main university library. In other instances, such as at the University of Colorado and the University of Nebraska, the reader services for all students and faculty were organized into a divisional plan.[30] Open-shelf collections and service were divided according to broad subject areas (usually three divisions: humanities, social sciences, and sciences). Literary form (periodicals, monographs, reference volumes, or documents) or library function (reference assistance or circulation) were no longer the criteria for the library's organization. Improved library service for undergraduates was a factor in the conversion to a divisional plan. In still other universities with relatively small numbers of undergraduate students, such as Princeton, there was no need for separate collections or services for undergraduates.[31] Open access by undergraduates to the stacks was the policy.

Lamont Library, 1949

The previous excursions into the past history of college and university libraries in England and the United States confirm the fact that undergraduate libraries were not a new concept in university library service. The Lamont Library at Harvard was not a new idea. It was rather the scale on which Lamont was envisioned and then built that was the new development.

The background of this new development began in 1937 when Keyes D. Metcalf was appointed as Librarian of Harvard College and Director of Harvard University Library. By that time, the Widener Library was regarded as too large and impersonal for undergraduates. It was also full. Metcalf's first decision was whether or not to plan on the construction of a new central library for Harvard. He later wrote:

> This, let us say, would have been the conservative thing to do. It would have followed standard practice, and would have made possible greater centralization in a university library system which had become too decentralized. But all idea of a new, central library building at Harvard was given up 'for our time.' To start with, the cost was prohibitive. It was then [1938] estimated that $10,000,000 would be required for the first unit of a new building.[32]

No suitable site in a central location was another deterrent. "A third and equally important reason was that a building of the size needed would be so large as to be unwieldly from the standpoint of service."[33] For these reasons, the idea of a new central library was dropped and another plan was developed.

A study of Harvard's library situation revealed that more space was needed for books, staff, and readers. Two other problems demanded solutions. The Widener Library also lacked adequate quarters for valuable collections of rare books and manuscripts, and it did not provide adequate quarters and services for undergraduates in a building where the needs of researchers were so demanding, where undergraduates had to use a catalog containing millions of cards, and where, it was thought, they could not be given direct access to the stacks.

With all this in mind, a master plan was developed to house parts of the Harvard Library. Four new units were recommended:

1. The New England Deposit Library for the storage of little used material;

2. The Houghton Library for rare books and manuscripts;

3. Undergraduate Library;

4. Underground stacks in the college yard for the expansion of the Widener collection.[34]

The Houghton Library for rare books and manuscripts and the New England Deposit Library were both opened in 1942, leaving the undergraduate library and underground stacks for Widener's collections until post-World War II completion. The Lamont Library was not an isolated event in itself, but was part of a four-pronged solution to the many library problems facing Harvard.

Lamont was planned on three suppositions:

1. That undergraduates will make more and better use of a library designed expressly for them;
2. That this was the best way to relieve the pressure in the Widener building and make unnecessary

a new central library building; and
3. That if that pressure were relieved, the Widener Library building would become a more satisfactory research center than it has been in the past.[35]

In the words of the architect for Lamont:

> The philosophy on which the functioning of the Library was based required, first, that it be conveniently located and inviting of access. It should be on one of the main undergraduate traffic routes, and there should be no flights of steps to the entrance or monumental vestibules or foyers to traverse before coming to the books. Second, once within the Library, the student should find the entire book collection as accessible as possible.[36]

Construction of the "first library building to be devoted primarily to undergraduate needs"[37] began with the announcement of a major gift from Thomas W. Lamont. Ceremonies dedicating the completed Lamont Library were held on January 10, 1949[38] and a conference on "The Place of the Library in a University," March 30-31, 1949, celebrated the completion of the building program which had included the Houghton, Deposit, and Lamont Libraries.[39]

Era of Separate Undergraduate Libraries

Thus, what might be pompously labeled as the new Age of the Separate Undergraduate Library began with the opening of the Lamont Library in 1949. Almost overnight Lamont became a living legend. It was idealized. Librarians from all over the world made pilgrimages to the shrine. Although university librarians were keenly interested in this separate approach to library services for undergraduate students, no university was financially able to build a separate undergraduate library during the next nine years. The University of Minnesota did open its Freshman-Sophomore Library in 1952 in a classroom building.[40]

In 1955, Taylor[41] surveyed the libraries of thirty-six institutions belonging to the Association of American Universities to ascertain the current status of library services for undergraduate students. Responses were received from twenty-nine large university libraries throughout the United

States. She found that only ten of the twenty-nine libraries had their stacks open to undergraduates.[42] However, "fifteen of the twenty-nine universities responding to the questionnaire have developed separate collections for undergraduates."[43] These were usually in the main university library.

Within a few years, this situation was to change radically. In 1958, Lamont's eldest son was born: the University of Michigan opened its Undergraduate Library. During the next decade, in rapid succession, many other universities opened separate undergraduate libraries. Undergraduate libraries in new buildings were built on the campuses of the University of South Carolina,[44] Indiana University,[45] the University of Texas,[46] Stanford University,[47] the University of North Carolina at Chapel Hill,[48] the University of Illinois,[49] Ohio State University, Pennsylvania State University, the University of Tennessee, and the University of California at Berkeley. New buildings are planned or under construction at the Universities of Wisconsin, Oklahoma, Maryland, British Columbia, and Washington (Seattle).[50]

Other universities built new research libraries, extensively remodeled their original main libraries, and reopened them as undergraduate libraries. Cornell University,[51] the University of California at Los Angeles,[52] and Michigan State University took this route. The University of Nebraska[53] remodeled over one-half of the largest building on the campus into an undergraduate library-museum-classroom facility. Hawaii, Emory,[54] and Duke[55] Universities recently completed new research libraries and are now renovating their former main library buildings into undergraduate libraries. The University of Florida constructed a graduate library and uses its older main library as an undergraduate library, but did not refurbish it. The University of California, San Diego, also created a new research library and moved its Cluster I Library into the building formerly occupied by the research collection.

It has not been a totally unquestioned trend toward separate undergraduate libraries. The University of South Carolina, which opened its undergraduate library in 1959, is now planning to centralize library services and eliminate the undergraduate library as a separate entity.[56] Indiana University, which created an undergraduate library in 1961, has now vacated it upon the completion of a new university library designed to serve the entire university community. A five-story tower provides undergraduate service and collection; an eight-floor tower houses the general book collection, seminars, carrels, and faculty studies. Connecting the two wings are public service departments and staff work areas.[57] New York University and the Universities of Notre Dame, Miami, and Iowa have also elected the same approach as Indiana. The University of Massachusetts[58] is contemplating the construction of area libraries for undergraduate service in place of one large central undergraduate library.

Kuhn has compiled information on the undergraduate libraries already in operation as well as those in some planning phase or actually under construction. His essay,[59] with data ranging from project costs and seating capacity to the number of volumes and staff members, is a summary of the status of undergraduate libraries in the United States in the late 1960's. The source for the most current information is the UGLI Newsletter,[60] edited by John R. Haak. Under the leadership of Haak, undergraduate librarians met together at the American Library Association convention in June, 1969 to discuss their work. The 1970 ALA convention in Detroit was the scene of a program on undergraduate libraries sponsored by the University Libraries Section of the Association of College and Research Libraries. This widespread interest in undergraduate libraries was further confirmed by the approval and funding by the U.S. Office of Education of the Institute on Training for Service in Undergraduate Libraries,[61] held at the University of California at San Diego, August 17-21, 1970, under the direction of Melvin J. Voigt. In addition to Voigt, Irene A. Braden, Patricia B. Knapp, Warren B. Kuhn, John R. Haak, and Billy R. Wilkinson served as instructors and delivered papers.[62] Thirty librarians were selected to participate in the institute. A preconference on undergraduate libraries was held prior to the American Library Association's 1971 convention in Dallas.

Literature of the Movement

In the published literature and in less formal discussions of undergraduate libraries during the past twenty years, little attention has been given to the services available in these libraries. The use made of the services by students has also received scant coverage. The chroniclers have devoted themselves to more tangible data (i.e., architectural plans, seating, selection of initial collection, audio equipment, and number of volumes circulated). Only Braden[63] has probed into the services of undergraduate libraries and attempted any evaluation of them. In her study of the undergraduate libraries at Harvard, Michigan, South Carolina, Indiana, Cornell, and Texas, she included reference services as one of the topics in her descriptive analysis of each library. Her findings concerning reference services at the first modern undergraduate library, Lamont, are not the uncritical descriptions typically written for the readers of alumni magazines or as glowing announcements to the library profession of a new building or service.

Braden, after interviewing Harvard librarians, wrote:

> For several reasons, the demand for reference services proved to be less than was expected in the Lamont Library. First, Lamont is largely used as a study hall; second, a major use of the library is for reserve books; third, students can serve themselves in getting books from the open stacks; and fourth, students have learned that to do research in depth, it is necessary to use the larger collections in Widener. Another reason for the lack of demand for reference service may be attributed to the nature of Harvard students. Most of the students are self-reliant and can find what materials they need by themselves. Only when they have exhausted their own resources do they ask for help.[64]

In 1949 the assistant librarian in charge of reference work in Lamont had stated that:

> The primary concern of the reference staff is to aid students in the use of the library. The whole staff joins with the reference staff in implementing this principle. The reference staff is available throughout the time the library is open to assist students in locating the materials they require for course work, for collateral reading, for special reports or term papers, or for leisure time enjoyment.[65]

When this philosophy of service was written, there were seven professional staff members in Lamont (three in reference, three in circulation, and the head librarian). When Braden studied Lamont, there were only two librarians on the staff, with reference assistance being provided by trainees.[66]

Instruction in the use of the library also declined over the years. By 1965, there was "little instruction in library use. Students are helped as individuals when they ask for aid, but there are few such requests."[67]

Braden's final conclusions concerning the Lamont Library were:

> It succeeded in providing a building that was suited to the undergraduates' needs. The book collection began as a basic collection of general literature but has been broadened to meet the expanding student needs. However, the division of the collection into so many distinct segments proved to be a detriment to its use. The proliferation of multiple copies for reserve has been extended too far. The reserve system appears to be a contradiction of the original plan of simplicity. Neither the division of the collection into three parts nor the unclassified order provide ease of use if a particular item is sought.
>
> The decrease in reference staff has accompanied a decrease in demand for service. The circulation system in use has satisfied the students' needs. Lamont has been generous in the special services provided for the undergraduates and has succeeded in centralizing undergraduate services, but the efforts at simplification seem to have backfired at Lamont. The decrease in professional staff and the removal of the remaining professional staff from contact with the students does not conform to the standards originally set up for the Lamont Library. Perhaps this has been in part the reason for the decline in use of the library.[68]

The phenomenal development of undergraduate libraries has continued to occur without any detailed studies of their various services. Are undergraduate libraries only an unqualified success as study halls? Are the collections meeting the needs of present-day undergraduates? Have the reference services of undergraduate libraries been successes or failures? These and many other questions must be asked; answers must be attempted.

The following case studies of reference services for undergraduate students are presented in the hope that the data will bring somewhat closer the answer to the question of the success or failure of reference services.

Notes

1. Frederick H. Wagman, "Library Service to Undergraduate College Students, a Symposium: The Case for the Separate Undergraduate Library," College and Research Libraries, XVII (March, 1956), 150.

2. Donald G. Davis, Jr., "Problems in the Life of a University Librarian: Thomas James, 1600-1620," College and Research Libraries, XXXI (January, 1970), 44.

3. Sir Thomas Bodley, Letters of Sir Thomas Bodley to Thomas James, ed. with an Introduction by G. W. Wheeler (Oxford: Clarendon Press, 1926), p. 183.

4. Sir Edmund Craster, History of the Bodleian Library, 1845-1945 (Oxford: Clarendon Press, 1952), p. 145.

5. Ibid.

6. Ibid., pp. 240-41.

7. Samuel A. Eliot, A Sketch of the History of Harvard College and of Its Present State (Boston: C. C. Little and J. Brown, 1848), p. 6.

8. Louis Shores, Origins of the American College Library, 1638-1800 ("Contributions to Education, George Peabody College for Teachers," No. 134; Nashville, Tennessee: George Peabody College for Teachers, 1934).

9. Ibid., p. 229.

10. Keyes D. Metcalf, "The Undergraduate and the Harvard Library, 1765-1877," Harvard Library Bulletin, I (Winter, 1947), 29-30.

11. Harvard University. College Book No. 7, pp. 145-150, quoted in Louis Shores, Origins of the American College Library, 1638-1800 ("Contributions to Education, George Peabody College for Teachers," No. 134; Nashville, Tennessee: George Peabody College for Teachers, 1934), p. 186.

12. Shores, pp. 224-25.

13. Kimball C. Elkins, "Foreshadowings of Lamont: Student Proposals in the Nineteenth Century," Harvard Library Bulletin, VIII (Winter, 1954), 42.

14. Harvard University. Harvard College Papers, 1857, "Considerations in Favor of an Undergraduate Library and Reading-Room," quoted in Kimball C. Elkins, "Foreshadowings of Lamont: Student Proposals in the Nineteenth Century," Harvard Library Bulletin, VIII (Winter, 1954), 43.

15. Ibid.

16. Harvard University. Harvard College Papers, 1857, [Petition], quoted in Elkins, p. 46.

17. Elkins, pp. 49-51.

18. Ibid., p. 52.

19. Robert W. Lovett, "The Undergraduate and the Harvard Library, 1877-1937," Harvard Library Bulletin, I (Spring, 1947), 222-23.

20. Ibid., pp. 223-24.

21. Columbia University. Library. "A Description of the Libraries" (Columbia University Library, February, 1967), p. 6. (Mimeographed.)

22. Columbia University. Library. Report of the Librarian for the Academic Year Ending June 30, 1905. pp. 243-44.

23. Ibid., ...June 30, 1907, pp. 184-85.

24. Lovett, pp. 233-34.

25. Clark Kerr, The Uses of the University (Cambridge: Harvard University Press, 1964), pp. 16-17.

26. Frank N. Jones, "The Libraries of the Harvard Houses," Harvard Library Bulletin, II (Autumn, 1948), 362.

27. Ibid., p. 374.

28. Keyes D. Metcalf, "The Undergraduate and the Harvard Library, 1937-1947," *Harvard Library Bulletin*, I (Autumn, 1947), 289.

29. *Ibid.*, p. 296.

30. Frank A. Lundy, "Library Service to Undergraduate College Students, a Symposium: The Divisional Plan Library," *College and Research Libraries*, XVII (March, 1956), 145.

31. William S. Dix, "Library Service to Undergraduate College Students, a Symposium: Undergraduates Do Not Necessarily Require a Separate Facility," *College and Research Libraries*, XVII (March, 1956), 149.

32. Keyes D. Metcalf, "Harvard Faces Its Library Problems," *Harvard Library Bulletin*, III (Spring, 1949), 185.

33. *Ibid.*

34. Philip J. McNiff, "Library Service to Undergraduates, a Symposium: Lamont Library, Harvard College," *College and Research Libraries*, XIV (July, 1953), 269.

35. Metcalf, "Harvard Faces Its Library Problems," p. 187.

36. Henry R. Shepley, "The Lamont Library, Part I: Design," *Harvard Library Bulletin*, III (Winter, 1949), 5.

37. Keyes D. Metcalf, "The Lamont Library, Part II: Function," *Harvard Library Bulletin*, III (Winter, 1949), 29.

38. "The Dedication of the Lamont Library," *Harvard Library Bulletin*, III (Spring, 1949), 304.

39. "Conference on the Place of the Library in a University," *Harvard Library Bulletin*, III (Spring, 1949), 305.

40. Robert H. Rohlf, "The Freshman-Sophomore Library at Minnesota," College and Research Libraries, XIV (April, 1953), 164-66.

41. Constance M. Taylor, "Meeting the Needs of Undergraduates in Large University Libraries" (unpublished Master's thesis, Graduate School of Library Science, University of Texas, 1956).

42. Ibid., p. 51.

43. Ibid., p. 74.

44. J. Mitchell Reames, "Undergraduate Library, University of South Carolina," Southeastern Librarian, X (Fall, 1960), 130-36.

45. Irene A. Braden, "The Undergraduate Library, Indiana University," in her The Undergraduate Library ("ACRL Monographs," No. 31; Chicago: American Library Association, 1970), 78-92.

46. Harry H. Ransome, "Academic Center: A Plan for an Undergraduate Library," Library Chronicle of the University of Texas, VI (Winter, 1960), 48-50.

47. Warren B. Kuhn, "The J. Henry Meyer Memorial Library, Stanford University," California Librarian, XXIX (April, 1968), 93-99.

48. "There are No Barriers Between Students and Books," University of North Carolina, Chapel Hill Alumni Review, LVII (October, 1968), 12-18.

49. Lucien W. White, "University of Illinois Award Winning Library," Illinois Libraries, L (December, 1968), 1042-46.

50. Kenneth S. Allen, "Proposed Undergraduate Library-Food Services Building, University of Washington, Seattle" (American Library Association, 1967 Library Buildings Institute, Buildings Committee for College and University Libraries, June 5, 1967). (Mimeographed.)

51. "A Second Youth for Main Library," Cornell Alumni News, LXV (January, 1963), 4-17, 20.

52. Elizabeth Mills, "The Separate Undergraduate Library," College and Research Libraries, XXIX (March, 1968), 152-54.

53. Frank A. Lundy, "The Undergraduate Library at the University of Nebraska: the Nebraska Hall Project, 1969." February, 1969. (Mimeographed.)

54. "Advanced Studies Library at Emory University," Library Journal, LXXXXIV (December 1, 1969), 4400.

55. Benjamin E. Powell, "Redoubled Gothic for Duke," Library Journal, LXXXXIV (December 1, 1969), 4397-98.

56. Letter from Kenneth E. Toombs, Director of Libraries, University of South Carolina, to Billy R. Wilkinson, March 4, 1970.

57. Robert A. Miller, "Indiana's Three-In-One," Library Journal, LXXXXIV (December 1, 1969), 4399.

58. Mary Jo Lynch and Gary L. Menges, "A Proposal for Undergraduate Library Service, 1970-1980" (University of Massachusetts/Amherst Library, February 2, 1970). (Mimeographed.)

59. Warren B. Kuhn, "Undergraduate Libraries in a University," Library Trends, XVIII (October, 1969), 188-209.

60. UGLI Newsletter. No. 1, July, 1969- . (Edited by John R. Haak, University of California at San Diego, La Jolla, California.)

61. California University. San Diego. Library. "Proposal [to the U.S. Office of Education] for an Institute Entitled Training for Service in Undergraduate Libraries, August 17-21, 1970." Director: Melvin J. Voigt. La Jolla, California, University Library, University of California at San Diego, 1969. (Mimeographed.)

62. Papers presented at the Institute of Training for Service in Undergraduate Libraries, University of California, San Diego, August 17-21, 1970:

Irene A. Braden, "The Undergraduate Library-The First 20 Years."
John R. Haak, "Goal Determination and the Undergraduate Library."
Patricia B. Knapp, "The Library, the Undergraduate and the Teaching Faculty."
Warren B. Kuhn, "Planning the Undergraduate Library."
Melvin J. Voigt, "The Undergraduate Library; The Collection and Its Selection."
Billy R. Wilkinson, "The Undergraduate Library's Public Service Record: Reference Services."

63. Irene A. Braden, _The Undergraduate Library_ ("ACRL Monographs," No. 31; Chicago: American Library Association, 1970).

64. _Ibid._, p. 18.

65. Morrison C. Haviland, "The Reference Function of the Lamont Library," _Harvard Library Bulletin_, III (Spring, 1949), 299.

66. Braden, _The Undergraduate Library_, p. 19.

67. _Ibid._, p. 21.

68. _Ibid._, pp. 25-26.

Chapter 3

CASE I: THE UNIVERSITY OF MICHIGAN

> The multiversity is an inconsistent institution. It is not one community but several--the community of the undergraduate and the community of the graduate; the community of the humanist, the community of the social scientist, and the community of the scientist; the communities of the professional schools; the community of all the nonacademic personnel; the community of the administrators. Its edges are fuzzy--it reaches out to alumni, legislators, farmers, businessmen, who are all related to one or more of these internal communities. As an institution, it looks far into the past and far into the future, and it is often at odds with the present.... A community should have a soul, a single animating principle; the multiversity has several--some of them quite good, although there is much debate on which souls really deserve salvation.
>
> Clark Kerr, The Uses of the University (Cambridge: Harvard University Press, 1964), pp. 18-19.

Brief History of the University

When Michigan was still a Territory, an elaborate educational plan was devised. The territorial government established the "Catholepistemiad,[1] or University of Michigania" on August 26, 1817.[2] With this erudite name, the University of Michigan was born. The University was to be the capstone of an elaborate educational system of colleges, academies, libraries, museums, and other institutions. From the plan would emerge "the foremost university of the great West and indeed the first model of a complete state university in America."[3] The University's actual development did not begin until after Michigan was admitted to the United States. A group of Ann Arbor residents, who formed the Ann Arbor Land Company, offered forty acres as a site for the University. On March 20, 1837, the offer was accepted by the legislature. A Board of Regents was then appointed and held its first meeting in Ann Arbor on June 5-7. At this organizational meeting, the first appointee to the University staff was the librarian.[4]

On September 25, 1841, the University opened with a completed building, three professors, a librarian, and seven students. During the first decade "the University was... merely a small country college with a curriculum based on the classics and mathematics."[5]

During the past century the University of Michigan has developed into one of the outstanding universities of the country, with eighteen colleges and schools and more than 120 teaching departments. The University of Michigan grants more degrees than any other university in the nation.[6] The original Ann Arbor campus has been supplemented with the North Campus of 874 acres.

Actual enrollment statistics for the sixteen schools and colleges on the Ann Arbor campus during the Fall term, 1969, were 20, 299 undergraduate students and 11, 704 graduate students, a total of 32, 003 students.[7] The other two campuses enrolled 2, 323 students (Flint College: 1, 501 students; and Dearborn Campus: 822).[8] During the same autumn term in Ann Arbor, 2, 362 full-time faculty members and 1, 865 part-time faculty were employed.[9]

The University of Michigan is accredited by the North Central Association of Colleges and Secondary Schools.

The College of Literature, Science, and the Arts

Prominently situated in this environment of a multiversity is its largest unit--the College of Literature, Science, and the Arts. During the nineteenth century, the Department of Literature, Science, and the Arts was a small but prominent part of American Academe. (The name was officially changed to the College of Literature, Science, and the Arts in 1915.) The twentieth century brought an increasing complexity to the College. New departments were created; old departments were divided. By 1937, there were 5,000 students and more than 300 faculty members in the College.[10] The College now surpasses in size many universities. In the 1969 Fall term, 12,442 undergraduates were enrolled and 3,600 graduate students were studying under the direction of the College faculty.[11] The faculty included 668 full-time members, 207 part-time teachers, and 1,100 part-time teaching fellows.[12] Courses were offered in twenty-eight departments.

In capsulated form, this is the University of Michigan and its largest unit, the College of Literature, Science, and the Arts. These are the institutions which the university libraries serve. These are the thousands of undergraduate students who are potential library users.

The University of Michigan Library

The University of Michigan Library began with the very founding of the University in Ann Arbor. At the Regents' first meeting in 1837, the Reverend Henry Colclazer, an Ann Arbor minister, was designated as librarian even before any faculty members were appointed.[13] There was little progress in developing the library until 1856, when it was installed in remodeled quarters. For the first time, the library had a reading room and daily library service.[14] John L. Tappan, the son of the President, was appointed as Librarian in 1856. He "may properly be called the first Librarian of the University."[15] In June, 1877, the entire collection consisted of 23,909 volumes and 8,000 pamphlets.[16] The Reverend Andrew Ten Brook served as Librarian from 1864 until 1877.

In 1881 the legislature appropriated $100,000 for the first separate library building on the Ann Arbor campus. Completed and opened in 1883, the brick structure was "situated a little to the south of the geometric centre of the campus [and] as its purpose requires, easily accessible from the buildings of all Departments."[17] Raymond C. Davis, University Librarian (1877-1905), in an address at the dedication, appealed for books to accompany the new building:

> A great library, rich in all literature, and in all science, is needed in this wide Northwest, to which the <u>litterateur</u> and the scientist may resort

> with a reasonable certainty of finding what they want.
>
> This needs no argument, no amplification. The seats of great libraries in this country are few. Away to the east is Boston, with Cambridge hard by. This is one, and the best; New York is two; Philadelphia, three; Washington, four; and these are all, and they are all distant from us. Why may not Ann Arbor become five, and in one collection meet the wants of the students under tuition here, and of independent workers elsewhere whose convenience will be best served by coming here?[18]

Davis was prophetic. Although not the fifth "seat of great libraries," the University of Michigan was the fifth largest university library in the United States on July 1, 1969.[19] Table 1 shows the growth of collections and use of the libraries for the years 1877-1969.

Byron A. Finney was appointed Reference Librarian in 1891, and after 1900, professionally trained librarians began joining the staff.[20] Service to the University thus began to increase. Davis was succeeded as Librarian by Theodore W. Koch (1905-1915). Bookstacks were added to the south of the building in 1910. Two innovations were made by Koch: some 3,000 additional reference volumes were added to the meager collection of dictionaries, encyclopedias, and atlases which had been contained in one small case in the main reading room, and students were now allowed to borrow books for home use.[21]

In 1915 William W. Bishop was appointed University Librarian and an appropriation was secured from the legislature for a new building. The new General Library was built on the same site as the 1883 building, with only the fireproof bookstacks being retained in the new design.[22] Wilhelm Munthe described the building:

> The factory-like and yet refined design of Michigan University Library still represents the end of an era of library building. How long will we have to wait for an architect to carry on from there? How long before we have a book tower without the architectural camouflage of historical styles?[23]

The University of Michigan had to wait fifty years. In 1970 a seven-floor book tower was added.

Table 1.--Volumes and Home Loans, University of Michigan Libraries, 1877-1969[a]

Year	Volumes on June 30	Home Loans During Previous Academic Year
1877	31, 909	. .
1883	ca. 40, 000	. .
1890	ca. 90, 000	. .
1915	352, 718	. .
1929	ca. 700, 000	. .
1941	1, 134, 052	. .
1953	1, 550, 914	313, 897
1954	2, 277, 620[b]	343, 340
1955	2, 350, 353	392, 394
1956	2, 411, 628	429, 092
1957	2, 512, 731	479, 268
1958	2, 603, 074	537, 175
1959	2, 669, 733[c]	632, 120
1960	2, 791, 041[c]	663, 362
1961	2, 908, 206[c]	682, 164
1962	3, 013, 015	774, 668
1963	3, 177, 940	814, 479
1964	3, 308, 866	895, 750
1965	3, 440, 799	946, 390
1966	3, 584, 331	1, 002, 408
1967	3, 714, 642	1, 025, 661
1968	3, 889, 066	1, 065, 061
1969	4, 084, 677	1, 085, 336

[a]Michigan. University. Library. Annual Reports of the Director. 1953/54-1968/69.

Raymond C. Davis, "The Growth of the Library," Michigan. University. Public Exercises on the Completion of the Library Building of the University of Michigan, December 12, 1883 (Ann Arbor: University of Michigan, 1884).

William W. Bishop, "The Library Service to the University," Michigan Alumnus, XXXV (May 18, 1929), 611-14.

[b]Monographs, chiefly unbound material which had not been previously reported, now included in record of holdings.

[c]Corrected figures.

William Warner Bishop, who has been called "a Nestor among American librarians,"[24] guided the Library for twenty-six years. It developed from a good university library into a great research library. In 1915 the Library had 352, 718 volumes; an annual book budget of $32, 000; a staff of 30; a salary appropriation of $26, 774; and a minimum salary of $450. At Bishop's retirement in 1941, "the Library holdings had risen to 1, 134, 052 volumes and the budget appropriation to $216, 685, of which more than a third--in addition to substantial trust funds--was available for book purchases; the staff numbered 118, with a minimum salary of $1, 034."[25]

The University Library, 1941-1952

Professor of English Warner G. Rice became librarian in September, 1941. "The wartime period of emergency measures was followed by a period during which even greater emergencies were caused by the sudden 'explosion' in student population and the wholly unprecedented burdens placed on library service."[26] The number of faculty members increased and the volume of sponsored research projects grew. The rise in costs of books and other materials, the increase in the number of publications each year to be acquired, and the need for more staff to select, process, and service the collections all became problems for the University Library.

Even though departmental libraries continued to spring up about the campus, the need for sufficient space for books, readers, and staff became more and more crucial. Rice summarized the situation:

> Small additions were made to divisional libraries; some space for new libraries and reading rooms (usually much less than was asked for) was assigned in new buildings planned for the campus.... In August, 1946, Michigan obtained a federal loan, to be expended in planning an extension to the General Library.... Complete plans were ultimately drawn, and approved, for the extension of the existing building on the east, south, and west, with the raising of the stack tower. In 1952, however, this project was finally discarded. For it, there was substituted in 1953 a plan to erect a storage library on the North Campus. This met, in part, the difficulty of finding space for books; but the larger problem of getting really adequate accommodations for readers, for library operations,

> and for book collection in constant use remained. The expedient suggested, but not immediately feasible, was the construction of an undergraduate library.[27]

The University Library, 1953-1969

Frederick H. Wagman became Director of the Library in August, 1953 when Professor Rice returned to the English Department as Chairman. Plans were drawn for a storage library on the North Campus to house 300, 000 volumes and the bindery which would move from the basement of the General Library.[28] When the building was completed in January, 1955, the congested conditions of the stacks in the General Library and the departmental libraries were relieved.

In 1967 Wagman summarized the previous fifteen years of library development.[29] From 1951 to 1967 the collections grew by 70%. In 1950/51 there were 152 staff members (in full-time equivalents) compared with 425 in 1966/67, an increase of 180%. Using home loans as a limited indicator of use of the libraries, loans jumped from 334, 000 in 1950/51 to 1, 024, 909 in 1966/67--an increase of 200%.

Director Wagman singled out two important developments during the period:

> Among the noteworthy developments of the past fifteen years are first and foremost the qualitative improvement of the collections and their expansion to include publications in broad new subject areas....
>
> Perhaps the most dramatic development of the past fifteen years, however, has been the effect of the Undergraduate Library on patterns of library use and of undergraduate instruction. The liberal attitude toward the library user which characterizes the Undergraduate Library has extended to all other libraries in the University Library system, which now admit to their collections all members of the University community.[30]

Profile of Users

Two studies conducted in 1961 and 1968 furnished details concerning library users. The first[31] was a mail questionnaire sent to the faculty. It was determined that:

> Three-fifths of the 1,355 respondents to the questionnaire say that they use University libraries at least once a week. Almost all phases of library activities are evaluated very favorably. The courtesy and cooperation of the libraries' staff are rated particularly favorably. The quality of book collections is also rated highly. The library buildings and facilities, however, meet with considerable criticism....
>
> The most favorable over-all ratings are given to the library by the Medical and Dental Schools and the College of Engineering; the least favorable by the College of Literature, Science, and the Arts. Within the latter College, the social science and humanities departments are considerably more critical of the library than the physical and biological science departments. Those departments with their own branch libraries tend to be more satisfied with the existing system than those which depend on the General Library.[32]

The second study, a General Library Utilization Survey,[33] was devised, pre-tested, and then conducted on four days in 1968. Its major findings were:

> An overwhelming percentage of the surveyed patrons (71.7) were enrolled in the School of Literature, Science, and the Arts. By class, the undergraduates accounted for over half of the surveyed General Library users (56.1%). A combination of class standing and field of study showed the L.S.&A. undergraduates to be the highest at 42.3%, compared to graduates...at 29.4%.... The highest percentages of surveyed L.S.&A. students majored in History, English, Science and Library Science [the last was at that time a department of L.S.&A.]....
>
> ...Use of the General Library throughout the semester did not change significantly among... those four days the survey was conducted.
>
> ...The greatest percentage of patrons reported "Studying, using personal materials." The other activities accounting for over 10% of the survey were, in descending order: searching the card catalog, using the books from the stacks, withdrawing books, using the periodical collection,

> using books on reserve, looking for a book that couldn't be found, and using reference materials.... The third section of the questionnaire asked the patron where he sat in the General Library during this visit. The second floor reference room ranked highest, the graduate reserve reading room second and open carrels third....
> The final section of the questionnaire deals with the patrons' reasons for using the General Library rather than any of the other university libraries. The two overwhelming reasons were first, "Only this library had my books and periodicals" and second, the General Library was quieter....[34]

Profile of Staff

Through these surveys, an accurate profile of the users, particularly of the General Library, developed. A profile of the library staff is necessary to complete the picture.

In July, 1968, the staff of 567 persons was composed of 147 professional positions, 275 full-time non-academic positions, 26 Work-Study Scholars,[35] and part-time employees (119 full-time equivalents).[36] The professional staff members have the title "Librarian" ranked in five levels (III-A, III-B, IV-A, IV-B, and V). These staff members work in the General Library, the Undergraduate Library, and approximately 41 other libraries and collections on the Ann Arbor campus.

Library Budget

The "largest budget increase in its history"[37] was received by the Library for 1964/65. Funds were granted for thirteen new professional jobs and eighteen additional clerical positions. A sum of $150,000 was added to the book funds. From fiscal 1966 to 1967, another large increase of 17% was appropriated. By fiscal 1969 the budget, exclusive of federal and foundation grants, income from trust funds, and internal service funds was $4,231,023.[38]

The Future

In 1965 the General Library housed 1,400,000 volumes (41% of the total holdings of the University). It was overcrowded by 200,000 volumes.[39] As early as 1962, Director Wagman had submitted a plan for an annex. The new building, officially named the Harlan Hatcher Graduate Library in honor of the former University president, was finally begun in 1967 and completed in 1970, at a cost of approximately $5, 517, 000 for construction and furnishings. The high-rise building has a book capacity of 800, 000-900, 000 volumes and 532 carrels assigned to doctoral candidates, faculty, and masters students, in that priority.[40] The first step in improving the General Library complex had been achieved.

Another step toward improved library facilities will be the interior renovation of the General Library. Planning funds were appropriated on July 1, 1969 by the legislature, but had not been released by March, 1970. Approximately $1, 000, 000 was also included in the Governor's 1970/71 budget request for the first phase of construction.[41]

The General Library has long functioned as the capstone of the library system. It now serves as a library for graduate students, advanced undergraduates, and faculty in the humanities and social sciences. The Hatcher Graduate Library will enlarge this service. However, the General Library remains the central library with the Public Catalog listing campus holdings; extensive collections of government documents, journals, society and academy publications; and over 90% of the microforms in the library system.[42]

The Undergraduate Library

William Warner Bishop, University Librarian, has been credited with the idea for a Michigan undergraduate library.[43] Frederick Wagman has also attributed the Michigan proposal to Harlan Hatcher, University President, and Charles Odegaard, Dean of the College of Literature, Science, and the Arts.[44] It was clear to University administrators by 1951 that undergraduates should no longer be ignored. They drew up a plan for a storage library on the North Campus and for a separate undergraduate library on the main campus. Actual planning did not begin until the arrival of Wagman as Director in 1953.

In November, 1953, nine faculty members representing six schools and colleges were designated as an Advisory Committee on the Undergraduate Library. They deliberated with Wagman in preparation for the writing of a program for the architects. The discussions were far-ranging: smoking regulations, content of the book collection, reserve books, listening facilities, and a host of other areas.[45]

By August, 1954, a preliminary program[46] had been drafted. It was revised and the final program[47] was submitted in February, 1955. The program called for a flexible, inviting building where books would be "arranged in such fashion that the reader is constantly aware of their proximity and their accessibility."[48] Requests were made for 2,500-3,000 seats, 150,000 volumes in free-standing cases, an audio room, exhibit areas, a multipurpose room seating 200 people, and a student lounge with coffee and soft drinks available. A card catalog in a prominent location in the ground floor lobby or between the lobby and reading room was specified. The program envisioned these reference facilities:

> On the ground floor directly adjacent to the catalog, with no door separating them, there should be a reference center with room for two desks and chairs, four bookcases, and four file cases. The reference librarians should be visible to the people using the catalog.
>
> Within the reading rooms on each of the other floors, ... there should be a prominently located reference alcove with space for one desk and chair, two bookcases, and a file case.[49]

The location of the building had already been determined--a site on the southeast section of the campus near the General Library. The program also requested that 350 seats and space for the collection of the Engineering Library be located on one floor.

The Building

The architects, Albert Kahn Associates, began preparations of working drawings by June, 1955; excavation began on April 3, 1956.[50] The second separate undergraduate library in the country was completed during the next twenty-one months. Wagman recorded the climax:

> At 8 A.M. on January 16, 1958, President Hatcher turned the key in a front door of the Undergraduate Library, officially opening it for use. This simple ceremony, witnessed by a small audience of faculty, University administrators, and students, was the culmination of four years of planning and construc-

> tion. It symbolized the University's effort to come to grips with one of the more elusive and frustrating problems of higher education and of librarianship. At various universities in this country it has become apparent that the old university library buildings with their huge, inaccessible collections and complicated catalogs do not offer a satisfactory means of providing good library service at the undergraduate level. It is becoming increasingly clear that, if students are to be stimulated to read and professors to teach with books, special facilities must be designed with the needs of these students in mind.[51]

The University of Michigan Undergraduate Library was built at a cost of $3, 105, 000 for the building, furniture, and equipment with the entire amount furnished by the legislature. A building of 145, 036 square feet in five floors was achieved.[52] The initial cost of the book collection was $200, 000, with another $200, 000 invested in acquiring and cataloging the opening day collection. Staff salaries amounted to $138, 000 during the first year of operation.[53]

The Collection

Rolland C. Stewart, then Head of the Book Selection Department, was responsible for the selection of the Undergraduate Library collection. He had some assistance from faculty members, librarians, and a small clerical staff, but he deserves major credit for the selection during the two and one half years before the Library's opening. Packard,[54] Braden,[55] and Stewart[56] have documented the complex selection process.

Periodicals, a reference collection, phonorecords, and duplicate copies for reserve use also had to be selected. After consultation with the faculty, 160 periodical titles were agreed upon by opening day.[57] By November, 1957, 800 reference volumes were acquired.[58] For the Audio Room, the School of Music chose approximately 1, 000 recordings.[59] Duplicate copies for reserve were purchased during the first semester in the building.

"On November 18, [1957], 44, 321 volumes... in 890 cartons were piled in a mountain in the lobby of the Undergraduate Library."[60] The collection has since grown to 155, 986 volumes (June 30, 1969). Table 2 traces the yearly growth.

Each professional on the Undergraduate Library staff was assigned responsibility for book selection in subject areas in which he had a background or interest.

Subscriptions for periodicals grew rapidly from 160 to 224 in 1959. Of these, some 142 had fairly extensive back files; 82 began with 1957 or 1958. Ten years later in October, 1969, 306 periodicals were received.[61] Another 24 subscriptions were received for binding copies.

Table 2.--Volumes in the Undergraduate Library, University of Michigan, 1956-1969[a]

Year	Volumes on June 30
1957	30, 910
1958	54, 388
1959	68, 590[b]
1960	74, 222
1961	81, 521
1962	86, 072
1963	98, 554[b]
1964	107, 817
1965	120, 080
1966	125, 822
1967	133, 227
1968	146, 129
1969	155, 986

[a]Michigan. University. Library. Annual Reports of the Director. 1956/57-1968/69.

[b]Corrected figures.

In 1969 the Undergraduate Library received thirteen newspapers. Another fifteen local Michigan papers were gifts.[62] During the first years, the Library did not have any microforms. In 1962/63, The New York Times on microfilm was added. By May, 1969, the Library had acquired 1, 233 reels of the Times and 18 reels of Scientific American.[63]

The Staff

The 1955 "Program for an Undergraduate Library" called for prominently located reference alcoves on at least three floors. An author catalog of the books on that floor would be located near the alcove. By August, 1956, this plan for decentralization of the professional staff throughout the building had been abandoned. The Committee on the Undergraduate Library Staff, a group of five senior librarians appointed to assist in the planning, "was told that it had been decided to have only one complete catalog--on the first floor."[64] The majority of the Committee "expressed concern that the Catalog Department had decided that the duplication and upkeep of complete [sic] catalogs on each floor would be too expensive."[65] Only one member held that students would not use the catalogs very much if they were provided.

The Committee then agreed to continue planning for a professional staff to be located on three floors. Margaret I. Smith, Head of the Reference Department, was commissioned to estimate the "size of staff needed to give good reference service."[66] It was suggested that one librarian be placed in charge of all reference service, and was surmised that the Head of the Undergraduate Library, having other responsibilities, would not be available for reference duty.

Robert H. Muller, Associate Director, then asked for reconsideration of the original plan of dispersed reference services. He envisioned the reference librarian's becoming competent in the subjects and materials on the particular floor, guiding students in their use, maintaining liaison with faculty in these fields, and selecting books to support the teaching of the subjects.[67]

When the Library opened, a compromise had been effected. There were five card catalogs for the Undergraduate collections: a complete dictionary catalog (author, title, and subject cards) in the lobby, three author catalogs (at the rear of the main floor and on the lower and second floors, each for locating books only on that floor), and a catalog for the phonorecords in the Audio Room.[68] However, the reference librarians were stationed only on the main floor--one at a Catalog Information Desk in the lobby with the main catalog and two at Reference Desks on the main floor adjacent to the reference collection.[69] Neither the reference collection nor the staff had been decentralized.

A time factor also entered the picture:

> We knew that we were going to open in the middle of the academic year. Obviously, we knew that, although we had to hire the staff before we opened the doors, we did not need a budget for a full year's complement of people.... So we estimated what we would need for the rest of that year.[70]

The Undergraduate Librarian was the first staff member employed. Roberta Keniston assumed her duties on July 1, 1957. She immediately familiarized herself with all aspects of the development of the Library to that point--three to six months from opening day. Her next major project was selection of the professional staff. When Mrs. Keniston accepted the librarianship, plans called for fourteen professionals.[71] This number was derived from the estimate by Margaret Smith for staffing the original three reference alcoves. Another estimate predicted that the reference services in the Undergraduate Library would probably average 750 questions per week. This forecast assumed that the Library would continue to occupy the same size quarters for seven or eight years, that no reference desks would be added, and that the student enrollment would not grow to more than 40, 000 by 1965.[72] But by July, 1957, there were only seven positions including Mrs. Keniston. The University had received a large cut in its appropriations. After an analysis of sample schedules for reference service, Mrs. Keniston found that it was impossible to keep open the desired hours with a staff of only seven.[73] She requested that the professional staff be increased to nine by reducing the rank of some positions. The Director of the University Library approved this request in August, 1957.[74]

The librarians were then selected: six transferred from other campus libraries, one came from the Ann Arbor Public Library, and another from the University of Illinois. Applicants were also invited for clerical positions and part-time student assistantships. During the first term, the staff consisted of nine librarians, seven full-time library assistants, one permanent half-time employee, and sixty-seven part-time student assistants.[75]

Although professional positions remained constant for several years, there was a large increase in clerical positions. On April 30, 1969, the staff members were ten librarians,[76] seventeen full-time assistants, and three Work-

Study Scholars. The part-time hours had increased to about 50,000 per year.[77]

Until November 15, 1965, the Head of the Undergraduate Library reported directly to the Director of the University Library; the Undergraduate Library is now under the supervision of Rolland C. Stewart, Associate Director.

Most processing of materials for the Undergraduate Library has been done in the General Library's Technical Services Department. The Undergraduate Library staff selects, searches, and prepares orders for its own monographs and serials. The Technical Services Department does all further processing and returns materials ready for use. However, the staff of the Audio Room of the Undergraduate Library receives phonorecords and tapes directly and completes their processing.[78] Vertical file materials are processed entirely in the Undergraduate Library.

Keniston's Librarianship, 1957-1963

If credit were limited to individuals, Rolland C. Stewart would be singled out for his work on the book collection. Frederick H. Wagman would be named for his planning of the building. And Roberta Keniston would stand as the person who organized and inspired the public services of the Undergraduate Library.

Wagman evaluated the first Undergraduate Librarian in these words:

> It would be difficult to say enough in praise of Mrs. Roberta Keniston, head of the Undergraduate Library, who came to the job as the furniture was being delivered in July and, within the space of six months, set up all the procedures, selected the personnel, and anticipated almost all the problems that would arise. By mid-January she was prepared to open the doors and begin operations in a new library, with a new collection, a new staff, and using completely new procedures in which all reserve books are kept on the open shelves in locations called for by their classification.[79]

It was evident from the beginning that the UGLI (as the Undergraduate Library was soon christened by the students) was answering a need frustrated for years at the University. Mrs. Keniston hoped that the Undergraduate Library would become an intellectual center for the campus and a stimulus to learning. She told one interviewer, "This is not just another place to check out books. We view it as a tremendous new educational force on the Michigan campus."[80] It is a matter of subjective opinion as to the fulfillment of this goal, but there is no question as to the immediate success of the Library when measured in objective terms of how many students entered the building, used volumes, listened to phonorecords, and asked for reference assistance. During the first complete academic year (1958/59) the UGLI recorded an attendance of 1,543,435; 368,789 volumes used in the Library; 143,105 home loans; 59,844 listeners in the Audio Room; and 44,894 questions asked at the reference desks.[81]

During its first years, the UGLI replaced Lamont Library as the showplace of undergraduate library service. Librarians from around the world journeyed to Ann Arbor to examine the building and services. The filming of the shelflist made it readily available to other universities as a selection tool. The UGLI had a great influence on American university libraries.

During the Keniston librarianship, a study of the University Library system was undertaken by Richard L. Meier.[82] Students using the UGLI were studied to ascertain human behavior in an information-rich environment. At the time of the study in 1959, the Library was open 100 hours each week. On average days 6,000 persons entered the building and seats were filled 40% of the time; during peak periods, 9,000 persons entered and 60% of the seats were occupied. The demand for seats went unsatisfied for two to three hours on the busiest days.[83] By means of observation, student behavior was analyzed during a peak period. Meier found that students spent 65-70% of their time in UGLI at work, 10-13% sleeping or staring into space, approximately 10% in settling down, and the rest in socializing and other activities.[84]

The Undergraduate Library under Mrs. Keniston's direction was a busy, active library, meeting for the first time many of the needs of Michigan undergraduates. (Her contribution to undergraduate reference services is discussed later in this chapter.) At the conclusion of five years as Head of the Library, Roberta Keniston resigned to accept the position of Associate Librarian at Eastern Michigan University.

Rose-Grace Faucher, Librarian, 1963-

Rose-Grace Faucher was appointed Head of the Undergraduate Library on July 1, 1963. She had been Assistant Head of UGLI since October, 1961, having transferred from the Dentistry Library. She had also worked in the General Library. In her familiarity with the University and its library system plus her experience in the Undergraduate Library, a continuity of direction and leadership was maintained.

Among the highlights of her administration was the introduction of an automated system of charging books. Two problems--abuse of the open-shelf reserve system and constant turnover in the staff--also continued during these years. In October, 1967, the UGLI moved into the age of automation with a computer-assisted system in its reserve book service. The records of reserve use maintained by the computer have been helpful in "identifying the reserve books that are little used and reducing the number of needless purchases."[85] The next step in automation was taken in 1968 when an IBM 1030 data collection system was introduced for the control of loans from the main book collection.[86]

Perhaps the noblest concept of the Undergraduate Library, and its greatest frustration, has been the reserve book service. No other undergraduate library has ever attempted on such a massive scale the almost totally unrestricted access to assigned readings. The Michigan system was to shelve reserve books in their ordinary places in the main collection. Distinctive markings were used to identify them. Only a small number of out-of-print volumes and personal copies loaned by instructors were placed behind the charging desk. The great educational advantage of this open-shelf system was to expose students to all volumes held by the Library on a specific subject instead of only the one reserve title. In housekeeping terms, it meant that the staff would be continually reshelving books in place of constantly charging and discharging volumes. The disadvantages of open access were the monopolization of books by a few students to the detriment of the class and actual theft of the volumes.

Director Wagman described the Library's attempt to overcome the problem:

> The effort to cope with the theft of reserve books from the Undergraduate Library this year [1962/63] by providing a higher ratio of books to class enrollment apparently has been relatively successful in reducing the number of complaints regarding unavailability of copies. The rate of books stolen has not declined, however. Just as the supermarkets and the department stores find it painful but necessary to pay a price in terms of stolen merchandise for the benefit of free access to the shelves, there seems to be no way to reduce the rate of theft without incurring both the educational disadvantage of a closed library and the higher cost of serving a closed collection.[87]

Michigan continued open access to reserve books at this high cost until the Fall term, 1967, when self-service was ended. An area to the rear of the first floor was remodeled with a service desk and closed shelving.

Another problem has been the turnover in staff--professionals, non-professionals, and part-time students. During the first four years the professional staff remained stable. This cycle ended in 1962/63 when the UGLI "suffered a turnover of 55 percent of its non-administrative professional staff in 14 months and had a complete staff on hand for only 7 weeks during the year."[88] Since 1963, a more normal pattern of turnover has occurred. Each year brought a few resignations and their replacements. Turnover brings loss of valuable experience, a lack of continuity, and the recurring need to train new staff, particularly for reference service.[89] Viewed from another perspective, new life and new ideas are gained. The turnover in clerical and part-time staff has been much higher than in the professional staff.[90]

Other aspects of the Faucher administration are discussed in the following sections on the Undergraduate Library's functions as campus study hall, social center, reserve book dispenser, browsing collection, audio-visual facility, and reference center. Before describing these functions, it should be noted that the University maintains an elaborate library system for undergraduates outside the administration of both Undergraduate and the University Libraries.

Residence Halls Libraries

The Office of University Housing has developed small libraries in twelve residence halls. The average holdings of each are 1,200 books, 500 phonorecords, and 35 periodical subscriptions.

Virginia J. Reese, Coordinating Librarian, Residence Halls Libraries, summarized the current situation:

> Each of the twelve libraries is in the charge of a student head librarian who has a staff of students to man the desk. The Coordinating Librarian acts as a consultant and advisor to the twelve libraries and the Office of University Housing, conducting a fall orientation for head librarians as well as in-service training.... Throughout the year, the head librarians use the Coordinating Librarian as a resource person in all problems. But, it is the head librarian who formulates policy, orders materials, plans programs, and works with the students to provide facilities which enhance their life in the residence halls and their University experience in general.... The total head count for the Fall term [1969] was 124,969.[91]

UGLI as Study Hall

The UGLI became an immediate success as the University of Michigan's study hall. On its first day--January 16, 1959, just before term exams--7,678 persons streamed into the building. The staff naively thought that the opening day attendance would not be surpassed for years.[92] However, daily attendance figures of 9,000-10,000 became routine. Millions of students have now used the Library (Table 3).

As early as 1960/61, the Director of the University Library credited the UGLI with being "one of the most intensively used library buildings in the United States."[93] The Ann Arbor News, exhibiting not too much local pride, classed it as the "second busiest library in the U.S. Only New York City's public library counts more users."[94]

Great success begat a great problem--not enough study seats. As partial relief, 377 additional seats were placed in UGLI in 1965, bring the total study positions to 1,357. (The building, including the two other libraries housed there, had a total capacity of 2, 620; 2, 315 were study positions, with the other seats in the coffee lounge and multi-purpose room.)[95]

Table 3. --Attendance, Undergraduate Library Building, University of Michigan, 1958-1969[a]

Year	Number of Persons Entering Building[b]	Percentage of Increase or Decrease
Feb. -June, 1958	708, 813	. .
1958/59	1, 457, 441	. .
1959/60	1, 556, 277	+ 6.8
1960/61	1, 548, 837	- 0. 5
1961/62	1, 731, 283	+11. 8
1962/63	1, 807, 896	+ 4.4
1963/64	1, 883, 083	+ 4. 2
1964/65	1, 969, 935	+ 4.6
1965/66	2, 070, 269	+ 0. 5
1966/67	2, 051, 655	- 0. 8
1967/68	1, 987, 069	- 3. 1
1968/69	1, 899, 461	- 4.4

[a]Michigan. University. Library. Undergraduate Library. Annual Reports. 1957/58-1968/69.

[b]The Engineering-Transportation and Education Libraries are also housed in the Undergraduate Library.

But what are these millions of students doing in the UGLI? Are they studying their own materials which they brought with them or are they using library materials? In a one-day survey in 1965, 59% of the sample in UGLI used library materials. This was in contrast to the General Library where only 22. 5% of the readers in the Main Reading Room and 25% at carrels in the stacks were using library materials. When the use of the library system was averaged, 34. 5% of those surveyed were using library materials and 65. 5% were studying from their own books.[96]

Extrapolating from the studies at Michigan and other universities, the study hall function accounts for 40 to 60% of UGLI's use. If this estimate lacks exactness, there is no question among thirteen Michigan librarians and administrators that the Undergraduate Library has been a great success in fulfilling its study hall role. In interviews they unhesitatingly called it a success. Typical comments were:

> The Undergraduate Library is heavily used as a study hall; so if we judge success by that, it's a great success.
>
> There is a problem now with lack of seats because it is so successful as a place to study.

One librarian, who had used the UGLI when she was an undergraduate, declared that:

> It is a thousand percent more successful now [1969]. When I was a student here, you could have your choice of seats. Now, that's impossible.

The first Undergraduate Librarian summarized the situation:

> The whole attitude towards libraries as a place to study has changed.... It is now accepted that the library is not just a place to go and use books; it's also supposed to provide a place to study. At the time [the Undergraduate Library was built] this was frowned upon. Some of the staff in other parts of the library system said we were just operating a big study hall. My feeling has always been that if students study amidst books, they are going to begin using the books.[97]

UGLI is open exclusively as a study hall with no desk services from 12 Midnight until 2 A.M. seven nights per week. During the Fall and Winter term examination periods, it is open until 5 A.M.

UGLI as Social Center

> The UGLI boasts 70,000 different titles and a total of 135,000 books, had a home circulation of 276,088 during 1967....
>
> The statistics don't tell the whole UGLI story, however. More than an educational institution, the UGLI is a social institution, complete with a built-in caste system. History of art students find

> themselves gathered together with the prints on the fourth floor; engineers hover primarily on the third. Fraternities and sororities have house annexes, setting up at the same group of tables every night, and the koffee klatch meets from 9 to 9:30 P.M.[98]

These are the words of a student commemorating the tenth anniversary of the Undergraduate Library. Two years later in the same student newspaper, a writer under the pseudonym of "The Ugli Crew" confessed:

> As a freshman, I derived a certain satisfaction from hearing that when my parents called, I was always at the library. My friends tell them I spend much of my time there, and I do.
>
> The UGLI isn't such a bad place to live. You can arrange your whole life at the University to fit into the 8 A.M. to 2 A.M. syndrome....
>
> Last year, during finals week somebody released a dozen chickens on the main floor. They must have known the UGLI subculture because they did it around nine, when few students study. At nine, everyone's sick of philosophy and in need of coffee, or a walk.
>
> Girls screamed and a couple guys tried to catch the chickens and didn't. I don't think anybody wanted to because the UGLI is sort of home, a play place, where it's necessary and quite acceptable to break all the rules.
>
> I know it would be better to study in an apartment with no coffee lounges and overheard collect telephone calls to New York City. But I can't bring myself to stay home.[99]

Although these descriptions are from those who certainly know the most about the social aspects of the Undergraduate Library, the accounts may give an exaggerated impression that the UGLI is only a "play place." The previously mentioned study by Meier furnishes more scientific data. From direct observations, he estimated the socializing and other miscellaneous activities took up approximately 7-15% of the students' time.[100] He also distributed a brief questionnaire to a sample of students entering the Library on one day. From this data, he estimated that 5% of the students' time in the morning was spent socializing, with the afternoons and evenings much higher at 19% and 12% respectively.[101]

Interviews with the Michigan staff substantiated the social aspects reported by the students and documented by Meier. The popularity and heavy use of the Student Lounge were stressed and there was general agreement that a much larger lounge was needed. And there was total recognition and acceptance of the facts of life at a coeducational university--socializing has been going on since the founding and will continue. The librarians were unanimously agreed that they were not monitors.

UGLI as Reserve Book Dispenser

If the reserve book service is added to the study hall and social center functions, they form a trinity which probably accounts for the amazing numbers of students using the UGLI. There is no question that the opportunity to place books on reserve in the UGLI stimulated many faculty members to broaden their former one-textbook courses into courses with additional assigned or suggested readings. Reading lists received from the faculty increased by one-third in the first year.[102] "The reserve system stimulated a tremendous increase in the formal and assigned use of books."[103]

The reserve book system has also been the major communications link between librarians and the faculty. From 539 lists for books and 73 for periodical articles submitted in 1958/59, requests from the faculty have grown to 854 book lists and 318 periodical literature lists in 1968/69. In another saga of growth, the number of books on reserve has more than tripled in ten years (14,470 in 1958/59; 50,149 in 1968/69) while the periodical articles, thanks to developments in reprinting and photocopying, have had a nine-fold increase (1,095 in 1958/59; 9,863 in 1968/69).[104]

Have the students used these thousands of reserve items? Since the vast majority of reserve books were shelved under their classification numbers in the main collection during the first years, there is no separate record of reserve book use for 1958/59 through 1966/67. An accurate count of reserve use has been possible since the change to a closed reserve system. The total reserve use of 276,136 in 1968/69 consisted of 226,826 books; 31,434 periodical articles; and 17,876 other items (faculty copies, materials borrowed from other libraries, and uncataloged items).[105]

Thousands of reserve volumes have been ordered each year. Of the volumes ordered for UGLI in 1968/69, 80.6% were for the Reserve Desk (8,680 volumes out of 10,769).[106]

UGLI as Browsing Collection

How have Michigan students responded to the carefully selected main collection in the Undergraduate Library? Do they read only required assignments or have they been stimulated to go beyond the required?

During its first three years, the UGLI gathered data on course-related reading. (A note on the charge cards requested patrons to give the course for which the book was being used or to indicate that it was for no course.) It was found that 35-40% of the home loans to undergraduates were for voluntary, non-course related readings.[107] During the first year, "further analysis of the course-related reading [revealed] that a very large part of this also was not required but apparently was stimulated by the course work."[108] The total book use in UGLI has reached over one million for several years (Table 4).

Another healthy indication is that home loans are not overshadowed by total reserve loans. This is not the pattern in some undergraduate libraries. In 1968/69 the use of the main collection--in the Library and at home--amounted to an amazing 70% of the total book use.[109]

Branscomb concluded that the "average student draws from the general collection of his college or university library about 12 books per year."[110] How do the Michigan undergraduates compare?

During 1968/69, an average of 9.5 home loans from the main collection were charged to each of the 20,000 undergraduates.[111] However, when it is assumed that the UGLI primarily serves the 12,500 undergraduates in the College of Literature, Science, and the Arts, each L.S.&A. undergraduate averaged about 15 home loans from UGLI. When the home loans and the building use of the main collection are combined, the L.S.&A. undergraduates had a per capita use of 40 books in 1968/69. These computations do

Table 4.--Home Circulation and Book Use within the Library, Undergraduate Library, University of Michigan, 1958-1969[a]

Year	Home Circulation[b]	% Increase or Decrease	Book Use in Library[b]	% Increase or Decrease	Total Book Use	% Increase or Decrease
1958/59	141, 036	. .	340, 476	. .	481, 512	. .
1959/60	164, 998	+17.0	479, 958	+40.9	644, 956	+33.9
1960/61	167, 008	+ 1.2	498, 938	+ 3.9	665, 946	+ 3.3
1961/62	196, 391	+17.6	516, 643	+ 3.5	713, 034	+ 7.1
1962/63	213, 429	+ 8.7	629, 141	+21.8	842, 570	+18.2
1963/64	249, 272	+16.8	724, 028	+15.1	973, 300	+15.5
1964/65	257, 425	+ 3.3	765, 659	+ 5.7	1, 023, 084	+ 5.1
1965/66	276, 176	+ 7.3	755, 988	- 1.3	1, 032, 164	+ 0.9
1966/67	268, 934	- 2.6	800, 258	+ 5.9	1, 069, 192	+ 3.6
1967/68	286, 917	+ 6.7	659, 112	-17.6	946, 029	-11.5
1968/69	308, 359	+ 7.5	614, 098	- 6.8	922, 457	- 2.5

[a]Michigan. University. Library. Undergraduate Library. Annual Reports. 1958/59-1968/69.

[b]Includes Reserve Books.

not account for volumes borrowed by undergraduates from other campus libraries.

The budget rose from $25,000 for main collection and reserve books in 1959/60 to $81,000 for books, periodicals, binding, phonorecords, and tapes in 1968/69. Because fewer copies were purchased in 1968/69 for closed reserve, only $69,000 was spent. Consequently, $73,140 was allocated for 1969/70.[112]

During interviews, undergraduate librarians and University Library administrators at Michigan pronounced the main collection a success. One librarian indicated that current fiction, poetry, and avant-garde literature need improvement. Also radical periodicals were lacking, but were being reviewed by the staff in the 1969 Fall term for possible subscription. Another librarian pointed to an imbalance in the collection because of heavy purchases of reserve books. All librarians completely agreed that the collection should be totally open and freely accessible; closed stacks in an undergraduate library were inconceivable to them.

UGLI as Audio-Visual Facility

There was a substantial commitment to audio services in planning UGLI, with a more limited provision of visual materials. Recordings and tapes, with listening equipment, became a special collection. Films and other visual media have never been collected.

Opportunity for contact with visual materials, however, has not been entirely lacking. A film preview room was originally one of the UGLI services, but was discontinued in 1965 because of little use and the need for the space.[113] The Multipurpose Room is used for showing some films by student groups. The viewing of prints and other art was incorporated in three areas. The print study gallery displays reproductions of art being studied in fine arts courses.[114] Off the main lobby is an exhibit area used by the Museum of Art to mount special exhibitions. The Multipurpose Room has a display wall for exhibits connected with programs held there. In most instances, the selection and actual presentation of visual materials is left to other University departments and groups.

Michigan was a leader in the development of audio services in libraries.

> The idea of making available for student use so many recordings and tapes was quite novel in the mid-1950's. At the time if you wandered around undergraduate facilities or other general libraries, you might find four or five stations at which students could listen to records. It was an extra-curricular adjunct to a great extent. At Michigan, we decided that this should be part of the instructional program with a library program to support the instruction.[115]

There were difficulties in designing the equipment because engineering companies lacked experience in providing for so many listeners. Eventually engineers on the University faculty designed the Audio Room.[116] It contained 144 seats and 72 record players (each player has two seats). The listener can hear via headphones the single disc he plays, or can listen to any of the 13 other channels piped from a control room. One of the channels is FM radio; others carry programs scheduled for particular courses or individual requests.

From 1958 the number of listeners rose steadily each year until a peak of 84, 059 patrons was reached in 1962/63. During the next five years, listeners declined to a low of 53, 881. This trend was reversed in 1968/69 when there were 56, 413 listeners.[117]

With annual additions, the collection contained 6, 217 recordings and 1, 157 tapes in April, 1969.[118] The collection has both music (classical, folk, rock, and musical comedies) and spoken word recordings (drama, poetry, and other literary forms in English and foreign languages). The musical recordings serve the College of Literature, Science, and the Arts; the Music Library provides audio facilities for the School of Music.[119] Recordings and tapes for learning foreign languages are not included.

When the Michigan librarians were asked to rate the Audio Room, they all stated that it was a successful operation. Many pointed out the urgent need for additional channels. No one mentioned the decline in listeners. One librarian recommended an additional service: a separate collection of recordings and tapes which could be charged for home use. Only two librarians had visions of a greatly expanded multi-media program, calling for the UGLI to learn from the community college libraries which were considered to be years ahead in the use of non-print media.

Statistical Summary of First Decade

In order to summarize many UGLI services--except reference assistance--the first complete academic year of operation is compared with the tenth year in Table 5.

Table 5.--Percentage Changes in Fifteen Variables, First Decade of Service, Undergraduate Library, University of Michigan[a]

Variable	First Complete Year of Operation (1958/59)	Tenth Year of Operation (1967/68)	% Increase
Attendance	1,457,441	1,987,069	+ 36.3
Home Loans from Circulation and Reserve Desks	141,624	286,917	+ 102.5
Book Use in Library-Main Stacks and Reserve Books	339,888	659,112	+ 93.9
Total Book Use	481,512	946,029	+ 96.4
Total Number of Listeners in Audio Room	47,587	53,881	+ 13.2
Collection Growth:			
Titles	40,000	69,000[b]	+ 72.5
Volumes	68,590	140,000[b]	+ 104.1
Total Seating Capacity	1,938	2,315	+ 19.5
Average Weekly Hours Open	100[c]	121[c]	+ 21.0
Books on Reserve	14,470	44,869	+ 210.1

Table 5.--Continued.

Variable	First Complete Year of Operation (1958/59)	Tenth Year of Operation (1967/68)	% Increase
Periodical Articles on Reserve	732	10,377	+1317.6
Reserve Lists Received	539	834	+ 54.7
Reserve Office Processing Staff	4.85 FTE	6.95	+ 43.3
Total Undergraduate Library Staff	38.4 FTE	54.8	+ 42.7
Undergraduate Enrollment, College of Literature, Science and the Arts[d]	7,357	11,839	+ 60.9
Undergraduate and Graduate Enrollment, College of Literature, Science and the Arts[d]	12,828	16,048	+ 25.2

[a]Michigan. University. Library. Undergraduate Library. Annual Reports. 1958/59, Statistical Appendix; 1967/68, Appendices B and D.

[b]Estimates.

[c]Irregularities occurred during both years.

[d]An average representative gross enrollment for both Fall and Winter terms furnished by the Statistical Services Office, University of Michigan.

The decade was one of growth in every category: from a 13.2% increase in listeners to a spectacular advance (1317.6%) in periodical articles on reserve. When the ten-year totals are computed, the Undergraduate Library's first decade is even more impressive. From January 16, 1958 through January 15, 1968, the UGLI had an attendance of 17,670,890 persons; circulated 2,157,974 books for home use; and had 5,922,381 volumes used in the library for a total book use of 8,080,355.[120]

In contrast to the growth exhibited in other areas, reference assistance in UGLI has decreased during the decade.

Reference Services for Undergraduate Students: The Undergraduate Library

When the Undergraduate Library opened, a staff member who transferred from the General Library Reference Department was placed in charge of the UGLI reference collection and service.

All professionals, including the Head of UGLI, have worked at the public reference desks in addition to their other responsibilities. The head of the Reference Collection and Service has provided orientation to the reference area for new librarians, been responsible for the selection of the reference collection, compiled annotated lists for the staff of new reference books, maintained statistical records of reference assistance, written detailed annual reports, and has other responsibilities in addition to duty at the desks.[121]

Contact with General Library Reference Department

Limited contact with the other major reference service for undergraduates--the General Library's Reference Department--has been maintained. The head of UGLI Reference has extensive knowledge of the reference collection of the General Library.[122] He returns periodically to review its new additions and he is acquainted with some of the General Library reference staff. Other contact between the two groups of reference librarians has been limited to an occasional orientation session given by one of the General Library reference librarians; for example, Janet F. White, documents specialist, spoke to the Undergraduate librarians on document holdings.[123]

In interviews, the librarians indicated little acquaintanceship with each other. One librarian estimated the contact as no more than would be gotten in a meeting of the staff association or at a meeting of the entire staff called by the library administration. In a series of luncheons for campus librarians, the reference librarians from the two libraries might see each other informally. There is no separate organization of reference librarians.

The interviews revealed no joint projects undertaken by the two staffs. No exchange of staff as a means of familiarizing each with the other's collection and service has been effected. Persons applying for reference positions at Michigan are not jointly interviewed. Relations between the two reference departments have been cordial, but there has never been a program of vigorous cooperation. One librarian traced the present distinctiveness of the two reference services to the years prior to the opening of the UGLI when the General Library was very crowded with both undergraduates and graduate students. An attitude developed then on the part of some librarians to survive until UGLI opened and took care of the undergraduates.

In order to keep the staff in UGLI from becoming isolated or unfamiliar with resources of other campus libraries, the Undergraduate Librarian has scheduled visits to various libraries. The Map Collection, a part of the General Library Reference Department, was visited in this series.

Communications With Faculty

When asked, "Is there much communication between the staff in the Undergraduate Library and the faculty concerning reference services for their students, or is it fairly minimal?" the librarians of UGLI unanimously agreed that the contact was minimal at best. The lack of contact extended to the many teaching fellows who give introductory courses. Several librarians replied that they knew of no contact with the faculty, except for communications concerning reserve lists.

One valuable contact with the faculty was lost with the resignation of Roberta Keniston. She was a member of the Honors Council, a faculty group which worked with the undergraduate honors program in the College of Literature, Science, and the Arts. Another librarian did not replace her on the Council.[124]

It was not until November, 1968 that professional staff in the upper three grades (Librarian IV-A, IV-B, and V) became members of the University Senate.[125] This potential contact with faculty was not possible for the UGLI reference librarians. Only the Head and the Assistant Head of the Undergraduate Library could become members of the Senate; eight other librarians were ineligible.

UGLI Publications

In addition to daily reference service, the staff has maintained two other programs to acquaint undergraduates with library services. Of the two--a series of publications and a library instruction program--the publications have been sustained over a longer period. During the first years, the staff prepared information leaflets on various aspects of UGLI. It was believed that a leaflet devoted to one subject, i.e., the card catalog or periodical indexes, had "an immediacy which inclines students to read it through"[126] at the time of need. Typical library "handbooks appear more formidable, and students have a tendency to take them and set them aside for later reading, which is sometimes never done."[127]

In succeeding years, a comprehensive and more elaborately printed handbook was prepared to use with the library instruction program. The *Guide to the University of Michigan Undergraduate Library*, in the revised edition of 1969, consisted of 20 pages. A short quiz--"Finding One in Three Million"--was included for students to test themselves on their library skills.

UGL's Automated Reserve System, designed for student use, and *Reserve Information*, prepared and distributed to the faculty as a means of acquainting them with procedures for requesting reserve materials, are other UGLI publications.

In response to requests from incoming freshmen for a list of books they might read during the summer before coming to Ann Arbor, the UGLI staff compiled in 1962 the first edition of *Read, Read, Read*. The 1969 edition contained an annotated list of 158 twentieth century titles arranged by subject.

Library Orientation and Instruction

UGLI has used a variety of approaches to library orientation. A tour with an upperclassman guide was the first approach. Although the Undergraduate Librarian held a training session for the student guides, less than 40% attended. Groups of 20-30 new students were then shown through UGLI. Much incorrect information was dispensed. In a university as large as Michigan, the staff found it "impossible to provide the careful orientation of new students which would be desirable."[128] When the professor in charge of Freshman English courses expressed an interest in having the reference staff instruct each second semester class in library methods, the Library could not cooperate because of the large number of classes. As a first step in developing an instruction program, the Undergraduate Librarian gave two lectures on the use of libraries to foreign students.[129]

The possibility of producing a film for library instruction in all Freshman English classes was investigated. The idea was abandoned because of costs--approximately $10, 000 for a 45-minute sound film.[130]

In 1961 UGLI became a part of the University's academic orientation. During the Summer session, 2, 100 students (freshmen in the coming Fall term) came in groups of 80 for a two-day campus visit. A well-trained, salaried student counselor brought students to UGLI where a librarian spoke briefly on the uses of the catalog and periodical indexes and also explained how the students might use UGLI in the Fall. Then the counselors led a tour of the Library. For students unable to attend the summer orientation, 2, 500 brochures--"Welcome to the Undergraduate Library"--were mailed by the Orientation Office in a packet of material on the University. Tours were also given during Fall and Spring registration. The results of the Summer orientation were immediately evident on the first day of classes, with the Library "crowded with freshmen going busily about their work, in contrast to other fall semesters when freshman library use had been low during the first weeks of classes."[131]

Many students had asked for a list of books they might read during the remainder of the Summer. The Orientation Office agreed to pay for the printing and mailing of a booklet if the librarians would select the titles to be recommended. A committee of five selected the titles, the criteria for selection being "timeliness, authoritativeness, readability, and relevance to the intellectual and cultural atmosphere of the University of Michigan."[132] Titles available in paperback were emphasized. Approximately 9,000 copies of Read, Read, Read were ordered and mailed to all freshmen and transfer students or distributed to campus organizations which had requested copies. As publicity for the bibliography, copies of the titles were requested from publishers and exhibited in the Honors Study Lounge, where students were taken at the end of their tour of UGLI. Discussions of four of the books were led by faculty members during the 1962 Autumn registration. Attendance averaged 200 at each session.[133] The list has continued to be a highly successful part of UGLI's orientation.

The 1962 Autumn orientation "was far from a success."[134] Searching for improvements, a staff committee meeting with the Director of the Orientation Office decided upon a program of slides explained by a librarian using a prepared script. Guide to the Undergraduate Library, the first comprehensive handbook, would also be given to students. This new format, used twice at the beginning of the Spring term, 1964, "was well received by the orientation group leaders, students, and librarians. The real test [would] come in the Fall orientation."[135] In the Fall, the counselors evaluated the slide presentation as being very good.[136] The UGLI staff also gave a two-hour orientation for disadvantaged students in the University's Pre-College Program.

The next development in UGLI's orientation was not successful. A tape recording was made in 1966 of the script which accompanied the slides. It was planned for the librarian to introduce the program and leave the student guides to show the slides and play the tape. For their own amusement, the guides mixed up slides so that illustrations did not match narration. Librarians returned; they usually preferred to explain the slides rather than use the tape. In their continued search for a way to introduce 5,000-6,000 students each year to UGLI, the staff reviewed two films used at other university libraries. Hopes of producing a film for Michigan were again dashed because of high costs and recognition that annual changes in UGLI would immediately date the film.[137]

A completely voluntary system evolved by 1968/69. During the Summer, Autumn, and Winter orientation, tours were led through UGLI by upperclassmen. Since the tours were optional, they were usually "more frequently and conscientiously [given] by the summer leaders whose schedule is less hectic than by the fall and winter leaders, who must orient greater numbers of students in less time."[138] No librarians participated in this first encounter. After the second week of classes, the Library offered an hour-long lecture on fundamental library skills. Held at four different times in the Multipurpose Room, the lectures were illustrated via an overhead projector. The Undergraduate Librarian recorded the dilemma facing the staff:

> Many students are not reached who should be, because the entire program is voluntary. Many group leaders give incorrect information on the tours, or do not give tours at all. The talk itself is directed at an audience of such diverse backgrounds that it sails over the heads of some members and grossly insults the intelligence of others.
>
> The remedy for these ills is not obvious. Requiring students to attend a library talk in their Orientation sessions would at least insure their setting foot in the building; but the program itself would have to be descriptive only of library service and locations, and of the 5, 800 or so gruding attendees, very few would gain any information of a useful sort....
>
> In any event, library orientation continues to be unsatisfactory and the great part of library instruction is given individually to students who approach the Reference Librarian on duty at the desk.[139]

In September, 1969, two bibliographical lectures were added. One lecture covered library resources in current affairs, American history, sociology, psychology, and science and technology.[140] The second dealt with biography, literature, and music.[141] Each subject was developed by an individual librarian; the parts were then edited into a script. Each lecture was given twice. Table 6 shows the chronology and attendance of the Summer and Autumn, 1969 orientation events.

The staff of UGLI was pessimistic before the September, 1969 library lectures, foreseeing a small response. When approximately 930 students attended--300 at one lecture, causing some students to be turned away--the staff members

Table 6.-Orientation Programs and Attendance, Undergraduate Library, University of Michigan, Summer and Fall 1969[a]

Program	Date	Attendance
Library Tours given by Student Guides for Freshmen Enrolling in September, 1969	June 15-Aug. 15, 1969	Not known
Slide Lecture (General Introduction to the Undergraduate Library)	Sept. 4, 1969[b]	
	10 A.M.	300
	2 P.M.	200
	Sept. 5, 1969[b]	
	10 A.M.	55
	2 P.M.	90
Bibliographical Lectures Part I: Social Science and Science	Sept. 16, 1969	
	3 P.M.	60
	7:30 P.M.	85
Part II: Biography, Literature, and Music	Sept. 17, 1969	
	3 P.M.	60
	7:30 P.M.	80
Total Attendance at 8 Lectures		930

[a]Information furnished by Patricia Kay, Librarian in charge of Orientation, Undergraduate Library, University of Michigan.

[b]Fall term classes began on September 5, 1969.

had a "feeling that they had accomplished something."[142] With the limited goal of UGLI's orientation program (it is the staff's "responsibility to acquaint students with the library and to offer assistance in its use; it is the student's responsibility to evaluate his library competence and determine the kind of help he will seek"[143]), the librarians considered the orientation as somewhere between a success and a failure. They all agreed that library instruction should remain voluntary, even though a small number of freshmen took advantage of the lectures. The 930 students were 29.7% of the 3,131 freshmen in the College of Literature, Science, and the Arts, or 20% of the University's 4,615 freshmen.[144] Some students may have attended more than one lecture, decreasing the number of individuals reached. Some transfer students may have attended.

When asked if UGLI should do more orientation, the librarians all replied affirmatively. Several qualified this by saying that more staff would be necessary. In response to the question: "Would you personally be willing to do more teaching--both lectures and discussions in the Library and integrated with the work of a particular course?" only half of the staff gave an unqualified "yes." Some did not want to appear before any class, but offered to work on the preparation of scripts; others wished to speak to small groups in the Library, not in a classroom. One librarian summarized her reluctance by saying that faculty members did not highly respect librarians; no faculty would ever dream of introducing a librarian to the class with "Isn't this wonderful? Today, we have ________________, the distinguished librarian, to discuss...."

Individual librarians disagreed as to the effectiveness of having tours led by upperclassmen. One view held that only librarians should give the orientation, to prevent the spread of misinformation. The opposing view found student guides during 1969 to be good and believed that there was a great advantage gained "if an upperclassman first gets across to the students the need to use a library." The problem of the large number of undergraduates influenced any discussion of improvements or expansion of library orientation.

Few attempts have been made to integrate bibliographical lectures by librarians with University courses at the exact time students have need of such assistance. Only tentative steps have been made: one librarian was asked to speak on science bibliography to students in a microbiology course.[145] The invitation came as a result of friendship with the instructor. No library instruction has been provided for advanced undergraduates, such as honors students in the College of Literature, Science, and the Arts or the Residential College students. Only a few orientation lectures have been given for disadvantaged students.

The Reference Collection

The Undergraduate Library opened in 1958 with some 800 reference volumes. Within the first year, it was "necessary to augment the reference collection rapidly. The problem of helping a student halfway to an answer and then referring him to the General Library for additional assistance becomes intolerable in practice if not in theory."[146] In 1958/59, 426 volumes (213 titles) were added. During succeeding years, the average yearly additions have been 240 volumes (161 titles).[147] By April 30, 1963, the collection of 2,860 volumes was considered a "strong, well-balanced collection which meets the needs of undergraduates."[148] The staff in April, 1969, worked with approximately 3,549 volumes.

An analysis of 1968/69 expenditures revealed that $2,311.55 was spent on 192 volumes (140 titles) added to the collection. The UGLI also maintains an extensive pamphlet file (25,077 items) as part of the reference collection. During 1968/69, 6,857 items were added at a cost of $473.94. The total cost of reference materials in 1968/69 was $2,784.49.[149]

The reference collection is housed on open shelves; no volumes are kept back of the desks giving only limited access. Magill's masterplot volumes, usually accorded this "honor" in some libraries, are simply not in the UGLI collection. The pamphlet file is freely accessible except for several folders in current, heavy demand. These are kept in drawers of a reference desk and students must sign for them. Several very popular university catalogs are also treated in this way.

To supplement the reference collection, the staff maintains several special indexes for material not indexed in the Essay and General Literature Index, Ottemiller's Index to Plays in Collections, and the Speech Index.[150] Short stories have also been indexed.

No formal evaluation of the reference collection was attempted in this study. However, librarians in UGLI were asked for their evaluations. When asked if the UGLI reference collection was adequate for full reference service without a large number of referrals to the General Library's reference desk, there was agreement that full service was not possible. Referrals were most often necessary when questions concerned the sciences, government documents, statistical sources, law (especially Michigan law), and other subjects having a divisional library on campus. Reference materials in literature and the other humanities were judged most adequate. Two of ten librarians stated that some reference volumes were now superseded and should be replaced. Lack of telephone books caused referrals to the General Library. One librarian found her personal theory of what should be in an undergraduate library reference collection going considerably beyond the Michigan practice.

> I would like to see the kind of reference collection that could give an undergraduate almost everything he would need in the way of bibliographical searching tools. He might have to go to other libraries to get the actual material, but at least he would go armed with precisely what he wanted.

The staff members were also asked if they would include a reference collection in a new undergraduate library. One librarian questioned the construction of a separate undergraduate library, preferring one large building with the undergraduate library on several floors of it. The other librarians unanimously agreed that a reference collection was essential in the separate undergraduate library. To the next question of how many volumes they would have in this hypothetical undergraduate library, the following eight responses were given comparing their ideal collection with the 3, 500 volumes in the UGLI reference collection:

Much larger	2
Somewhat larger	4
Somewhat larger, with more multiple copies of heavily used items	1
About the same size	1

Several librarians pointed out the heavy use by both students and librarians of the check-in records of periodical issues. This file was conveniently and freely accessible near the reference desks; undergraduates were encouraged to use it. Roberta Keniston recalled evidence that the students had learned its uses:

> The undergraduates became more expert at using libraries. For example, after the Undergraduate Library opened, the Head of the Catalog Depart-

> ment in the General Library was quite amused when undergraduates began to come into the Technical Services area to consult the Checklist of complete holdings. They had become accustomed to having that information easily available in the Undergraduate Library.[151]

Description of Reference Area and Desks

The reference collection has always been shelved, along with periodicals, on the first floor. In 1958 two desks, each labelled "Reference Desk," were near the collection; a third desk, marked "Catalog Information Desk," was adjacent to the catalog in the Lobby and separated by a glass partition from the other desks. During peak periods, all three desks were staffed. Only one desk was manned during slack hours.[152]

After a semester's experience, the reference librarian believed:

> that the centralization of reference service, reference collection, periodical collection and indexes on the first floor is working very well and at the moment would be reluctant to break up the collection and divide service among the other floors, since many requests for assistance are so vaguely formulated, general in nature, and even mistakenly-identified as to subject area, that a divided service would mean constant referral of students from one floor to another, with resulting duplication of staff effort and discouragement and even embarrassment to the students.[153]

By 1959/60, the reference area was even more centralized when the catalog was moved from the Lobby into an alcove near the reference collection. Two reference desks were placed immediately inside the doors from the Lobby with the reference collection and periodicals to one side and the catalog to their rear. A strategic location for reference services had been devised (Figure 1).

Standard office desks in grey metal were used. Librarians sat in swivel chairs; no chairs were provided beside the desks for the patron's use.

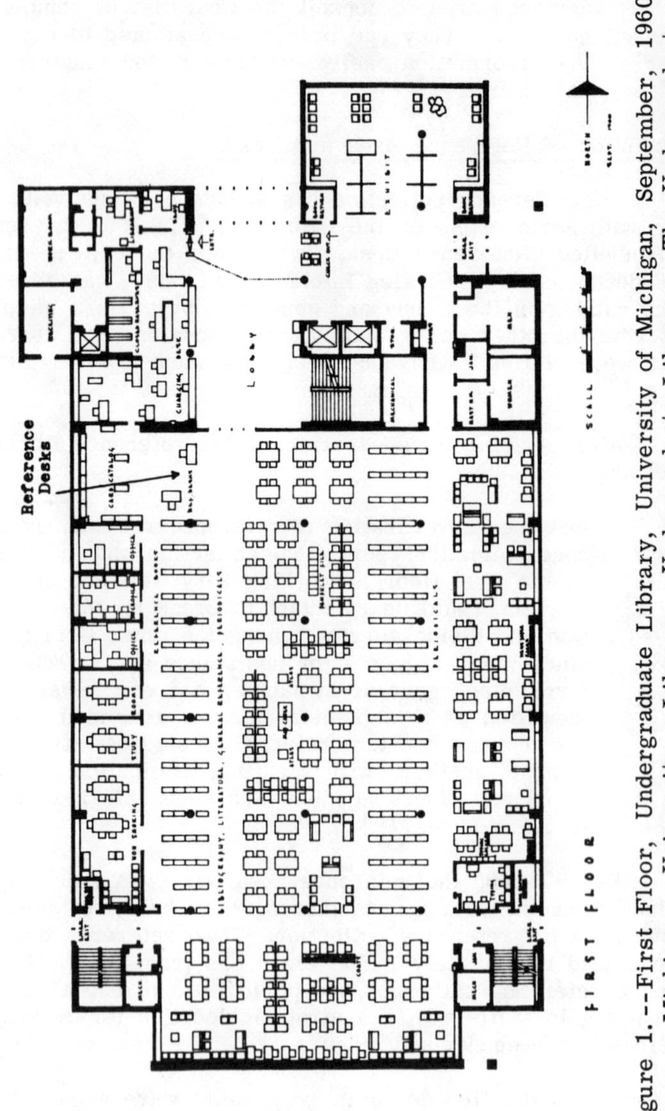

Figure 1.--First Floor, Undergraduate Library, University of Michigan, September, 1960. Source: Michigan. University. Library. Undergraduate Library. The Undergraduate Library Building of the University (Ann Arbor: University Library, 1960).

The reference services remained in the northwest corner of the first floor until crowded conditions in the building forced the addition of more seats. The library administration commissioned the Community Systems Foundation--young engineers at the University who had formed a non-profit group--to design new furniture layouts for UGLI.[154] Finding the reference desks to be in an area of high traffic and noise, the engineers designed a new location for reference services. The proposal was accepted and introduced in 1965 (Figure 2). In order to solve the traffic and noise problems,

> the reference/catalog area was moved from the alcove and placed in the center-front of the main floor. The reference desks were placed adjacent to the catalog with traffic flow designed to go in any direction through the catalog area without having to pass through the reference area first. Placement of the reference area was designed to make the reference librarians' jobs significantly easier and provide better reference service. Layout design placed reference librarians in the center of all activities common to their job. For example, previously the reference librarians had to cross a main traffic aisle to give students assistance with some of the reference aids. The new design placed the librarians adjacent to or near the catalog, indices, reserve notebooks, periodical lists, clipping file, reference collections, and other reference aids.[155]

The new arrangement was "functioning efficiently"[156] after the first year. During interviews in 1969, librarians complained that the reference desks were not as visible from the card catalog as in the previous arrangement.

Staffing of Reference Desks

Each librarian is on duty at the reference desks from ten to thirteen hours per week, or about one-third of his 37.5 hour work-week. The Head and the Assistant Head of UGLI spend less time at the desks. Daily reference duty is usually two hours, except when the librarian works at night or on weekends.[157] Coverage of the desks is by professional staff and four Work-Study Scholars. Although the Scholars' primary assignment is assisting with reserve book service or another function, they also work several hours per week at

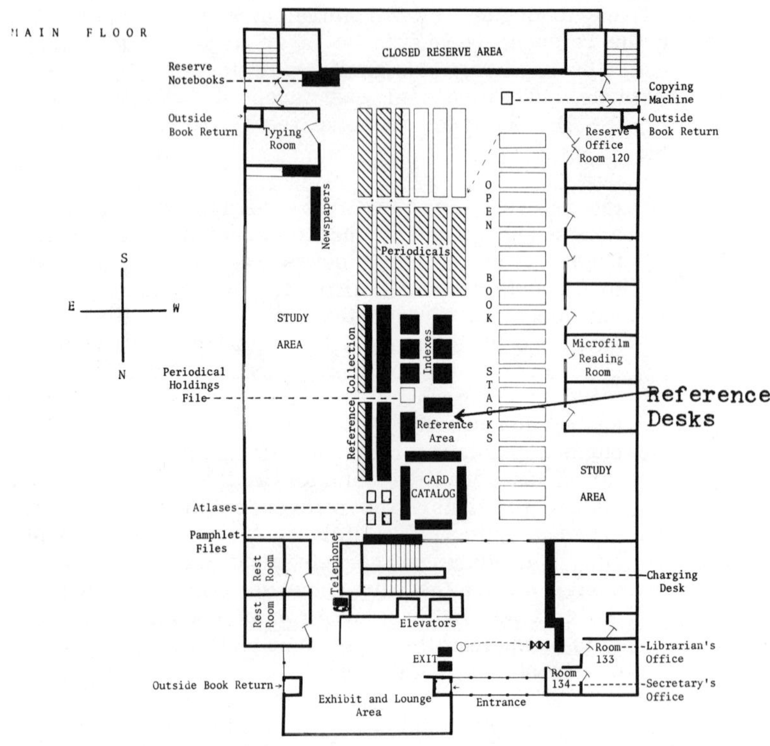

Figure 2.--First Floor, Undergraduate Library, University of Michigan, 1969. Source: Michigan. University. Library. Undergraduate Library. Guide to the University of Michigan Undergraduate Library (Ann Arbor: University Library, 1969).

the reference desks with one of the librarians. One Scholar is the only staff member on reference duty on Sunday nights and during a few other hours each week.[158]

Hours of reference service during a regular week in the Fall term, 1969, totalled 76 hours, 62.8% of the 121 hours UGLI was open. The UGLI hours were Monday-Saturday: 8 A.M.-2 A.M. and Sunday: 1 P.M.-2 A.M., with no service available at the reserve and circulation desks after midnight.[159] Reference service was available on Mondays-Fridays from 8 A.M.-12 Noon, 1-5 P.M. and 6-10 P.M.; Saturdays, 8 A.M.-12 Noon and 1-5 P.M.; and Sundays, 1-5 P.M. and 6-10 P.M. No reference assistance was provided during lunch and supper hours. Two staff members were on duty at the reference desks during 36 (47.3%) of the 76 reference service hours; only one person was on duty the other 40 hours.

Qualifications of Staff in 1969/70

A composite profile of the reference librarians in the Undergraduate Library in October, 1969 would portray an attractive young woman who had worked there for one or two years.[160] She received her Master's degree in library science from the University of Michigan; almost her entire professional experience was also at Michigan. She had done no subject graduate work, except for two courses required as cognates for the library degree. Her undergraduate major was English at an institution other than the University of Michigan.

Individual education, length of experience, and other qualifications should be noted to guard against over-simplification in the profile. Only one of nine librarians in UGLI received the Master's degree in library science from a school other than the University of Michigan. One staff member had not yet received the library degree; the last course was being taken at the time of this study. Two librarians had received a Master's degree in English from Michigan. For their undergraduate degrees, six persons majored in English, two in French, and one in History. The alma maters were a variety of institutions (Loyola University at Chicago, Michigan State, Northwestern, William and Mary, and Colorado, Brooklyn, and Hiram Colleges with one librarian each; two librarians from the University of Michigan).

One librarian had considerable experience in the General Library and a divisional library before joining the UGLI staff. Another person had worked for several years at the Detroit Public Library and also in the General Library. Two others had a year's experience elsewhere: one in Florida and one in the Canal Zone. Two had preprofessional experience: one at the Brooklyn Public Library and the other with teenagers at the Toledo Public Library. Most of the accumulated experience, however, had been gained in the Undergraduate Library. One staff member had been employed in UGLI since 1958; another, for eight years. These were exceptions; the other seven librarians ranged from one month to twenty-six months of service in UGLI. Four of the seven began in August, 1968.

One member of the 1969 staff was male; eight were female. Several men have been on the staff throughout the years, but women have always been in the majority.

Other characteristics are not as easy to summarize as formal education and experience. The youthfulness of most of the staff has limited their work experience. However, their age may give them a certain advantage. Undergraduates seeking reference assistance may feel that young staff are more easily approached. In response to an interview question concerning this, one librarian said, "We're extremely approachable; if we are nothing else, we're approachable." Another thought that the "youth of the staff makes them a lot more flexible." Other responses were:

> We are young and therefore do not have a great deal of experience, but I think that because we are aware of this, we know our own limitations. We do not just stop when we individually can't go any further. We go to a more experienced staff member.
>
> There's such good rapport among this particular group of librarians that I am not ashamed or afraid to run into an office and ask for help on a specific reference question.... We pool our experience.

Scope of Reference Services

The Undergraduate Library offers reference assistance at two formal desks previously described. The assistance must be requested by the student in person. There is no telephone reference service. Nor do the librarians make it a practice to call to other campus libraries or offices on behalf of students. On rare occasions the librarians approach students who show signs of needing assistance, but the great majority of information-seeking encounters are initiated by students. Most of the reference services are performed in the immediate area of the reference desks. The major exception to this was during the first two weeks of the Fall term in 1968 and 1969 when a librarian, wearing a small "Reserve Information" sign, stationed himself in front of the reserve desk at the rear of the first floor. For the first thirty minutes of each hour (after classes change), the librarian gave assistance in the use of reserve lists and acquainted students with reserve procedures. It was an individual approach, with the librarian asking the students if they needed help.[161]

Philosophy of Service

Reference service philosophy was established before the Library opened with a statement by Roberta Keniston--"Reference Service to Undergraduates." The new staff then discussed implementation of the philosophy.[162] The philosophy can be distilled into one word: teacher. The complete text, which is still official Undergraduate Library policy, follows:

> ### REFERENCE SERVICE TO UNDERGRADUATES
>
> The reference librarian working with undergraduates serves as adjunct teacher for all departments, acting as interpreter and intermediary between professor and student. He has a unique opportunity to help students expand their intellectual horizons, see relationships between the various areas of their studies, appreciate books as a means of intellectual stimulus and growth, clarify their assignments, learn expert use of a library's resources and become aware of the utility of individual reference works. In some cases, the help he can give to students is crucial to their success in college.
>
> With this in mind, reference work is practiced in the following manner:
>
> 1. Each student is considered as a person of worth and is treated in a friendly manner with respect for his

requests for help, whatever they may be.

2. When necessary, the student is led by discussion and tactful questioning to clarify and sharpen his request for information.

3. Contacts with students are regarded as teaching opportunities: all searches of the card catalog, periodical indexes and other indexes and bibliographies are made jointly with the student, with informal description of the methods followed and indications of the information ascertained, so that the student is at one time receiving the requested information and learning techniques of library use.

4. Students are made aware of the utility of special bibliographies and of bibliographies in individual books.

5. Whenever an individual reference book is consulted, effort is made to point out its special usefulness, unusual features and its relationship to other reference books in its own and related areas.

6. When examination of the catalog by librarian and student reveals that books containing the desired information are not identifiable and it is clear that the student will have further difficulties, the reference librarian will go to the shelves to assist him in his search.

7. Referrals of students to larger or more specialized collections are accompanied by indications of specialized bibliographies and of methods of conducting an intensive search in a research collection.

8. Every effort is made to become informed about the scope and special assignments in courses. Cooperation is given faculty members in preparing library materials for their classes and assisting their students in such a way that maximum support is given to the instructional program.

The purpose of this method is to teach students to use library resources to the maximum and to develop in them a conviction that books are a necessary part of their lives. Since the alertness of the reference staff is essential to the success of such a program, it is important that the reference librarians continue to grow in

> their work. They should take every opportunity to become familiar with the existing library collection and with new books being added to the collection, should read their professional publications, keep abreast of current affairs and be aware of new developments in the fields of learning.[163]

Michigan's Definitions of Questions

In 1958 the Undergraduate staff decided to use the same categories of questions as were used in the General Library Reference Department. All questions were categorized for purposes of statistical recording into one of three types: (1) spot questions; (2) reference questions taking less than five minutes to answer; and (3) reference questions requiring over five minutes to answer.

Spot questions are those requests for information or directions which were "usually very simple, often answerable in a few words plus some directional motions."[164] Reference questions are more substantial questions for which the librarian "explains in some detail the mechanics"[165] of a reference volume, the catalog, the holdings records of periodicals, or other resource, perhaps going to the shelves or catalog to assist the student. These definitions have been used for the entire eleven years in UGLI.

It was assumed by the Undergraduate staff that there "will be relatively few questions in category 3. The bulk of the questions fall into the other two categories."[166]

Recorded Use of Reference Services, 1958-1969

As is usual at the opening of a new library, the number of spot questions is far larger than the quantity of reference questions. The UGLI was no exception. In 1958/59, 69.5% (32,537) of the total questions (46,825) asked were spot questions; 30.5% (14,288) were recorded as reference questions. During the next five years, the spot questions decreased until an all-time low of 11,610 such questions was reached in 1963/64 (Table 7). In the same five-year period, reference questions[167] increased in number each year until an all-time high of 31,844 reference questions was attained in 1963/64. A phenomenal 73% of the total were reference questions while only 27% were spot questions.

Table 7.-Types of Questions Received at Reference Desks, Undergraduate Library, University of Michigan, 1958-1969[a]

Year	Spot Questions[b]	Increase or Decrease %	Reference Questions[c]	Increase or Decrease %	Total Questions	Increase or Decrease %	Reference Questions (% of Total)
1958/59	32,537	. .	14,288	. .	46,825	. .	30.5
1959/60	24,958	-23.3	16,899	+18.3	41,857	-10.6	40.4
1960/61	30,162	+20.9	18,404	+ 8.9	38,566	- 7.9	47.7
1961/62	15,103	-49.9	23,327	+26.7	38,430	- 0.3	60.7
1962/63	12,164	-19.5	26,950	+15.5	39,114	+ 1.8	68.9
1963/64	11,610	- 4.6	31,844	+18.2	43,454	+11.1	73.3
1964/65	14,726	+26.8	25,550	-19.8	40,276	- 7.3	63.4
1965/66	19,623	+33.3	19,112	-25.2	38,745	- 3.8	49.3
1966/67	19,177	- 2.3	17,011	-11.0	36,188	- 6.6	47.0
1967/68	21,920	+14.3	15,631	- 8.1	37,551	+ 3.8	41.6
1968/69	22,410	+ 2.3	14,110	- 9.7	36,520	- 2.7	38.6

[a]Michigan. University. Library. Undergraduate Library. Annual Report, Reference Collection and Service. 1968/69, p. 8.

[b]Spot questions are simple questions for directions or information answered by the librarian in a few words.

[c]In the Undergraduate Library, these are the more substantial questions and are divided into two categories: those which require under five minutes to answer and those requiring more than five minutes. A large majority take less than five minutes. For purposes of this table, the time element is ignored and the "under five" and "over five" questions are added together.

In succeeding years, there was a reversal of the previous trend. Reference questions decreased each of the last five years; spot questions increased in four of the five years. During the period there was an overall decrease in the total number of questions asked. Comparing 1968/69 with 1958/59, reference questions returned to the same level (Table 8). While the reference services have suffered drops of 31.1% in spot questions, 1.2% in reference questions, and 22% in total questions, the undergraduates enrolled in the College of Literature, Science, and the Arts have increased by 69.9%. During the same eleven years, home loans from UGLI have grown by 117% and total book use has increased by 91%.

On a per capita basis, each L.S.&A. undergraduate asked about two reference questions in 1958/59 and only one question in 1968/69. What are the reasons for this lack of growth in reference services of UGLI during a period when undergraduate enrollment has been expanding?

First, have the hours of reference service been cut? In 1958/59 reference service was available during 76 hours each week; this was unchanged in 1968/69. Two librarians were on duty during 59 of these hours in 1958/59. Double staffing has been discontinued during early morning hours, Monday-Thursday; 8 A.M.-12 Noon on Friday;[168] and on Friday, Saturday, and Sunday afternoons. By 1968/69 double staffing had been cut to 36 hours. Has this been a major factor in the decline of UGLI reference questions? This is doubtful. The cuts were made because of lack of demand for assistance.[169] Since some cuts were made in the very early years, lack of a second librarian during slack periods has probably not been detrimental to the quantity of service. In interviews, most librarians thought the current schedule correct except that an additional librarian might be needed on Sundays.

Did the relocation of the reference desks and catalog have a dampening effect on the number of questions? A marked decline in reference questions had begun a year before the relocation. Instead of being one of the triggering factors, the new location may have been a contributing cause. In the old plan (Figure 1), the two desks were in the reading room adjacent to the main doors from the lobby--one of the most heavily used traffic routes in UGLI. The main charging desk was located on the Lobby side of the doors. The charging desk may have been an excellent referral agent to the reference desks. The most striking arrangement of the

Table 8.-Percentage Changes in Types of Questions Received at Reference Desks of the Undergraduate Library and Undergraduate Enrollment, University of Michigan from 1958/59 to 1968/69[a]

Variable	1958/59	1968/69	% Increase or Decrease
I. Questions at Reference Desks:			
Spot Questions	32,537	22,410	-31.1
Reference Questions	14,288	14,110	- 1.2
Total Questions	46,825	36,520	-22.0
II. Student Enrollment:			
Undergraduate Students in the College of Literature, Science, and the Arts	7,357[b]	12,500[c]	+69.9

[a]Michigan. University. Library. Undergraduate Library. Annual Report, Reference Collection and Service. 1968/69, p. 8.

[b]Average representative gross enrollment for Fall and Spring terms. Data furnished by University of Michigan Statistical Services Office.

[c]Estimated enrollment.

pre-1965 layout was the location of the desks in relationship to the public catalog so that students had to walk between the desks to consult the catalog. In the new layout (Figure 2), the catalog is located in front of the desks as students enter from the Lobby. It is now possible for students to use the catalog without being conscious of the reference desks.

Did changes in the orientation program precipitate the reference decline? A definite "no" can be answered. During the first year of decline, the 1964/65 orientation program was judged to be very good by both student guides and librarians.[170]

Have changes in the staff over the years affected the number of reference questions? Roberta Keniston evaluated the first staff:

> I think you'll find everyone endowed with a great sense of service. It's a strong staff of professional librarians, each of whom is deeply interested in helping students. We hope that we'll be able to do a great deal in this direction.[171]

In interviews in 1969, the librarians also projected a "sense of service." Personal observations confirmed the presence of this characteristic in most of the librarians. One notable difference in the first and present staff is age. As a whole, the group in 1958-1962 was older and more experienced.[172] Their replacements have been younger.

The first staff may have had an advantage, not because of any superiority over later staffs, but simply because of the circumstances of time. They opened a bright, new building--the second undergraduate library in the country. A sense of adventure and having a role in something significant may have carried over to the individual encounters with students.

Have student attitudes changed in the eleven years UGLI has been open? It is generally agreed that American college students of the 1950's were the silent generation. One group of sociologists found them to be "politically disinterested, apathetic, and conservative. Social movements and social philosophies [did] not arouse their interest and command their commitment."[173] The UGLI opened at the end of this decade.

By the mid-sixties, students were changing. Kenneth Keniston wrote in 1967:

> A small but growing number of American students ...exhibit a peculiar responsiveness to world-historical events--a responsiveness based partly on their own broad identification with others like them throughout the world, and partly on the availability of information about world events via the mass media. The impact of historical events, be they the world-wide revolution for human dignity and esteem, the rising aspirations of the developing nations, or the war in Vietnam, is greatly magni-

> fied upon such students; their primary identification is not their unreflective national identity, but their sense of affinity for Vietnamese peasants, Negro sharecroppers, demonstrating Zengakuren activists, exploited migrant workers, and the oppressed everywhere. One of the consequences of security, affluence, and education is a growing sense of personal involvement with those who are insecure, non-affluent, and uneducated.[174]

The Reference Librarian, in the 1966/67 annual report on the Michigan Undergraduate Library reference service, reflected on student attitudes:

> During this past year I have noted in many (all too many) of the students an odd sort of ennui. The boys, in particular, have displayed this overall boredom, plus a certain lackadaisical approach to matters in general. When helping some of them, one often senses in their make-up a frightening brand of *carpe diem* attitude, which is, I suppose, dictated by our Viet Nam-oriented world and its attendant and merciless *bête noire*, the military service.[175]

Two years earlier, the decline in reference questions had been noted and the reasons for the decline were sought:

> As a matter of personal curiosity, I questioned during March and early April, 1965, some 37 students, and they, in general, seemed to register complaints of their own about the same annoying factors in their lives--the pressures of the trimester plan with the little time it leaves for one's "personal" life (five vehemently protested that for the first time in their lives they had no time at all to read books of their own choosing); the excessive length of Reserve readings and Reserve lists; the discomfort of the physical facilities in the Undergraduate Library (this seemed to be primarily a complaint about overcrowding at peak hours; several deeply lamented the denial to them of the General Library carrel space after the new locked gates were installed); the use of "pre-chewed" bibliographical lists on which to base term papers (one boy almost bitterly, and probably correctly so on the basis of what I saw, said that

> he could write a much better and more inspired paper if he were not restricted by the rather elementary list of books which his professor had outlined for his and his classmates' use on a mimeographed list). It would seem that students are in some ways being denied the rights and opportunities to think, read, and choose for themselves, and as a result of this, and owing to the time pressures experienced by the students, the reference desks are receiving fewer genuine reference questions, and instead receive what seems like a steadily increasing flow of simple directional questions....[176]

In summarizing 1968/69, the Reference Librarian of UGLI wrote:

> The Undergraduate Library reference service has just passed through the 'Year of the Big Quiet.' ...The reason for this remains an enigma to me. Are students more apathetic about library use today? (Certainly they are more mature than the students of 10 or 15 years ago, and they have a driving moral outrage over many issues and institutions.) Are today's students perhaps better able to use the library without professional help? (They are certainly more experienced in many things than their counterparts of the 1950's.) Are students, as restless citizens of the almost surrealistic world which the campus of today has become, illustrating their independence in one more way--that is, by not asking an elder for help? Do students in spite of our high turnstile counts simply use the Undergraduate Library more as a social club than as a place to study?[177]

Samples of Questions: October and November, 1969

As a first step in attempting to answer the questions which have been raised concerning the quantity and quality of reference services, the two reference desks of the Michigan Undergraduate Library were monitored during the sixth week (October 6-10, 1969) and the eleventh week (November 10-14, 1969) of the University's Fall term. The methodology and definitions used in recording the questions are given in Chapter I.

During the 38 hours of the first week's monitoring, 940 questions were asked by undergraduates, an average hourly rate of 24.7 questions. Graduate students, faculty, and others asked 36 questions during the week, but these questions were excluded from the study. Questions by undergraduates increased to 1,003 during the second week, an hourly average of 26.3. Non-undergraduates asked 26 questions during the second week. All questions were asked in person; the Undergraduate Library gives no telephone reference service. In the 1,943 questions by undergraduates, students approached the librarian in 1,939 cases. In only four situations did the librarian approach a student who seemed to need assistance.

The evening hours were busier than afternoon hours. Morning hours were least busy. Fridays and Mondays were the slowest days; Tuesdays, Wednesdays, and Thursdays were considerably more active.

The data reveal that only a short time was spent with each student seeking reference assistance. No search[178] questions (over 30 minutes) were recorded and only one problem question (over one hour) occurred. Information questions, often lasting only a few seconds, were a large part of the reference activity (Table 9). During the first week, 53.4% were information questions while 46.6% were reference questions. Reference questions increased to 52.1% during the second week. However, of the 961 reference questions asked in both weeks, only in 19 instances did the librarian spend more than five minutes with the student.

Bibliographical assistance with the library's own catalog and holdings (R-1) constituted the bulk of the reference questions (Table 9). There was very little assistance with holdings of other campus libraries (R-2). There were no requests for assistance with non-campus holdings (R-3). Although the Michigan philosophy of reference service for undergraduates portrays the librarian as teacher, little personal instruction was given in the use of the library or any of its resources (R-6). Retrieval of factual, non-bibliographical information (R-4) took place more often than instruction. Librarians rarely counseled students in a reader's advisory capacity (R-5).

In order to evaluate the calibre of questions and service given, information and reference questions were further

Table 9.--Questions Asked by Undergraduates at Reference Desks, Undergraduate Library, University of Michigan, in Two One-Week Samples, 1969

Type of Question	Oct. 6-10, 1969		Nov. 10-14, 1969	
	No.	%	No.	%
Information	502	53.4	479	47.8
Reference:				
R-1	262	27.9	348	34.7
R-2	39	4.1	47	4.6
R-3	. .	. .	. .	. .
R-4	91	9.7	75	7.5
R-5	12	1.3	22	2.2
R-6	34	3.6	31	3.1
R-7	. .	. .	. .	. .
Sub-total	438	46.6	523	52.1
Search	. .	. .	. .	. .
Problem	. .	. .	1	0.1
Total	940	100.0	1003	100.0

analyzed. Almost half of the information questions concerned collections or services with the librarian responding with brief directions (Table 10). Requests for the location of periodicals were the most numerous items in this category. The librarians also did a brisk business in directing students, who already had call numbers, to the proper location of volumes in the main collection. Students asked very few of the simplest of all questions concerning physical facilities ("Where is the pencil sharpener?" and other similar questions).

An analysis of the R-1 questions (Table 11) shows that assisting students at the catalog or at the records of periodical holdings constituted the largest number of reference questions. R-1 questions accounted for 59.8% of all reference questions during the first week and 66.6% in the second week. Most of this assistance (55-60%) was with the records of periodical holdings. Requests for general bibliographical assistance in which the librarians responded by using the

Table 10. --Types of Information Questions Asked by Undergraduates at Reference Desks, Undergraduate Library, University of Michigan, in Two One-Week Samples, 1969

Type of Information Question	Oct. 6-10, 1969		Nov. 10-14, 1969	
	Number	% of Total Information Questions Asked	Number	% of Total Information Questions Asked
Assistance with physical facilities of library:				
Location of pencil sharpener or request to borrow pen, stapler, etc.	21	4.1	16	3.3
Request for keys or unlocking of rooms	10	2.0	18	3.7
Location of areas in library	14	2.8	11	2.2
Sub-total	45	8.9	45	9.2
Requests for location of particular volume (librarian gave directions):				
Monographs in main collection (student had call number)	115	22.9	79	16.5
Reference books (student usually requested by title)	51	10.1	65	13.5
Sub-total	166	33.0	144	30.0

Table 10. --Continued.

Type of Information Question	Oct. 6-10, 1969		Nov. 10-14, 1969	
	Number	% of Total Information Questions Asked	Number	% of Total Information Questions Asked
Requests for information or publication (student did not have call number):				
Librarian knew answer without referring to any source	18	3.6	20	4.2
Librarian referred student to catalog or reference collection, giving no additional assistance	19	3.7	18	3.8
Librarian knew that question would be better answered in another library and referred student to it	23	4.6	23	4.8
Sub-total	60	11.9	61	12.8

Table 10.--Continued.

Type of Information Question	Oct. 6-10, 1969 Number	Oct. 6-10, 1969 % of Total Information Questions Asked	Nov. 10-14, 1969 Number	Nov. 10-14, 1969 % of Total Information Questions Asked
Questions concerning collection or services (librarian responded with brief directions or information):				
Periodicals	60	11.9	102	21.3
Newspapers	12	2.4	12	2.5
College catalogs	16	3.2	16	3.3
Catalog or record of periodical holdings	12	2.4	18	3.8
Reserve books	26	5.2	21	4.4
How and where to charge out books	45	8.9	33	6.9
Use of reference volume in another part of library	2	0.4	5	1.1
Photocopying machine	17	3.4	7	1.5
Exam file	27	5.4	3	0.6
Location of another library	10	2.0	4	0.8
Sub-total	227	45.2	221	46.2

Table 10. --Continued.

Type of Information Question	Oct. 6-10, 1969		Nov. 10-14, 1969	
	Number	% of Total Information Questions Asked	Number	% of Total Information Questions Asked
Miscellaneous information questions	4	1.0	8	1.8
Total information questions	502	100.0	479	100.0

reference collection or pamphlet file were the second most numerous sub-category of R-1 questions.

R-2 questions (bibliographical assistance with holdings of other campus libraries) accounted for 9% of the reference questions during each week. They were almost exclusively concerned (93%) with periodical titles and were answered with the use of special lists of periodical titles held by campus libraries.

There were no requests for bibliographical verification of material not on the campus (R-3).

During the first week, 20.7% of the reference questions were requests for retrieval of factual, non-bibliographical information (R-4). This category dropped to 14.3% in the second week. These questions were widely varied--ranging through requests for addresses, biographical data, maps, pictures, and many other items. No particular subject or type of material dominated the questions.

R-5 questions (counseling of students in a reader's advisory capacity) were very infrequent. Only 2.7% of the first week's reference questions and 4.2% of the second week's were classified in this category. In most cases, the student was beginning a paper and requested advice on appropriate sources.

Table 11.--Bibliographical Assistance with Library's Own Catalogs and Holdings (R-1 Questions) Requested by Undergraduates at Reference Desks, Undergraduate Library, University of Michigan, in Two One-Week Samples, 1969

	Oct. 6-10, 1969		Nov. 10-14, 1969	
Type of Response by Type of R-1 Question	Number	% of Total Reference Questions Asked	Number	% of Total Reference Questions Asked
Request for particular volume or type of volume; librarian gave assistance by:				
Checking list of frequently used reference titles and giving student call number	10	2.2	9	1.7
Charging out heavily used item from drawer of desk or from office	27	6.2	47	9.0
Going to reference shelves and producing particular volume for student who had usually given title or described type	30	6.9	48	9.2

Table 11.--Continued.

Type of Response by Type of R-1 Question	Oct. 6-10, 1969 Number	Oct. 6-10, 1969 % of Total Reference Questions Asked	Nov. 10-14, 1969 Number	Nov. 10-14, 1969 % of Total Reference Questions Asked
Going to main collection shelves and locating monograph, periodical, or newspaper which student had been unable to find	20	4.6	11	2.1
Sub-total	87	19.9	115	22.0
Request for general bibliographical assistance; librarian responded by:				
Using reference collection or pamphlet file	34	7.8	50	9.6
Assisting student at catalog or record of periodical holdings	104	23.8	116	22.2
Using *Subject Headings Used in... the Library of Congress* (or library's own subject headings list for pamphlet file)	10	2.2	15	2.8

Table 11. --Continued.

Type of Response by Type of R-1 Question	Oct. 6-10, 1969 Number	Oct. 6-10, 1969 % of Total Reference Questions Asked	Nov. 10-14, 1969 Number	Nov. 10-14, 1969 % of Total Reference Questions Asked
Assisting in use of microfilm	17	3.9	39	7.5
Assisting in use of print-out of circulation and reserve charges	10	2.2	13	2.5
Sub-total	175	39.9	233	44.6
Total R-1 Questions	262	59.8	348	66.6
Other Reference Questions (R-2 through R-7)	176	40.2	175	33.4
Total Reference Questions	438	100.0	523	100.0

R-6 questions (informal, personal instruction in use of the library or any of its resources) comprised 7.7% of the reference questions during the first week and 5.9% during the second week. The questions were about equally divided into instruction in three resources: the catalog and record of periodical holdings, individual reference volumes, and the reserve book system.

It was unnecessary to place any of the reference questions into a miscellaneous category (R-7).

Other UGLI Activities During Reference Monitoring

In order to place the two weeks of monitoring questions at the reference desks into the over-all context of the Undergraduate Library, Table 12 provides the appropriate data.

Table 12.-Attendance, Home Loans, and Reserve Use during Two Weeks of Monitoring Questions at Reference Desks, Undergraduate Library, University of Michigan in 1969[a]

Variable	Oct. 6-10, 1969[b]	Nov. 10-14, 1969[b]
Total Attendance	44,906	40,562
Average Daily Attendance	8,981	8,112
Total Home Loans from Main Collection (Students Only)	5,102	6,466
Average Daily Home Loans (Students Only)	1,020	1,293
Total Home Loans	5,913	7,477
Average Daily Home Loans	1,182	1,495
Total Reserve Use	6,772	5,435
Average Daily Reserve Use	1,354	1,087

[a]Michigan. University. Library. Undergraduate Library. Weekly Statistical Reports. October and November, 1969.

[b]18 hours each day (8 A.M.-2 A.M.).

Although the attendance and reserve use were larger during the October week, more home loans were made during the November week. The number of questions asked at the reference desks was also greater during November 10-14. This may denote that during October students were using the library as a study hall and for reserve reading. During November students asked more questions and made greater use of the main collection, perhaps in preparation of term papers.

Reference Services for Undergraduate Students: The General Library

All members of the university community, including undergraduates, were provided with assistance by the Reference Department in the General Library from 1891, when the first Reference Librarian was appointed, until the opening of the Undergraduate Library in 1958. Margaret I. Smith served as head of the Department in the years immediately preceeding the UGLI's completion.

Extremely crowded conditions existed in the reference room in 1957. Requests for reference assistance were more than could be sustained if they had lasted "for a more protracted period of time. With the opening of the Undergraduate Library this pressure at the desk was eased somewhat and the crowded condition of the room was gone."[179] At that time, statistics of use were kept only during March of each year. In March, 1958 (one and one-half months after UGLI opened) the Reference Department answered a daily average of 204 questions. This total consisted of 85 spot questions, 84 reference questions requiring under five minutes to answer, and 35 reference questions requiring over five minutes. In March, 1957, the average daily number of questions was 263.[180] This was a 21.6% decrease from 1957 to 1958.

Agnes N. Tysse was head of the Department from 1958 until her retirement in August, 1970. During 1958/59 the staff at the reference desk answered an estimated 32, 856 questions with an additional 4, 560 telephone questions.[181] By 1968/69, questions by patrons at the main reference desk totalled 45, 486 with 9, 075 telephone questions. A separate information desk near the catalog recorded 15, 308 inquiries.[182]

Michigan undergraduates may use the reference collection and staff of the General Library as well as those in the Undergraduate Library. What is the extent of these reference resources and how much use do undergraduates make of them?

A long rectangular main reading room on the second floor, typical of monumental university libraries built in the early years of this century, housed the Reference Department in 1969. Approximately 300 seats were available for readers at large tables. Most of the 15,000 volumes[183] in the reference collection were shelved along the walls of the room. Heavily used reference books (about 850 volumes) were shelved behind the reference desk.

As a result of the great distances to the catalog and parts of the reference collection, the librarians spent most of their time behind the reference desk. An information desk, supervised by the Reference Department, was located near the catalog in the main corridor. Graduate students manned this desk. Members of the Technical Services Department also answered questions concerning the catalog as they filed during weekdays.

In addition to reference volumes in all subject fields and a large bibliography collection, the Reference Department housed current Congressional hearings, slip laws, House and Senate documents, and many other current United States Government publications. The Department was also responsible for United Nations and foreign documents. Telephone directories, college catalogs, and an extensive vertical file containing pamphlets and newspaper clippings were in the reference collection. The map collection, located on the third floor and totalling over 123,000 accessioned items, was administered by the Reference Department.[184] The Human Relations Area Files were also housed in the map room.

Another major responsibility was the borrowing from other libraries of volumes lacking at the University of Michigan. The Reference Department did not borrow from other libraries for undergraduates. Nor did it answer questions via telephone from undergraduate or graduate students. Telephone service was restricted to faculty, university offices, campus libraries, and non-university callers.

The General Library's Reference Department also performed some technical processing. Maps were selected, cataloged, and serviced. United States, United Nations, and foreign documents were received and prepared for binding.[185]

The reference desk was staffed by two librarians from 9 A.M.-12 Noon and 1-5 P.M., Monday through Friday. One professional staff member was on duty from 8-9 A.M., 12

Noon-1 P.M., 5-6 P.M., and 7-10 P.M., Monday-Friday. A graduate student was at the desk from 6-7 P.M. and 10 P.M.-12 Midnight each weekday night. On Saturdays, one professional worked from 8 A.M.-1 P.M. and another professional worked from 1-6 P.M. Sunday hours from 1 P.M.-12 Midnight were covered by graduate students. Librarians were available for 75 hours, or 74.2% of the 101 hours the General Library was open each week during the regular school year.

The information desk was staffed by a graduate student from 10 A.M.-12 Noon, 1-5 P.M., and 7-10 P.M., Monday-Thursday. Friday hours were 10 A.M.-12 Noon and 1-5 P.M. On Saturdays and Sundays the hours were 1-5 P.M.

The professional staff of the Reference Department in the Fall term, 1969 was composed of nine librarians. In addition to public service at the desk, each was assigned a special area of responsibility (such as government documents, the map collection, interlibrary borrowing, the clipping file, or other administrative duties). Five reference librarians had extensive experience at the University of Michigan, ranging from eight to thirty-two years continuous service. Four librarians had less experience in the Department: one to four years. Eight of the nine were women. Six librarians received their library science degrees from the University of Michigan with Columbia, Drexel, and Illinois being the professional schools of the other three. Two staff members had masters degrees in subject areas from Michigan. None of the General Library reference librarians had worked in the Undergraduate Library.

In May, 1969, the Reference Department employed three full-time clerical assistants; another staff member worked one-half time. Several graduate students also worked part-time.

Undergraduate Use of the General Library's Reference Department

No formal studies have ever been undertaken to ascertain the number of undergraduates asking questions at the reference desk in the General Library. When asked if they had impressions of the undergraduates who ask questions, the reference librarians all agreed that it was extremely difficult to distinguish informally between undergraduate and graduate students. One librarian, however, believed that reference work with undergraduates in the General Library was increasing rather than decreasing. Several staff members pointed out that government documents was one area where they assisted undergraduates.

An elaborate study[186] of the users of the General Library was undertaken in 1968. The survey showed that 56.1% of all users were undergraduates. Most of the undergraduates came to the General Library to study their own personal materials (33.1%) or to use the main catalog (16.2%).[187] Approximately 5% of the undergraduates and 6.5% of the graduate students said that they came to the General Library to "use reference materials."[188] The number of undergraduates who asked a reference librarian for assistance was not determined.

Samples of Questions: October and November, 1969

How many undergraduates ask questions at the General Library's reference desk? What types of questions do they ask? To answer these questions, all requests for assistance were monitored, with questions by undergraduates being recorded during the same 38 hours of both October 6-10 and November 10-14, 1969 as was done in the Undergraduate Library.

During the first week, 135 questions were received from undergraduates, an average hourly rate of 3.5 questions. Questions by undergraduates increased to 189 during the second week, an hourly average of 4.9. All questions were asked in-person. In all instances the questions were student-initiated; no librarians approached students.

During the October monitoring, undergraduates asked 21.8% of the total in-person and telephone questions (617) asked at the reference desk of the General Library. During the week in November, undergraduate questions rose to 28.4% of the total questions (665). Three questions by undergraduates from other colleges have been excluded from the data.

Table 13 categorizes the questions by undergraduates. Once again, only a short time was spent with each student. One search question[189] was undertaken; there were no problem questions. Brief information questions were 48.1% of the total during the first week and 44.4% in the second. Of the 174 reference questions in both weeks, the librarian spent at least five or more minutes with the student on only five occasions.

Table 13.--Questions Asked by Undergraduates at Reference Desk, General Library, University of Michigan, in Two One-Week Samples, 1969

	Oct. 6-10, 1969		Nov. 10-14, 1969	
Type of Question	No.	%	No.	%
Information	65	48.1	84	44.4
Reference				
R-1	43	31.9	60	31.9
R-2	. .	. .	. .	. .
R-3	3	2.2	5	2.6
R-4	18	13.4	35	18.5
R-5	1	0.7	. .	. .
R-6	4	3.0	5	2.6
R-7	. .	. .	. .	. .
Sub-total	69	51.2	105	55.6
Search	1	0.7	. .	. .
Problem	. .	. .	. .	. .
Total	135	100.0	189	100.0

In an analysis of information questions, three types are clearly dominant (Table 14). In the largest number of cases, students asked for particular reference books. The next most frequent situation was a request by the student for information or a publication (student did not have call number). The librarian referred him to the catalog or reference collection, giving no additional assistance. Questions concerning the location of periodicals were also numerous.

R-1 questions (bibliographical assistance with the library's own catalog and holdings) constituted 31.9% of all questions asked in both weeks, or 62.3% and 57.1% of the more substantive reference questions. Assistance was rarely given students at the main catalog because of its distance

Table 14.--Types of Information Questions Asked by Undergraduates at Reference Desk, General Library, University of Michigan, in Two One-Week Samples, 1969

Type of Information Question	Oct. 6-10, 1969		Nov. 10-14, 1969	
	Number	% of Total Information Questions Asked	Number	% of Total Information Questions Asked
Assistance with physical facilities of library:				
Location of pencil sharpener or request to borrow pen, stapler, etc.	..	..	1	1.2
Request for keys or unlocking of rooms	..	..	..	..
Location of areas in library	2	3.1	5	5.9
Sub-total	2	3.1	6	7.1
Requests for location of particular volume (librarian gave directions):				
Monographs in main collection (student had call number)	9	13.9	6	7.1
Reference books (student usually requested by title)	21	32.3	24	28.6
Sub-total	30	46.2	30	35.7

Table 14.--Continued.

Type of Information Question	Oct. 6-10, 1969		Nov. 10-14, 1969	
	Number	% of Total Information Questions Asked	Number	% of Total Information Questions Asked
Requests for information or publication (student did not have call number):				
Librarian knew answer without referring to any source	. .	. .	1	1.2
Librarian referred student to catalog or reference collection, giving no additional assistance	14	21.5	18	21.5
Librarian knew that question would be better answered in another library and referred student to it	3	4.6	3	3.5
Sub-total	17	26.1	22	26.2

Table 14.--Continued.

Type of Information Question	Oct. 6-10, 1969		Nov. 10-14, 1969	
	Number	% of Total Information Questions Asked	Number	% of Total Information Questions Asked
Questions concerning collection or services (librarian responded with brief directions or information):				
Periodicals	12	18.5	16	19.1
Newspapers	. .	. .	1	1.2
College catalogs	1	1.5	. .	. .
Catalog or list of periodical titles	. .	. .	. .	. .
Reserve books	. .	. .	. .	. .
How and where to charge out books	3	4.6	4	4.8
Use of reference volume in another part of library	. .	. .	. .	. .
Photocopying machine	. .	. .	1	1.2
Exam file	. .	. .	1	1.2
Location of another library	. .	. .	3	3.5
Sub-total	16	24.6	26	31.0

Table 14. --Continued.

Type of Information Question	Oct. 6-10, 1969 Number	Oct. 6-10, 1969 % of Total Information Questions Asked	Nov. 10-14, 1969 Number	Nov. 10-14, 1969 % of Total Information Questions Asked
Miscellaneous information questions	. .	. .	. .	. .
Total information questions	65	100.0	84	100.0

from the reference desk. Most of the questions in this category are assistance with reference volumes (Table 15). For half of the R-1 questions, the librarian responded by charging out one of the reference books shelved back of the desk.

There were no questions during the two weeks of monitoring at the General Library's reference desk in which the librarians assisted undergraduates with the holdings of other campus libraries (R-2).

R-3 questions (bibliographical verification of material not on the campus) accounted for approximately 4.5% of the reference questions each of the weeks.

During the first week, 26% of the reference questions were requests for retrieval of factual, non-bibliographical information (R-4). This category increased to 33.3% in the second week. As in the Undergraduate Library, these questions varied greatly with no subject area or type of material dominant.

Only once during the monitoring did a librarian counsel a student in a reader's advisory capacity (R-5).

R-6 questions (informal personal instruction in use of the library or any of its resources) were also infrequent. Only 5.8% of the first week's reference questions and 4.8%

Table 15.--Bibliographical Assistance with Library's Own Catalog and Holdings (R-1 Questions) Requested by Undergraduates at Reference Desk, General Library, University of Michigan, in Two One-Week Samples, 1969

Type of Response by Type of R-1 Question	Oct. 6-10, 1969		Nov. 10-14, 1969	
	Number	% of Total Reference Questions Asked	Number	% of Total Reference Questions Asked
Request for particular volume or type of volume; librarian gave assistance by:				
Checking list of frequently used reference titles and giving student call number	..	..	..	..
Charging out heavily used item from back of reference desk	23	33.3	22	20.9
Going to reference shelves and producing particular volume for student who had usually given title or described type	..	..	..	..

Table 15. --Continued.

Type of Response by Type of R-1 Question	Oct. 6-10, 1969		Nov. 10-14, 1969	
	Number	% of Total Reference Questions Asked	Number	% of Total Reference Questions Asked
Going to main collection shelves and locating monograph, periodical, or newspaper which student had been unable to find	. .	. .	. .	. .
Sub-total	23	33. 3	22	20. 9
Request for general bibliographical assistance; librarian responded by:				
Using reference collection or pamphlet file	14	20. 3	29	27. 6
Assisting student at catalog or list of periodical titles	6	8. 7	8	7. 6
Using *Subject Headings Used in... the Library of Congress*	. .	. .	1	1. 1

Table 15. --Continued.

Type of Response by Type of R-1 Question	Oct. 6-10, 1969 Number	Oct. 6-10, 1969 % of Total Reference Questions Asked	Nov. 10-14, 1969 Number	Nov. 10-14, 1969 % of Total Reference Questions Asked
Assisting in use of microforms	. .	. .	. .	. .
Assisting in use of print-out of circulation charges	. .	. .	. .	. .
Sub-total	20	29.0	38	36.3
Total R-1 Questions	43	62.3	60	57.2
Other Reference Questions (R-2 through R-7)	26	37.7	45	42.8
Total Reference Questions	69	100.0	105	100.0

of the second week's were classified in this category. In all cases, it was instruction in use of a reference volume.

No reference questions required classification in a miscellaneous category (R-7).

Other General Library Activities During Reference Monitoring

Undergraduates could have also requested assistance from the graduate student at the information desk or from a staff member filing at the main catalog. During October 6-10, the graduate students at the information desk recorded

246 questions by undergraduates during the same 38 hours the reference desk was monitored. This was 47.7% of the total questions (515) asked. Although the number of questions by undergraduates declined slightly to 234 during November 10-14, the percentage of undergraduates' questions rose to 52.5% of the total questions (445). Table 16 gives the questions by undergraduates. The majority of the questions were brief and informational in nature. Only two types of questions--catalog aid (accounting for 12.6% during the first week and 11.1%, the second week) and identification questions (4.5% and 6.4%)--could qualify as reference questions.

Users of the main catalog during mornings and afternoons of weekdays may also ask for assistance from technical services staff. During 37.5 hours of October 6-10, 1969, 216 questions were answered. From November 10-14, there were 261 questions.[190] The number of questions by undergraduates is not known.

Other pertinent statistics of General Library use (attendance and book use) during the two periods of monitoring questions are shown in Table 17.

The Two Michigan Reference Services

Are there significant differences between the reference services in the Undergraduate Library and the General Library? What are the similarities?

The Undergraduate Library reference librarians served a much larger number of undergraduate students than did their counterparts in the General Library. During October 6-10, 1969, the librarians in UGLI assisted almost seven times as many undergraduates as were assisted by the reference staff in the General Library. From November 10-14, over five times as many undergraduates were served at the UGLI reference desks.

Three of the greatest differences between the reference services are the result of the long distances from the reference desk in the General Library to the reference collection and the catalog. The General Library staff members often responded to inquiries by charging out books from behind the desk (33.3% and 20.9% of the reference questions during the two weeks). In UGLI this accounted for only 6.2% and 9% of the reference questions. Second, librarians in the General Library did not often go to the reference or

Table 16.--Questions Asked by Undergraduates at the Information Desk, Second Floor Corridor, General Library, University of Michigan, during Two Weeks of Monitoring Questions in 1969 at Main Desk of Reference Department[a]

Type of Question	Oct. 6-10, 1969		Nov. 10-14, 1969	
	No.	%	No.	%
Stack Directions	61	24.8	64	27.4
Catalog Aid	31	12.6	26	11.1
"Where Is?" Questions	96	39.0	87	37.2
Identification Questions[b]	11	4.5	15	6.4
Campus Information	18	7.3	19	8.1
Referrals to the Reference Desk, Periodical Reading Room, or Other Library Departments	29	11.8	23	9.8
Total Information Desk Questions	246	100.0	234	100.0

[a]Data compiled by graduate students on duty for the following hours: Monday-Thursday, 10 A.M.-12 Noon, 1-5 P.M., and 7-9 P.M.; Friday, 10 A.M.-12 Noon and 1-5 P.M.

[b]This category was used for identification of items in the printed catalogs of the Library of Congress and other bibliographies which were once shelved near the information desk.

Table 17. -Attendance, Home Loans, and Reserve Use during Two Weeks of Monitoring Questions at Reference Desk, General Library, University of Michigan, in 1969[a]

Variable	Oct. 6-10, 1969[b]	Nov. 10-14, 1969[b]
Total Attendance	17, 400	17, 881
Average Daily Attendance	3, 480	3, 576
Total Home Loans (Students Only)	2, 828	3, 998
Average Daily Home Loans (Students Only)	565	799
Total Home Loans	5, 123	6, 662
Average Daily Home Loans	1, 024	1, 332
Total Reserve Use	2, 426	2, 188
Average Daily Reserve Use	485	437

[a]Michigan. University. Library. Circulation Department. "Monthly Statistical Sheets." October and November, 1969.

________. Graduate Reserve Service. "Monthly Statistics." October and November, 1969.

[b]16 hours each day (8 A. M. -12 Midnight).

main collections to assist students in finding specific items; the Undergraduate staff members did this fairly frequently. Third, General Library personnel rarely assisted students at the catalog or with a rotary list of periodical titles (although the periodical list was mounted on the reference desk). These R-1 questions, in contrast, were 23. 8% and 22. 2% of all reference questions in UGLI.

Other differences were:
R-2 questions: 9% during each week in UGLI; none in General Library;

R-3 questions: none in UGLI; 4.5% during each week in General Library;

R-4 questions: 20.7% in first week and 14.3% in second week in UGLI; 26% and 33.3% in General Library.

Similarities were also evident. A large proportion of all undergraduate questions at both reference services was information questions--usually about one-half. R-1 questions were the most numerous of reference questions at both desks. Undergraduate and General Library reference librarians spent a brief time with each student, giving extended assistance only on rare occasions. Neither group of reference librarians extensively counseled students in a reader's advisory capacity (R-5) nor did they give informal, personal instruction to students (R-6).

Undergraduate Users of Union Catalog

An additional investigation was conducted in the General Library to test the hypothesis that unassisted use by undergraduates of the union catalog of campus holdings increases use of the General Library and decreases use of the Undergraduate Library. Methods, hours, and other procedures used in interviewing 474 University of Michigan undergraduate students are described in Chapter 1.

The Public Catalog, located on the second floor of the General Library, is a card record of "all books held by the complex of University of Michigan divisional libraries."[191] Monographs, serials, government documents, and micro-reproductions are included. However, some libraries (Law, Clements, Michigan Historical Collections, and other smaller collections) are "independent of the University Library system, and their holdings are only partly represented in the Public Catalog."[192] Not all newspapers are included. Sound recordings in the Undergraduate and Music Libraries, maps in the General Library, and many documents of international organizations are excluded. Cards for Chinese, Korean, and Japanese publications are also not filed in this union catalog.[193]

Undergraduates accounted for 28.3% of all union catalog users during the 38 hours of the study (Table 18).

In percentages, the 474 undergraduates interviewed were members of the following university classes:

Freshman	16.9%
Sophomore	21.8
Junior	29.7
Senior	31.6
Special Unclassified	. .

Table 18.--Union Catalog Users in the General Library, University of Michigan, September 29-October 3, 1969[a]

Union Catalog User	Number	%
Undergraduates Interviewed	474	26.2
Undergraduates Refusing Interview	5	0.3
Undergraduates Who Had Been Previously Interviewed	33	1.8
Total Undergraduate Users	512	28.3
Graduate Students, Faculty, and University Staff (Excludes Library Staff)	1,281	70.9
Non-University Users (Local Residents, Students and Faculty from Other Institutions)	15	0.8
Total Users of Union Catalog	1,808	100.0

[a]Interviews conducted during week of September 29-October 3, 1969. Hours on Monday-Thursday were: 10 A.M.-12 Noon, 1-5 P.M., and 7-9 P.M. On Friday: 10 A.M.-12 Noon and 1-5 P.M.

They were enrolled in the following schools and colleges:

College of Literature, Science, and the Arts	83.6%
College of Engineering	6.3
School of Education	4.2
College of Architecture and Design	2.1
School of Nursing	1.9
School of Natural Resources	1.1
School of Business Administration	0.4
College of Pharmacy	0.4

All undergraduates were asked: "Did you use the Undergraduate Library catalog before coming here?" Forty-one percent responded "Yes" and 59% said "No."

The 194 undergraduates who replied that they had used the UGLI catalog before coming to the union catalog were then asked: "Why are you now using this main catalog?" The 199 reasons given were:

Undergraduate Library did not have material	47.2%
Material in use in Undergraduate Library (out, on reserve, etc.)	32.7
Wanted additional material	16.1
Referred to Union Catalog by Undergraduate reference librarian	1.5
Did not use Undergraduate catalog properly	1.0
Wanted different edition	0.5
Had wrong citation	0.5
Subject headings in Undergraduate catalog not specific enough	0.5

The 280 students who said they had not used the Undergraduate Library catalog before coming to the union catalog in this particular instance were asked: "Do you usually by-pass the Undergraduate Library catalog and come to the main catalog first?" The responses were:

Yes	65.8%
No	23.3
About half the time, I by-pass it	6.0
Depends on the material I am seeking	3.9
Depends on which is closer	0.7
First time in any campus library	0.3

The 184 undergraduates who affirmed that they usually by-passed the UGLI catalog were next asked: "Why do you not use the Undergraduate Library catalog first?" 208 varied reasons were given:

This is a union catalog listing holdings of all campus libraries	21.7%
Have found through experience that the UGLI lacks what I want	19.3
Most of the university's books are here in the main library	15.9
I do not like the Undergraduate Library	12.1
Undergraduate collection is too small	11.6
I like the General Library better	9.1
Too much on reserve in UGLI	3.8
The General Library is closer to my living quarters	1.9
My professor sent me here to use union catalog	1.4
I did not know the UGLI existed	1.4
I work here in the General Library	0.9
It depends on the material I am seeking	0.9

The final question posed to all 474 undergraduates interviewed was: "If the Undergraduate Library had a catalog like this which includes holdings of all campus libraries, would you use it there or still come here?"

Still come here to General Library	41.8%
Use it in UGLI	51.3
I do not know	2.8
Would use whichever is closer	2.5
Does not matter to me	1.0
Depends on material sought	0.6

Comparison of the foregoing data on undergraduate users of the General Library's union catalog is made with Cornell undergraduates in Chapter 7. Conclusions are also drawn there.

Notes

1. Catholepistemia, or universal science.

2. Howard H. Peckham, *The Making of the University of Michigan, 1817-1967* (Ann Arbor: University of Michigan Press, 1967), pp. 4-5.

3. Frank W. Blackmar, *The History of Federal and State Aid to Higher Education in the United States,* Contributions to American Educational History, No. 9; U.S. Bureau of Education Circulars of Information, 1890, No. 1, Whole Number 161 (Washington: U.S. Government Printing Office, 1890), p. 238.

4. Peckham, pp. 17-18.

5. Michigan. University. Official Publications, *General Information, 1970-71* ("Official Publications," Vol. LXX, No. 146; Ann Arbor, University of Michigan, 1969), p. 9.

6. Michigan. University. *President's Report.* January, 1969, p. 4.

7. Letter from Harris D. Olson, Associate Registrar, University of Michigan, to Billy R. Wilkinson, March 6, 1970.

8. "University Enrollment Increases...," *Michigan Daily* (Ann Arbor), October 10, 1969, p. 6.

9. Letter from Robert P. Souve, Office of the Vice-President for Academic Affairs, University of Michigan, to Billy R. Wilkinson, February 6, 1970.

10. Edward H. Krause and Lloyd S. Woodburne, "The Administration and Curriculums of the College of Literature, Science, and the Arts," Michigan. University. *The University of Michigan, an Encyclopedic Survey,* ed. Wilfred B. Shaw. 9 vols. (Ann Arbor: University of Michigan Press, 1941-1958), III, 437.

11. Interview with the Assistant Dean, College of Literature, Science, and the Arts, University of Michigan, November 14, 1969.

12. Letter from Ruth A. Brown, Statistician, College of Literature, Science, and the Arts, University of Michigan, February 19, 1970.

13. William W. Bishop, "The University Library to 1941," in Michigan. University. *The University of Michigan, an Encyclopedic Survey*, VIII, 1369.

14. *Ibid.*, pp. 1370-71.

15. Raymond C. Davis, "The Growth of the Library," Michigan. University. *Public Exercises on the Completion of the Library Building of the University of Michigan, December 12, 1883* (Ann Arbor: University of Michigan, 1884), 15.

16. *Ibid.*

17. Michigan. University. *Public Exercises on the Completion of the Library Building of the University of Michigan, December 12, 1883* (Ann Arbor: University of Michigan, 1884), p. 43.

18. Davis, p. 17.

19. Association of Research Libraries. *Academic Library Statistics, 1968/69* (Washington: Association of Research Libraries, 1969).

20. Bishop, "The University Library to 1941," p. 1375.

21. *Ibid.*

22. Wilfred B. Shaw, "General Library Building," in Michigan. University. *The University of Michigan, an Encyclopedic Survey*, VIII, 1633.

23. Wilhelm Munthe, *American Librarianship from a European Angle* (Chicago: American Library Association, 1939), p. 180.

24. Michigan. University. Regents. *Proceedings of the Board of Regents..., 1939-42*, p. 652 as quoted in Warner G. Rice, "The University Library, 1941-53," Michigan. University. *The University of Michigan, an Encyclopedic Survey*, VIII, 1385.

25. Warner G. Rice, "The University Library, 1941-53," in Michigan. University. *The University of Michigan, an Encyclopedic Survey*, VIII, 1384.

26. "The General Library," Research News [University of Michigan Office of Research Administration], XV (April, 1965), 5.

27. Rice, pp. 1386-87.

28. Michigan. University. Library. Annual Report of the Director. 1953/54, p. 3.

29. Ibid., 1966/67, pp. 1-10.

30. Ibid., p. 4.

31. Michigan. University. Survey Research Center. Faculty Appraisal of a University Library, A Report of the Responses of the University of Michigan Faculty to a Mail Questionnaire Concerning the University Library's Collections, Services, and Facilities as of April, 1961. Prepared for the Library Council of the University under the Direction of Charles F. Cannell and Jack M. McLeod, in Collaboration with a University Library Committee Consisting of Fred L. Dimock, Roberta C. Keniston, Warren S. Owens, and Robert H. Muller, Chairman (Ann Arbor: University of Michigan Library, 1961).

32. Ibid., p. 3.

33. Michigan. University. Library. Operations Research Unit. General Library Utilization Survey. [Final Report of a Survey of 2,705 Library Patrons, Winter Term, 1968. Prepared by Pat Fulford and Noel M. Ernst. November 13, 1969.] (Typewritten.)

34. Ibid., pp. 5-6.

35. Work-Study Scholars are students registered half-time in the School of Library Science who work 30 hours per week in the libraries. They receive a stipend and their instructional fees are paid by the Library.

36. Michigan. University. Library. Organization Charts, University Library of the University of Michigan (Ann Arbor: University Library, 1968), [p. 1].

37. Michigan. University. Library. Annual Report of the Director. 1964/65, pp. 3-4.

38. *Ibid.*, 1968/69, p. 16.

39. "The General Library," *Research News*, p. 10.

40. Letter from Connie R. Dunlap, Head, Graduate Library, University of Michigan, to Billy R. Wilkinson, March 17, 1970.

41. *Ibid.*

42. Michigan. University. Library. *The University of Michigan General Library Building*. [Ann Arbor: University Library, n.d.], p. 1.

43. Irene A. Braden, *The Undergraduate Library*, ACRL Monographs, No. 31 (Chicago: American Library Association, 1970), p. 29.

44. *Ibid.*

45. Michigan. University. Library. Advisory Committee on the Undergraduate Library. Minutes of Meetings. 1954-1956.

46. Michigan. University. Library. Advisory Committee on the Undergraduate Library. "Preliminary Program for the Undergraduate Library." August 18, 1954. (Mimeographed.)

47. Michigan. University. Library. Advisory Committee on the Undergraduate Library. "Program for an Undergraduate Library," Submitted by Frederick H. Wagman, Director of the University Library, for the Advisory Committee on the Undergraduate Library, February 1, 1955. (Mimeographed.)

48. *Ibid.*, p. 3.

49. *Ibid.*, p. 12.

50. Michigan. University. Library. *Annual Report of the Director*. 1955/56, p. 3.

51. *Ibid.*, 1957/58, p. 3.

52. Roberta Keniston, "The University of Michigan Undergraduate Library," Michigan Librarian, XXV (June, 1959), 24-25.

53. Frederick H. Wagman, "The Undergraduate Library of the University of Michigan," College and Research Libraries, XX (May, 1959), 188.

54. [James Packard], "The Undergraduate Library," Research News, XV (May, 1965), 3-10.

55. Braden, The Undergraduate Library, pp. 43-47.

56. Rolland C. Stewart, "The Undergraduate Library Collection." Paper presented at the Institute on Book Selection and Acquisitions, University of California, San Diego, August 25-September 5, 1969.

57. Braden, The Undergraduate Library, p. 46.

58. Michigan. University. Library. Undergraduate Library. Annual Report. 1957/58, p. 4.

59. Braden, The Undergraduate Library, p. 47.

60. Michigan. University. Library. Undergraduate Library. Annual Report. 1957/58, p. 4.

61. Interview with Rose-Grace Faucher, Head, Undergraduate Library, University of Michigan, October 10, 1969.

62. Michigan. University. Library. Undergraduate Library. Annual Report. 1968/69, p. 18.

63. Ibid.

64. Michigan. University. Library. Committee on the Undergraduate Library Staff. Minutes of Meeting, August 1, 1956. p. 2. (Mimeographed.)

65. Ibid., p. 3.

66. Ibid., p. 4.

67. Memorandum from Robert H. Muller, Associate Director, to Frederick H. Wagman, Director, University

of Michigan Library, August 16, 1956.

68. Braden, The Undergraduate Library, p. 54.

69. Michigan. University. Library. Undergraduate Library. Annual Report. 1958/59, p. 18.

70. Interview with Frederick H. Wagman, Director, University of Michigan Library, October 1, 1969.

71. Interview with Roberta Keniston, former Head, Undergraduate Library, University of Michigan; then Associate Librarian, Eastern Michigan University, October 1, 1969.

72. Michigan. University. Library. Undergraduate Library. Annual Report, Reference Collection and Service. 1967/68, p. 2.

73. Interview with Roberta Keniston, October 1, 1969.

74. Michigan. University. Library. Undergraduate Library. Annual Report. 1957/58, p. 3.

75. Ibid., p. 12.

76. The position of Assistant Head of the Library was vacant in 1969 when this study was done.

77. Michigan. University. Library. Undergraduate Library. Annual Report. 1968/69, p. 2.

78. Michigan. University. Library. Organization Charts..., [p. 8].

79. Michigan. University. Library. Annual Report of the Director. 1957/58, p. 5.

80. "A New Intellectual Center," Michigan Alumnus, LXIV (December 14, 1957), 151.

81. Michigan. University. Library. Annual Report of the Director. 1958/59, p. 19.

82. Richard L. Meier, Social Change in Communications-Oriented Institutions, University of Michigan Mental

Health Research Institute Reports, No. 10 (Ann Arbor: University of Michigan, 1961).

83. Ibid., pp. 26-27.

84. Ibid., p. 28.

85. Michigan. University. Library. Annual Report of the Director. 1967/68, p. 4.

86. Ibid., 1968/69, p. 9.

87. Ibid., 1962/63, p. 24.

88. Ibid., p. 18.

89. Michigan. University. Library. Undergraduate Library. Annual Report, Reference Collection and Service. 1966/67, p. 3.

90. Michigan. University. Library. Undergraduate Library. Annual Report. 1964/65, p. 3.

91. Letter from Virginia J. Reese, Coordinating Librarian, Residence Halls Libraries, Office of University Housing, University of Michigan, to Billy R. Wilkinson, January 13, 1970.

92. Michigan. University. Library. Undergraduate Library. Annual Report. 1957/58, p. 11.

93. Michigan. University. Library. Annual Report of the Director. 1960/61, p. 13.

94. Ann Arbor News, January 4, 1966.

95. Michigan. University. Library. Undergraduate Library. Annual Report. 1965/66, Appendix C-2.

96. Braden, The Undergraduate Library, p. 58.

97. Interview with Roberta Keniston, October 1, 1969.

98. Meredith Eiker, "Ten Years in Circulation," Michigan Daily (Ann Arbor), January 12, 1968.

99. "The 'Ugli' Routine: Student Subculture," *Michigan Daily* (Ann Arbor), February 16, 1969.

100. Meier, p. 28.

101. *Ibid.*, p. 30.

102. Wagman, "The Undergraduate Library...," p. 188.

103. Interview with Roberta Keniston, October 1, 1969.

104. Michigan. University. Library. Undergraduate Library. *Annual Reports*. 1959/60, [Statistical Supplement, p. 1]; 1968/69, Appendix A, p. 1.

105. Michigan. University. Library. Undergraduate Library. *Annual Report*. 1968/69, Appendix B.

106. *Ibid.*, p. 15 and Appendix C-2.

107. Michigan. University. Library. Undergraduate Library. *Annual Report*. 1960/61, [Statistical Supplement, p. 2].

108. Wagman, "The Undergraduate Library...," p. 186.

109. Letter from Rose-Grace Faucher, Head, Undergraduate Library, University of Michigan, to Billy R. Wilkinson, April 2, 1970.

110. Harvie Branscomb, *Teaching With Books* (Hamden, Connecticut: Shoe String Press, 1964 [Reprint of Chicago: Association of American Colleges and American Library Association, 1940]), p. 27.

111. The basis for computation is that for 21 semesters from 1958-1968 undergraduates have charged out 77.72% of the total home loans from the Undergraduate Library.

112. Interview with Rose-Grace Faucher, November 12, 1969.

113. Michigan. University. Library. Undergraduate Library. *Annual Report*. 1964/65, p. 16.

114. Roberta Keniston, "Circulation Gains at Michigan," Library Journal, LXXXIII (December 1, 1958), 3359.

115. Interview with Frederick H. Wagman, October 1, 1969.

116. Ibid.

117. Michigan. University. Library. Undergraduate Library. Annual Report. 1968/69, Appendix A.

118. Ibid.

119. Interview with Rose-Grace Faucher, September 29, 1969.

120. Michigan. University. Library. Undergraduate Library. Annual Report. 1967/68, Appendix A.

121. Michigan. University. Library. Undergraduate Library. Annual Report, Reference Collection and Service. 1968/69, pp. 2-4.

122. Interview with Rose-Grace Faucher, September 29, 1969.

123. Interview with Janet F. White, Reference Department, General Library, University of Michigan, October 6, 1969.

124. Interview with Roberta Keniston, October 1, 1969.

125. Michigan. University. Library. Annual Report of the Director. 1968/69, p. 15.

126. Michigan. University. Library. Undergraduate Library. Annual Report. 1958/59, p. 34.

127. Ibid.

128. Ibid., p. 38.

129. Ibid.

130. Ibid., 1959/60, p. 23.

131. Ibid., 1961/62, p. 20.

132. Ibid., p. 21.

133. Ibid., 1962/63, p. 20.

134. Ibid., 1963/64, p. 20.

135. Ibid.

136. Ibid., 1964/65, p. 18.

137. Ibid., 1966/67, p. 20.

138. Ibid., 1968/69, p. 28.

139. Ibid.

140. Michigan. University. Library. Undergraduate Library. "Making the Most of Library Resources, Part I." Ann Arbor, Fall Term, 1969. (Typewritten.)

141. Ibid., Part II.

142. Interview with Patricia Kay, In Charge of Orientation, Undergraduate Library, University of Michigan, October 2, 1969.

143. Michigan. University. Library. Undergraduate Library. [Untitled Paper Describing the Orientation Program of the Undergraduate Library.] n. d.

144. Letter from Harris D. Olson, Associate Registrar, University of Michigan, to Billy R. Wilkinson, April 10, 1970.

145. Interview with Michele Cone, Undergraduate Library, University of Michigan, October 2, 1969.

146. Wagman, "The Undergraduate Library...," p. 185.

147. Michigan. University. Library. Undergraduate Library. Annual Reports, Reference Collection and Service. 1958/59-1968/69.

148. Michigan. University. Library. Undergraduate Library. Annual Report. 1962/63, p. 4.

149. Letter from Rose-Grace Faucher to Billy R. Wilkinson, December 9, 1969.

150. Michigan. University. Library. Undergraduate Library. Annual Reports. 1967/68, p. 6; 1968/69, p. 5.

151. Interview with Roberta Keniston, October 1, 1969.

152. Michigan. University. Library. Undergraduate Library. Annual Report. 1957/58, p. 18.

153. Ibid., pp. 18-19.

154. Michigan. University. Library. Annual Report of the Director. 1964/65, p. 3.

155. J. J. Cook, "Increased Seating in the Undergraduate Library: A Study in Effective Space Utilization," Case Studies in Systems Analysis in a University Library, ed. by Barton R. Burkhalter (Metuchen, New Jersey: Scarecrow Press, 1968), p. 151.

156. Michigan. University. Library. Undergraduate Library. Annual Report. 1965/66, p. 3.

157. Interview with Paula de Vaux, Undergraduate Library, University of Michigan, October 1, 1969.

158. Interview with Rose-Grace Faucher, September 29, 1969.

159. During a ten-day exam period at the end of the Fall and Winter terms, UGLI is open until 5 A.M. This practice of opening 40 extra hours was begun in 1967/68.

160. Data in this section are from personal interviews held September 29-October 3, 1969 with eight of nine librarians on the staff and from a letter from Rose-Grace Faucher, April 5, 1970.

161. Interview with Rose-Grace Faucher, September 29, 1969.

162. Michigan. University. Library. Undergraduate Library. Annual Report. 1957/58, p. 8.

163. Michigan. University. Library. Undergraduate Library. "Reference Service to Undergraduates [with] Appendix 1, The Recording of Reference Statistics." [Ann Arbor, n. d.]. (Mimeographed.) Originally appeared as a supplement to the 1957/58 Annual Report of the Undergraduate Library.

164. *Ibid.*, Appendix 1, p. 1.

165. *Ibid.*

166. *Ibid.*

167. There are so few "over 5 minute" reference questions that they have been combined with the "under 5 minute" questions.

168. Michigan. University. Library. Undergraduate Library. *Annual Report*. 1959/60, p. 3.

169. *Ibid.*

170. *Ibid.*, 1964/65, p. 18.

171. "A New Intellectual Center," pp. 151-52.

172. Interview with Roberta Keniston, October 1, 1969.

173. Rose K. Goldsen, *et al.*, *What College Students Think* (Princeton: Van Nostrand, 1960), p. 199.

174. Kenneth Keniston, "The Sources of Student Dissent," *Journal of Social Issues*, XXIII (July, 1967), 130.

175. Michigan. University. Library. Undergraduate Library. *Annual Report, Reference Collection and Service*. 1966/67, p. 4.

176. *Ibid.*, 1964/65, pp. 6-7.

177. *Ibid.*, 1968/69, p. 1.

178. Definitions of search questions as well as information, reference (R-1 through R-7), and problem questions are given in Chapter 1. Hereafter in this section, these definitions are used.

179. Michigan. University. Library. Reference Department. Annual Report. 1957/58, p. 1.

180. Ibid.

181. Ibid., 1958/59, p. 24.

182. Ibid., 1968/69, [p. 16].

183. An estimate of reference volumes; interview with Agnes N. Tysse, Head, Reference Department, General Library, University of Michigan, September 30, 1969.

184. Michigan. University. Library. Reference Department. Annual Report. 1968/69, [p. 20].

185. Michigan. University. Library. Organization Charts..., [p. 7].

186. Michigan. University. Library. Operations Research Unit. General Library Utilization Survey. [Final Report of a Survey of 2,705 Library Patrons, Winter Term, 1968. Prepared by Pat Fulford and Noel M. Ernst. November 13, 1969.] (Typewritten.)

187. Ibid., pp. 48-49.

188. Ibid., p. 55.

189. Definitions of search questions as well as information, reference (R-1 through R-7), and problem questions are given in Chapter 1. Hereafter in this section, these definitions are used.

190. Michigan. University. Library. "Weekly Reports, Catalog Information Desk, Technical Services Department." October 6-10, 1969; November 10-14, 1969.

191. Michigan. University. Library. The University of Michigan General Library Building, [Ann Arbor: University Library, n.d.], p. 1.

192. Michigan. University. Library. "How to Use the

General Library Card Catalog." [Mimeographed Guide, n. d.], p. 1.

193. Ibid.

Chapter 4

CASE II: CORNELL UNIVERSITY

...this easy-going, loose-jointed institution...

> Carl L. Becker, Cornell University: Founders and the Founding (Ithaca: Cornell University Press, 1943), p. 200.

Brief History of the University

Two very dissimilar men--Ezra Cornell and Andrew Dickson White--founded Cornell University in 1865. Cornell, an upstate New York mechanic and farmer, left Ithaca in 1842 to seek his fortune. When he returned thirteen years later, he had made a considerable one as a builder of telegraph systems with Samuel F. B. Morse.[1] He purchased land and began to farm it scientifically. Wishing to benefit his fellow citizens, Cornell in 1863 "proposed to build, and to endow, a great public library for Ithaca and Tompkins County."[2] Later in November, he was elected to the New York State Senate. Here he met Andrew D. White, Chairman of the Senate's Committee on Literature when Cornell's bill to incorporate the library was referred to White's committee. A partnership unique in the annals of American higher education was formed.

White, a wealthy and scholarly Yale graduate who had taught at the University of Michigan, already had an

> idea of the great work that should be done in the great State of New York. Surely...in the greatest state there should be the greatest of universities; in central New York there should arise a university which by the amplitude of its endowment and by the whole scope of its intended sphere, by the

> character of the studies in the whole scope of the curriculum, should satisfy the wants of the hour.[3]

After Cornell's first philanthropic venture--the public library--he still had a great desire

> to dispose of so much of my property as is not required for the reasonable wants of my family, in a manner that shall do the greatest good to the greatest number of the industrial classes of my native state, and at the same time to do the greatest good to the state itself, by elevating the character and standard of knowledge of the industrial and productive classes.[4]

Thus a university "where any person can find instruction in any study"[5] became a reality with Ezra Cornell's endowment, plus funds from the sale of western lands provided in the Morrill Act of 1862, and with the leadership of Andrew Dickson White as the first President. Cornell University opened on October 7, 1868 with 412 students (332 freshmen, 80 with advanced credit); a small faculty (one member being Daniel Willard Fiske, Professor of North European Languages, Librarian, and Director of the University Press); and two completed buildings.[6]

From these auspicious and innovative beginnings, the University has flourished during the past century.

> For perhaps the first time in history, courses in agriculture, engineering, and veterinary medicine were taught on a level with the humanities. It is unique today in its peculiar and diverse organization, where we find certain units--the College of Arts and Sciences, the Medical College, the Law School and the School of Hotel Administration, and the Colleges of Architecture and Engineering--existing as private, endowed colleges, while others [the College of Agriculture for example] are supported as "contract colleges" by the State of New York.[7]

The main Ithaca campus of more than 90 major buildings and 700 acres is now home to twelve schools and colleges. The School of Nursing and the Medical College are in New York City. During the Fall semester, 1969, 10,042 undergraduates and 4,098 graduate students were enrolled for a total of 14, 140 students on the Ithaca campus. Men numbered 10, 743; there were 3, 397 women.[8] During the same semester, 1, 805 full-time faculty members were employed in Ithaca.[9] The number of part-time faculty was approximately 2, 000.

Cornell University is accredited by the Middle States Association of Colleges and Secondary Schools.

The College of Arts and Sciences

A single faculty guided Cornell until 1887 when the College of Law separated. In 1896 other departments and colleges were formed with the Academic Department as the forerunner of the College of Arts and Sciences.[10] (The official renaming came in 1903.) The College had 631 undergraduate students by 1898/99; 1, 424 by 1915/16.[11] Throughout its history, the College has attracted a distinguished faculty and offered its students, through one of the freest of elective systems, a wide range of courses. In addition to the education of its own students, the College plays a second role as a university college and is responsible for the education of all Cornell students in liberal subjects.

In the 1969 Fall semester, 3, 241 undergraduate students were enrolled in the College of Arts and Sciences. There were 1, 139 women and 2, 102 men. The freshmen numbered 770.[12] The full-time College faculty members totalled 622 in the same semester.[13]

This, briefly, is Cornell University and its largest component, the College of Arts and Sciences. The 10, 042 university undergraduates, and more particularly the 3, 241 underclassmen of the College, are the largest group of potential library users at the University.

The Cornell University Library

Few universities have had a President who believed so strongly in and worked so successfully for a great university library as Cornell had in its first President, Andrew Dickson White. To White "the ideas of a university and a great library were so inseparably related that one predicated the other."[14] In his organizational plan for the University, he wrote:

> A large library is absolutely necessary to the efficiency of the various departments. Without it, our men of the highest ability will be frequently plodding in old circles and stumbling into old errors.[15]

The Board of Trustees backed White with funds, appropriating in February, 1868, $11,000 for the purchase of books. In the Spring, White traveled over Europe shopping for books and equipment. Having already collected a fine personal library, "he knew how to buy well, occasionally indulging in a bibliophile's weakness for the rare and scholarly volumes which are today Cornell's treasures."[16] When he had spent the appropriated funds, he used his own money or appealed to Ezra Cornell.

The first of the Library's great collections was a gift by Cornell before the University opened. He purchased in July, 1868, the 7,000-volume library of classical literature collected by Charles Anthon of Columbia College. White recorded that Cornell's

> liberality was unstinted.... Nothing could apparently be more outside his sympathy than the department needing these seven thousand volumes; but he recognized its importance in the general plan of the new institution, bought the library for over twelve thousand dollars, and gave it to the university.[17]

The President and the Founder were soon joined by the first Librarian to form a trinity of extraordinary library benefactors. White invited Willard Fiske, an old friend from their boyhood days in Syracuse, to the staff of the University.

> An excellent linguist, he was fitted for his professorship of north European languages. Well trained in the best American scholarly library [seven years as Assistant Librarian of the Astor Library in New York], and a true bibliolater, he was equally well equipped to establish Cornell's Library. A practiced journalist, he could supervise Cornell's publications and serve as an unofficial Director of Public Information.[18]

The University Library's home was in Morrill Hall, the first building on the campus. "By January, 1869, the Library numbered 15,400 volumes--more than Columbia College had acquired in a hundred years."[19] In June, 1871, there were 27,500 volumes. The Library then moved to McGraw Hall when it was completed in 1872.

The Cornell Library was a reference library, patterned on the Astor and the Bodleian Libraries. With this concept of non-circulation, there was a need to make the volumes available to the faculty and students. Fiske from the first had the Library open nine hours each day--longer, he boasted, than in any other American university.[20]

Together Fiske and White continuously and systematically strengthened the collection. Goldwin Smith, the brilliant professor from England who taught at Cornell, gave his personal library. The Franz Bopp philological library and the Kelly Collection of the history of mathematics and the exact sciences were purchased; Samuel Joseph May, the abolitionist, gave his Antislavery Collection; the Jared Sparks Collection in American History and the 13,000-volume Zarncke library of German literature came to Cornell; and other collections enriched the holdings.[21]

This progress in the development of the Cornell Library, however, was interrupted. Rita Guerlac has recorded the extraordinary events:

> In the 1880's the Cornell University Library was the center, and Willard Fiske one of the principal figures, of a drama which rocked the University and the community. John McGraw, one of the first trustees of the University and the donor of the building which first housed the Library, died in 1877, leaving his whole estate to his only daughter Jennie. Jennie McGraw had been a friend of the University since its founding, and had given the chime of nine bells that rang out for the first time at the inauguration exercises.... In 1880 she married Willard Fiske in Berlin; she died a year later. Her will, after bequests to her husband and her McGraw cousins, left to Cornell University the residue of her estate, amounting to almost two million dollars, part of which was designated for a library and other gifts and the rest for unrestricted use. It was a princely bequest. 'The creation of such a library would have been the culmination of my work,' wrote White. 'I could then have sung my *Nunc dimittis*.'

> But a question arose as to the legality of the University's accepting the bequest, because its Charter restricted the size of the Corporation's endowment. While the University turned its attention to this problem, personal complications arose between two of the trustees and Willard Fiske. Mr. Fiske, indignant, and not without provocation, resigned from the University in 1883 and undertook to break his wife's will; the McGraw cousins, on the advice of trustee Henry Sage, joined him in his suit. Ithacans took sides and feeling ran high; outsiders followed the story in the press. The case was contested over seven years, and went finally to the Supreme Court of the United States, which, in May 1890, decided against the University. The litigation had by then consumed almost a quarter of the estate; half went to the McGraw heirs and the final quarter to Willard Fiske.[22]

All was not lost to the University and its Library. The legal limitation on the size of the University's endowment was removed. But more importantly, Henry W. Sage decided to pay for the new library building which Jennie McGraw Fiske had intended in her will. A site on the main quadrangle was selected and William Henry Miller was chosen as architect. The stone building with its tower was completed and opened on October 7, 1891. Sage gave the University $260,000 for the construction costs and $300,000 as an endowment--the interest would purchase books annually for the collection.[23] The local newspaper described the building as being "somewhat in the form of a Greek cross, ... treated in a style that may be called modified Romanesque."[24] The Library had a stack capacity of 475,000 volumes, or over four times the 1891 holdings (ca. 114,330; 84,330 volumes in the main collection and some 30,000 in the White Historical Library).[25] The new Library

> soon enjoyed a national reputation... when Secretary Thwaites of the Wisconsin Historical Society returned to Madison in 1895 from a visit to fourteen Eastern and two Southern cities... he reported to the Wisconsin Board of Library Building Commissioners regarding the Cornell Library: '... This is by far the best planned and best built university library building in this country.'[26]

President White gave his personal collection of 30,000 volumes, 10,000 pamphlets, and many manuscripts. "Called the most valuable private historical library collected in the United States,"[27] it was installed in a special room--"a delightful example of Millerian gothic-romanesque-baroque"[28]--in the new building.

Willard Fiske, who had retired to a villa in Florence, left the University a large bequest upon his death in 1904. But to the Library he bequeathed four magnificant collections which are particular treasures: his 7,000-volume Dante Collection, a 3,500-volume Petrarch Collection, a library of Rhaeto-Romantic literature, and his 10,000-volume Icelandic Collection.[29]

In his 1905 Autobiography, Andrew Dickson White wrote of his pride in the development of the Library:

> The library has become, as a whole, one of the best in the country. As I visit it, there often come back vividly to me remembrances of my college days, when I was wont to enter the Yale library and stand amazed in the midst of the sixty thousand volumes which had been brought together during one hundred and fifty years. They filled me with awe. But Cornell has now, within forty years from its foundation, accumulated very nearly three hundred thousand volumes, many among them of far greater value than anything contained in the Yale library of my day.[30]

George William Harris succeeded Fiske as Librarian. He served the Library for forty-two years, thirty-two of them as head Librarian. After the move into the new building, there was a period of "largely uneventful years, devoted to keeping the Library going rather than growing."[31] Harris continued the policy of a non-circulating, reference library until 1908 when the Library Council decided to permit home loans. The inevitable flaws were found in the building: poor ventilation in certain rooms, the need for more radiators in the stacks, and an over-estimation of the stack capacity (by 1904 Harris began requesting more stack space). Harris is most remembered, however, for the book classification system he adopted--a fixed shelf location device based on the British Museum scheme.[32]

The period from 1915 until 1946 was a general decline into chaos. The Librarians--Willard Austin, 1915-1929, and Otto Kinkeldey, 1930-1945--pleaded for more space, more funds, and more staff, but their pleas were unanswered by University administrators. "The space nightmare took on a Kafkaesque quality. The Library was bulging."[33]

The University Library, 1946-1969

Once again, a "forceful and imaginative Librarian and a President who [believed] in the Library and its central importance to the intellectual life of the University"[34] came together to bring order out of chaos. President Edmund Ezra Day in 1946 invited Stephen A. McCarthy to take charge of the Library. With Day's promised support, McCarthy directed the Library toward recovery. The administration of the Library was reorganized and new staff members were appointed: Felix Reichmann and G. F. Shepherd, Jr. in two key positions and Frances W. Lauman and Josephine M. Tharpe as Cornell's first reference librarians. Studies were made of the space problem and a survey[35] by outside experts gave recommendations for improving the Library and "strong support to the initiative of the new Librarian."[36] On January 1, 1948, the staff began the use of the Library of Congress classification and the long task of reclassifying all pre-1948 holdings from the Harris system to that of the Library of Congress.

It was President Deane W. Malott, 1951-1963, however, who "saw the central importance of the Library and the urgency of its problems, made their solution his first priority, and quietly carried it through to a splendid conclusion."[37]

During the McCarthy years, all campus libraries were completely rehoused in new or renovated quarters. Beginning in 1950 with the A. R. Mann Library, which serves the Colleges of Agriculture and Human Ecology, the building program culminated with the 1961 opening of the John M. Olin Library (the "first university library building in this country designed and constructed for research"[38]) and the 1962 reopening of the renovated main library building as the Uris Undergraduate Library. The Olin Library, built and furnished at a cost of $5, 700, 000, occupies a prominent position on the College of Arts and Sciences quadrangle. Its seven floors and two lower levels have a stack capacity of two million volumes.

When Stephen A. McCarthy resigned as Director of Libraries in 1967 to become Executive Director of the Association of Research Libraries, a distinguished era in the development of the Cornell Libraries ended. Under his leadership the collections more than doubled (1, 206, 195 volumes in June, 1946; 3, 067, 073 in June, 1967); the number of professional staff members doubled (62. 5 in October, 1947; 120 in 1967); reference questions tripled (28, 939 in 1950/51; 92, 217 in 1966/67); total recorded use was 2. 2 times greater (526, 361 in 1950/51; 1, 172, 530 in 1966/67); and library expenditures in his last year were eleven times more than his first year ($361, 251 in 1946/47; $4, 096, 779 in 1966/67).[39]

During 1967/68, G. F. Shepherd, Jr., Associate Director, was Acting Director. David Kaser became Director of Libraries on August 1, 1968.

Table 19 shows the growth and use of the University Libraries during their first century.

The Users

A survey[40] of all persons entering the Olin Library was conducted January 10-13, 1967. Of the 5, 251 persons who answered the brief questions concerning their status at the University and their purpose in coming to the Library, undergraduate students were most numerous (47. 3%). Graduate students (38. 2%) and faculty members (11. 7%) were the other major users with the research staff (0. 5%) and others (2. 3%) forming very small proportions.

When all users were asked what they planned to do in the Library, the responses were:

Course assignment or class preparation	25. 3%
Research	27. 4
Some of both	11. 4
Other plans	10. 1
No response to question	25. 8

During the same period, 511 persons asked questions at the Olin Library reference desks. Their university statuses were:

Undergraduates	42. 7%
Graduate students	31. 9
Faculty	17. 0
Others	8. 4

Table 19.--Volumes and Recorded Use, Cornell University Libraries, 1869-1969[a]

Year	Volumes on June 30	Total Recorded Use of Materials During Previous Year
1869	18,000	. .
1876	39,000	. .
1891	96,000	. .
1900	250,000	. .
1920	655,000	. .
1940	1,063,000	. .
1946	1,206,195	. .
1951	1,505,728	526,361
1958	1,967,599	744,656
1959	2,043,026	811,182
1960	2,116,230	873,903
1961	2,198,654	958,946
1962	2,278,046	967,515
1963	2,413,369	1,060,554
1964	2,577,296	1,140,085
1965	2,725,624	1,203,690
1966	2,892,539	1,178,885
1967	3,067,073	1,172,530
1968	3,257,399	1,269,052
1969	3,444,570	1,310,509

[a]Cornell University. Library. The Cornell University Library, Some Highlights (Ithaca: The Library, 1965).

Cornell University. Library. Reports of the Director of the University Libraries. 1950/51-1968/69.

The categories of borrowers of 3, 906 volumes at the Olin circulation desk during January 10-13, 1967 were:

Undergraduates	40. 3%
Graduate students	40. 8
Faculty	12. 3
Others	6. 6

The Staff

In 1969, the staff of the University Libraries was composed of 136 professionals and 251 full-time non-academic employees. Many part-time employees (in full-time equivalents: 92. 25) worked a total of 189, 915. 75 hours during 1968/69. The total number of FTE staff members was 479. 25.[41] The professionals have the following titles: Assistant Librarian, Senior Assistant Librarian, Associate Librarian, and Librarian. These staff members work in the Olin Library, the Uris Library, and thirteen other libraries on the Ithaca campus.

Library Budget

During the early 1960's, with the opening of the Olin and Uris Libraries, substantial increases in funds were allocated by the University for library personnel. Funds for books and other materials were also increased. In 1959/60, the total library expenditures (including the Medical Library in New York City and other non-Ithaca libraries) were $1, 650, 995. By 1962/63, when both new libraries were in operation, the total library expenditures were $2, 711, 166. During 1968/69, $5, 011, 500 was expended for the entire library system.[42]

The Future

Adequate space for housing the Cornell collections has again become a problem. Six linear miles of new shelving are required each year to keep pace with the present rate of growth in the campus libraries. In order to plan for the future needs of the libraries, the University appointed a 15-member faculty-administration Library Study Committee in the Fall Semester, 1969. Under the chairmanship of Professor Francis E. Mineka, the Committee began a year-long study of the problem.[43]

The Uris Library

There were a series of abortive plans going back to 1925 for relieving the crowded conditions of the University Library. The schemes were either additions to the building, the use of Boardman Hall (the neighboring building on the quadrangle) as an annex, or the construction of a new building. After the appointment of McCarthy as Librarian, further efforts were made to solve the Cornell library problem. Finally, Keyes D. Metcalf and Frederic C. Wood[44] were retained as consultants to restudy the situation.

> The two consultants visited the campus, conferred with library and administrative officers, reviewed previous plans, studied the present library building, proposed sites, etc. The consultants also conferred with each other. Each consultant submitted his own report, and both participated in a joint meeting of the Administration and the Library Board on July 21 [1955], at which the reports were presented orally and discussed. The recommendations of the consultants won the full support of the Administration and the Library Board.[45]

The recommendations made by Wood and Metcalf were:

> 1. Retention of the main library by conversion into an undergraduate library, and
>
> 2. demolition of Boardman Hall and use of its site for the construction of a new research library which would primarily serve graduate students and faculty.[46]

Their plan had excellent points in favor of its adoption: the old Library with its tower which had become a landmark and the symbol of Cornell would be preserved; Libe Slope, a lovely hill behind the Library, would not be violated (it had become hallowed ground to many generations of Cornellians as the scene of commencements and reunions in the Spring and tray-sliding in Winter); and the two-building central library complex could serve all members of the University community in its choice location on the main quad.

The plan had one great disadvantage: the demolition of Boardman Hall. Although the building was old, needed extensive repair work, and had much unusable space, it was also venerated as the previous home of the Law School and later as home to the Departments of History and Government with the offices of such illustrative professors as Carl Becker.

The Executive Committee of the Cornell University Board of Trustees adopted the Wood-Metcalf proposals on October 13, 1955--"a two-building central library, consisting of a new Graduate and Research Library on the site of Boardman Hall and the present Library Building remodeled and converted into an undergraduate library"[47] became official policy.

Efforts were concentrated on the research library building after the drafting in 1956 of a preliminary program[48] for the undergraduate library which "served as a basis for the schemative plans developed by the architect in connection with the planning of the Research Library."[49] In 1958 a Committee on the Undergraduate Library, organized as a subcommittee of the Library Board (an advisory group of faculty members), was appointed by the Provost of the University. Professor Robert M. Adams chaired the committee of six faculty members and three librarians (Stephen A. McCarthy; G. F. Shepherd, Jr.; and Charles A. Carpenter, Jr., Librarian of the Goldwin Smith Library). The subcommittee reviewed the preliminary program and approved a final program[50] for the conversion of the old Library into an undergraduate library. The program called for 1,000-1,200 seats, capacity for 100,000-150,000 volumes, audio equipment, a room for library orientation and other lectures, and various reading rooms. The program stated that

> The Reference Department performs the chief teaching function of the Library. The Reference Collection will consist of 2000-3000 volumes of bibliographies, indexes, encyclopedias, handbooks, etc. The Reference Room should be close to the card catalog and the Circulation Department.[51]

The Building

The architects of the new John M. Olin Library--Warner, Burns, Toan, and Lunde--were appointed in June, 1959 to draw plans for the major renovation. When the Olin Library was completed in early 1961, all volumes and equipment were moved through a new tunnel connecting the two libraries. The old Main Library was closed on February 1, 1961 after seventy years of service. Later that year, work was begun on interior renovation; the exterior of the 1891 building was to remain unchanged.

For a total expenditure of $1, 232, 192 (including $144, 375 for furnishings),[52] Cornell University created an undergraduate library of 50, 000 square feet with 1, 067 seats and a book capacity of 125, 000 volumes. A major portion of the costs was given by Harold D. and Percy Uris, for whom the building was named the Uris Library. Arthur H. Dean also contributed substantially and the main reading room was named in his honor.

At 8 A.M., September 19, 1962, the Uris Library quietly opened for use (the fanfare being saved until October 9-10, when the Olin and Uris Libraries were dedicated in a long-remembered program climaxed with a special concert by the Philadelphia Orchestra). In contrast to its forebears --the Lamont Library and the University of Michigan Undergraduate Library--the Uris Library was not a modern building designed to meet the needs of undergraduates, but

> it is generally agreed that architect Charles Warner and his associates were peculiarly sensitive in planning the remodeling in that they preserved and enhanced many of the fine architectural features of the building and yet produced a good, functional, modern library.[53]

The Collection

The Goldwin Smith Library--a select collection of 8, 000 volumes (6, 200 titles) strong in American and English literature, philosophy, and drama, situated in a classroom building with a reading room for undergraduate students, and the reserve book desk of the University Library for courses in the Departments of English, Speech and Drama, Romance Literature, German Literature, Philosophy, and Classics--was the foundation upon which the collection for the Uris Library was built. In May, 1959, the Subcommittee on the Undergraduate Library proposed to the faculty of the College of Arts and Sciences that the shelflist of a recently established undergraduate library be obtained, divided among the various disciplines, and distributed to the departments for revisions and additions. Assured of the faculty's cooperation, the shelflist of the University of Michigan Undergraduate Library was distributed in September, 1959, to be used in the selection of titles. Charles A. Carpenter, Jr., Goldwin

Smith Librarian, also compiled a list of approximately 11,000 titles. To his file were then added titles from reserve book lists, syllabi, and recommended reading lists. When the faculty recommendations were returned, the Library had its shopping list for the undergraduate collection.

The purchase of the stock of the Pyetell Bookshop in Pelham, N. Y., the transfer of duplicate copies from the research library's collection, the purchase of in-print titles, the cataloging and processing of the volumes, and other details of assembling the collection--all done under the direction of Felix Reichmann--are described by Irene A. Braden.[54]

A committee of the library staff selected the periodical titles which would be duplicated in the Uris Library. Approximately 250 titles were initially selected (some 80 of these were designated to have complete or 10-year backfiles). A list of the desired backfiles was sent to the faculty and also appeared in the Cornell Alumni News. These appeals prompted numerous gifts.

Recommendations for the reference collection were made by the reference staff in the Olin Library. When Frances W. Lauman, Associate Reference Librarian, was named Reference Librarian-designate of the Uris Library in July, 1961, she assumed the task of final selection for the reference collection, which numbered approximately 1,780 volumes during the first year of operation.[55] The spoken arts recordings for the Listening Rooms were selected by the Uris Library staff. No musical recordings were included because the Music Library maintained an extensive collection.

The Uris Library was to contain no microforms or bound backfiles of newspapers. The Department of Maps, Microtexts, and Newspapers, in the adjacent Olin Library, would serve undergraduates needing these materials.

The Uris Library opened with a book collection of 42,722 volumes. The main collection was housed in one wing of the building on seven levels of bookstacks. The holdings have increased to 83,485 volumes (June 30, 1969). Table 20 traces the yearly growth.

Upon the opening of Uris Library, the professional staff members began to assist the Undergraduate Librarian in selecting titles to be added to the collection. In addition to recommending current publications, several librarians with special subject backgrounds strengthened portions of the collection by recommending retrospective titles. Individual faculty members have also surveyed a subject area and suggested purchases.

Table 20.--Volumes and Titles in the Uris Library, Cornell University, 1962-1969[a]

Year	Volumes on June 30 of Each Year	Titles
1962	ca. 30, 000[b]	. .
1963	46, 404	. .
1964	52, 032	. .
1965	57, 103	. .
1966	64, 517	42, 587
1967	71, 906	47, 493
1968	79, 038	52, 421
1969	83, 485	55, 123

[a]Cornell University. Library. Uris Library. Annual Reports. 1962/63-1968/69.

[b]On September 19, 1962 (Opening day) there were 42, 722 volumes.

Subscriptions for additional periodicals were also continually considered. By June 30, 1965, the number of periodicals received had reached 282; by June 30, 1969, 347 periodicals were received.[56] In 1969, the Uris Library received 10 newspapers.

The Staff

No formal studies were done of undergraduate use of the old Main Library in order to gather data for estimating the size staff necessary for the Uris Library.[57] The chaotic, crowded conditions during the building's last ten years of service precluded any meaningful studies. As the planning of the Uris Library progressed, the top University administrators asked Director McCarthy and his associates for an estimate of the staff needed to operate Uris Library for its first several years, not just the opening-day staff. The University administrators realized that the Library "had been running at a very low level for a long time and was staffed at approximately that low level."[58] It was completely understood that the two new buildings would require a substantial increase in the number of staff members. During 1960/61, McCarthy submitted an estimated salary budget for the Undergraduate Library staff. It was then planned that the staff would "consist of 23-25 members, approximately 10 of whom will be professional librarians and the remainder clerical or subprofessional."[59] Funds were then officially allocated for a staff of 22 full-time persons (9 librarians and 13 sub-professionals). All were new positions in the library system. Wages for part-time student assistants were also budgeted.

Several years before the opening of Uris Library, Charles A. Carpenter, Jr. was named as Librarian-designate of the Undergraduate Library. When he resigned to work on a doctorate in the Department of English at Cornell, Billy R. Wilkinson was appointed in July, 1961 to succeed him. During the 1961/62 academic year, Wilkinson was in charge of the small Goldwin Smith Library and assisted the Library administration in planning the service program and assembling the book collection of Uris Library, then under renovation. Frances W. Lauman was also designated as the future head of reference services in Uris Library, over a year in advance of the opening. During 1961/62, she continued as Associate Reference Librarian in the Olin Library. By April 4, 1962, five additional staff members had been selected to transfer to Uris Library on September 1, 1962.[60] Experienced librarians thus formed the nucleus of the first Uris Library staff. A search was then begun for librarians for the other positions. During the summer of 1962, applicants for the non-professional positions were invited.

During 1962/63, the Uris staff was comprised of 9 librarians, 13 non-professional staff members, and approximately 50 part-time student assistants. By June 30, 1969, the full-time staff still numbered 22 persons, but the professional positions had decreased from 9 to 7 and the non-professional positions had increased from 13 to 15. Part-time student and non-student employees worked a total of 16,116 hours during 1968/69.[61]

The Librarian of the Uris Library has always reported to G. F. Shepherd, Jr., Assistant Director for Readers Services and later Associate Director of University Libraries.

The technical service departments of the John M. Olin Library perform most of the acquiring and processing tasks for Uris Library materials. The Uris staff selects, searches, and prepares orders for its own monographs and serials, which are then acquired, processed, and returned to Uris ready for use. Two exceptions, however, have existed to this general rule: beginning in 1966, orders for Reserve Desk copies were taken directly by the Uris staff to a local bookstore and when the books were received, they were sent to the Olin Acquisitions and Catalog Departments for rush processing. From the beginning, recordings for the Listening Rooms were ordered and received directly by the Uris staff who also cataloged the recordings.

Wilkinson's Tenure, 1962-1967

Billy R. Wilkinson served as Librarian of the Uris Library during its first five years. He and the staff saw the building win acceptance by the Cornell undergraduates during the first year. During 1962/63, Uris Library had an attendance of 705, 251 persons; 125, 488 volumes used in the Library; 64, 072 home loans; 2, 247 listeners in the Listening Rooms; and 6, 609 questions asked at the reference desk.[62]

During the first years, the Library had an unusually experienced staff who knew the University and its library system and who were interested in working with undergraduate students. The staff members were also flexible; during the summers when Uris Library was completely or partially closed, various staff members worked in departments of the Olin Library or other campus libraries.

The collection and access to it were kept in good order by complete annual inventories. Only approximately 1% or less of the volumes in the main collection was missing each year.

Physical improvements were made in the building. The large Dean Reading Room and other areas on the main floor were carpeted in December, 1965. One of the reading rooms on the lower level was completely redecorated and carpeted in 1966/67 with a gift from Allan P. Kirby as a memorial to his brother, Sumner M. Kirby, who had attended Cornell.

Progress was also made in improving the book funds. Allocations from the University were gradually increased and then Uris Library was endowed by Allan P. Kirby with the Sumner M. Kirby Memorial Fund of $100, 000 (the yearly income would purchase volumes in American history, economics, and sociology and also refurbish the Kirby Room as necessary). Another generous benefactor was the Iota Chapter of Kappa Alpha Theta Sorority which gave in 1966 a fund of $35, 000 for the establishment and support of a Cornelliana Collection in the President Andrew D. White Library--the triple-tiered "gothic-romanesque-baroque"[63] room which had been preserved in the conversion of the building into an undergraduate library. The annual income from the Kappa Alpha Theta Fund purchased books concerning the University as well as those by and about its faculty and students. The University Press also helped in establishing a collection of its publications.

Arthur H. Dean, Chairman of the University Board of Trustees, also continued his generous support. As one of his many gifts to the Library, he began a series of book collection contests in 1966. Cash awards were presented to six undergraduate students who were judged to have the best private collections. The Uris Library staff organized and conducted the competitions and the receptions held in the White Library for the participants.[64]

All was not sweetness and light, however, during this period in the Uris Library. Complaints were received from students and staff about noise in the Library, particularly at night and in the main lobby, Dean Reading Room, and adjacent areas. Installation of additional acoustical tile in the lobby and carpeting of the main floor partially alleviated the noise problem created by many socializing students.

Another problem during the first years of the Uris Library was the lack of a formal means of communication with a representative group of students. No attempt was made during 1962-1965 to initiate a committee of undergraduate students who would advise the Librarian and the staff concerning the policies and services of Uris Library. When a Committee on Undergraduate Library Service--two students, two librarians (the Undergraduate Librarian and the Associate Director of Libraries), and one faculty member--was formed in 1966, it was a substitute for the students' request for representation on the all-faculty Library Board. Five meetings[65] were held during 1966/67, but

> From the view point of both the students and the librarians, it would probably be agreed that the committee was not a smashing success. The reasons for the failure were many and complicated, but basically the whole intemperate climate of student-administration relationships kept hovering over the meetings. Perhaps the committee should be given a second year in order to function more successfully.[66]

There was no second year.

Other problems (the decline in use of the Listening Rooms, the decline in the number of questions asked at the reference desk, and the failure to develop a program of library instruction other than the one-hour orientation lecture for freshmen) are discussed in succeeding sections.

Rucker's Librarianship, 1967-

Ronald E. Rucker was appointed Acting Librarian of Uris Library on September 1, 1967 upon the resignation of Wilkinson who became a doctoral student at the Columbia University School of Library Service. Rucker had previously directed the Central Serial Record Department in the Olin Library. He was named Librarian of Uris Library in 1968.

During Rucker's tenure, the collection has reached 83,485 volumes (June 30, 1969) and the staff "embarked on a program of selective retirement"[67] of obsolete volumes. Books of little interest to undergraduates were removed from the collection, with additional weeding to be done in the future.

Improvements continued to be made in physical facilities. The lecture room on the lower level was redecorated and carpeted in 1968 with funds given by Mrs. Oscar Seager as a memorial to her husband. A long-neglected room on the ninth level of the bookstack was also refurbished the same year, with the aid of a special grant, and became the seminar room of the Greek Civilization Study Program.

The Cornelliana Collection in the White Library grew to 1,112 volumes by June 30, 1969. Frances W. Lauman was appointed Curator of the Collection in the Autumn of 1967.

The Uris staff worked intimately with small groups of undergraduates through the continuation of the Arthur H. Dean Book Collection Contest. Contact was established with three fraternities by assisting with their house libraries. Suggestions were made as to material which might be discarded and purchases were recommended for improving the small libraries. Recommendations of titles were also made for a small collection in the Noyes Center, the second student center on the campus.

Tentative planning was done for a new Commons Library, which would be a Uris Library branch situated in the residence hall complex under construction on the North Campus. Scheduled for completion in Fall, 1971, the Commons Library was envisioned by Ronald Rucker as a library of several thousand volumes where "the emphasis will be placed on a solid reference section, recreational reading and congenial study space with a highly selective collection providing the basic materials for the teaching fields of undergraduate concern."[68] However, after an indefinite postponement of the branch library because of a lack of funds, it was decided in November, 1970 to eliminate completely the Commons Library.[69]

As the financial problems of the University have affected the Uris Library in its projected branch in the new student residence area, other contemporary University problems have directly touched the Library's users and staff.

> In December [1968] the deep-seated dissatisfaction with life at Cornell felt by many black students brought them to Uris among other libraries to protest the alleged irrelevance of the book collections. The demonstration, which involved piling books taken at random from the shelves on the Circulation Desk, seemed to be an early skirmish in the sequence of events that led to the occupation of Willard Straight Hall in April [1969]. As the atmosphere of tension on campus reached a peak on the Tuesday evening following the weekend of occupation, there were rumors that Uris was among the buildings to be seized.[70]

There was no take-over of Uris Library, but

> In the days that followed, the Library was deserted most of the time and in fact normal levels of usage

> were not experienced during the remainder of the term. This situation allowed the staff considerable time to talk among themselves and a number of specific proposals were put forward concerning our response to campus events.[71]

Several of the proposals were acted upon, such as assembling a collection of books, periodicals, pamphlets, and newspaper clippings on student dissent. The materials were intensively used. However,

> There remain within the Uris staff considerable differences of opinion as to the role of the Library. Some strongly support its apolitical stance; some believe we are too bound to passivity; and others probably have simply refrained from speaking their minds. Probably to all, however, it seems necessary to re-examine what we are doing and why.[72]

Other aspects of the Rucker administration are discussed in the following sections on Uris Library's roles as campus study hall, social center, reserve book dispenser, browsing collection, audio-visual facility, and reference center.

Uris as Study Hall

The first *Annual Report* of the Uris Library recorded that:

> the Library immediately began fulfilling its functions as the much needed open-stack basic book collection and study space for the Cornell undergraduates.
>
> During the first year, the Uris Library had a total attendance of 705, 251--an average of 2, 722 for each of the 259 days open during the 1962/63 year. The highest single day's attendance on January 15, 1963 was 5, 959.[73]

The attendance increased by 7. 5% during the second year and then remained basically the same until 1967/68 when there was a 6. 8% decrease (Table 21). The attendance decreased another 7. 7% during 1968/69.

Table 21.--Attendance, Uris Library, Cornell University, 1962-1969[a]

Year[b]	Number of Persons Exiting Building	Percentage of Increase or Decrease
Sept. 19, 1962- June 15, 1963	705,251	. .
1963/64	758,331	+7.5
1964/65	752,583	-0.8
1965/66	739,126	-1.8
1966/67	742,596	+0.5
1967/68	691,624	-6.9
1968/69	638,344	-7.7

[a]Cornell University. Library. Uris Library. Annual Reports. 1962/63-1968/69.

[b]Uris Library has usually been completely or partially closed from the end of the Spring semester in late May or early June until mid-September.

Although no formal studies have been done to ascertain the exact number of students who come to Uris Library to study exclusively from their own materials, the number is large. One survey[74] conducted January 10-13, 1967 does support this deduction. Persons entering the Library were asked "What do you plan to do in the Library today?" and were asked to check one of the following four responses: (1) Course assignment or class preparation; (2) Research; (3) Some of both; or (4) Other. Undergraduate students outnumbered graduate students 14 to 1 (5,990 undergraduates: 420 graduate students) in the Uris Library. In the Olin Library during the same four days, the number of undergraduates only slightly outnumbered the graduate students (2,483 to 2,007). In the two libraries, the undergraduates gave the following responses as to their library plans:

	Uris Library (N= 5, 990)	Olin Library (N= 2, 483)
Course Assign. or Class Prepar.	53. 5%	35. 9%
Research	5. 7	16. 3
Some of Both	8. 5	10. 7
Other Plans	7. 8	10. 2
Left Blank	24. 5	26. 9

Although the percentage of those who left the question blank is high, over half of the undergraduates in the Uris Library were doing course assignments. Much of this was probably with materials they brought with them or with reserve books. The significant difference between the undergraduates in the Uris and Olin Libraries is the larger number who intended to do "research" in the Olin Library.

If there is no exact data on the number of students using Uris Library as a place to study their own materials, the observations of past and present Uris staff members confirm that large numbers of students use it as a study hall. When asked in interviews whether the Library was a success as a study hall, the librarians unanimously agreed that it was extremely successful as a study hall. The Director of University Libraries summarized for many of the staff:

> Uris Library is very effective as a study place; the variation and kind of accommodations--the totally "camp" atmosphere of the whole building with its little nooks and crannies--make it extremely functional as a study hall.[75]

During the past three years, the Uris Library has not been open past its regular closing at 12 Midnight as a late-night study hall. In 1966/67 when the closing hour was 11:30 P.M., a study hall from 11:30 P.M. until 1 A.M. was provided during examination periods in several rooms on the lower level.

Uris as Social Center

The rites of Spring were celebrated in the Uris Library in April, 1968 when someone anonymously distributed over the building many mimeographed copies of the poem on page 163. (Two references in the poem may need explication for non-Cornellians: Alan Funt gave the Psychology Department video tapes prepared for his "Candid Camera" television program; Straight-shooters connotes Willard Straight Hall, the student union.)

IT'S ALL HAPPENING AT THE ZOO

Welcome to Uris
Did you ever visit the zoo
Animals are ever so amusing
And Art Linkletter is quite right, you know
Ferlinghetti's island has my mind, you see
If I knew Alan Funt was coming
I'd of burnt a cake
But the smoke would be blinding
And there's ever so much smog about
What with kappa cool
sigma skin
pi protest
et al.
But the minstrels are asking
Have you noticed you're alive
And the Straight-shooters are asking
Are you happy
But they don't care
Nor do the animals
Of course it is said that hamsters
Turn on frequently
And Art Linkletter is quite right, you know
Though sad might be a better term
They say spring is best
Birds come out in the spring
Like a peculiar game of show and tell
And people watch
To keep their minds from wandering
Instead of fixing a hole
But people should realize
You can't keep the rain from coming in a cage
Make sure you see the shaven thighs
And the shaven minds
That's very painful to see, you understand
But so many dead people live at the zoo
So it won't bother them
Then how is it that a perceptive few can say
The beauty of the human race is here
And you have created
After all
Can't animals
Think

Characterizing Uris Library as a zoo is too harsh, but the lines

They say spring is best
Birds come out in the spring
Like a peculiar game of show and tell
And people watch
To keep their minds from wandering

captures beautifully the social aspects of an undergraduate library not only in the Spring, but on some week-day nights throughout the year.

The Librarian had earlier and more prosaically described the Uris Library:

> The Library is a fine place to study from 8 o'clock in the morning until 7 o'clock in the evening.
>
> It is an impossible place to study from 7 P.M. until 10 P.M. on some nights of the week. Usually, there is just too much activity, too much coming and going, too much socializing. In short, too many lively and restless undergraduates. The good study conditions are shot down by the students themselves.
>
> Around 7 P.M. or a little earlier, the great entrance begins. It takes the next hour for everyone to settle down. When this is almost accomplished, it's time to wander around, smoke and talk in the lobbies and stairways, go to the Straight, etc., etc. This is the agenda for the next hour. We finally go through the settling down period again.
>
> From 10 P.M. until 11:30 P.M., the Library is a good study place again.[76]

The Librarian was naturally showing his age--perhaps he and the other librarians on duty at night at the reference desk, which is only separated by glass from the main lobby where most of the socializing takes place, were the ones who found it difficult to concentrate; the undergraduates who wanted to study may have had no difficulty.[77] But it is more likely that the Librarian was slightly exaggerating in order to make a stronger case for carpeting the Dean Reading Room, the reference room, the lobby, and other rooms on the main floor. Funds were appropriated for carpeting which allowed the continuation of the socializing at several decibels lower in volume.

During interviews in 1969, the Uris staff agreed that the Library continues to be a social center for the campus, but that it is no great problem. Ronald Rucker attributed the decrease in attendance during the past two years to a decline in socializing in Uris Library. The librarians also agreed that they did not act as monitors.

Uris as Reserve Book Dispenser

Throughout the history of Uris Library, the volumes circulated at the Reserve Desk have outnumbered the home loans from the main collection. Even when the main collection volumes used within the Library (not charged out) are added to the home loans, the reserve usage still outdistanced main collection use during the first six years. During the first year, reserve use amounted to 144, 480 loans--over three times the 45, 080 volumes used from the main collection (31, 268 home loans and 13, 812 volumes reshelved after use in the stacks). Reserve use rose during the next two years, reaching its high point in 1964/65 when 170, 375 reserve transactions occurred. Since then, however, reserve use has declined during the four most recent years to a low point of 111, 229 in 1968/69. For the first time, use of the main collection surpassed reserve use (111, 229 at Reserve Desk; 113, 758 volumes used from the main collection-- 63, 225 home loans and 50, 533 volumes used within the Library in 1968/69).[78]

This pattern of declining reserve use was greatly assisted by a concentrated effort, begun by the Reserve Book Librarian in 1965/66, to call faculty members' attention to specific reserve titles which were never or rarely used. This pointing out of the "deadwood" was continued each year. By 1967, results began to show:

> A strong plea was made to more than eighty faculty members in the Spring of 1967 asking that they eliminate unused items from future reserve lists. The response was very good as the total of 7, 391 volumes placed on reserve for the Fall, 1967 semester represents a 36% reduction over the previous Fall term. Under these conditions, much better and faster service was possible at the Reserve

> Desk. Whether or not our plea will have a lasting effect is uncertain.[79]

The number of items on reserve in the Fall semester, 1968, did increase to 8,661 from 7,391 in the previous Fall semester, but by 1969, Librarian Ronald Rucker saw "decreased dependence on reserve reading assignments and the limited exploration of library resources which this teaching approach engenders."[80] He also pointed out that

> The proportion of uncataloged items, mainly duplicated journal articles provided by the faculty member, is increasing rapidly while the number of books declines...[and] as has been true for years, too many works are placed on reserve and receive little or no use, rendering considerable staff time wasted.[81]

Judith H. Bossert, Reserve Book Librarian, recently worked with several professors who were willing to experiment with leaving the books to be used by their students in the open stacks of Uris Library. She also saw another trend in reserve book use with students who are themselves running their seminars under the direction of a faculty member. The students bring only the books and articles which will be used during a particular two-week period to the Reserve Desk for circulation to the seminar members.[82]

No records have been kept of the number of reserve titles and volumes purchased each year and their proportion of the total titles and volumes acquired during the year. However, expenditures for reserve books have never exceeded 36% of the total expenditures for books and recordings (this occurred in 1965/66 when $11,217.42 was spent on reserve books, out of a total budget of $31,237.72).[83] During most years, reserve book expenditures ranged from 20% to 29% of the total.[84]

In summary, definite progress has been made in whittling down the importance of Uris Library's role as reserve book dispenser, but much more progress must be made before the battle is won.

Uris as Browsing Collection

As noted in the preceding section, use of the carefully selected main collection has been overshadowed by the heavier reserve use during the early Uris years. During 1962/63, use of the main collection accounted for only 23.7% of the total book use. Use of the main collection gradually increased each year: by 1968/69, it was 50.5% of the total use.

Using Branscomb's finding that the "average student draws from the general collection of his college or university library about 12 books per year,"[85] how do Cornell undergraduates compare in their use of the Uris Library? During 1968/69, an average of 6.3 home loans from the main collection was charged to each of the 9,993 undergraduates on the Ithaca campus. However, when it is assumed that Uris primarily serves the 3,207 undergraduates in the College of Arts and Sciences, each of the College's undergraduates averaged about 19.7 home loans.[86] When the home loans and the building use of the main collection are combined, Arts and Sciences undergraduates had a per capita use of 35.5 Uris books in 1968/69. These computations do not account for volumes borrowed by undergraduates from other campus libraries.[87]

The home loans and book use within the Uris Library are detailed in Table 22.

The expenditures for the Uris main collection, reference collection, and reserve books in 1962/63 totalled $18,214.61 (additional amounts were spent: $1,000 for recordings and tapes; $3,836.78 for back files of periodicals; and $4,999.44 for binding).[88] By 1968/69, the total expenditures for the main collection, reference collection, and reserve books had increased to $26,276.45 (2,702 titles and 4,954 volumes were received during the year). A total of $16,227.89 was spent on additions to the main collection--61.7% of the expenditures for books. Reserve books accounted for 27.3% ($7,185.71) of the expenditures and 10.9% ($2,862.85) was for additions to the reference collection. Additional amounts were also spent: $360.68 for recordings and tapes; $1,111.18 for back files of periodicals; and $2,576.61 for the Cornelliana Collection, for a grand total of $30,324.92.[89] Both binding and current subscriptions for periodicals are paid by general library funds and do not come from Uris Library allocations.

Although not a part of the main collection, an extensive collection of catalogs from both American and foreign universities and colleges is maintained on open shelves in Uris Library. In 1966, the collection contained 3,786 cata-

Table 22. --Home Circulation and Book Use within the Library, Uris Library, Cornell University, 1962-1969[a]

Year	Home Circulation[d]	% Increase or Decrease	Book Use in Library[d]	% Increase or Decrease	Total Book Use	% Increase or Decrease
1962/63	64, 072	. .	125, 488	. .	189, 560	. .
1963/64	87, 009	+ 35. 8	130, 297	+ 3. 8	217, 306	+ 14. 6
1964/65	83, 277	- 4. 3	183, 823[b]	+ 41. 1[b]	267, 100[b]	+ 22. 9[b]
1965/66	77, 099	- 7. 4	174, 109	- 5. 3	251, 208	- 5. 9
1966/67	76, 752	- 0. 4	169, 493	- 2. 6	246, 245	- 3. 0
1967/68	79, 673	+ 3. 8	168, 677	- 0. 5	248, 350	+ 0. 8
1968/69	76, 786	- 3. 6	148, 201[c]	- 12. 1[c]	224, 987[c]	- 9. 4[c]

[a]Cornell University. Library. Uris Library. Annual Reports. 1962/63-1968/69.

[b]27, 227 of the increase was of college catalogs which were included for the first time.

[c]Does not include 20, 000-30, 000 uses of college catalogs.

[d]Includes Reserve Books.

logs representing over 1,500 institutions. During 1966/67, in-library use amounted to 28,443.[90]

When questioned about the open-shelf main collection, Uris librarians and Cornell University Library administrators replied that in their estimation the collection was a success. Several librarians pointed to its increasing use each year during a period when undergraduate enrollment had not greatly increased as one indication of its success. Several of those interviewed thought that its greatest disadvantage had been the necessity to house the collection in a tiered book-stack because of the use of a renovated building. Although the stacks have been open to all users and have adjacent reading rooms, the arrangement was not as ideally suited to browsing as recently designed undergraduate libraries.

Uris as Audio-Visual Facility

As was the case at the University of Michigan Undergraduate Library, there was a substantial commitment to audio services and equipment in creating the Uris Library. However, whereas Michigan made limited provisions for visual materials, Cornell, in contrast, did nothing. Recordings and tapes with listening equipment became a special collection in Uris Library, but films and other visual media have never been provided. A projection booth and equipment were planned for the lecture room on the lower level, but they were deleted from the plans for lack of funds. No exhibition space for art was included in the Library.

A suite of three rooms--a central control room with audio equipment and two listening rooms (one exclusively for sixteen individual listeners at carrels and the other for classes or group listening which can accommodate sixteen individual listeners when not in use by a group)--was designed on the upper level above the Library's main entrance. Eight desks in the adjacent White Library were also wired for sound, bringing to 40 the number of seats for individual listening available at one time. The lecture room (seating 50-70 persons) on the lower level was wired for group listening.

The Listening Rooms were first provided with six channels (one AM-FM radio, two phonograph record players, and three tape recorder-players). Two channels were later added, with further expansion still possible. The listener, after using the card catalog[91] of audio holdings, presents his request to the staff member in the control room who secures the tape or recording from storage, charges out a pair of earphones to the listener, and informs him of the channel number to which he should dial at the seat.

The collection in June, 1969 consisted of 1,140 albums of discs and 1,514 tapes (1,140 are duplicates of the albums). The collection consists of poetry, drama, speeches, prose literature, and other material in the "spoken arts" field. Most of the recordings are in English, but foreign literature in its original language is also included. However, there are no recordings for learning foreign languages; the Division of Modern Languages houses these. No musical recordings are included; the Music Library provides recordings and equipment for music and Willard Straight Hall also has a collection of musical recordings.

The number of listeners grew steadily during each of the first four years of operation. In 1962/63, 2,247 patrons (1,599 individual listeners and 648 students in 31 classes meeting in the Listening Rooms) were served. By 1965/66, 8,845 persons (5,571 individual listeners and 3,274 students in classes) used the Listening Rooms. Then, beginning in 1966/67 and continuing through 1968/69, the number of listeners declined each year, reaching a low of 4,102 (3,105 individual listeners and 952 students in classes) in 1968/69.[92]

Two factors may explain this substantial decline. During the Library's first five years, all freshmen attended an orientation lecture in the Uris classroom. At the end of the hour, an excerpt was played from one of the recordings in the Listening Rooms collection and a brief description was given of the audio facilities and their out-of-the-way location. This advertisement for the Listening Rooms was lost when the orientation lectures for freshmen were discontinued in 1967/68. Another factor is also important in the decline. Judith H. Bossert explained:

> We are not in the audio age. We're in a visual age--this is not the generation of students who grew up listening to the radio. I did; they watched television. The Listening Rooms should be showing films and television sets should be available. We should show films at four o'clock every afternoon in the Seager Room. University libraries are dragging their feet, absolutely dragging their feet over this.... The Listening Rooms, however, serve a

> function. The students seem to listen most to plays because listening, rather than just reading, brings them alive and brings an immediacy to them which the printed page lacks.[93]

David Kaser concurred:

> The kids who are with us today as undergraduates are totally visually oriented. They grew up, not with a radio as I did, but with a screen in front of them. They do not want to listen to anything; they want to watch.[94]

To revive use of the Listening Rooms, there has been an effort toward promoting the collection and facilities during the past two years:

> Several displays of new acquisitions were exhibited in Uris and bookmarks featuring an important new recording were available at several places in the building. In addition, spot announcements produced by the Listening Rooms staff were played on radio station WVBR during the Fall term. As in past years, copies of the holdings list were sent to new faculty members in the humanities and social science disciplines.[95]

Statistical Summary of First Seven Years

As a summary of many Uris Library services--except reference assistance--the first year of operation is compared with the seventh year in Table 23.

The years were ones of growth in all areas, except for attendance in the Library, which decreased by 9.4% and the number of full-time staff, which remained the same. The increases ranged from a modest rise in the number of hours open to substantial increases in the size of the book collection, number of students using the Listening Rooms, home loans, and total book use.

The concluding sections of this chapter will place the reference services for Cornell undergraduate students in the context of these previously described functions and services of the Uris Library.

Table 23.--Percentage Changes in Thirteen Variables From First to Seventh Years of Service, Uris Library, Cornell University[a]

Variable	1st Year (1962/63)	7th Year (1968/69)	% Increase or Decrease
Attendance	705, 251	638, 344	- 9.5
Home Loans from Circulation and Reserve Desks	64, 072	76, 786	+ 19.8
Book Use in Library-Main Stacks and Reserve Books	125, 488	148, 201	+ 18.1
Total Book Use	189, 560	224, 987	+ 18.7
Total Number of Listeners in Listening Rooms	2, 247	4, 102	+ 82.5
Collection Growth:			
Titles	Unknown	55, 123	. .
Volumes	46, 404	83, 485	+ 79.9
Total Seating Capacity	1, 115	Slight Decrease	. .
Average Weekly Hours Open	104.5	107	+ 2.4
Books and Periodical Articles on Reserve	14, 000[b]	16, 000[b]	+ 14.3[b]
Reserve Lists Received	325	406	+ 24.9

Table 23.--Continued.

Variable	1st Year (1962/63)	7th Year (1968/69)	% Increase or Decrease
Total Full-Time Uris Library Staff (Does Not Include Part-Time Student Assistants)	22	22	0.0
Undergraduate Enrollment, College of Arts and Sciences	2,904[c]	3,207[d]	+ 10.4
Total Undergraduate Enrollment, Ithaca Campus, Cornell University	8,836[c]	9,993[d]	+ 13.1

[a]Cornell University. Library. Uris Library. Annual Reports. 1962/63 and 1968/69; Letter from Ronald E. Rucker, Librarian, Uris Library, to Billy R. Wilkinson, September 21, 1970; Letter from Jack D. McFadden, Associate Registrar, Cornell University, to Billy R. Wilkinson, November 10, 1970.

[b]Estimate.

[c]Fall semester, 1962.

[d]As of October 4, 1968.

Reference Services for Undergraduate Students: The Uris Library

Before the Uris Library opened, Frances W. Lauman, transferring from the Olin Library Reference Department, was appointed Reference Librarian of the Undergraduate Library. She continues in the position.

From the beginning, all professional staff members have worked at the public reference desk in addition to another major responsibility, i.e., in charge of acquisitions, public catalog, circulation desk, reserve desk, or listening rooms. Miss Lauman has been responsible for selection of the reference collection, provided training and orientation to the reference area for new librarians, maintained desk schedules and statistical records of reference assistance, and worked at the reference desk. In addition to these duties, she has assisted the Undergraduate Librarian in the administration of Uris Library and acted as Curator of the Cornelliana Collection.

Cooperation with Olin Library Reference Department

Close contact has been maintained with the other major campus reference service for undergraduates--the Olin Library's Reference Department. Miss Lauman has extensive knowledge of the reference collection of the Olin Library. The first Librarian of Uris Library had worked in the Olin department. Other Uris librarians have also become familiar with that collection through an informal but extensive program of working at the Olin reference desks in addition to their duties in Uris. Each year, with few exceptions, several Uris librarians have been oriented to the larger Olin reference collection and then been on duty at the reference desks there for ten or more hours each week. These Uris librarians attended the weekly staff meetings of the Olin department. No Olin reference librarians have come to the Uris Library to work at its reference desk. Several librarians who began their Cornell careers in the Uris Library have later been appointed to positions in the Olin Reference Department.

Other forms of cooperation between the two reference services exist. Fairly frequent phone calls are exchanged between the two reference staffs concerning a patron's question or about internal operations. Calls are made to alert the librarian on duty at the other desk that a student is being referred. Purchases of new editions of certain major encyclopedias are alternated by the two departments. In past years, candidates for reference positions in the Cornell libraries were jointly interviewed by the senior staff of Uris Library and the Olin Reference Department. Lists of holdings of telephone directories held in each of the reference collections have been prepared. The Librarian and the Reference Librarian of Uris Library attend a regular meeting of the department heads and designated assistants of the Olin and Uris Libraries in which there is an exchange of information and discussion of problems in the Central Library. Several local organizations of librarians also afford opportunities for Olin and Uris reference librarians to become acquainted with each other: (1) the meetings of the Cornell University Libraries Staff Association, (2) the monthly meetings of the Academic Staff of the Libraries, and (3) the smaller, informal meetings of reference librarians from all campus libraries.

In interviews in 1969, the reference librarians in Olin and Uris indicated that they were acquainted with each other. The interviewer detected a sense of trust between the two groups.

Communications with Faculty

When the Uris librarians were asked "Is there much communication between the staff in the Uris Library and the faculty concerning reference services for their students or is it fairly minimal?" they unanimously replied that there was almost no contact with faculty members about reference services. They pointed to the Reserve Book Librarian who knew and worked with faculty members, and to the staff of the Listening Rooms who were in touch with a much smaller number of instructors, but these relationships had not been established with the faculty concerning reference services.

The Reference Librarian summarized the situation:

> What typically happens in the reference service is that we suddenly realize that there has been an assignment, but by this time it is a little late to call the faculty member and discuss the matter with him.[96]

As a step in attempting to communicate with the faculty, a letter of invitation to visit the Uris Library was sent to some 60 new faculty members joining the College of Arts and Sciences in the Fall semester, 1969. Only two or three faculty members responded with visits.[97]

The professional staff of the Cornell Libraries do not have faculty status, but rather academic status, which means that

> The university administration definitely separates the librarians from the non-professional or supporting staff and recognizes the librarians as professional people. While not yet ready to confer any faculty titles or ranks, the administration saw the need and justification to classify the professional library staff as academic.[98]

The lack of faculty status closes a possible avenue of contact for Uris librarians with the faculty in meetings and committee work.

Uris Publications

As supplements to daily reference service, the Uris Library has provided other programs designed to acquaint undergraduates with library services. Instruction in library use for all freshmen in the Fall semester will be discussed in the following section. An elaborate exhibition detailing the services offered by the Uris Library and other campus libraries has also been displayed annually in the exhibit cases in the main and lower lobbies.

The publications of the Uris Library are the other major supplement to individual assistance at the reference desk. The *Basic Library Handbook* was first produced in 1962. This 36-page guide to the Uris Library, with additional material on Olin and other campus libraries, was usually revised and up-dated yearly. A major revision with a change of title (*Uris Library Handbook*) and format occurred in 1969. Approximately 2,000-2,500 copies have been distributed each year through various means: at the freshmen library lectures, in the dormitories, and at various points within Uris Library.

The Collection, Uris Library Listening Rooms, a complete list of holdings, was also compiled in 1962. Supplements were published often, with cumulations less frequently. The latest cumulation--running to 49 pages--was distributed, as were earlier editions, to selected College of Arts and Sciences faculty members and was made available in the Library for students.

Throughout the years, other publications have been distributed: finely printed brochures inviting competitors for the Dean Book Collection Contests and less elegant leaflets which were guides to the use of a particular service, such as the Reserve Desk.

In the Spring of 1969, Uris librarians prepared and made available to students seven basic bibliographies. Entitled "Selected Reference Sources" and covering economics, history, literature, political science, psychology, sociology and anthropology, and general reference sources, the bibliographies were revised and refined in November, 1969.

Library Orientation and Instruction

> Instruction in use of the library for first year students began in the Fall of 1947. It was initiated by a request from a new English instructor for a tour for his classes. Other instructors then expressed interest and sixteen classes with 320 students heard the lecture. In the Fall of 1948, library instruction as a responsibility of the University Library Reference Department was given to all Freshman English classes after planning by the Assistant Director for Public Services and the faculty member in charge of Freshman English. From 1950 through 1957, the program included a library problem follow-up to the fifty-minute lecture and tour. In 1962 with the opening of the Undergraduate Library, the orientation lectures for freshmen became the responsibility of the Uris Library staff.[99]

Frances W. Lauman has been in charge of instruction given by the Uris Library staff since the first Fall semester in the building when she and four other librarians gave orientation lectures of fifty minutes, the last ten minutes of which were used for a building tour. A basic script was prepared for the use of individual instructors.[100] The lecture, given in the Uris Library classroom, furnished information on the library system in general, more specific information on the resources and services of Olin Library, and then dealt in detail with the services of Uris Library. There was little time to discuss specific reference resources; they were only briefly mentioned and students were invited to ask for assistance in the Reference Room. Approximately 2,250 students in 103 sections of Freshman English were scheduled in 51 lectures over one and one-half weeks during October, 1962.[101]

By October, 1963, the lecture was cut to 35 minutes followed by a 15-20 minute tour of Uris. The lecture staff now included eight of the nine librarians on the staff. Four non-professional staff members also assisted in conducting 163 groups of 12-16 students each on the tours. For the first time, an individual letter was sent to the 63 English Department instructors, asking them to stress the importance of the library in a class meeting preceding the scheduled lecture and also inviting the instructors to attend the lecture with their students. A large percentage of the instructors accompanied their students. The orientation lecture was also given on a voluntary attendance basis to 40 transfer students (out of a possible 140) during the Orientation Week preceding classes. The Undergraduate Librarian evaluated the 1963 program as the most successful to that point.[102]

For three years, beginning in September, 1963, the Undergraduate Librarian spoke briefly at the first meeting of the freshman class of the College of Arts and Sciences, extending a welcome to the Uris Library and urging its use during their ensuing Cornell careers.

In October, 1965, the tour part of the instruction was discontinued (it was believed that the time could be better spent in the lecture because students quickly found their own way around the building). The use of an overhead projector for illustrative materials, such as pages from periodical indexes, was begun in 1965. The librarians did not attempt to communicate an overwhelming amount of detail during the lecture, but rather an understanding of the library system, and stressed that Uris Library or one of the other college libraries on the campus was the place to start in their search for material. The lectures particularly tried to create an impression that there were "helpful and pleasant people to call upon at the Reference Desk whenever the student could not find something or needed help."[103]

To acquaint students with the Listening Rooms, an excerpt from one of the spoken arts recordings was played at the end of each lecture. The visual became a part of the lecture in 1966 when a five-minute film--written and directed by David Shearer, Librarian of the Fine Arts Library at Cornell--was first used to introduce the session. The film was an excellent addition to the instruction program. Done by Shearer with wit and humor, its contemporaneity seemed to capture the interest of the freshmen.[104]

The year 1966 was significant for another reason. After almost twenty years of cooperation between the Library and the English Department in library instruction, nine departments were now involved in the program. During 1965/66, the College of Arts and Sciences faculty had

> voted to abolish Freshman English and to establish instead a number of small courses or colloquia in the humanities.... It was very generally felt that the course, in its conventional format, had outlasted its usefulness; it was going a little stale. Moreover, the program (administered by a single department) had become increasingly difficult to staff with qualified and experienced instructors.
>
> The new program represents a collaborative enterprise by nine departments.... Instead of directing all students into one and the same course, it offers the freshmen more than thirty different subject-courses from which to choose.
>
> At the same time...the [new] program is emphatically designed to be a composition course. ...In abolishing Freshman English, therefore, the faculty had no intention whatever of diminishing the practice of writing. On the contrary, it intended to encourage the stimulus to composition by providing the freshmen with stimulating subjects to write about.[105]

From October 6-25, 1966, the Uris librarians, joined by a librarian from Olin, gave 65 lectures to 110 sections of the Freshman Humanities Program. Two departments (History and Philosophy) chose not to give an hour of their class time to the Uris staff and several sections failed to appear at their scheduled time.[106]

After the 1966 program, an English professor, who was speaking for four or five other instructors with whom he had consulted, expressed doubt as to the effectiveness of the library lecture. He reported that the "students groan when it is mentioned and display their jaded sophistication."[107] The professors also did not want to give up an hour of their class time and suggested that the lecture be offered on a voluntary basis. After discussions with the Uris staff, the Associate Director of Libraries, and the Dean of the College of Arts and Sciences, the decision was made to discontinue library lectures in conjunction with the Freshman Humanities Program.

During September 14-20, 1967, the lecture was offered at seven different times on a voluntary basis, with two librarians as the instructors. Only 116 students attended. In September, 1968, attendance was even smaller: 46 students at ten lectures.[108]

Trying a different time and approach, two Uris librarians offered six 30-minute "cram sessions" on how to locate materials for term papers during December 2-5, 1968. Basic reference resources in the social sciences and humanities were discussed. Different advertisements were also used. Borrowing a line--"I get high with a little help from my friends"--from a song by John Lennon and Paul McCartney of the Beatles, posters were designed by a staff member inviting students to "GET HIGH grades on late term papers WITH A LITTLE HELP FROM YOUR FRIENDS at Uris Library." Announcements were broadcast on the student-run radio station, an ad was placed in the student newspaper, and notices were sent to department offices to be placed in faculty mailboxes. Once again, 46 students attended. In the Spring semester, similar sessions were scheduled, with two sessions each during the weeks of April 21, May 5, and May 12, but only nine students came to them.[109] Disturbances on the Cornell campus contributed to the low attendance.

During the week of September 22, 1969, four orientation sessions for new students were offered, and 25 students attended--only 3.2% of the 770 freshmen in the College of Arts and Sciences or 0.9% of the 2,584 freshmen in all colleges and schools on the Ithaca campus.[110]

After the "cram sessions" in December, 1968, the two librarians who led the sessions asked the small number of students who attended how they had learned of the program. The posters displayed over the campus and the ad in the student newspaper were most successful. At least half the students said there had been no announcement in any of their classes by their instructors. Other comments from the students revealed that

> Approximately one quarter of the forty-six students did not know where the reference room was. When those who did know were questioned why they did not ask a librarian for help, the answer was invariably, 'I don't want to disturb you.'[111]

When the instruction program of the Uris Library was held in conjunction with the English Department and reached 2,300-2,500 freshmen each year, the librarians were unhappy with the situation--it was too compulsory and too many students were bored with the lecture. Now, with the voluntary program in which so few students chose to participate, the large number of undergraduates who receive no library instruction worries the staff. However, in interviews in 1969, the Uris librarians did not believe that library instruction should be compulsory. For all the arguments which can be cited against the compulsory program, it did, however, acquaint many students with the Uris Library and its services. After it was discontinued in 1967, the reference librarians in Olin Library noticed many more undergraduates attempting to use the Olin Library with little success. Some students using Olin Library did not know the Uris Library existed, or thought they were in Uris Library.[112] The discontinuation of the lectures was discussed earlier as one of the factors in the sharp decline in use of the Listening Rooms.

Many of the librarians agreed that the instruction had never come at the right time for students--the time of real need. As a means to solve this problem, the Cornell Libraries may experiment with recordings and video tapes which could be used by an individual student when he needs an explanation of a particular library resource.[113] As a first step, a Video Center was established on September 1, 1970 in Uris Library with David Shearer as its Acting Director. His responsibilities will include:

> 1. Managing the Libraries' activities with video tapes and encouraging innovative use of the medium in teaching, learning, and research;
>
> 2. Bringing together such motion pictures and motion picture equipment as are or as become available and developing a service center for them;

3. Developing support both inside and outside the University for the staged extension of resources and services toward an advanced and comprehensive audio-visual library program.[114]

When asked if Uris staff should do more teaching, the librarians all replied in the affirmative. In response to the question, "Would you personally be willing to do more teaching--both lectures and discussions in the Library and integrated with the work of a particular course?" all the Uris librarians again replied affirmatively. One person qualified his "Yes" with "I would be happy to do more teaching if I thought it would get us anywhere, if we were reaching anybody. I still have a skeptical view of it doing any good."

No attempts have been made to integrate bibliographical lectures or discussions by Uris librarians with particular undergraduate courses at the time students have need of such information. No library instruction has been provided for advanced undergraduates, such as honors students in the College of Arts and Sciences. Uris librarians have also failed to give library orientation for disadvantaged students at Cornell. Library instruction for undergraduates from minority groups, who were recruited by the Committee on Special Educational Projects, has instead been given by the Reference Department of the Olin Library. Olin reference librarians also provided orientation and prepared materials for the library committee of the Black Liberation Front. In addition to these Cornell students, Olin librarians have oriented high school students during the summers in the Cornell Upward Bound Program (conducted by the U.S. Office of Economic Opportunity) and the Reading and Study Skills Program (for local and nearby students who intend to apply for college admission).[115]

Library instruction and orientation programs are also provided by librarians in the A.R. Mann Library (for students in the Colleges of Agriculture and Human Ecology) and by librarians in other Cornell schools and colleges.

The Reference Collection

The Uris Library had approximately 1,780 volumes in its separate reference collection during the first year of operation--1962/63. By December 31, 1964, the reference collection numbered 2,549 volumes. (A complete set of the Loeb Classical Library--408 volumes--is included in the count because it is non-circulating and considered to be part of the reference collection.)[116] By June 30, 1969, the collection had grown to 1,688 titles in 3,294 volumes.[117]

An analysis of the 1968/69 expenditures of the Uris Library for books showed that $2,862.85 was spent during the year on 138 volumes (71 titles) added to the reference collection.[118]

Most of the reference collection is housed on open shelves around the periphery of a separate room. A small number of duplicate volumes--including an unabridged dictionary, several foreign language dictionaries, statistical abstracts, almanacs, and older editions of encyclopedias--are shelved for the convenience of students in six other Uris reading rooms. Only Magill's masterplot volumes, and the current issues of Consumer Reports, Consumer Bulletin, Cornell Freshman Register, Cornell student and staff directories, and Manning's city directory of Ithaca are kept back of the reference desk, requiring students to request their use. A clipping and pamphlet file exclusively devoted to Cornell University is maintained, with a subject index in the Reference Room. Limited access is available to the file because it is also housed back of the reference desk.

To supplement the reference collection, the librarians maintained a special index to eight journals of literary criticism for several years. When the Social Sciences and Humanities Index incorporated most of the journals, the local indexing was stopped.

No formal evaluation of the reference collection was undertaken in this study. Librarians in the Uris Library were, however, asked for their evaluations. When asked, "Is the reference collection in the Uris Library adequate for full reference service without a large number of referrals to the Olin Library's reference desk?" the librarians agreed that full reference service was not possible, pointing out such areas as government documents, scientific subjects, and African literature, in which referral had to be made to Olin Library or one of the other campus libraries. Reference materials in most of the humanities and social sciences were judged to be adequate.

The Uris staff members were also asked if they would include a reference collection in a new undergraduate library. Two librarians questioned the building of a separate undergraduate library, suggesting instead one large library for the whole university community and a greatly expanded reference collection and staff for all patrons in that building. The four other librarians agreed that a reference collection was essential if they were building a separate undergraduate library. Replying to the next question of how many volumes they would have in this hypothetical undergraduate library reference collection, three librarians believed that the present size of the Uris reference collection (approximately 1, 700 titles in 3, 300 volumes) was appropriate. One librarian would select a slightly smaller reference collection, weeding some titles from the Uris holdings.

Description of Reference Room and Desk

In the 1956 preliminary "Program for the Undergraduate Library," the reference collection was planned for an attractive room (with views of Lake Cayuga) which had previously housed the Catalog Department. The room was adjacent to the main lobby and to the large main reading room where the circulation desk would be located. The final 1959 program and then the architectural drawings continued this arrangement. Upon the appointments in 1961 of Billy R. Wilkinson as Librarian and Frances W. Lauman as Reference Librarian, it was suggested that the reference area be moved from the assigned room and placed in an alcove of the large main reading room so that the reference desk would be located beside the circulation desk. The theory was to locate the reference desk in the middle of a heavily used area, rather than off to the side in the separate room. Periodicals which had been assigned this alcove would occupy the separate room which had been designed for reference. The renovation of the building had progressed too far, however, to permit the change. When the Library opened in September, 1962, the reference collection was housed according to the original plan. The public catalog was located immediately outside the reference room in the main reading room; a small open arch at the southern end of the reference room permitted the reference librarian on duty to see the catalog (Figure 3). This arrangement of the reference area has continued to the present. The room was named the E. R. B. Willis Reference Room after the Associate Librarian who had served the University for thirty-three years.

Two standard office desks in black metal with simulated wood tops were used as reference desks. Librarians on duty sat in swivel chairs with no chairs provided beside

Figure 3.--Main Floor, Uris Library, Cornell University, February, 1968. Source: Cornell University. Department of Buildings and Properties, 1968.

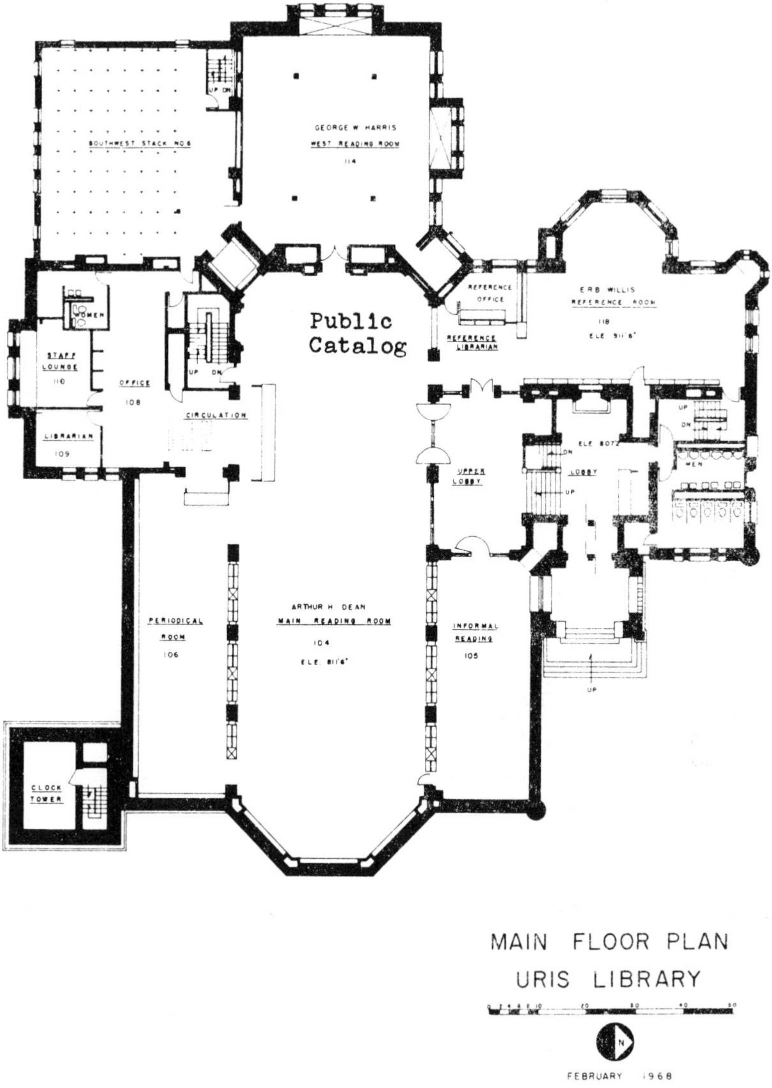

GEORGE W HARRIS
WEST READING ROOM
114
SOUTHWEST STACK NO 6
Public
Catalog
REFERENCE
OFFICE
REFERENCE
LIBRARIAN
ERB WILLIS
REFERENCE ROOM
118
WOMEN
STAFF
LOUNGE
110
OFFICE
108
LIBRARIAN
109
CIRCULATION
UPPER
LOBBY
LOBBY
MEN
PERIODICAL
ROOM
106
ARTHUR H DEAN
MAIN READING ROOM
104
INFORMAL
READING
105
CLOCK
TOWER
MAIN FLOOR PLAN
URIS LIBRARY
FEBRUARY 1968

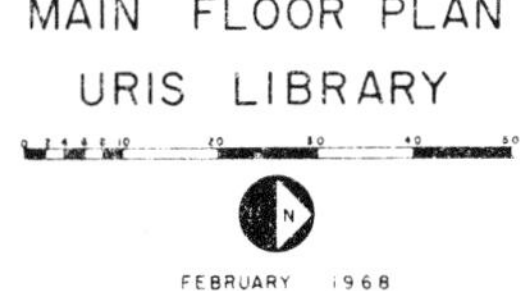

the desks for the inquirer who might wish to be seated. The reference desks were in the southern end of the room with glass doors and panels to the front (separating the room from the lobby) and to the rear was a small office for the Reference Librarian and three other librarians. The office was completely enclosed, with no glass permitting vision out of the office. To the librarian's right was the public catalog and to the left was the largest part of the room which provided seats for 39 readers at four eight-seat tables and seven individual carrels. Two of the tables held periodical and other indexes. General encyclopedias were shelved in a counter-high, free-standing case and the other reference volumes were in call number sequence on wood shelving along the walls of the room.

Staffing of Reference Desk

The Reference Librarian and two other professional staff members were on duty at the reference desk for 13-15 hours each week in the Fall semester, 1969. The Librarian, Reserve Book Librarian, and Circulation Librarian spent less time at the desk. Daily reference duty was usually performed in two-hour blocks of time, except for nights and Sundays when the time was longer and rotated among the librarians. Coverage of the desk was by professional staff during most of the hours: a senior non-professional staff member was on duty Friday nights (6-10 P.M.) and Saturdays (9 A.M.-1 P.M. and 2-6 P.M.).

Hours of reference service during a regular week in the Fall semester, 1969 totalled 76 hours (71%) of the 107 hours Uris was open. (The total Uris Library hours on Monday-Saturday were: 8 A.M.-12 Midnight; Sunday: 1 P.M.-12 Midnight.) Reference service was available from 10 A.M.-10 P.M. (Monday-Friday), 9 A.M.-1 P.M. and 2-6 P.M. (Saturday) and 1-5 P.M. and 6-10 P.M. (Sunday). Only one staff member was on reference duty at all times.

Qualifications of Staff in 1969/70

A composite profile of the Uris reference staff in the Fall semester, 1969, would portray a young woman who had worked there from seven months to seven years.[119] She had received her library degree from one of five schools scattered over the country. She had not received a master's degree in a subject area although some graduate courses had been taken. The undergraduate major was in the humanities at an institution other than Cornell University.

To guard against over-simplification in the profile, individual education, experience, and age should be noted. Two librarians were graduates of the Columbia School of Library Service, with the library schools at the University of California at Berkeley, Carnegie Institute of Technology, Oklahoma, and Rutgers educating one staff member each. One librarian had received a Master's degree in music from Harvard; two others had taken some graduate courses in a subject. For their undergraduate degrees, two librarians majored in music and one each in mathematics, medieval history, philosophy and German literature. The undergraduate alma maters varied (Bryn Mawr, Pomona, Wooster, and Oklahoma with one librarian each; two graduated from Cornell).

Four librarians had previous experience in the Cornell University libraries before joining the Uris staff (two in technical services, one in the Olin Reference Department, and one in the Music Library). One person had experience in the Buffalo Public Library. Only one librarian began his professional career in Uris Library. Two librarians had worked in Uris since it opened in 1962 and the other four librarians had less experience in Uris (two had worked two years, one for one year, and one for seven months).

Two members of the 1969 staff were male; four were female. Several other men have been on the staff in past years (in 1965/66 four men and four women worked at the reference desk), but in most years women have been in the majority.

Another characteristic of the Uris librarians in 1969 was their youthfulness. Almost all ranged in age from their early twenties to early thirties. This has also been true of the professional staff in past years.

Scope of Reference Services

The Uris Library offers reference assistance at a desk in the Willis Reference Room which has been previously described. Students request assistance in person or they may telephone for help. The librarians only infrequently approach students who show signs of needing assistance; the vast majority of information-seeking encounters are initiated by students. Most of the reference services are performed in the Reference Room or at the nearby public catalog in the Dean Reading Room. The librarians telephone the Olin Reference Department and departmental libraries for information for students and also receive calls from other libraries concerning the requests of individual patrons.

Philosophy of Service

Before the Uris Library opened, its first Librarian promised that the staff would provide Cornell undergraduate students

> with a very simple, yet very difficult to achieve thing--something called good library service. We shall get the books, periodicals, and answers to their questions which they need.[120]

Another tenet of the philosophy was stated in the handbook provided for undergraduates:

> Although the Uris Library and the John M. Olin Library occupy separate buildings, there is no intention of confining undergraduates to the one and faculty and graduate students to the other. It is hoped that at some time in his career every undergraduate will be drawn to the larger collections in the Olin Library in pursuit of game started in the open shelves of the Uris Library. The two collections are planned to complement each other in service to the University's program of teaching and scholarship.[121]

The handbook also stated that:

> The librarians in the Reference Room are especially prepared to assist students in using reference books, periodical indexes, and the card catalog; in locating books, documents, pamphlets, and periodicals; in obtaining material for term papers; in getting information on a specific subject; and in compiling bibliographies.[122]

The Uris Library staff did not prepare a formal statement of reference service philosophy as was the case at the University of Michigan Undergraduate Library.

Cornell's Definitions of Questions

On July 1, 1962, all libraries on the Cornell campus began using the same definitions of questions when they reported to the central library administration the number of inquiries at their reference desks. A committee of reference librarians devised the following categories and definitions:

1. General Reference Question

   A General reference question is one which is answered through the use of library resources. The answering of a general reference question requires a specialized knowledge of library resources. The source of information used is most frequently one which is obvious to the staff member at the time inquiry is made. The general reference question requires less than fifteen minutes to answer. Ordinarily no more than two sources of information are used.

2. Search Reference Question

   A Search reference question is one which requires more than fifteen minutes of time to answer and, ordinarily, the use of three or more library resources.

3. Other Reference Question

   An Other reference question is one which concerns library resources and/or their use. It is answered from the personal knowledge of the staff member without his consulting any other library resource.

4. Bibliography

   A Bibliography is a systematic list of writings relating to a given subject or author and is the original work of a reference staff member. It is compiled by using several library resources and requires at least an hour of work.

5. Problem Question

> A Problem question is one which requires more than an hour of time to answer. The answering of such a question employs the specialized knowledge of a trained librarian, as well as an extensive use of library resources which extends beyond the general reference collection.[123]

"Other Reference Questions" (No. 3 above) were later referred to as "Information and Directional Questions" in the annual reports of the Director of University Libraries..

These definitions have been used throughout the history of the Uris Library.

Recorded Use of Reference Services, 1962-1969

As was the case at the University of Michigan Undergraduate Library and at the opening of most new library buildings, the number of brief information and directional questions at the Uris Library reference desk far exceeded the number of general reference questions during the first year. In 1962/63, 57.4% (3,792) of the total questions (6,609) asked were information and directional questions; 42.4% (2,800) of the total were recorded as general reference questions (Table 24). Only 0.2% (17) was categorized as the longer search question. There were no problem questions during 1962/63 nor were any bibliographies prepared.

In five of the next six years, information and directional questions decreased with the all-time low of 2,130 occurring in 1968/69. General reference questions grew for two years reaching a high of 3,951 in 1964/65. This was 61.5% of all questions (6,420) asked; 2,423 information and directional questions were 37.7%, and 46 search questions were 0.7%. However, during three of the four most recent years, general reference questions have declined (Table 24). By 1968/69, general reference questions numbered 3,248; still above the level of 1962/63, but 17.8% below the best year of 1964/65. In 1968/69, general reference questions (3,248) accounted for 60.3% of the total questions (5,385) while information questions (2,130) were 39.6%. Search questions (7) accounted for only 0.1% of the total. Table 25 compares the reference activity of the first year (1962/63) with 1968/69.

Table 24.--Types of Questions Received at Reference Desk, Uris Library, Cornell University 1962-1969[a]

Year	Information and Directional Questions	% Increase or Decrease	General Reference Questions[b]	% Increase or Decrease	Total Questions	% Increase or Decrease	General Reference Questions (% of Total)
1962/63	3,792	. .	2,817	. .	6,609	. . .	42.6
1963/64	2,446	- 35.5	3,889	+ 38.1	6,335	- 4.1	61.4
1964/65	2,423	- 0.9	3,997	+ 2.8	6,420	+ 1.3	62.3
1965/66	2,227	- 8.1	3,555	- 11.1	5,782	- 9.9	61.5
1966/67	2,727	+ 22.5	3,406	- 4.2	6,133	+ 6.1	55.5
1967/68	2,471	- 9.4	3,447	+ 1.2	5,918	- 3.5	58.2
1968/69	2,130	- 13.8	3,255	- 5.6	5,385	- 9.0	60.4

[a]Cornell University. Library. Uris Library. _Annual Reports._ 1962/63-1968/69.

[b]A small number of Search Questions are included in the General Reference Questions: 1962/63-17; 1963/64-59; 1964/65-46; 1965/66-22; 1966/67-19; 1967/68-15; and 1968/69-7.

While the Uris Library's reference services in its first seven years declined by 18.5% in total questions asked, although increasing by 16% in number of general reference questions, the undergraduate enrollment in the College of Arts and Sciences increased by 10.4% (Table 25). During the same time period, home loans from the main collection more than doubled.

Table 25. -Percentage Changes in Types of Questions Received at Reference Desk of Uris Library and Undergraduate Enrollment, Cornell University from 1962/63 to 1968/69[a]

Variable	1962/63	1968/69	% Increase or Decrease
I. Questions at Reference Desk:			
Information Questions	3,792	2,130	-43.8
General Reference Questions	2,800	3,248	+16.0
Search Questions	17	7	-58.8
Total Questions	6,609	5,385	-18.5
II. Student Enrollment:			
Undergraduate Students in the College of Arts and Sciences	2,904[b]	3,207[c]	+10.4

[a]Cornell University. Library. Uris Library. Annual Reports. 1962/63 and 1968/69.

[b]Fall semester, 1962.

[c]As of October 4, 1968.

On a per capita basis, each undergraduate in the College of Arts and Sciences asked approximately one general reference question in both 1962/63 and 1968/69. What are the reasons for this lack of growth in the number of substantial reference questions asked in Uris Library?

First, have the hours of reference service been cut? In 1962/63 reference service was available for 90.5 hours each week (the building was open 103.5 hours per week). Only on Saturday and Sunday nights that first year were there no professional staff members at the reference desk. Two librarians were on duty at the reference desk Monday through Thursday nights; one stayed until closing time at 11:30 P.M. During 1963/64, professional reference service was added on Sundays from 7-10 P.M., bringing the total to 92.5 hours per week.

In 1965/66, the hours of reference service were decreased by 7.5 hours when the hours from 10-11:30 P.M., Monday-Friday nights, were discontinued. A survey of the number of inquiries made during these late evening hours indicated almost no requests by students for reference assistance. The second reference librarian on Monday-Thursday nights was also discontinued.[124]

By 1966/67, Uris provided 82 hours of reference service by the professional staff and four additional hours on Friday night when a non-professional was on duty at the reference desk.[125] The same hours were maintained during 1967/68.

In 1968/69, the hours from 8-10 A.M., Monday-Friday were discontinued. A non-professional also replaced a professional on Saturdays from 9 A.M.-1 P.M. and 2-6 P.M. The undergraduate student, thus, had 76 hours of reference service available to him during each week, but 12 of the hours were staffed by non-professionals.[126] Although the hours of service which have been discontinued were usually slack periods, this decrease from 92.5 hours of professional reference service in 1963/64 to 64 hours of professional coverage of the reference desk in 1968/69 may be one factor contributing to the lack of growth in the reference services.

Has the location of the Reference Room in Uris Library been detrimental to the quantity of reference service? In interviews with Uris librarians in 1969, two expressed strong dissatisfaction with the location. One staff member said:

> I would place the reference area smack in the middle of the traffic pattern and smooth flow of traffic be damned. The Reference Room is now stuck off in a corner and most people haven't seen it because

> they go straight up the stairs in the lobby and across the Dean Room to the circulation desk.

Another librarian agreed:

> One thing that may have been a factor in the relatively few requests by students for reference assistance from the very beginning is the placement of the reference desk. Being nearer the circulation desk might have helped stimulate reference services. Many questions come to the circulation desk. A lot of students do not have the foggiest notion what the books in the Reference Room are. It is doubly confused by the fact we now have the Kirby Room downstairs which also happens to be a room with books. Many students think the Reference Room is just a room with another collection.

Did discontinuation of the library orientation lectures to all freshmen contribute to the lack of growth of reference services? The orientation was discontinued in 1967/68 while the number of general reference questions had already decreased in each of the two previous years. There was instead a slight increase of 1.2% in the quantity of general reference questions during the first year of voluntary orientation.

Have changes in the staff over the years affected the number of general reference questions? The best years statistically for reference services were 1963/64 and 1964/65. The original professional staff who had experienced the excitement of opening Uris Library in 1962 were then at their peak levels of performance. During the first year, they had internally organized library procedures and routines and during the second and third years were perhaps better able to devote themselves to public services. Then immediately at the conclusion of the third and best year, four of nine librarians resigned or requested a leave of absence. During the fourth year (1965/66), the first decrease (11%) in the number of general reference questions occurred. During 1965/66, the four experienced and full-time librarians who had departed were replaced with one full-time librarian who had just graduated from library school, one experienced reference librarian who worked only part-time, a library trainee (full-time staff member who was going to a near-by library school and taking one course per semester), and a full-time senior non-professional staff member. Although these new members of the staff had excellent qualifications, they could not match the experience of those they replaced. Two lacked professional training in a library school. This break-up of the original professional staff was a major factor in the lack of growth of reference services.

Have students changed in the seven years the Uris Library has been open? There is general agreement among scholars that undergraduate students have changed greatly (see the discussion of this topic in Chapter 3: The University of Michigan, with the quotations from Rose K. Goldsen and Kenneth Keniston). Patricia B. Knapp has summarized the past several years and their significance for undergraduate libraries:

> The student protest movement has moved so rapidly, changing direction as it goes, now breaking into factions, later coalescing as a result of dramatic and tragic events, that it is almost impossible to keep up with. In the process it has stimulated floods of print, some few examples of careful and objective analysis, and only a very little empirical research. It has met with more success in its attempt to change the university than one would have thought possible ten years ago, and yet the final outcome of the movement is certainly in doubt.
>
> Nevertheless, one might venture the suggestion that most of the goals of the student movement have significance for the undergraduate library, some of them quite positive. The call for a greater emphasis on teaching instead of research surely portends a more important role for the undergraduate library. The demand for a share in the power governing the university, as it becomes more sophisticated, may undermine the enormous influence of the graduate departments. This, too, should mean more attention would be paid to the undergraduate program. The hostility toward bureaucracy in the university may stimulate the library to de-emphasize its own bureaucratic tendencies. Surely these are goals we should support.[127]

The student movement began in the mid-1960's at the same time when the reference services of Uris Library were reaching a zenith and then beginning a decline. Uris reference services, however, have changed remarkably little from 1965 to 1969. This lack of adaptation to the new life styles of undergraduates or to the protest movement may be a major factor in the non-growth of reference services.

Samples of Questions: November and December, 1969

In order to ascertain what actually occurs at the reference desk of the Uris Library, all questions asked of the reference librarian on duty were monitored during the eighth week (November 3-7, 1969) and the thirteenth week (December 8-12, 1969) of Cornell's Fall semester.

The methodology and definitions used in recording the questions are given in Chapter 1.

During the 38 hours of the first week's monitoring, 167 questions were asked by undergraduates, an average hourly rate of 4.4 questions. Graduate students, faculty, and others asked six questions during the week, but these were excluded from the study. Questions by undergraduates increased to 196 during the second week, an hourly average of 5.2. Non-undergraduates asked eight questions during the second week. Telephone calls accounted for only seven questions (1.9%) of the total questions (363) during the two weeks. In the 363 questions by undergraduates, students approached the librarian in 361 cases. In only two situations did the librarian take the initiative by approaching a student who seemed to need assistance.

The evening hours were busier than the afternoon hours. Morning hours were least busy. Mondays and Tuesdays were the most active days and Wednesdays were almost as busy. Thursdays and Fridays were the slowest days.

The monitoring revealed that only a brief time was spent with each student seeking reference assistance. Only two search[128] questions (over 30 minutes) were recorded--one each week. No problem questions (over one hour) occurred. Information questions, often lasting only a few seconds, accounted for 40.1% of all questions during the first week, with the longer reference questions amounting to 59.3% (Table 26). Information questions decreased to 32.7% and reference questions increased to 66.8% during the second week. However, of the 230 reference questions asked in both weeks, only on eight occasions did the librarian spend more than five minutes with the student.

Table 26.--Questions Asked by Undergraduates at Reference Desk, Uris Library, Cornell University, in Two One-Week Samples, 1969

Type of Question	Nov. 3-7, 1969 No.	Nov. 3-7, 1969 %	Dec. 8-12, 1969 No.	Dec. 8-12, 1969 %
Information	67	40.1	64	32.7
Reference				
R-1	69	41.3	90	45.9
R-2	6	3.6	7	3.6
R-3	1	0.6	. .	. .
R-4	18	10.8	30	15.3
R-5	1	0.6	1	0.5
R-6	3	1.8	3	1.5
R-7	1	0.6	. .	. .
Sub-total	99	59.3	131	66.8
Search	1	0.6	1	0.5
Problem	. .	. .	. .	. .
Total	167	100.0	196	100.0

Bibliographical assistance with the Uris Library's own catalog and holdings (R-1) accounted for the largest number of reference questions (Table 26). There were few assists with the holdings of other campus libraries (R-2) and only once did a librarian help an undergraduate with non-campus holdings (R-3). Retrieval of factual, non-bibliographical information (R-4) constituted the second largest number of reference questions. Uris librarians rarely counseled students in a reader's advisory capacity (R-5). Personal instruction in the use of the library or any of its resources (R-6) was also extremely infrequent.

A further analysis of the information questions reveals that nearly half of them (46.4% in first week; 45.4% in second week) were very simple questions concerning the physical facilities of the building (Table 27). The next most frequent type of information question concerned the collections or services of Uris Library and was answered by the librarian with brief directions or information (17.8% in first week;

Table 27.--Types of Information Questions Asked by Undergraduates at Reference Desk, Uris Library, Cornell University, in Two One-Week Samples, 1969

Type of Information Question	Nov. 3-7, 1969		Dec. 8-12, 1969	
	No.	% of Total Information Questions Asked	No.	% of Total Information Questions Asked
Assistance with physical facilities of library:				
Location of pencil sharpener or request to borrow pen, stapler, etc.	14	20.9	17	26.7
Request for keys	17	25.5	12	18.7
Location of areas in library	. .	. .	. .	. .
Sub-total	31	46.4	29	45.4
Requests for location of particular volume (librarian gave directions):				
Monographs in main collection (student had call number)	4	6.0	1	1.6
Reference books (student usually requested by title)	3	4.5	7	10.9
Sub-total	7	10.5	8	12.5

Table 27.--Continued.

Type of Information Question	Nov. 3-7, 1969		Dec. 8-12, 1969	
	No.	% of Total Information Questions Asked	No.	% of Total Information Questions Asked
Requests for information or publication (student did not have call number):				
Librarian knew answer without referring to any source	6	8.9	7	10.9
Librarian referred student to catalog or reference collection, giving no additional assistance	. .	. .	. .	. .
Librarian knew that question would be better answered in another library and referred student to it	6	8.9	5	7.8
Sub-total	12	17.8	12	18.7

Table 27. --Continued.

Type of Information Question	Nov. 3-7, 1969 No.	Nov. 3-7, 1969 % of Total Information Questions Asked	Dec. 8-12, 1969 No.	Dec. 8-12, 1969 % of Total Information Questions Asked
Questions concerning collection or services (librarian responded with brief directions or information):				
Periodicals	4	6.0	3	4.7
Newspapers	..	..	..	..
College catalogs	2	2.9	1	1.6
Main catalog or serials catalog	..	..	2	3.1
Reserve books	2	2.9	..	..
How and where to charge out books	..	..	..	..
Use of reference volume in another part of library	3	4.5	7	10.9
Photocopying machine	1	1.5	2	3.1
Exam file	..	..	..	..
Location of another library	..	..	..	..
Sub-total	12	17.8	15	23.4

Table 27. --Continued.

Type of Information Question	Nov. 3-7, 1969 No.	Nov. 3-7, 1969 % of Total Information Questions Asked	Dec. 8-12, 1969 No.	Dec. 8-12, 1969 % of Total Information Questions Asked
Miscellaneous information questions	5	7.5	. .	. .
Total information questions	67	100.0	64	100.0

23.4% in second week). These questions ranged in type of content from periodicals to photocopying machines with no collection or service asked about very often. Fewer students asked the reference librarian for the location of a book after they already had the call number or requested the location of a specific title in the reference collection (10.5% and 12.5%).

Analysis of the R-1 questions (Table 28) shows that the largest number were requests for the librarian's assistance in use of volumes in the reference collection. The response of going to the reference shelves and producing a particular volume for a student who had given the title or described the type of volume he was seeking was made to 21% and 19.1% respectively of the total reference questions received during the two weeks of monitoring. In 16% and 21.4% of the reference questions in which the student asked for general bibliographical assistance, the librarian responded by using the reference collection. Assisting students at the main and serials catalogs also formed a substantial portion of the reference questions (19% in first week; 18.3% in second week). Of the 43 questions in which the librarian assisted at the catalogs, 27 (62.8%) were at the serials catalog and 16 (37.2%) with the main catalog.

R-2 questions (bibliographical assistance with holdings of other campus libraries) amounted to 6% and 5.3% of the

Table 28.--Bibliographical Assistance with Library's Own Catalogs and Holdings (R-1 Questions) Requested by Undergraduates at Reference Desk, Uris Library, Cornell University, in Two One-Week Samples, 1969

Type of Response by Type of R-1 Question	Nov. 3-7, 1969		Dec. 8-12, 1969	
	No.	% of Total Reference Questions Asked	No.	% of Total Reference Questions Asked
Request for particular volume or type of volume; librarian gave assistance by:				
Checking list of frequently used reference titles and giving student call number	..	..	..	..
Charging out heavily used item from drawer of desk or area back of desk	11	11.0	4	3.1
Going to reference shelves and producing particular volume for student who had usually given title or described type	21	21.0	25	19.1

Table 28.--Continued.

Type of Response by Type of R-1 Question	Nov. 3-7, 1969 No.	Nov. 3-7, 1969 % of Total Reference Questions Asked	Dec. 8-12, 1969 No.	Dec. 8-12, 1969 % of Total Reference Questions Asked
Going to main collection shelves and locating monograph, periodical, or newspaper which student had been unable to find	..	..	9	6.8
Sub-total	32	32.0	38	29.0
Request for general bibliographical assistance; librarian responded by:				
Using reference collection	16	16.0	28	21.4
Assisting student at main catalog or serials catalog	19	19.0	24	18.3
Using *Subject Headings Used in...the Library of Congress*	2	2.0	..	..
Assisting in use of microform[a]	..	..	..	..

Table 28. --Continued.

Type of Response by Type of R-1 Question	Nov. 3-7, 1969 No.	Nov. 3-7, 1969 % of Total Reference Questions Asked	Dec. 8-12, 1969 No.	Dec. 8-12, 1969 % of Total Reference Questions Asked
Assisting in use of circulation records	. .	. .	. .	. .
Sub-total	37	37.0	52	39.7
Total R-1 Questions	69	70.0	90	68.7
Other Reference Questions (R-2 through R-7)	30	30.0	41	31.3
Total Reference Questions	99	100.0	131	100.0

[a]Uris Library has no microforms.

total reference questions. They were all concerned with periodical titles and were answered by consulting special union lists of periodicals currently received by the Cornell Libraries.

There was only one request for bibliographical verification of material not on the campus (R-3).

During the first week, 18% of the reference questions were requests for retrieval of factual, non-bibliographical information (R-4). These questions increased to 23% in the second week. The R-4 questions varied greatly, ranging through requests for addresses, biographical data, maps, pictures, and many other items. No particular subject or type of material dominated these questions.

Only twice during the two weeks (once each week) did librarians counsel students in a reader's advisory capacity (R-5). In both cases, the student was beginning a paper and sought advice from the librarian as to the appropriate sources.

R-6 questions (informal, personal instruction in use of the library or any of its resources) were almost as rare as the R-5 category. Only six students (three in each week, for 3% and 2.3% of the total reference questions) received any extensive personal instruction from the librarian.

One question was placed in the miscellaneous category (R-7).

Other Uris Activities During Reference Monitoring

The data presented in Table 29 make it possible to view with some perspective the reference questions asked

Table 29.--Attendance, Home Loans, and Reserve Use during Two Weeks of Monitoring Questions at Reference Desk, Uris Library, Cornell University in 1969[a]

Variable	Nov. 3-7, 1969[b]	Dec. 8-12, 1969[b]
Total Attendance	14,622	14,260
Average Daily Attendance	2,924	2,852
Total Home Loans from Main Collection[c]	1,431	2,041
Average Daily Home Loans[c]	286	408
Total Reserve Use	2,954	2,280
Average Daily Reserve Use	590	456

[a]Cornell University. Library. Uris Library. Daily Statistical Reports. November and December, 1969.

[b]16 hours each day (8 A.M.-12 Midnight).

[c]No separate records are kept of home loans to undergraduates, graduate students, faculty, and others. Studies in 1965 and 1967, however, showed that 82-87% of the home loans was to undergraduates.

during the two weeks of monitoring questions at the reference desk of the Uris Library and to place the reference activity within the context of Uris Library as a whole.

Although the attendance was slightly larger during the November week, significantly more home loans were made during the December week. The number of questions asked at the reference desk was also greater during the December week. Reserve book use was higher during the first week when the attendance was higher. This may suggest that during the earlier part of the semester students were using the library as a study hall and for reserve book reading, but during the later part of the semester students, perhaps in preparation of term papers, made greater use of the reference librarians and the main collection.

Reference Services for Undergraduate Students: The Olin Library

When the Cornell University Library was surveyed by a team of outside experts in October, 1947, they found reference services to be

> relatively undeveloped when compared with reference work in institutions of similar rank. Actually, the Reference Department of the University Library is a creation of the summer of 1947. Prior to that time, no organized reference staff was available to handle exclusively the normal responsibilities of a reference department in a university library. Since the Department is new and finding its way, several services usually rendered by comparable institutions have not yet been fully developed.[129]

There had been some reference service provided for faculty members prior to 1947:

> a special type of reference assistance has been provided to faculty members through a faculty research assistant since 1932. This staff member, originally appointed at Cornell through a subvention of the Carnegie Corporation of New York, has had the responsibility of aiding faculty members in various editorial, bibliographic, and research pro-

> jects. This service has been significant and should be continued. At present the service is arranged on the basis of faculty needs as determined by a committee of the Graduate School, with the cooperation of the Director of the Library.[130]

However, Cornell students, both undergraduate and graduate, had to depend on the reference services of the college and departmental libraries scattered over the campus until the founding of the Reference Department in the main library.

> In 1947 the newly organized Reference Department consisted of three professional staff members and one clerical assistant. It began with only a handwritten shelf list as a record of its 4,000 volumes, and with the knowledge that the already apparent lack of space would continue to restrict expansion until a new building appeared. During the fourteen years between its founding in 1947 and the move to Olin Library in 1961, three important characteristics marked the Department's development: a continuity of staff, an unceasing effort to increase its public service activities, and an ever-increasing volume of 'extra-mural' activity--i.e. Interlibrary Loan and Photoduplication.
>
> Professional reference positions were few until 1960. To the original three-member staff was added in 1948 a fourth, whose primary responsibility was to the Map Collection and who was to give 35 percent of her time to Reference activities. In 1954/55, a fifth position was budgeted, and the Map Librarian was to contribute desk time only to Reference. This essentially four and one-half person staff remained constant in number until 1960, when the projected expansion of Reference activity called for seven professional positions. The Reference Librarian, Miss Josephine Tharpe, served the Department from 1947 through 1963; the Associate Reference Librarian, Miss Frances Lauman, from 1947 through [the summer of] 1962; the Map Librarian, Miss Barbara Berthelsen, from 1948 to 1961. In February 1965 Mrs. Caroline Spicer succeeded Miss Tharpe as Reference Librarian and Miss Evelyn Greenberg was appointed Associate Reference Librarian. As Mrs. Spicer and

> Miss Greenberg had functioned in an acting capacity for some time there was no break in the continuity of departmental services.[131]

Caroline Spicer, the present Reference Librarian, has also chronicled the development of the reference collection and services:

> By 1950 the collection totalled 9,000 volumes, the original shelf list had become a more conventional author catalog and typed shelf list, and a firm start had been made in assessing and strengthening the quality of the collections. At the end of the first year of service [1947/48] almost 10,000 questions from patrons were recorded; by 1959/60, this total was 17,000. In addition to desk service, the Department staff with the aid of other staff members gave orientation lectures to entering freshmen yearly until 1962, when the Undergraduate Library assumed this responsibility.[132]

In 1962, a series of voluntary orientation lectures for graduate students was initiated. The lectures, held at the beginning of each semester, have emphasized bibliographical sources. When the Reference Department moved in February, 1961 to spacious quarters in the John M. Olin Library, the map collection became a part of the new Department of Maps, Microtexts, and Newspapers, but the Reference Department

> assumed responsibility for servicing the Periodical Room's 425 titles and the United Nations document collection. In 1962-63 outposts were acquired when the Zoology Collection (on the seventh floor) and the Human Relations Area File (on the second floor) were put under the Department's administration. The former collection was removed to the Mann Library in the summer of 1966, but use of the HRAF files--now physically located in Reference--continued to increase and servicing it required a full-time non-professional staff member. Finally, to celebrate its twentieth anniversary, the Department in 1966/67 entered the Machine Age by installing a teletypewriter and participating in FACTS [Facsimile Transmission Pilot Project] and NYSILL [New York State Interlibrary Loan Network]. While FACTS ceased, the TWX facilities and membership in NYSILL remained as refinements of traditional Interlibrary Loan Service.[133]

During 1961/62, when the old library was being renovated into an undergraduate library, the reference librarians in the Olin Library served both undergraduate and graduate students, answering 21,995 questions (information questions, 40.3%; general reference questions, 57.9%; correspondence questions and correspondence referrals to other campus libraries and offices, 1.6%).[134] During 1962/63, the number of questions increased to 24,798--a 12.7% gain even with the Uris Library also open for the first time and providing reference services during the entire academic year.[135] Information questions had decreased to 30.7% while general reference questions had substantially risen to 67.1% of the total questions. Search questions were 0.7%; correspondence questions and referrals were 1.4%. By 1968/69, questions at the Olin reference desks totalled 26,610 (information questions, 29.8%; general reference questions, 67.5%; search questions, 0.7%; and correspondence questions and referrals, 1.9%). This was a decrease of 11.7% from the previous year's total of 30,160 questions.[136]

The Reference Department is strategically located in the center of the main floor of Olin Library--halfway between the building's only entrance and a sculpture court. Two low wood desks, where the reference librarians on duty are seated, are clearly visible from the main entrance. The reference collection of 13,722 volumes (June, 1969) is shelved in free-standing cases to the sides and rear of the reference desks. Immediately in front of the desks are special tables and counters for periodical and other indexes, and bookcases housing an additional 2,500 volumes in the Bibliography Collection (national and trade bibliographies from various countries). Also in front of the desks are the public catalogs listing the holdings of Olin Library as well as those of all campus libraries. The reference desks and collections plus the union catalogs are, thus, in close proximity to each other.

Only 28 volumes are kept on closed shelves in the Reference Department office. Patrons must specifically request these items and sign for their use. An additional 25 volumes are kept handy in drawers of the reference desks; seven of them are not duplicates of copies on the open shelves of the main reference collection. Patrons must also ask the reference librarians on duty for unbound issues of some periodicals. The current issues of the journals are shelved in the Periodical Room, but some non-current issues are kept in the Reference office awaiting binding preparation.

All inquirers, including undergraduate students, may request assistance in-person or may telephone their questions to the reference librarians. The only restriction on undergraduates is that they may not borrow volumes from other libraries through the Department's interlibrary loan service.

The reference desks were staffed in the Fall semester, 1969, by two librarians from 10 A.M.-12 Noon and 1-4 P.M., Monday-Friday. From 12 Noon-1 P.M. and 4-5 P.M., one librarian was on duty with the second on stand-by call. From 8-10 A.M. and 5-9 P.M., only one librarian was on duty. A graduate student manned the desks from 9 P.M.-12 Midnight, Monday-Thursday nights, and from 6 P.M.-12 Midnight on Fridays. On Saturdays, one professional staff member worked from 8 A.M.-1 P.M. Another professional worked from 1-7 P.M. A graduate student assisted the professional from 2-6 P.M. The Saturday hours from 7 P.M.-12 Midnight were then covered by a graduate student. On Sundays, one librarian worked from 1-5 P.M. and 6-10 P.M. During 2-5 P.M. and 7-10 P.M., he was assisted by a graduate student. From 5-6 P.M. and 10 P.M.-12 Midnight on Sundays, a graduate student gave reference assistance. Librarians were available for 81 hours, or 75.7% of the 107 hours the Olin Library was open each week during the regular academic year.

The professional staff of the Reference Department in the Fall semester, 1969 was comprised of nine librarians--two persons worked one-half time for a FTE of eight librarians. In addition to public service at the desks, each was responsible for another reference function (such as maintenance of the reference and bibliography collections, supervision of photoduplication requests from other libraries, interlibrary lending of Cornell materials, borrowing from other libraries for Cornell graduate students and faculty, or other administrative duties). Five of the nine librarians have had several years experience in the Olin Reference Department, ranging from two to eight years. The other four had less experience in the Department; one person had just joined the staff and three had worked there one year. Six librarians had worked in other academic or public libraries before coming to Cornell. Two of these six staff members had worked in the Uris Library before transferring to the Reference Department. Seven librarians were female; two were male. Three were graduates of the Columbia School of Library Service and six were from other library schools (Carnegie Institute of Technology, Michigan, North Carolina, Rutgers, Simmons, and Toronto). Three librarians had also earned a master's degree in a subject and one other person had done extensive graduate work not for credit toward a degree.

The Olin Reference Department also had 7.5 permanent clerical positions. Three graduate students worked on a part-time basis.

Undergraduate Use of the Olin Reference Department

Several formal studies at the Olin Library reference desks have shown the number of undergraduate students asking questions of the librarians. The most recent data are for the month of July, 1969 when inquirers were asked their university status. Undergraduates accounted for only 13.8% of the 1,161 persons who asked general reference questions. This proportion was small in relation to the other users:

Undergraduates	13.8%
Graduate students	23.1
Faculty	8.2
University and Library staff	24.5
Persons not connected with Cornell	16.6
Persons whose status was not determined by the librarian	13.7[137]

Information and directional questions were excluded from the above data.

A month during the Summer session--when most undergraduates are away and when University staff and non-Cornellians asked 24.5% and 16.6% of the general reference questions--is, however, not typical of the regular academic year.

Earlier studies,[138] conducted for four-day periods in May 1965, December 1965, and January 1967, revealed that during these selected weeks of the Fall and Spring semesters undergraduates constituted 42-57% of the inquirers at the Olin reference desks. All questions asked (information and directional, general reference, and search questions) were included in these studies. The exact data for the three periods were:

January 10-13, 1967

Undergraduates	42.7%
Graduate students	31.9
Faculty	17.0
Others	8.4

May 17-20, 1965

Undergraduates	57.3%
Graduate students	19.4
Faculty	7.2
Others	16.0

December 6-9, 1965

Undergraduates	47.2%
Graduate students	26.7
Faculty	10.2
Others	15.8

"Others" include both University staff and non-Cornellians.

When only general reference questions are considered, undergraduates asked 40.3% of these more substantial questions during January 10-13, 1967.

Samples of Questions: November and December, 1969

Are undergraduate students the most numerous inquirers at the Olin Library reference desks? What types of questions do they ask? To answer these questions, all requests for reference assistance were monitored at Olin Library's Reference Department during the same 38 hours of both November 3-7 and December 8-12, 1969 as was done in the Uris Library.

During the first week, 130 questions were received from undergraduates, an average hourly rate of 3.4 questions. Questions by undergraduates increased to 188 during the second week, an hourly average of 4.9. The overwhelming majority of the 318 questions asked by undergraduates during the two weeks was asked in-person; only five questions from undergraduates were via telephone. With the exception of one question, all were student-initiated; only once did a librarian approach a student.

During the November monitoring, undergraduates asked 23.5% of the total in-person and telephone questions (554) received at the Olin reference desks. During the week in December, undergraduate questions rose to 34.3% of the total questions (548). During the two weeks, nine questions were asked by undergraduates from other colleges and universities. They have been excluded from the data.

Table 30.--Questions Asked by Undergraduates at Reference Desks, John M. Olin Library, Cornell University, in Two One-Week Samples, 1969

Type of Question	Nov. 3-7, 1969 No.	Nov. 3-7, 1969 %	Dec. 8-12, 1969 No.	Dec. 8-12, 1969 %
Information	42	32.3	56	29.8
Reference				
R-1	60	46.2	90	47.8
R-2	2	1.5	1	0.5
R-3	1	0.7	5	2.7
R-4	21	16.2	34	18.1
R-5	. .	. .	. .	. .
R-6	4	3.1	2	1.1
R-7	. .	. .	. .	. .
Sub-total	88	67.7	132	70.2
Search	. .	. .	. .	. .
Problem	. .	. .	. .	. .
Total	130	100.0	188	100.0

Table 30 categorizes the undergraduate questions. As in the Uris Library, only a short time was spent with each student. There were no search[139] or problem questions. Brief information questions were 32.3% of the total during the first week and 29.8% in the second. For the 220 reference questions in both weeks, the librarian spent at least five or more minutes with the student on only five occasions.

In an analysis of information questions, four kinds of questions were dominant (Table 31). The most numerous requests were for information concerning the main or serials

Table 31.--Types of Information Questions Asked by Undergraduates at Reference Desks, John M. Olin Library, Cornell University, in Two One-Week Samples, 1969

Type of Information Question	Nov. 3-7, 1969		Dec. 8-12, 1969	
	No.	% of Total Information Questions Asked	No.	% of Total Information Questions Asked
Assistance with physical facilities of library:				
Location of pencil sharpener or request to borrow pen, stapler, etc.	1	2.4	. .	. .
Request for keys	. .	. .	. .	. .
Location of areas in library	2	4.8	1	1.8
Sub-total	3	7.2	1	1.8
Requests for location of particular volume (librarian gave directions):				
Monographs in main collection (student had call number)	2	4.8	1	1.8
Reference books (student usually requested by title)	9	21.4	8	14.3
Sub-total	11	26.2	9	16.1

Table 31. --Continued.

Type of Information Question	Nov. 3-7, 1969 No.	Nov. 3-7, 1969 % of Total Information Questions Asked	Dec. 8-12, 1969 No.	Dec. 8-12, 1969 % of Total Information Questions Asked
Requests for information or publication (student did not have call number):				
Librarian knew answer without referring to any source	9	21.4	6	10.7
Librarian referred student to catalog or reference collection, giving no additional assistance	1	2.4	7	12.5
Librarian knew that question would be better answered in another library or department and referred student to it	2	4.8	1	1.8
Sub-total	12	28.6	14	25.0

Table 31.--Continued.

Type of Information Question	Nov. 3-7, 1969		Dec. 8-12, 1969	
	No.	% of Total Information Questions Asked	No.	% of Total Information Questions Asked
Questions concerning collection or services (librarian responded with brief directions or information):				
Periodicals	5	11.9	8	14.3
Newspapers	1	2.4	2	3.6
Main catalog or serials catalog	6	14.3	15	26.7
Reserve books	. .	. .	. .	. .
How and where to charge out books	3	7.1	4	7.1
Use of reference volume in another part of library	. .	. .	. .	. .
Photocopying machine	1	2.4	1	1.8
Exam file	. .	. .	. .	. .
Location of another library	. .	. .	2	3.6
Sub-total	16	38.1	32	57.1

Table 31. --Continued.

Type of Information Question	Nov. 3-7, 1969 No.	Nov. 3-7, 1969 % of Total Information Questions Asked	Dec. 8-12, 1969 No.	Dec. 8-12, 1969 % of Total Information Questions Asked
Miscellaneous information questions	. .	. .	. .	. .
Total information questions	42	100. 0	56	100. 0

catalogs, with the librarian responding with brief directions but no actual assistance at the catalogs. The other frequently occurring situations were: requests by title of a particular reference volume, with the librarian giving directions to its location; requests for information in which the librarian knew the answer without referring to any source; and questions about periodicals in the Olin Library.

R-1 questions (bibliographical assistance with the library's own catalogs and holdings) accounted for 46. 2% and 47. 8% of all questions asked during the first and second weeks of monitoring, or 68. 2% of the more substantive reference questions during each week. Assisting students at the main or serials catalogs was the most frequent kind of response to R-1 questions (Table 32). During the first week of monitoring, 56. 7% of the R-1 questions required assistance at the catalogs; during the second week, 48. 9%. This assistance was about equally divided between the main catalog and the serials catalog. The next most numerous R-1 questions were requests for general bibliographical assistance to which the librarian responded by using the reference collection. Going to the shelves with a student who had requested a particular reference title or type of reference volume and producing the volume was a response that also occurred fairly frequently.

Table 32. --Bibliographical Assistance with Library's Own Catalogs and Holdings (R-1 Questions) Requested by Undergraduates at Reference Desks, John M. Olin Library, Cornell University, in Two One-Week Samples, 1969

Type of Response by Type of R-1 Question	Nov. 3-7, 1969		Dec. 8-12, 1969	
	No.	% of Total Reference Questions Asked	No.	% of Total Reference Questions Asked
Request for particular volume or type of volume; librarian gave assistance by:				
Checking list of frequently used reference titles and giving student call number	. .	. .	. .	. .
Charging out heavily used item from drawer or from office	10	11.4	10	7.6
Going to reference shelves and producing particular volume for student who had usually given title or described type	8	9.1	14	10.6

Table 32. --Continued.

Type of Response by Type of R-1 Question	Nov. 3-7, 1969 No.	Nov. 3-7, 1969 % of Total Reference Questions Asked	Dec. 8-12, 1969 No.	Dec. 8-12, 1969 % of Total Reference Questions Asked
Going to main collection shelves and locating monograph, periodical, or newspaper which student had been unable to find	. .	. .	1	0.7
Sub-total	18	20.5	25	18.9
Request for general bibliographical assistance; librarian responded by:				
Using reference collection	7	7.9	19	14.4
Assisting student at main catalog or serials catalog	34	38.7	44	33.4
Using _Subject Headings Used in... the Library of Congress_	1	1.1	2	1.5
Assisting in use of microform	. .	. .	. .	. .

Table 32. --Continued.

Type of Response by Type of R-1 Question	Nov. 3-7, 1969 No.	Nov. 3-7, 1969 % of Total Reference Questions Asked	Dec. 8-12, 1969 No.	Dec. 8-12, 1969 % of Total Reference Questions Asked
Assisting in use of circulation records	. .	. .	. .	. .
Sub-total	42	47.7	65	49.3
Total R-1 Questions	60	68.2	90	68.2
Other Reference Questions (R-2 through R-7)	28	31.8	42	31.8
Total Reference Questions	88	100.0	132	100.0

There were only three occasions during the two weeks when Olin reference librarians directly assisted undergraduates with the holdings of other campus libraries (R-2). Some of this kind of assistance may have been given when the librarian helped the student at the catalogs, but usually the search was for a copy in the Olin Library.

R-3 questions (bibliographical verification of material not on the campus) were also infrequent among undergraduate students. Only once in the November week and five times during the December week was this kind of assistance requested.

During the November week, 23.8% of the reference questions were requests for retrieval of factual, non-bibliographical information (R-4). This category increased slightly to 25.8% in the December week. As in the Uris Library, these questions varied greatly, with no subject area or type of material dominant.

At no time during the hours of monitoring did an Olin reference librarian counsel an undergraduate student in a reader's advisory capacity (R-5).

R-6 questions (informal personal instruction in use of the library or any of its resources) were also rare: only four instances during the first week and two during the second week.

No reference questions required classification in a miscellaneous category (R-7).

Table 33.--Attendance, Home Loans, and Building-Use of Volumes Paged from Stacks During Two Weeks of Monitoring Questions at Reference Desks, John M. Olin Library, Cornell University in 1969[a]

Variable	Nov. 3-7, 1969[b]	Dec. 8-12, 1969[b]
Total Attendance	14, 919	15, 098
Average Daily Attendance	2, 983	3, 019
Total Home Loans	3, 387	4, 056
Average Daily Home Loans	677	811
Total Volumes Paged From Stacks and Charged Out for Building Use	382	541
Average Daily Volumes Paged from Stacks and Charged Out for Building Use	76	108

[a]Cornell University. Library. Olin Library. Circulation Department. "Daily Statistics." November and December, 1969. (Typewritten.)

[b]16 hours each day (8 A.M.-Midnight).

Other Olin Library Activities During Reference Monitoring

No separate information desk is maintained by the Reference Department at another location in the Olin Library. Undergraduate students ask occasional questions of the technical services staff members working at the public catalogs, but there is no formal system as at the General Library of the University of Michigan.

Data on Olin Library attendance, building-use of volumes paged from the stacks for use by undergraduates and non-Cornellians without stack permits, and home loans during the two weeks of monitoring questions at the reference desks are shown in Table 33.

The Two Cornell Reference Services

Are there significant differences and/or similarities in the reference services for undergraduates in Uris Library, Cornell's undergraduate library, and the Olin Library, the research library?

The reference librarians in the Uris Library during the first week of monitoring served 37 (28.5%) more undergraduates than did the Olin reference librarians. However, during the second week, Olin librarians almost pulled even with the Uris staff (188 questions by undergraduates in Olin; 196 questions in Uris).

More of the questions in Uris were brief information questions (40.1% and 32.7% were information questions in Uris versus 32.3% and 29.8% in Olin during the two weeks).

In the R-1 category of reference questions, the Olin librarians assisted students at the main or serials catalogs in a much larger proportion of the situations (Olin: 38.7% and 33.4% of all reference questions during the first and second weeks; Uris: 19% and 18.3%). In contrast, the Uris librarians used the reference collection to answer questions more often than did the Olin librarians (Uris: 16% and 21.4%; Olin: 7.9% and 14.4%). The Uris librarians also went to the reference shelves to produce a particular volume for a student about twice as often as did the reference librarians in Olin (Uris: 21% and 19.1%; Olin: 9.1% and 10.6%). These R-1 questions constituted about the same percentages of all questions asked by undergraduates at the two reference services (Uris: 41.3% and 45.9%; Olin: 46.2% and 47.8%). When the R-1 questions are taken as percentages of the total reference questions asked by undergraduates in the two libraries, they are almost identical (Uris: 70% in first week and 68.7% in second week; Olin: exactly 68.2% during each week).

Other differences in the questions by undergraduates in Uris and Olin Libraries:

R-2 questions: 3.6% during each week in Uris; only 1.5% and 0.5% in Olin;

R-4 questions: 10.8% and 15.3% in Uris; 16.2% and 18.1% in Olin.

The R-3, R-5, and R-6 questions were very small in number at the reference desks of both Uris and Olin. The search and problem questions were almost non-existant in both libraries. Only a brief time was spent with each student (Uris: in 10 instances--2.7% of the 363 questions--a librarian spent 5 or more minutes with the student; Olin: on 5 occasions--1.6% of the 318 questions--a librarian assisted for 5 or more minutes).

Undergraduate Users of Union Catalog

An investigation was conducted in the Olin Library to test the hypothesis that unassisted use by undergraduate students of the union catalog of campus holdings increases use of the Olin Library and decreases use of the Uris Library. Methods, hours, and other procedures used in interviewing 427 Cornell University undergraduates are described in Chapter 1.

The public catalogs--one is labeled "Old Catalog" and the other, though not labeled, is referred to as the "Main Catalog"--are located in the center of Olin's first floor. The Old Catalog lists a small number of pre-1948 publications which have not been reclassified from the Harris system to the Library of Congress classification. Both of "these catalogs are a record of the books, periodicals, newspapers, pamphlets, government publications, and other types of printed materials held by the various libraries on the Cornell University campus."[140] Both are, therefore, union catalogs.

The separate Serials Catalog lists the bound volumes of periodicals and other serials held by the Olin Library and the departmental and college libraries (with the exception of the Law Library) which are in the private and endowed parts of the University. In addition to the Law Library, the libraries of the New York State colleges and schools do not have their exact serial holdings listed in the Serials Catalog.

The weekly computer-produced "Master Status List of Current Acquisitions" is available opposite the reference desks and serves as a supplement to the Main Catalog. "It indicates under main entry those books on-order or in-process for the endowed college libraries (except Law). Documents and serials are not included."[141]

The Main Catalog lists the sound recordings of the Uris Library's Listening Rooms, but does not include many documents of the United Nations and other international organizations.

Undergraduate students constituted 32.7% of all union catalog users during the 38 hours of the survey from October 27-31, 1969 (Table 34).

The 427 undergraduates interviewed were members of the following Cornell classes:

Freshman	12.9%
Sophomore	19.3
Junior	29.9
Senior	37.7
Special Unclassified	0.2

They were registered in the following seven schools and colleges:

College of Arts and Sciences	64.9%
New York State College of Agriculture	11.5
New York State College of Human Ecology	7.2
College of Engineering	7.0
New York State School of Industrial and Labor Relations	4.7
College of Architecture, Art, and Planning	3.7
School of Hotel Administration	0.9

Table 34.-Union Catalog Users in the John M. Olin Library, Cornell University, October 27-31, 1969[a]

Union Catalog User	No.	%
Undergraduates Interviewed	427	27.6
Undergraduates Refusing Interview	None	. .
Undergraduates Who Had Been Previously Interviewed	78	5.1
Total Undergraduate Users	505	32.7
Graduate Students, Faculty, and University Staff (Excludes Library Staff)	958	62.0
Non-University Users (Local Residents, Students and Faculty from Other Institutions)	82	5.3
Total Users of Union Catalog	1,545	100.0

[a]Interviews conducted during 38 hours of the week of October 27-31, 1969. Hours on Monday-Thursday were: 10 A.M.-12 Noon, 1-5 P.M., and 7-9 P.M. On Friday: 10 A.M.-12 Noon and 1-5 P.M.

All undergraduates were asked: "Did you use the Uris Library catalog before coming here?" 24.4% responded "Yes" and 75.6% said "No."

The 104 undergraduates who replied that they had used the Uris catalog before coming to the Olin union catalogs were then asked: "Why are you now using this main catalog?" The reasons given were:

Uris Library did not have material	40.4%
Material in use in Uris (Out, on reserve, etc.)	41.4
Wanted additional material	17.3
Could not find catalog in Uris	0.9

The 323 students who said that they had not used the Uris Library catalog before coming to the Olin catalogs in this particular instance were asked: "Do you usually by-pass the Uris Library and come to the main catalog first?" Their responses were:

Yes	77.5%
No	12.4
About half the time, I by-pass it	7.1
Depends on material I am seeking	2.1
Depends on where I want to study	0.3
First time in any campus library	0.6

The 250 undergraduates who affirmed that they usually by-passed the Uris catalog were next asked: "Why do you not use the Uris Library catalog first?" 311 reasons were given:

This is a union catalog listing holdings of all campus libraries	32.8%
Have found through experience that Uris lacks what I want	10.7
Most of the university's books are here in Olin Library	17.4
I do not like Uris Library	3.6
Uris collection is too small	1.2
I like the Olin Library better	4.9
Too much is on reserve in Uris	0.6
Olin Library is closer to my living quarters	0.3
My professor sent me here to use the union catalog	0.3
I did not know Uris Library existed	0.3
I work here in Olin Library	3.6
It depends on the material I am seeking	2.2
I have an Olin Library stack permit[142]	14.8
I use a college or school library first	3.2
I do not know why	1.9
Miscellaneous (ranging from "Help is easier to get in Olin Library" to "I am interested in a boy who who studies here.")	2.2

The final question posed to all 427 undergraduates interviewed was: "If the Uris Library had a catalog like this which includes holdings of all campus libraries, would you use it there or still come here?"

Still come here to Olin Library	47.6%
Use it in Uris	35.7
I do not know	3.5
Would use whichever is closer	2.1
Does not matter to me	9.1
Depends on material sought	1.6
Depends on how noisy Uris Library is	0.2
It is unnecessary to duplicate because Uris is so close to Olin	0.2

Comparison of the foregoing data on Cornell undergraduate users of the Olin Library's union catalogs is made with University of Michigan undergraduates in Chapter 7. Conclusions are also drawn there.

Notes

1. Morris Bishop, A History of Cornell (Ithaca: Cornell University Press, 1962), p. 19.

2. Ibid., p. 21.

3. George William Curtis [Address at the Inauguration of Cornell University, October 7, 1868] as quoted in Bishop, p. 40.

4. Ezra Cornell, "Defense Against the Charge of Being the Founder of an 'Aristocratic' University, 1865" in Carl Becker, Cornell University: Founders and the Founding (Ithaca: Cornell University Press, 1943), p. 169.

5. The motto on the Seal of Cornell University: "I would found an institution where any person can find instruction in any study."

6. Bishop, p. 90 and p. 107.

7. Rita Guerlac, An Introduction to Cornell (Ithaca: Cornell University, 1962), pp. 8-9.

8. Cornell University. Office of the Registrar. "Registration--Fall Term 1969," October 17, 1969. (Mimeographed.)

9. Data furnished by Office of the Dean of the University Faculty, Cornell University, November 5, 1969.

10. Bishop, p. 323.

11. *Ibid.*, p. 352.

12. Cornell University. Office of the Registrar. "Undergraduate Enrollment by Class--Fall Term 1969," October 17, 1969. (Mimeographed.)

13. Data furnished by Office of the Dean of the University Faculty, Cornell University, November 5, 1969.

14. Rita Guerlac, "Cornell's Library," *Cornell Library Journal*, No. 2 (Spring, 1967), 1.

15. Andrew D. White, *Report of the Committee on Organization* (Albany, 1867) as quoted in Bishop, p. 77.

16. Guerlac, "Cornell's Library," p. 4.

17. Andrew Dickson White, *Autobiography of Andrew Dickson White* (2 vols.; New York: Century, 1905), I, p. 308.

18. Bishop, p. 108.

19. Guerlac, "Cornell's Library," p. 5.

20. Bishop, p. 108.

21. Guerlac, "Cornell's Library," pp. 8-9.

22. *Ibid.*, pp. 11-12.

23. Henry W. Sage "Presentation Address" in Cornell University, *Exercises at the Opening of the Library Building, October 7, 1891* (Ithaca: Cornell University, 1891), p. 30.

24. *Ithaca Journal*, June 18, 1888.

25. Sage, p. 29.

26. Jackson E. Towne, "Building the Cornell Library," *Cornell Alumni News*, LV (June 15, 1953), 533.

27. Bishop, p. 271.

28. *Ibid.*

29. Guerlac, "Cornell's Library," p. 13.

30. White, *Autobiography*, I, pp. 421-22.

31. Guerlac, "Cornell's Library," p. 18.

32. *Ibid.*, pp. 18-19.

33. *Ibid.*, p. 22.

34. *Ibid.*, p. 15.

35. Louis Round Wilson, Robert B. Downs, and Maurice F. Tauber, *Report of a Survey of the Libaries of Cornell University for the Library Board of Cornell University, October 1947-February 1948* (Ithaca: Cornell University, 1948).

36. Guerlac, "Cornell's Library," p. 27.

37. *Ibid.*, p. 30.

38. *Ibid.*, p. 31.

39. Wilson, Downs, and Tauber, pp. 20, 28, and 107; Cornell University. Library. *Reports of the Director of the University Libraries*. 1951/52, p. 19 and 1966/67, p. 40.

40. Cornell University. Library. "Library Use Survey, January 10-13, 1967." Ithaca, 1967. (Typewritten.)

41. U.S. Office of Education. "Higher Education General Information Survey, Library Collections, Staff, Expenditures, and Salaries." (Cornell University's Report for 1968/69.)

42. Cornell University. Library. *Reports of the Director of the University Libraries*. 1962/63, p. 33 and 1968/69, p. 29.

43. "Study Group Analyzes Libraries' Future Needs," *Cornell Chronicle*, I (November 6, 1969), 1.

44. Frederic C. Wood, "The Expansion of the Cornell Library" [Report of Frederic C. Wood, Consulting Engineer, to Cornell University, July 8, 1955]. Greenwich, Connecticut, 1955. (Typewritten.)

45. [Stephen A. McCarthy, "Introduction" to the] "Central Library Facilities: the Wood Report; the Metcalf Report." Ithaca, 1955, p. 2. (Typewritten.)

46. Wood, pp. 3-6.

47. Cornell University. Library. _Report of the Director of the University Library_. 1955/56, p. 1.

48. Cornell University. Library. "Program for the Undergraduate Library." Draft Program, March 26, 1956. (Mimeographed.)

49. Cornell University. Library. _Report of the Director of the University Library_. 1958/59, p. 4.

50. Cornell University. Library. "Program for the Undergraduate Library," July 13, 1959. (Mimeographed.)

51. _Ibid._, p. 2.

52. Cornell University. Library. Uris Library. "Costs of Remodeling the Building, 1961." [Statement prepared by Harold B. Schell, Assistant to the Director of University Libraries, July 3, 1964.] (Typewritten.)

53. Cornell University. Library. _Report of the Director of the University Libraries_. 1962/63, p. 3.

54. Irene A. Braden, _The Undergraduate Library_, ACRL Monographs, No. 31 (Chicago: American Library Association, 1970), pp. 101-05.

55. Cornell University. Library. Uris Library. _Annual Report_. 1962/63, p. 17.

56. _Ibid._, [Statistical Supplement], 1964/65, p. 4; 1968/69, p. 4.

57. Interview with Stephen A. McCarthy, former Director of the Cornell University Libraries, presently Executive Director of the Association of Research Libraries, Washington, D.C., December 29, 1969.

58. Ibid.

59. Cornell University. Library. Report of the Director of the University Libraries. 1960/61, pp. 21-22.

60. Cornell University. Library. Information Bulletin, No. 55 (April 4, 1962), 1.

61. Cornell University. Library. Uris Library. Annual Report. [Statistical Supplement], 1968/69, p. 5.

62. Ibid., 1962/63, pp. 3-4.

63. Bishop, p. 271.

64. Benjamin G. Whitten and Billy R. Wilkinson, "A Day of Books and Students," Cornell Alumni News, LXIX (July, 1966), 7-11.
Billy R. Wilkinson, "The Arthur H. Dean Book Collection Contest," Cornell Library Journal, No. 3 (Autumn, 1967), 55-56.

65. Cornell University. Library. Committee on Undergraduate Library Service. Minutes of Meetings, 1966/67. (Typewritten.)

66. Cornell University. Library. Uris Library. Annual Report. 1966/67, pp. 21-22.

67. Ibid., 1968/69, p. 6.

68. Ibid., 1967/68, p. 30.

69. Letter from Ronald E. Rucker, Librarian, Uris Library, to Billy R. Wilkinson, November 18, 1970.

70. Cornell University. Library. Uris Library. Annual Report. 1968/69, p. 1.

71. Ibid.

72. Ibid., p. 2.

73. Ibid., 1962/63, p. 3.

74. Cornell University. Library. "Library Use Survey, January 10-13, 1967." Ithaca, 1967. (Typewritten.)

75. Interview with David Kaser, Director of University Libraries, Cornell University, December 10, 1969.

76. Cornell University. Library. Uris Library. *Annual Report*. 1964/65, pp. 38-39.

77. In April, 1966, the Librarian decided it was very easy to forget about the large majority of students who were seriously studying even at the height of the social period and commissioned a head count for 8:30 P.M. on six nights. Over 500 students each evening were quietly seated and studying.

78. Cornell University. Library. Uris Library. *Annual Reports*. [Statistical Supplements.] 1962/63, p. 1; 1964/65, p. 1; and 1968/69, p. 1.

79. Cornell University. Library. Uris Library. *Annual Report*. 1967/68, p. 13.

80. *Ibid.*, 1969/70, p. 8.

81. *Ibid.*, p. 9.

82. Interview with Judith H. Bossert, Reserve Book Librarian, Uris Library, Cornell University, October 30, 1969.

83. Letter from Ronald E. Rucker, Librarian, Uris Library, Cornell University, to Billy R. Wilkinson, September 24, 1970.

84. During 1969/70, only 14.6% of the total expenditures for books and recordings was for reserve books ($4,171.14 for reserve books of a total of $28,535.02).

85. Harvie Branscomb, *Teaching with Books* (Hamden, Connecticut: Shoe String Press, 1964 [Reprint of Chicago: Association of American Colleges and American Library Association, 1940]), p. 27.

86. Cornell University. Office of the Registrar. "Registration-Fall Term 1968," October 4, 1968. (Mimeographed.)

87. In two studies of home loans from the research collection in the John M. Olin Library, where the stacks are closed to undergraduates except by special permission, undergraduate students accounted for 34% (December 6-9, 1965) and 39.8% (January 10-13, 1967) of all home loans. Of the 184,361 home loans from the research collection in 1966/67, undergraduates probably accounted for 70,000-75,000 loans.

88. Cornell University. Library. Uris Library. Annual Report. [Statistical Supplement.] 1962/63, p. 3.

89. Letter from Ronald E. Rucker, Librarian, Uris Library, Cornell University, to Billy R. Wilkinson, October 8, 1970.

90. Cornell University. Library. Uris Library. Annual Reports. 1965/66, p. 9; 1966/67, p. 8.

91. Christopher R. Barnes, "Classification and Cataloging of Spoken Records in Academic Libraries," College and Research Libraries, XXVIII (January, 1967), 49-52.

92. Cornell University. Library. Uris Library. Annual Reports. 1962/63, p. 13; 1965/66, p. 4; 1968/69, p. 13.

93. Interview with Judith H. Bossert, Reserve Book Librarian, Uris Library, Cornell University, October 30, 1969.

94. Interview with David Kaser, Director of University Libraries, Cornell University, December 10, 1969.

95. Cornell University. Library. Uris Library. Annual Report. 1969/70, p. 14.

96. Interview with Frances W. Lauman, Reference Librarian, Uris Library, Cornell University, October 31, 1969.

97. Interview with Ronald E. Rucker, Librarian, Uris Library, Cornell University, October 29, 1969.

98. Interview with G. F. Shepherd, Jr., Associate Director of Libraries, Cornell University, December 9, 1969.

99. Cornell University. Library. Uris Library. *Annual Report.* 1967/68, p. 23.

100. Cornell University. Library. Uris Library. [Script of Untitled Library Orientation Lecture Given by Reference Staff, Uris Library, to Freshman English Classes.] Fall Term, 1963. (Typewritten.)

101. Cornell University. Library. Uris Library. *Annual Report.* 1962/63, pp. 17-18.

102. *Ibid.*, 1963/64, p. 24.

103. *Ibid.*, 1964/65, p. 20.

104. *Ibid.*, 1966/67, p. 14.

105. Edgar Rosenberg, *The Freshman Humanities Courses* [Ithaca: Cornell University, 1966], p. 1.

106. Cornell University. Library. Uris Library. *Annual Report.* 1966/67, pp. 14-15.

107. Frances W. Lauman and Billy R. Wilkinson, "Annual Orientation Program for Freshmen, Memorandum to Stephen A. McCarthy and G. F. Shepherd, Jr.," October 26, 1966, p. 2. (Typewritten.)

108. Cornell University. Library. Uris Library. *Annual Report.* 1967/68, pp. 23-24; 1968/69, p. 12.

109. *Ibid.*, 1968/69, p. 12.

110. *Ibid.*, 1969/70, p. 12; Cornell University. Office of the Registrar. "Undergraduate Enrollment by Class--Fall Term, 1969," October 17, 1969. (Mimeographed.)

111. Frances W. Lauman and Susan Gauck, "Introductory Reference Lectures, Memorandum to G. F. Shepherd, Jr. and Ronald E. Rucker," December 30, 1968. (Typewritten.)

112. Interview with Caroline Spicer, Reference Librarian, John M. Olin Library, Cornell University, October 31, 1969.

113. Interview with Ronald E. Rucker, October 29, 1969.

114. "Video Center," The CUL Weekly Gazette, I (August 17, 1970), 3.

115. Cornell University. Library. John M. Olin Library. Reference Department. Annual Reports. 1967/68, p. 9; 1968/69, p. 3.

116. Cornell University. Library. Uris Library. Annual Report. 1964/65, p. 22.

117. Ibid., 1968/69, p. 12.

118. Letter from Frances W. Lauman, Reference Librarian, Uris Library, Cornell University, to Billy R. Wilkinson, May 14, 1970.

119. Data in this section are from personal interviews conducted October 29-November 7, 1969 with six librarians on the Uris Library staff.

120. Billy R. Wilkinson, "New Out of Old," Cornell Alumni News, LXIV (January, 1962), 12.

121. Cornell University. Library. Uris Library. Basic Library Handbook (1st ed.; Ithaca: Uris Library, 1962), p. 5.

122. Ibid., p. 25.

123. Cornell University. Library. Committee on Reference Statistics Terminology. "Definitions of Reference Statistics Terminology," July 1, 1962. (Mimeographed.)

124. Cornell University. Library. Uris Library. Annual Report. 1965/66, p. 12.

125. Ibid., 1966/67, p. 10.

126. Ibid., 1968/69, p. 12.

127. Patricia B. Knapp, "The Library, the Undergraduate and the Teaching Faculty" (Paper presented at the Institute on Training for Service in Undergraduate Libraries, University of California, San Diego,

August 17-21, 1970), pp. 14-15.

128. Definitions of search questions as well as information, reference (R-1 through R-7), and problem questions are given in Chapter 1. Hereafter in this section, these definitions are used.

129. Wilson, Downs, and Tauber, p. 89.

130. Ibid.

131. Cornell University. Library. John M. Olin Library. Reference Department. Annual Report. 1967/68, p. 1.

132. Ibid., pp. 1-2.

133. Ibid., pp. 2-3.

134. Ibid., 1961/62, p. 8; the Olin Reference Department uses the same definitions of reference questions as Uris Library.

135. Ibid., 1962/63, p. 5.

136. Ibid., 1968/69, p. 3.

137. Marcia Jebb, "Reference Desk Questions, July, 1969, Memorandum to Caroline T. Spicer," November 5, 1969, p. 2.

138. Cornell University. Library. "Library Use Surveys; May 17-20, 1965; December 6-9, 1965; and January 10-13, 1967," Ithaca, 1965 and 1967. (Typewritten.)

139. Definitions of search questions as well as information, reference (R-1 through R-7), and problem questions are given in Chapter 1. Hereafter in this section, these definitions are used.

140. Cornell University. Library. John M. Olin Library Handbook (Ithaca: Cornell University Library, September, 1969), p. 3.

141. Ibid., p. 4.

142. Although the stacks of the Olin Library are closed to most undergraduates, honors students, Phi Beta Kappas, and other undergraduates have stack permits.

Chapter 5

CASE III: SWARTHMORE COLLEGE

> Probably no college in America now has [an ideal teaching library]. Excellence in teaching, however, is a traditional goal at Swarthmore, and the College has developed, particularly in recent years, a library which will provide a sound base for future growth. The teaching library... is not something which may simply be bought tomorrow; it will take, especially its educational functions, years to develop.
>
> Swarthmore College. "Report of the Special Committee on Library Policy" in Critique of A College (Swarthmore: Swarthmore College, 1967), p. 345.

Historical Highlights of The College

Conceived in the early 1850's by Martha Tyson, Benjamin Hallowell, and other Friends of the Baltimore Yearly Meeting, Swarthmore's gestation was long. Its Charter was not granted until 1864 and classes did not begin until 1869.

> Unlike the multitude of frontier colleges which sprang almost literally from the wilderness, Swarthmore did not evolve from a vigorous religious evangelism. It was not the agency of a church intent upon extending its influence or enhancing its prestige; rather, it was the creation of modest Christians bent only upon the preservation of their beliefs against denominational competition and the inroads of secular influence. It was first and foremost a bastion of defense, and never a weapon of proselytism.[1]

One group of the Society of Friends, the Hicksites, were determined to provide an education for their children which would equal that of the best colleges in the country.[2]

Edward Parrish was appointed President in 1865. He labored to open the College and presided over the 199 students who were enrolled for part or all of the first year, 1869/70. Of these students, only 26 qualified as Freshmen; the others were in the Preparatory Department.[3] Parrish, however, served briefly as President. He was forced to resign by the Board of Managers in 1871 as a result of difficulties between him and Edward Hicks Magill, Principal of the Preparatory Department of the College.[4]

Magill was then appointed President and served until 1889. During these years, a system of elective courses was begun, the natural sciences were introduced as a major course of study, and coeducation of women and men flourished. Magill's major contribution was "not in these innovations which largely distinguish Swarthmore from its contemporary collegiate environment, but in his efforts to bring Swarthmore more closely into identification with that larger pattern of higher education."[5]

President Magill succeeded in getting the Board of Managers' approval to begin dropping the preparatory classes in 1884/85. During the previous year, 216 students were enrolled in the Preparatory School and 83 students in the College. In 1889/90, the proportions were reversed, with 163 College students and only 80 Preparatory students.[6] By the early 1890's, only college level courses were taught and the "primacy of the College function"[7] was established.

Charles De Garmo became President of Swarthmore in 1891 and for six years attempted to bring the College "fully abreast of the best colleges in requirements for admission and in work demanded for graduation [and to] match them in quality and quantity of teaching force and in all necessary equipment."[8] This plan for intellectual competition, however, did not appeal to the Board of Managers nor to the members of the Society of Friends. Unable to set Swarthmore upon this path, De Garmo resigned in 1897.

The Board selected as President William W. Birdsall, Principal of the Friends Central School in Philadelphia, "a sincere, faithful and somewhat unimaginative leader among local Quakers."[9] Not since 1870 had a Swarthmore President

> so clearly recognized a direct responsibility to the religious tradition of the institution.... What set him apart from his predecessors was a frank espousal of the existence of Swarthmore as a means of benefit to the Society of Friends, and his relegation of worldly ambition and material wealth to positions of contributing, secondary importance.[10]

Birdsall's critics were very outspoken in opposition to this philosophy and after four years, he resigned in March, 1902. The Board of Managers then abandoned the "last remnants of the conservative sectarianism which had stayed with them through four decades"[11] by inviting Joseph Swain to be President. Swain, who had been President of Indiana University, laid down two conditions--substantial increase of the endowment and the granting of Presidential power to hire and dismiss faculty members--to the Board before his acceptance of the position. Swain asked for and received the "two things Swarthmore never before had enjoyed--a material endowment adequate by contemporary educational standards, and a President with the power to lead."[12]

Swain, during the next two decades, defined the "role of Swarthmore as one which should apply the essential values of Quakerism to the changing circumstances of each succeeding generation"[13] and began to direct the College "out of the isolated charm of its cultural backwaters and into the swift moving main currents of higher education in America."[14]

Frank Aydelotte, who became Swarthmore's President in 1921, continued the College in the main currents of American higher education. He had been a Rhodes Scholar and studied at Oxford in a small residential college under an intimate tutorial system. Aydelotte's educational philosophy had three major premises: he had a strong belief in the small college; saw education as an active rather than a passive process, with self-education as the true education; and believed that the principles of democracy cannot be applied to values (all subjects are not as good as all others and although there should be equality of opportunity, not all students are equal in ability).[15] Swarthmore was soon to begin an educational experiment that would be closely watched by other American colleges and universities.

By the autumn of 1922, the now famous honors program was launched with eleven students who volunteered. The lock-step lecture method was being broken with the introduction of small seminars and independent study. In 1925/26, fifty-two students were reading for honors.[16] Under the guidance of President Aydelotte until his resignation in 1940, the program gradually developed, and by 1939/40, 44% of the juniors and seniors were reading for honors.[17]

John W. Nason succeeded Aydelotte as President, serving from 1940 to 1953. Having studied at Oxford, he maintained and advanced the honors program. Nason was followed by Courtney Smith. The Smith years, 1953-1968, were ones of continued academic excellence. They were also a period of great expansion of the College's physical facilities with the construction of the du Pont Science Building, Sharples Dining Hall, Worth Health Center, Dana and Hallowell Dormitories, McCabe Library, Tarble Social Center, and other buildings.

The last two years of President Smith's administration were one of the most important periods in the history of Swarthmore. In the summer of 1966, he appointed the Commission on Educational Policy to review the College's "entire academic program and make recommendations to the faculty and to the Board of Managers."[18] Not since the honors program was begun in 1922 "had there been a period of conscious and purposeful curricular change at Swarthmore."[19] The Commission--composed of five faculty members, two alumni, and one non-Swarthmorean--studied the College during 1966/67 and submitted its report in November, 1967. Two other groups, the Special Committee on Library Policy and the Special Committee on Student Life, also conducted self-studies during the period. The three reports were brought together and published as Critique of a College. Discussions of the recommendations in the reports were held by the entire College community during the week of December 1-7, 1967 (dubbed "Superweek"). There then ensued many faculty and Board of Managers' meetings. By June, 1968, President Smith could report that two of the reports (Educational Policy and Library Policy) "have been debated and refined by our Faculty, and heartily approved by our Board of Managers."[20] Smith saw a "prospect for significant change in shaping the Swarthmore of the decades ahead."[21]

Implementation of the recommendations in Critique of a College was then begun, but was interrupted by Courtney Smith's death on January 16, 1969. On May 6, 1969, announcement was made of the appointment of Robert Cross as the next President of Swarthmore College.

Contemporary Scene

The College is located on a campus of 330 wooded acres in the borough of Swarthmore in Delaware County, Pennsylvania. Primarily a residential school, there are nine dormitories for men and five for women. In the Fall semester, 1969, student enrollment was 1,114. All were undergraduates except for three graduate students. There were 330 freshmen.[22] During 1968/69, there were 1,062 undergraduates (488 women and 574 men), 10 special students, and 2 graduate students. Students from Pennsylvania numbered 211 and there were 179 from New York and 88 from New Jersey. There were 53 students from foreign countries.[23]

Full-time faculty numbered 118 in the Fall semester, 1969. There were 36 part-time faculty members.[24] Of the faculty members listed in the 1969/70 Swarthmore College Bulletin with ranks of assistant, associate, or full professor, 78.4% had doctorates.

The College grants the degree of Bachelor of Arts to students in the Humanities, Social Sciences, and Natural Sciences and the degree of Bachelor of Science to students majoring in Engineering. Six foreign languages are available. A pre-medical program is available for students considering the attendance of a medical or dental school after graduation from Swarthmore. The Master of Arts, Master of Science, and advanced degrees in Engineering are offered, but only three Master of Arts degrees were granted in 1969.

Swarthmore College is accredited by the Middle States Association of Colleges and Secondary Schools.

The honors program continues to be a distinctive feature of Swarthmore. Presently, all students during their first two years are introduced to the content and methods of a variety of subjects important to a liberal education. The students then choose the course program or the honors program for their last two years. Approximately 60% of the students decide to major in a single department (eight courses) and take at least twenty other courses outside the major field. These students must pass a comprehensive examination in their major before graduation. Some 40% of the students participate in the honors program. They are freed of the limitations of the classroom and allowed to work independently. During each semester, they concentrate upon only two subjects. There are no periodic examinations; instead, students prepare themselves for exams in six subjects at the end of the senior year. Their papers are read by visiting examiners. The honors work is carried on in small seminars which meet once a week, or in independent projects.[25]

At least two things may happen in the seminars:

> In the absence of syllabi, lectures, and textbooks, students will learn that they are not studying something final and complete, that the seminar is not like a chocolate cake prepared by the teacher to be eaten whole by the other members. A seminar may clearly be seen to be one small bite taken out of an infinity of knowledge.... It may also teach the fact that little worth learning can be taught by someone else. If an instructor obeys the rules and avoids both histrionics and lecturing, then the students in the seminar must be left with the frustrating sense of not having been taught, which is the point at which education begins.[26]

Swarthmore students may also study abroad through established programs administered by other American colleges and universities. Swarthmore also has exchange programs with the Universities of Keele and Warwick in England. Foreign study must meet the College's academic standards and "form a coherent part of the student's four-year plan of study. The Honors Program in particular demands a concentration of study which is not easily adapted to the very different educational systems of foreign universities."[27]

Students may take courses at Bryn Mawr or Haverford Colleges or the University of Pennsylvania at no extra cost. Advanced students in engineering and the physical sciences benefit from the Bartol Research Foundation of the Franklin Institute, which is on the Swarthmore campus.[28]

Swarthmore is recognized throughout the world for its academic excellence. In a study[29] of the collegiate alma maters of humanistic scholars who had earned the doctorate, both Swarthmore men and women ranked first in the productivity indexes for the period from 1946-1959. Swarthmore has ranked first among small colleges in Woodrow Wilson Fellowships. Many freshmen are the recipients of National

Merit Scholarships. In 1966/67, 90% of the freshmen were in the top quarter of their high school class; 80% were in the top tenth.[30] "Swarthmore applicants and entering freshmen are more highly selected in terms of College Board scores and intelligence quotients than those at all but a single other institution (Harvard-Radcliffe); and there is no evidence that the trend is down."[31]

Blended with Swarthmore's extraordinary academic attainment is its Quaker tradition:

> It is a tradition bound up in the basic faith of Quakers that there is something of the divine in every individual. It inheres in the sense of "caring" that characterizes Swarthmore. It is bound up with an insistence on the academically first-rate as against the merely passable. It inheres in the belief that education should consist of the simultaneous cultivation of intellectual and moral powers.... It encourages us to feel a deep concern for the individual student...[32]

The Swarthmore College Library

There were few significant developments in the College Library during the late 1800's. The collection was small and was presided over by a faculty member. For example, in 1885 the professor in charge of the Engineering courses received a $250 stipend (supplementing his regular $2,000 annual salary) to serve as Librarian.[33]

Substantial collections and buildings were not provided until the twentieth century. Commenting on the Library in 1941, the Swarthmore faculty wrote:

> The ingredients of college libraries vary greatly. Some collections, for example, have been considerably augmented by bequests of the personal libraries of deceased clergymen. Such collections--discussions of theological dogma and volumes of printed sermons--while they probably provide generous quantities of edifying texts, are not greatly helpful in supplying authoritative and recent information on most subjects included in the college curriculum.... Fortunately Swarthmore has little of this deadwood: inasmuch as the great

> bulk of the collection has been assembled in the last quarter-century (with the majority of that growth during the last eight years), the library is uncommonly rich in its provisions of books and periodicals live and pertinent to the college's present intellectual needs.[34]

The faculty in 1941 also summarized the housing of the collections:

> The library building was erected a third of a century ago in those less ambitious days when the structure was more nearly an ornamental campus mausoleum than a busy central workshop. It was built for the accommodation of a student body numbering about 225. In the past dozen years two annexes have been added to the original building. The Biddle Memorial Library, built in 1929, provided dignified, beautiful and spacious quarters for the particular functions of the Friends Historical Library--a rapidly growing collection of books and manuscripts devoted to the history of Quakers and to the concerns in which Quakers have been active participants: peace, race relations, prison reform, and so on. This annex released badly needed floor space in the main college library building and also provided additional reading room facilities for upperclassmen. The erection, in 1935, of a stackroom--a temporary expedient constructed chiefly of Truscon steel and glass--provided at a low cost the housing for the great bulk of the book collection and permitted at the same time alterations and rearrangements within the old main library building....[35]

The faculty did not fail to give their critique on the use of the Library:

> Another aspect of growth concerns the character and quantity of use of the superior materials which have been assembled. Statistics, which would be dull, could be devised to express some such unit as the per capita man-hours spent in the library. Perhaps no one will ever attempt this bit of educational research. In the absence of any such exact bibliothecal foot-candle, kilowatt, horsepower sort of rating one must be content with

> asserting the conviction without offering statistical proof, that reading for honors brings a higher percentage of its votaries to the library's resources and keeps man and book together for longer periods than is the case under any less exacting course of study.[36]

Charles B. Shaw as Librarian, 1927-1962

Charles B. Shaw served as Librarian of Swarthmore College for thirty-three years. The collection grew from 62,000 to 208,400 volumes during his tenure. In 1926/27, 2,750 volumes were added, subscriptions were held for 451 periodicals, and there were seven full-time staff members. By 1960/61, 6,786 volumes were added during the year, periodical subscriptions were 1,087, and the full-time staff was equivalent to 14 persons. Library expenditures for 1929/30 totalled $34,572; in 1960/61, $132,050. The number of volumes loaned (excluding reserve books) quadrupled: 12,242 in 1929/30, 47,580 in 1960/61. Interlibrary loans began in 1930 with 38 volumes borrowed from other libraries and two loans made to libraries. In 1960/61, Swarthmore asked other libraries for 662 loans and received 987 requests for loan.[37]

In notes prepared for his last annual report before his death in January, 1962, Shaw considered the important milestones of the period to be:

> the addition of a wing for the Friends Historical Library...; the reclassification of the book collection from Dewey Decimal to the Library of Congress system, a procedure which required twelve years to complete, 1931-1943; the establishment of reference service in 1932; the addition of a book stack in 1935; the merging of four of our science departmental libraries to form the du Pont Science Library in 1960; a current library budget four times the size of the 1927 budget.[38]

He also recorded his regrets:

> an inadequate library building; continued existence of departmental libraries; the failure to enlarge the Wells Wordsworth and Wells Thomson collections; the status of the professional staff; too little bibliographical instruction; the Librarian office-

bound rather than student-serving.[39]

Midway in the Shaw years, a study was made by Henry B. Van Hoesen, Fremont Rider, and Rudolph H. Gjelsness of possible cooperative efforts which might be undertaken among the libraries of Bryn Mawr, Haverford, and Swarthmore Colleges. The Committee's report[40] outlined a series of recommendations which served as a starting point for cooperation. Although the "findings of this committee remain substantially pertinent [they are] yet unimplemented."[41]

Shaw was also instrumental in the development of special collections in the Library: Swarthmoreana, British Americana, Private Presses, and others.[42]

In addition to the publication of articles, Charles Shaw made a substantial contribution to librarianship as compiler of <u>A List of Books for College Libraries</u>, 1931, and its 1931-38 supplement.

James F. Govan's Librarianship, 1965-

From 1962 until June, 1965, Martha A. Connor, Associate Librarian, served as Acting Librarian. During these years, a site was selected for a new library building, a planning committee was appointed, Keyes D. Metcalf was selected as a consultant, and the program for the building was completed. In June, 1963, Thomas B. and Jeannette L. McCabe announced the gift which made construction of the building possible.

James F. Govan was then appointed Librarian of Swarthmore College in 1965. Govan earned a doctorate in History at Johns Hopkins University and had served as Librarian of Trinity University, San Antonio, Texas before coming to Swarthmore. In addition to the final planning, beginning of construction of the McCabe Library in May 1966, and its completion and occupancy which are described in the following section, another outstanding achievement of Govan's tenure was the study and report of the Special Committee on Library Policy in 1967. As one of three special interrelated committees established by Swarthmore to study itself in 1966 (the other two were the Commission on Educational Policy and the Special Committee on Student Life), the Special Committee on Library Policy (SCOLP) considered the "function and operation of the library in a liberal arts college."[43] James Govan chaired the Committee. Carroll G. Bowen, Director of the M.I.T. Press and an alumnus and member of the Swarthmore Board of Managers; William S. Dix, Librarian of Princeton University; and four Swarthmore faculty members: Helen North, Chairman of the Classics Department; Clair Wilcox, Chairman of the Economics Department; Olexa-Myron Bilaniuk, Associate Professor of Physics; and George McCully, Assistant Professor of History, all served on SCOLP.

The Committee rejected the concept of the College Library as a passive repository. "The analogue of such a library is a warehouse, with [the librarian as] its custodian."[44] The other extreme, the library-college concept, was also rejected because of the "unnaturalness of this particular realignment of the faculty and the library."[45] They took instead as a model

> the kind of library training most of the faculty received in graduate schools. Operating in conjunction with a university research library, graduate students acquire bibliographic skills from necessity, in departmental bibliography courses, or in the process of fulfilling other curricular requirements, with the assistance of instructors in their departments or, occasionally, of library personnel. The interplay between the faculty and library systems works well in graduate training, because graduate students come to depend increasingly on the library as they cut loose from their dependence on courses and devote more of their study time to reading and research, on an increasingly independent basis.[46]

The Committee chose the concept of the teaching library as a moderate approach between the polarities of the warehouse and the library-college. The teaching library recommended for Swarthmore would have three major functions:

> (1) to assist the faculty in its teaching; (2) to teach students directly how to use the library; and (3) to serve students as they teach themselves.[47]

In order to implement the teaching library concept, SCOLP made twenty-six major recommendations ranging from general objectives, such as making proficiency in the use of library materials an integral part of courses, to the more specific: provision of photo-duplication equipment in branch libraries.

Of particular importance in this case study of reference services for undergraduate students are seven recommendations. Each recommendation is quoted as set forth in the SCOLP report[48] with progress toward its implementation (which had occurred by December, 1969) noted.

> Recommendation 3. That each student should be required to demonstrate some skill at independent inquiry as he progresses through the curriculum and as major prerequisite for graduation; and that he spend at least one semester with a reduced course load, appropriate to the scope and difficulty of his project, in order to be free for independent study.

When this was brought to the Swarthmore faculty for consideration, the requirement of demonstration of skill at independent inquiry by students as a prerequisite for graduation was defeated.[49]

> Recommendation 4. That reference services be provided during evening hours and that the entire building be open until midnight.

The library's hours were extended to midnight, but reference librarians do not provide any evening service.

> Recommendation 5. That there be appointed to the library staff two Divisional Librarians, one trained in the humanities and one in the social sciences, to assure proper response by the library to the teaching needs in these two divisions.

This was one of the most important recommendations. The two new positions would provide instruction and service to the students and faculty in the humanities and social sciences in the same way the Science Librarian presently performs. The three Divisional Librarians could "become the active educational officers of the library."[50] Ideally, the persons in these posts should have a doctorate in a relevant subject field, a library degree, and experience in libraries as well as classroom instruction. Although the two positions were given the highest priority by the President of Swarthmore among the SCOLP recommendations which requested new personnel, the two additional Divisional Librarians remain a future prospect.

> Recommendation 7. That a new student handbook to the library, containing bibliographic annotations on reference sources, be provided.

A brief four-page guide to the Library has not been supplemented or replaced by this more comprehensive handbook.

> Recommendation 14. That there be appointed a Special Projects Librarian, possibly beginning on a part-time basis, to coordinate library operations with extracurricular activities on campus.

This means of establishing contact with Swarthmore students in the person of a Special Projects Librarian and through the sponsorship of poetry readings, lectures, and discussions by the Library to emphasize the richness of its non-curricular collections has yet to be implemented. Faculty members were not enthusiastic when the recommendation was presented to them and the President made it the last priority in requests for additional personnel.[51]

> Recommendation 22. That the library staff include a specialist on technology affecting teaching methods and library operations to supervise the use of audio-visual materials and to keep the College community constantly abreast of new developments in these areas and to recommend adoption of appropriate innovations.

This position received a priority below that of the Divisional Librarians and also remains unimplemented.

> Recommendation 25. That members of the library staff be officially accorded status and benefits commensurate with their professional qualifications and the character of their responsibilities.

The College Librarian had always had faculty status as specified in the Charter of Swarthmore. As a result of this recommendation, three additional staff members--the Associate Librarian, the Reference Librarian, and the Science Librarian--were granted faculty status in 1968.[52]

The innovative recommendations made by SCOLP have faced the most difficulty in implementation. Several recommendations of a more traditional nature have been acted upon. The most important of these was:

> Recommendation 9. That the existing gaps in the collection be filled as soon as possible and that the collections be developed and maintained according to the functional standards described in this Report, as closely as possible.

A price list of library lacunae totaling $251, 061. 39 was compiled by the various departments of the College. The Board of Managers authorized in 1968 the allocation of $250, 000 from the Maud Perry Mills Fund for the purchase of the lacunae.[53]

The McCabe Library, 1967

The new Library, named for the donors--Thomas B. McCabe and his wife, Jeannette L. McCabe--was designed by Vincent G. Kling Associates. Containing 90, 000 square feet, it was the largest single addition of building space in Swarthmore's history. The McCabe Library is centrally located, near Parrish Hall, the main College building, and faces Clothier Memorial across the campus. The handsome four-story gray stone building provides study space for 600 students (210 individual carrels) and has a book capacity of 435, 000 volumes. The exterior stone is repeated extensively inside on the main floor and contrasts with a brilliant red-orange carpeting used through the building.[54] The approximate cost of the McCabe Library, including furnishings, was $3, 300, 000.[55] It was opened in September, 1967.

The main floor (Level II) houses the circulation/reserve desk, catalog, reference area, technical services room, student lounge, librarian's office, and the Friends Historical Library. The reference and bibliography collections are the only openly shelved books on the main floor. The lower level (Level I) includes a receiving room, seminars, faculty studies, and the Jane Addams Peace Collection. Government documents, college catalogs, maps, and the main collections in history, philosophy, and religion are shelved here in open stacks. The closed stacks of the Friends Historical Library are also on Level I. Level III contains seminars, faculty studies, two lounge areas for readers, and a staff lounge. Current issues and backfiles of periodicals and newspapers, the open-shelf reserves for honors courses, and the main collections in most of the social sciences are shelved here. The top floor, Level IV, houses seminars; faculty studies; a service desk and space for Special Collections, recordings, and microforms; and listening equipment. Volumes of literature, language, fine arts, music, education, psychology, and some science materials[56] are shelved on Level IV. The McCabe Library does not contain a classroom for library instruction.

Book and Microform Collections

The total holdings of the main Swarthmore collections, excluding the Friends Historical Library and the Peace Collection, numbered 337,261 on June 30, 1969 (287,730 books, periodicals, and microforms and an estimated 49,531 U.S. documents).[57] Table 35 illustrates the growth of the collections during the past four years.

Table 35.--Volumes, Microforms, and Current Periodicals Swarthmore College Library, 1966-1969[a]

	Holdings on June 30 of:			
Type of Material	1966	1967	1968	1969
Volumes	302,350	315,412	323,225	337,261
Reels of Microfilm	2,191	2,901	3,363	3,495
Physical units of other forms of microtext (cards, prints, fiche)	..	..	..	65,276[b]
Periodical titles being received (excluding duplicates)	1,492	1,407	1,400	1,513

[a]Data from Swarthmore's 1968/69 report to the U.S. Office of Education "Higher Education General Information Survey, Library Collections, Staff, Expenditures, and Salaries" and from Annual Reports of the Librarian, 1965/66-1968/69.

[b]47,273 of the total units are the Human Relations Area Files.

Expenditures for books and other library materials totalled $124, 602 in 1968/69.[58] (This excludes the special appropriation of $250, 000 from the Maud Perry Mills Fund for filling gaps in the collection.) The categories of expenditures were:

Books	$91, 173
Periodicals	23, 826
Microforms	9, 603
	$124, 602

Binding costs were $12, 416.

The McCabe Library is a depository for U.S. documents. Although some are cataloged as monographs or treated as regular periodicals, most are shelved as a separate collection. On June 30, 1969, the estimated holdings of U.S. documents were 49, 531 items. In 1968/69, 4, 664 documents were added with 1, 176 being withdrawn.[59]

The McCabe Library maintains two extremely large reserve book collections. On November 30, 1969, the general reserves, which are on closed shelves back of the circulation desk, amounted to 7, 917 volumes. They may be borrowed for one-hour periods and must be used within the Library during the day. An additional 10, 765 volumes were on open-shelf reserve on Level III for the honors seminars.[60] Arranged by seminars, they may be borrowed for one-day periods.

Outstanding special collections are housed in the McCabe Library. In addition to the separately administered Friends Historical Library and the Jane Addams Peace Collection, which are described in the next section, the Library has a separate department of Special Collections on Level IV. The three outstanding collections are the rare books (which include a definitive James Thomson Collection, a William Wordsworth Collection, a collection in the history of technology, and a noteworthy collection of private press books); British Americana, a collection of the accounts of British travelers in the United States; and Swarthmoreana, material about the College and by its faculty, alumni, and students.[61]

Swarthmore has extensive holdings in microforms (Table 35). The Human Relations Area Files in microfiche, and the _Times_ (London) and the _New York Times_ on microfilm are examples.

Other Campus Libraries

The Friends Historical Library occupies separate quarters on three levels in the north wing of the McCabe Library (Figure 4). Now under the direction of Frederick B. Tolles, the Friends Historical Library's origins go back to 1871. The collection of books, pamphlets, periodicals, manuscripts, pictures, and other historical source materials illuminating the history of the Society of Friends numbered approximately 35,000 volumes in 1969. In 1930 Jane Addams gave a part of her personal library and correspondence on peace and social problems to the Friends Historical Library. The gift, together with peace material already in the Library became the Swarthmore College Peace Collection: A Memorial to Jane Addams.[62] The Peace Collection included about 3,500 books in 1969 and had subscriptions to 150 periodicals.

In addition to the collections in the McCabe Library, Swarthmore students have available three other campus libraries. The Pierre S. du Pont Science Library, which opened in January, 1960 in du Pont Hall, houses the College's materials in mathematics, physics, chemistry, and engineering. On June 30, 1969, 27,422 volumes were in the du Pont Library. The Sproul Observatory Library had 5,139 volumes in astronomy. The Biology Library in Martin Hall possessed 8,566 volumes.[63] Psychology periodicals are shelved with the biological materials in Martin. Dr. Eleanor A. Maass, Science Librarian, is in charge of the three science libraries.

Library Staff and Budget

Ten professional staff members were employed full-time in the McCabe Library (excluding the Friends Historical Library) and the science libraries in 1969. Another professional worked three-quarters time.[64] These positions were: the Librarian, the Associate Librarian, the Reference Librarian, the Science Librarian, the Head of the Circulation Department, the Assistant Head of Circulation who also served as Special Collections Librarian, the Head of Cataloging Department, two catalogers, the Head of Order Department, and the Assistant Order Librarian.

During 1968/69, eight nonprofessional staff members worked full-time in the libraries with sixteen persons working part-time (7.9 in full-time equivalents). Over 70 students[65] worked 8,785 hours during 1968/69.[66]

Salaries and benefits totalling $172, 344 were paid to the regular library staff (excluding the Friends Historical Library) during 1968/69. Wages for student assistants amounted to $22, 732. The cost of personnel ($195, 076) was 54.3% of the total library expenditures ($340, 592) during the year. A total of $124, 602 was spent on books and other library materials (excluding the special appropriation of $250, 000) and $12, 416 on binding for a combined expenditure of $137, 018 (40.2% of the library budget). An additional $8, 498 went to other operating expenses.[67]

During 1968/69, the library expenditure per student was $369.00. Library expenditure as a percentage of the institutional budget during the year was an extraordinary 8.6%. This was the highest percentage in a survey of 34 leading college libraries in the United States.[68]

Technical Services

Until 1967, there were two major divisions--technical services and readers services--in the organization of the Library. The Associate Librarian, in addition to the duties of that position, was in charge of technical services. With the move into the McCabe Library, the Associate Librarian was freed of direct responsibility for technical services. Two departments, Cataloging and Order, are now each directed by a Head.

In October, 1969, five professional staff members worked in technical services; three persons were engaged in sub-professional work. Non-professional positions numbered 5.5 full-time equivalents. The regular technical services staff totalled 13.5. Nineteen part-time student assistants worked 98 hours each week.[69] This large technical services staff added 13, 491 volumes to the collections in 1968/69.

The Library of Congress classification has been used at Swarthmore since 1931. The public catalog is a dictionary catalog with author, title, and subject cards filed in one alphabetical sequence.

McCabe as Campus Study Hall and Social Center

No records are available of the attendance in the old Library. Although an exit inspection system was instituted in the McCabe Library, attendance statistics have not been kept. Swarthmore librarians, however, agree that the Library is heavily used as a study place.

> There was a dramatic increase when we moved into the new building. As heavily used as the old Library was, it was often over-crowded and uncomfortable. Students went back to their rooms. When we moved into the McCabe Library, the attendance went up.[70]

From 10 P.M. until midnight, McCabe Library remains open as a study hall. There is no desk service during these hours. At first only the main floor of the building was open, but presently all four levels are available for study.

In addition to Swarthmore students, students from surrounding high schools and colleges use McCabe Library. Because of complaints from Swarthmore students and faculty concerning "noise, crowding, and general nonserious use of the collection"[71] by the outsiders, a policy of enforcing the registration system was begun. During 1967/68, approximately 1,100 outsiders were registered to use the Library. Beginning on December 1, 1968, an annual registration fee of $10.00 was established and "resulted in far fewer casual borrowers."[72]

As in most residential colleges, students use the Library as a social center. During the first year of operation in McCabe, the old College Library building was renovated into the Tarble Social Center with recreational facilities, lounges, meeting rooms, and a snack bar. Tarble is next to the McCabe Library. When asked if there were noticeable decreases in the use of McCabe as a social center after Tarble was opened, only one librarian had detected such decreases. Other staff members, who were interviewed, saw no difference.

McCabe as Reserve Book Dispenser and Browsing Collection

The dispensing of reserve books greatly overshadows the circulation of material from the main collection at Swarthmore (Table 36). In 1968/69, the use of reserve books accounted for 62% of the total circulation (169,264) to students. During 1967/68, reserve circulation was an even larger proportion: 64%. During 1968/69, there was an

Table 36.--Circulation from Main, Periodical, and Reserve Collections, McCabe Library, Swarthmore College, 1967/68 and 1968/69[a]

Category of User by Type of Material	1967/68	1968/69
Use by Students		
Main Collection		
Home Loans	36, 139	37, 438
Use in Building	21, 372	18, 807
Sub-total	57, 511	56, 245
Periodicals		
Home Loans	3, 810	4, 152
Use in Building	. .	3, 675
Sub-total	3, 810	7, 827
Reserve Collections		
Honors Reserve (Open-shelf)	46, 540	41, 817
Course Reserve (Closed-shelf)	64, 946	63, 375
Sub-total	111, 486	105, 192
Total Circulation to Students	172, 807	169, 264
Use by Faculty	8, 767	9, 493
Use by Outsiders	10, 529	8, 828
Total Circulation	192, 103[b]	187, 585[c]

[a]Swarthmore College. Library. Annual Reports, Circulation Department. 1967/68, [p. 7]; 1968/69, [p. 11].

[b]An additional 717 volumes were circulated from Special Collections.

[c]An additional 508 volumes were circulated from Special Collections.

average of 99 reserve loans to each Swarthmore student.

The extraordinary large numbers of volumes placed on reserve at Swarthmore is explained in part by the 10, 765 volumes on open-shelf reserve for individual honors seminars. The Special Committee on Library Policy recommended

> that each instructor teaching a seminar be required to weed his Honors Reserve periodically, restricting the number of books removed from general circulation to the smallest number consistent with effective teaching.[73]

In the Spring of 1969, professors were requested to weed their Honors Reserves. Only 1,184 volumes from 30 seminars were removed. There were 104 seminars.[74]

In addition to the open-shelf reserves for seminars, there were 7,917 volumes for the regular College courses on closed reserve back of the circulation desk. The total volumes on reserve in November, 1969 were 18,682.[75]

The main collection of monographs and periodicals accounted for 41,590 home loans to Swarthmore students during 1968/69, or an average of 39 loans to each student. This was an increase of 4.1% over the 39,949 home loans to students during 1967/68.

McCabe as Audio-Visual Facility

The audio-visual materials of the McCabe Library are part of Special Collections. The new building made possible expansion of both service and collections in this area. Provision of phonorecords and tapes is the major endeavor; only one film has been purchased by the Library.

In an alcove of Level IV, ten turntables are provided for listening to recordings via headphones. Each turntable will accommodate several headphones for multiple listening to the same recording. Four tape recorder/players are also available. There are four major collections of recordings. The Potter Collection of Recorded Literature included 653 recordings of poetry, drama, and prose in June, 1969. Recordings of literary programs held at Swarthmore are also in the collection. The Cutting Memorial Collection of Recorded Music was begun in 1936 and now contains 1,705 recordings. Another collection of 894 musical recordings has been purchased by the Music Department, but they are housed in the Library. The final separate collection is the Perdue Jazz Collection consisting of 89 recordings. In June, 1969, the recordings totalled 3,341.[76]

The recordings are for use within the Library. During 1968/69, 45 headphones were charged out 7,621 times--an average monthly use of 953 during the school year.[77] The greatest use is of phonodiscs; tapes account for a much smaller number. During 1968/69 tapes were made of draft-counseling sessions held on the campus and students who could not attend came to listen to the tapes.[78]

The College's Language Laboratory of 35 stations is in Beardsley Hall and is not administered by the Library.

Reference Services for Undergraduate Students

Reference service was established in 1932 in the College Library. During 1950/51, "two major positions, that of Reference Librarian and that of Chief of the Circulation Department, were combined as Readers Services Librarian. Howard H. Williams advanced to this post."[79] From 1950 until the occupancy of the McCabe Library in 1967, Williams was in charge of all readers services: reference assistance, interlibrary lending and borrowing, the circulation desk and stacks, the reserve book processing and service, receipt and maintenance of the U.S. and Pennsylvania documents, and the Library's special collections. Two professional staff members assisted him with the circulation and reserve work. Then, in 1967, Williams was named Reference Librarian and Catherine J. Smith was promoted to be Head of the separate Circulation Department.

Library Publications

As a very brief introduction to the McCabe Library, the Swarthmore College Library is available for students. This four-page guide is in loose-leaf format for possible insertion into the student's personal notebook. A more comprehensive library handbook with bibliographical annotations to reference resources was recommended by the Special Committee on Library Policy, but had not yet been compiled in December, 1969.

The Library recently began issuing "New Books," which lists selected Library accessions made available during the previous months.

The Friends Historical Library of Swarthmore College, an eight-page booklet, was published as a guide to that library. A brochure describing the Jane Addams Peace Collection is also available.

The Science Librarian distributes a brief newsletter to the faculty in the sciences two or three times each academic year.

Interlibrary Borrowing

Interlibrary transactions--both the lending of Swarthmore materials and the borrowing of items from other libraries for Swarthmore students and faculty--occupy a considerable amount of the Reference Librarian's time. During 1968/69, 584 requests were made by Swarthmore to other libraries; 474 of these requests were received. Swarthmore students accounted for 241 requests (188 receipts); the other requests for interlibrary loan were made for faculty and staff. Inquiries for locations of titles made via phone to the Union Library Catalogue of Pennsylvania totalled 346. The Reference Librarian issued 166 letters (121 of these for the University of Pennsylvania Libraries) to Swarthmore students for use of other libraries.[80]

The Swarthmore College Library received an even greater number of requests for the loan of its materials. In 1968/69, 2,035 requests were received from other libraries; 1,690 of these were sent.[81]

Swarthmore's location in suburban Philadelphia is an excellent one for access to other libraries when Swarthmore collections lack a title needed by its students and faculty. The libraries of Bryn Mawr, Drexel, Haverford, University of Pennsylvania, Temple, and Villanova are rich in holdings and extremely near for in-person use.

Communications with Faculty

Progress has been made in the past two years in formal communications between Swarthmore librarians and faculty members. Three of the senior librarians joined the Librarian in having faculty status. An opportunity to serve on the standing committees of the faculty was one of the avenues opened to the librarians. In 1969, the Librarian served as Chairman of both the Bookstore Advisory Committee and the Library Committee. Faculty and students were on each of these committees. The Librarian was also on the Curriculum Committee. The Associate Librarian was a member of the Committee on Faculty and Staff Benefits. The Reference Librarian held membership on the Student Summer Research Committee. The Science Librarian served on the Library Committee and the Travel Allowance Committee.

In addition to going to all-college faculty meetings, the four librarians attended divisional luncheon meetings.

James F. Govan has also regularly taught English History in the Department of History. As a lecturer, he attended the departmental faculty meetings.

These formal contacts with the Swarthmore faculty were supplemented by informal associations with individual faculty members.

Six professional members of the library staff have not been granted faculty status.

Library Orientation and Instruction

During the College's Orientation Week for freshmen before the opening of the 1968 and 1969 Fall semesters, a tour of the McCabe Library was scheduled. The Swarthmore librarians, however, consider these attempts at library orientation a failure: they have come at the end of the Orientation Week, usually on Saturday, when the students have already been subjected to too much orientation; only an estimated 25-30% of the freshmen take part; and those who do participate take little information away with them because the orientation comes too early in their Swarthmore careers, not at a more critical time of real need such as when they are preparing their first long paper.

The library orientation was scheduled for approximately an hour. The students were addressed briefly at the beginning of the session and then groups of students were given tours throughout the building by professional staff members. Changes were planned for the 1970 orientation.

Another method has been used to acquaint new students with the Library. The brief library guide was placed in the students' campus mailboxes.

Swarthmore librarians have no library instruction program integrated with College courses. The major reasons for this derive from the strong tradition of honors work at Swarthmore and the faculty conception of their function.

> Faculty members believe that it is their place to direct the students' reading. They feel that if they do not do this, for what are they being paid? Because the honors program has been a very bibliographical program, the tradition on the faculty is that most evaluation of sources should come from the instructor.[82]

Only occasionally does a faculty member approach the Reference Librarian requesting library orientation or bibliographical instruction for his class. The Reference Librarian spent time with two groups of students in urban education, but this was the only request for library instruction from the Reference Librarian in the past two years.[83]

The Science Librarians have had more success in bibliographical orientation for students. The first Science Librarian, John G. Daley,

> experimented in the Spring [of 1963] with private lectures and discussions with students in the Chemistry Honors Program on the services and holdings of a science library. The response was extremely favorable and [he felt] the method or a similar approach should be an integral part of the Science Librarian's responsibility.[84]

During 1966/67, one laboratory period in the Physics I course was devoted to a library problem. After an hour lecture by Eleanor A. Maass, the second Science Librarian, the class "adjourned to the Science Library to work on a practical physics information problem."[85] With the cooperation and assistance of Mrs. Maass, the instructor of Physics 8 set up a reading week in the Library. It was "apparently very successful in arousing the students to an awareness of the variety and number of scientific periodicals, and the interesting reading to be found therein, even for non-science students."[86] In 1967/68, Mrs. Maass spoke to the Science faculty seminar on current developments in library science. She also attended the seminars throughout the year.

"Chemical Information Sources," a guide for chemistry majors using the du Pont Science Library, was prepared in 1969 by Mrs. Maass and submitted for review and criticism to the faculty of the Chemistry Department. It was not available for students in May, 1970, because one faculty member wanted to review the preliminary draft during the summer of 1970.[87]

Mrs. Maass was also asked to teach a course in the Chemistry Department on instrumental analysis during the Spring Semester of 1970.

The Reference Collection

An estimated 8, 000 volumes are in the reference collection of the McCabe Library.[88] This is a considerably larger reference collection than those at the two undergraduate libraries or the other college library under study. During 1968/69, $3, 000 was allocated for additions to the reference collection and $4, 787. 76 was actually spent during the year (neither amount includes the cost of continuations).[89] Approximately $8, 000 was spent in the past two years on additions to the reference collection from the special appropriation for filling in gaps in the collections. Large monumental sets and reprints were purchased with these special funds. As a result of the availability of funds, the Swarthmore reference collection approaches the scope of a university library's reference collection.

The general reference collection is housed on open shelves over an extensive area on the main floor of McCabe Library (Figure 4). Starting with the atlas cases against the entrance wall, the collection continues along the west and south of the floor in Library of Congress classified order, A-Z. The southwest bay contains the periodical, book review, and newspaper indexes. National and trade bibliographies and printed library catalogs are shelved separately, by national groupings, along the east wall of the public catalog area and adjacent to the technical services room. A pamphlet collection, containing current material in the social sciences, is part of the reference collection.

Description of Reference Area and Desk

Ellsworth Mason has described the McCabe Library:

> The main floor of this library is distinguished in my experience by the fact that from the main entrance you can see no library element at all, not

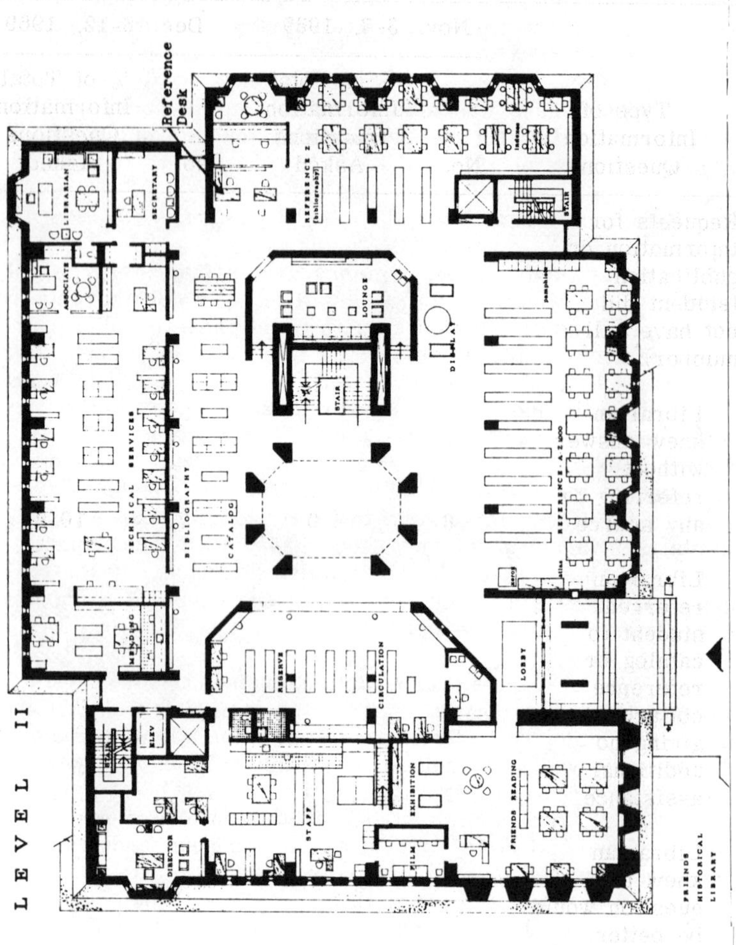

Figure 4.--Level II (Main Floor), McCabe Library, Swarthmore College, 1967. Source: Circulation Department, McCabe Library, Swarthmore College, 1969

> even the circulation desk, which is only 11 feet away, but well-hidden behind an internal fieldstone wall.
>
> There is nothing like a good solid, internal fieldstone wall to make for flexibility in a library. On this main floor there are three other internal fieldstone walls, plus a sunken level browsing room, plus a very interesting flexible formation directly in front of the circulation desk, a kind of Stonehenge, comprised of eight huge fieldstone pillars, two stories high, each one a triangle about three feet on each side. Of course, areas on this floor could easily be converted to other functions by the use of an atomic bomb.[90]

Mason may have never found the reference desk because it is located at the furthest possible point from the entrance--hidden by the "kind of Stonehenge," behind the sunken browsing room with its stone walls, and obscured by reference shelving and the public catalog. It is difficult to imagine a more unfortunate location for a college reference desk. The photocopying machine occupies the choicest location on the floor--immediately adjacent to the main entrance --while the reference desk rests in the most remote and inaccessible spot (Figure 4).

Two wood reference desks are in front of a small reference office in the southeast corner of the main floor. Only one of the desks is extensively used; the other is occasionally used by student assistants who work in the Reference Department. A chair is provided for the inquirer if he wishes to be seated while consulting the Reference Librarian.

Staffing of Reference Desk

The regular hours of professional reference service during a typical week of the Fall semester, 1969 were: Monday-Thursday, 8:30 A.M.-12 Noon and 1-4:30 P.M. and Friday, 8:30-10 A.M. and 1-4:30 P.M. (The Reference Librarian attends a meeting of library department heads each Friday from 10 A.M.-12 Noon.) There is no regular service at the reference desk at nights or on weekends. However, from 6:30-10 P.M., Monday-Thursday, a professional staff member (or a full-time staff member attending library school) is on duty at the circulation desk. The Reference

Librarian is also present at irregular hours during the weekend. Regular professional reference service totalled 33 hours (37.7%) of the 87.5 hours per week the McCabe Library was open for full service. The Library was also open from 10 P.M.-12 Midnight Sunday through Friday nights as a study hall.

The Reference Librarian is the only member of the McCabe staff who mans the reference desk.

Qualifications of Reference Librarian

The Reference Librarian majored in English, with a minor in History, at Lake Forest College. His other degrees are from Columbia University--a Master's degree in English Literature and a professional degree from the School of Library Service. In addition to the positions at Swarthmore as Readers Services Librarian and Reference Librarian, he had experience in the Teachers College Library at Columbia.

Scope of Reference Services

The Reference Librarian is available for in-person assistance at the desk previously described. Students, as well as others, may also call on the telephone.

In addition to serving Swarthmore students, faculty and staff, the Reference Librarian assists students from other colleges, high school students, local residents, and others. Many calls are made by the Reference Librarian to the Union Library Catalogue of Pennsylvania in Philadelphia and to other area libraries to assist patrons in the location of titles not in the Swarthmore collections.

Philosophy of Service

> Consistent with the Honors Program, there has long been a tradition of self-service in the Swarthmore College Library. This tradition of self-service [by the students] is something on which the library staff has long prided itself.... The result is that our reference services tend to be fairly minimal.[91]

The one phrase, self-service, succinctly summarizes the past philosophy of library service at Swarthmore.

Although self-education and independent study on the part of students have long been goals of Swarthmore College, the Special Committee on Library Policy found in its study in 1967 "strong indications, however, that many students pass their undergraduate years at the College without any substantial experience of independent learning."[92] Responses to a questionnaire by both students and faculty showed that the major portion of course readings was assigned in text-books or reserve books.

> While the students indicated a strong need for greater sophistication in the use of the library, the faculty indicated that the chief function of the library was to provide assigned and optional readings named by the instructor. Only a small majority reported that they made assignments which forced the student to prepare bibliographies, to familiarize himself with the bibliographic aids, or to call upon the services of the Reference Librarian.[93]

Faced with this situation, the Committee developed and recommended a philosophy of service for Swarthmore as a teaching library.

> The Reference Librarian should not merely find material for those students who are sufficiently knowing and enterprising to ask his aid. He and the Divisional Librarians [not yet appointed] should teach students to find materials for themselves, instruct them in the use and appraisal of bibliographic aids and all other resources, and provide assistance throughout the whole spectrum of independent study projects.[94]

At the time of this case study, Swarthmore's philosophy of library service was at an interim stage--slowly evolving from a tradition of self-service by the students to the more active role of a teaching library.

Use of Reference Services

No regular statistical records have been kept of the number or types of questions asked at McCabe Library's reference desk. However, two special studies of reference activity were undertaken after the move into the McCabe Library. During five separate weeks in 1967/68, the time spent on actual reference questions was recorded by the Reference Librarian. The total hours per week ranged from a high of 23.5 to a low of 14.25 hours.[95] More detailed records are available for one of the weeks: April 15-25, 1968.

The types of questions and the time spent on each were:

Simple reference questions	33	
More complicated reference/ bibliography questions	16	
Questions via telephone (9 from College offices in Parrish Hall, 2 from faculty, and 3 from outsiders)	14	
Sub-total	63	10.25 hours
Reference/bibliography questions in which instruction was given	9	3.25 hours
Complicated bibliography questions (1 faculty; 1 student)	2	2.00 hours
Bibliographical checking for other libraries	5	2.50 hours
Sub-total	16	7.75 hours
Total	79	18 hours[96]

It was estimated that another one-half hour was spent during the week answering brief directional and informational questions. Interlibrary borrowing took 5.75 hours and checking and approval of loans of Swarthmore material to other libraries accounted for 2.25 hours.[97]

During the Spring semester, 1969, an experiment with evening reference service was conducted on eleven nights during a six-week period. Some of the nights were announced in the student newspaper; others were unannounced. During the eleven nights a total of only 14 questions were asked of the Reference Librarian.[98]

The Reference Librarian estimated that Swarthmore undergraduates are by far the major users of the reference service with the faculty and non-Swarthmoreans asking much smaller proportions of the total questions asked.[99]

Samples of Questions: October and December, 1969

All questions asked at the McCabe Library's reference desk were monitored during two weeks of the Fall semester, 1969 (October 20-24 and December 1-5, 1969). The hours, methodology, and definitions used in recording the questions asked by undergraduate students are described in Chapter 1.

Undergraduates were the major users of the reference services. During the October week, they asked 64.8% of the total questions (108); faculty, staff, and others accounted for 35.2%. During the December week, 64% of the total (64) were undergraduate questions, and faculty, staff, and others asked 36%.

During the 27.5 hours of the first week's monitoring, 70 questions were asked by undergraduates, an average hourly rate of 2.5 questions. Questions by Swarthmore undergraduates decreased to 41 during the second week, an hourly average of 1.4. There was only one question from a student via telephone during the two weeks.

During October 20-24, Monday and Wednesday afternoons and Tuesday and Thursday mornings were considerably busier than the other time periods. During December 1-5, Monday morning and afternoon and Tuesday afternoon were the only busy periods, the rest of the week being extremely slow. Fridays were the slowest of all days.

Unlike the other case studies, the monitoring of activity at the Swarthmore reference desk does not include the hours of 7-9 P.M., Monday-Thursday. However, the McCabe Library's circulation desk was monitored on three nights from 7-9 P.M. to ascertain if the staff on duty there gave reference assistance to students. During these six hours, 17 information and reference questions[100] were asked but only eight of the inquiries were by Swarthmore students; the others were made by high school students and local residents who had registered to use the Library.

Table 37 categorizes the questions asked by Swarthmore students at the McCabe Library reference desk. Substantive reference questions (74.3% in the first week; 80.5%, the second week) greatly outnumbered the information questions (25.7% and 19.5%). There were no search questions (over 30 minutes) or problem questions (over one hour) undertaken for either students or faculty during the two weeks.

Table 37.--Questions Asked by Undergraduates at Reference Desk, McCabe Library, Swarthmore College, in Two One-Week Samples, 1969[a]

	Oct. 20-24, 1969		Dec. 1-5, 1969	
Type of Question	No.	%	No.	%
Information	18	25.7	8	19.5
Reference				
R-1	14	20.0	14	34.2
R-2	1	1.4	. .	. .
R-3	18	25.7	18	43.9
R-4	12	17.1	. .	. .
R-5	1	1.4	1	2.4
R-6	6	8.7	. .	. .
R-7	. .	. .	. .	. .
Sub-total	52	74.3	33	80.5
Search	. .	. .	. .	. .
Problem	. .	. .	. .	. .
Total	70	100.0	41	100.0

[a]The McCabe Library does not offer evening reference service. Therefore, the hours from 7-9 P.M., Monday-Thurday, are not included in the data.

Of the 85 reference questions asked by Swarthmore students in the two periods, the Reference Librarian spent over five minutes with the student in only two instances. The Reference Librarian approached the student only three times out of 111 questions; the students initiated the encounter in the other 108 instances.

A further analysis of the information questions shows a decrease of 55% from the first week of monitoring to the second week (18 information questions were asked October 20-24; only 8 during December 1-5, 1969). Table 38 lists the various types of information questions.

Table 38.--Types of Information Questions Asked by Undergraduates at Reference Desk, McCabe Library, Swarthmore College, in Two One-Week Samples, 1969

Type of Information Question	Oct. 20-24, 1969[a]		Dec. 1-5, 1969[a]	
	No.	% of Total Information Questions Asked	No.	% of Total Information Questions Asked
Assistance with physical facilities of library:				
Location of pencil sharpener or request to borrow pen, stapler, etc.	2	11.1	2	25.0
Request for keys or unlocking of rooms	. .	. .	. .	. .
Location of areas in library	3	16.7	. .	. .
Sub-total	5	27.8	2	25.0
Requests for location of particular volume (librarian gave directions):				
Monographs in main collection (student had call number)	. .	. .	. .	. .
Reference books (student usually requested by title)	4	22.2	3	37.5
Sub-total	4	22.2	3	37.5

Table 38.--Continued.

Type of Information Question	Oct. 20-24, 1969 No.	Oct. 20-24, 1969 % of Total Information Questions Asked	Dec. 1-5, 1969 No.	Dec. 1-5, 1969 % of Total Information Questions Asked
Requests for information or publication (student did not have call number):				
Librarian knew answer without referring to any source	1	5.6	..	..
Librarian referred student to catalog or reference collection, giving no additional assistance	4	22.2	2	25.0
Librarian knew that question would be better answered in another library and referred student to it	..	..	..	..
Sub-total	5	27.8	2	25.0

Table 38.--Continued.

Type of Information Question	Oct. 20-24, 1969		Dec. 1-5, 1969	
	No.	% of Total Information Questions Asked	No.	% of Total Information Questions Asked
Questions concerning collection or services (librarian responded with brief directions or information):				
Periodicals	. .	. .	. .	. .
Newspapers	. .	. .	. .	. .
College catalogs	. .	. .	1	12.5
Main catalog or serials catalog	. .	. .	. .	. .
Reserve books	. .	. .	. .	. .
How and where to charge out books	. .	. .	. .	. .
Use of reference volume in another part of library	. .	. .	. .	. .
Photocopying machine	. .	. .	. .	. .
Exam file	. .	. .	. .	. .
Location of another library	. .	. .	. .	. .
Sub-total	. .	. .	1	12.5

Table 38.--Continued.

Type of Information Question	Oct. 20-24, 1969 No.	Oct. 20-24, 1969 % of Total Information Questions Asked	Dec. 1-5, 1969 No.	Dec. 1-5, 1969 % of Total Information Questions Asked
Miscellaneous information questions	4	22.2	..	..
Total information questions	18	100.0	8	100.0

[a]Hours of survey: Monday-Thursday, 9:30 A.M.-12 Noon and 1-4:30 P.M.; Friday, 1-4:30 P.M.

A broad analysis of all questions asked by Swarthmore undergraduates (Table 37) shows that R-3 questions (bibliographical verification of materials not on the campus) accounted for 25.7% and 43.9% of the total questions. When the R-3 questions are considered as a part of only the reference questions, they form 34.6% and 54.5% of this group. Swarthmore's strategic location near other excellent collections, and its added advantage of having easy access to the Union Library Catalogue of Pennsylvania, are the factors which make bibliographic verification of materials not on the campus the most numerous type of reference question.

R-1 questions (bibliographical assistance with the catalog and holdings of Swarthmore) were next most numerous in the major categories of reference questions (Table 39). They were 20% and 34.2% of all questions, or 27% and 42.4% of the more substantive reference questions. About one-half of the R-1 questions during the two periods were requests for a particular reference title or type of reference book with the librarian going to the shelves and producing it for the student. The other half of the R-1 questions were requests for general bibliographical assistance in which the librarian either helped the student at the catalog or with the reference collection.

Table 39.--Bibliographical Assistance with Library's Own Catalogs and Holdings (R-1 Questions) Requested by Undergraduates at Reference Desk, McCabe Library, Swarthmore College, in Two One-Week Samples, 1969

	Oct. 20-24, 1969[a]		Dec. 1-5, 1969[a]	
Type of Response by Type of R-1 Question	No.	% of Total Reference Questions Asked	No.	% of Total Reference Questions Asked
Request for particular volume or type of volume; librarian gave assistance by:				
Checking list of frequently used reference titles and giving student call number	..	..	..	..
Charging out heavily used item from drawer of desk	..	..	..	..
Going to reference shelves and producing particular volume for student who had usually given title or described type	10	19.2	3	9.1

Table 39.--Continued.

Type of Response by Type of R-1 Question	Oct. 20-24, 1969		Dec. 1-5, 1969	
	No.	% of Total Reference Questions Asked	No.	% of Total Reference Questions Asked
Going to main collection shelves and locating monograph, periodical or newspaper which student had been unable to find	. .	. .	. .	. .
Sub-total	10	19.2	3	9.1
Requests for general bibliographical assistance; librarian responded by:				
Using reference collection	2	3.9	4	12.1
Assisting student at main catalog	2	3.9	7	21.2
Using *Subject Headings Used in... the Library of Congress*	. .	. .	. .	. .
Assisting in use of microforms	. .	. .	. .	. .

Table 39.--Continued.

Type of Response by Type of R-1 Question	Oct. 20-24, 1969 No.	Oct. 20-24, 1969 % of Total Reference Questions Asked	Dec. 1-5, 1969 No.	Dec. 1-5, 1969 % of Total Reference Questions Asked
Assisting in use of circulation records	. .	. .	. .	. .
Sub-total	4	7.8	11	33.3
Total R-1 Questions	14	27.0	14	42.4
Other Reference Questions (R-2 through R-7)	38	73.0	19	57.6
Total Reference Questions	52	100.0	33	100.0

[a]Hours of survey: Monday-Thursday, 9:30 A.M.-12 Noon and 1-4:30 P.M.; Friday, 1-4:30 P.M.

There was only one request for bibliographical assistance with the holdings of other campus libraries (R-2) during the two weeks of monitoring.

R-4 questions (requests for retrieval of factual, non-bibliographical information) formed a significant portion of the questions during the first week--17.1% of all questions or 23% of the reference questions. However, during the second week, not one of these questions was asked.

R-5 questions (counseling of students in a reader's advisory capacity) were very infrequent, occurring only once in each of the two weeks. It is possible that the Swarthmore faculty advise their students upon the selection of topics for papers and ways to gather materials, leaving almost none of this to the Reference Librarian.

Again in the case of R-6 questions (informal, personal instruction in use of the library or any of its resources), there was a significant number in the first week and none in the second week. During the first week, 8.7% of all questions, or 11.5% of the reference questions, were recorded in this category.

It was unnecessary to place any of the reference questions in a miscellaneous category (R-7).

Other Library Activities During Reference Monitoring

Table 40 presents some of the McCabe Library's other activities during the two weeks of monitoring questions at the reference desk.

Table 40. --Home Loans and Reserve Use During Two Weeks of Monitoring Questions at Reference Desk, McCabe Library Swarthmore College in 1969[a]

Variable	Oct. 20-24, 1969[b]	Dec. 1-5, 1969[b]
Attendance in Library	No Record Kept	No Record Kept
Total Home Loans from Main Collection (Swarthmore Students Only)	1,027	1,479
Average Daily Home Loans (Swarthmore Students Only)	205	295
Total Home Loans	1,385	1,828
Average Daily Home Loans	277	365
Total Reserve Use	1,350	1,427
Average Daily Reserve Use	270	285

[a]Swarthmore College. Library. Circulation Department Daily Statistics. October and December, 1969.

[b]13.75 hours each day (8:15 A.M.-10 P.M.).

The number of home loans from the main collection to Swarthmore students increased by 44% when October 20-24 is compared with December 1-5, 1969. In contrast, the number of questions asked at the reference desk decreased in the second week by 41.4% from the first week. The use of reserve books also was higher in the December period than in the October week. Swarthmore students were, therefore, actively using the collections in the later part of the semester, but they made little use of the services of the Reference Librarian.

Notes

1. Homer D. Babbidge, Jr. "Swarthmore College in the Nineteenth Century, A Quaker Experience in Education" (unpublished Ph.D. dissertation, Graduate School, Yale University, 1953), p. 42.

2. David Boroff, "Swarthmore: Use Thy Gumption!" in his _Campus U. S. A., Portraits of American Colleges in Action_ (New York: Harper, 1961), p. 60.

3. Babbidge, p. 77.

4. _Ibid._, pp. 85-100.

5. _Ibid._, p. 122.

6. Edward Hicks Magill, _Sixty-five Years in the Life of a Teacher, 1841-1906_ (Boston: Houghton Mifflin, 1907), p. 196.

7. Babbidge, p. 183.

8. Charles De Garmo, "College Training at Swarthmore vs. University Training in Cities," _Report of the President_, 1894 as quoted in Babbidge, p. 204.

9. Babbidge, p. 206.

10. _Ibid._, p. 207.

11. _Ibid._, p. 209.

12. _Ibid._, p. 211.

13. *Ibid.*, p. 216.

14. *Ibid.*

15. Swarthmore College. Faculty. *An Adventure in Education, Swarthmore College under Frank Aydelotte* (New York: Macmillan, 1941), pp. 4-17.

16. *Ibid.*, pp. 28-30.

17. *Ibid.*, p. 224.

18. Swarthmore College. "Report of the Commission on Educational Policy" in *Critique of a College* (Swarthmore, Pennsylvania: Swarthmore College, 1967), p. 9.

19. *Ibid.*, p. 3.

20. Swarthmore College. *President's Report*, 1967/68. p. 8.

21. *Ibid.*, p. 7.

22. Interview with Registrar, Parrish Hall, Swarthmore College, December 2, 1969.

23. Swarthmore College. *Bulletin, Catalogue Issue, 1969/70* ("Swarthmore College Bulletin," LXVII, September 1969), p. 215.

24. Interview with Registrar, Parrish Hall, Swarthmore College, December 2, 1969.

25. Swarthmore College. *Bulletin, Catalogue Issue, 1969/70*, pp. 56-61.

26. Lawrence D. Lafore, "Honors at Swarthmore: A Setting in Which Things May Go Well," *Swarthmore College Bulletin, Alumni Issue*, LXI (May, 1965), p. 2.

27. Swarthmore College. *Bulletin, Catalogue Issue, 1969/70*, p. 63.

28. *Ibid.*, pp. 13 and 63.

29. Robert H. Knapp, *The Origins of American Humanistic Scholars* (Englewood Cliffs, New Jersey: Prentice-Hall, 1964), pp. 38 and 56.

30. American Universities and Colleges, ed. by Otis A. Singletary (10th ed.; Washington, D.C.: American Council on Education, 1968), p. 1333.

31. Swarthmore College. "Report of the Commission on Educational Policy" in Critique of a College, p. 13.

32. "Swarthmore," Swarthmore College Bulletin, LXII (October, 1966), 6.

33. Babbidge, p. 181.

34. Swarthmore College. Faculty. An Adventure in Education, pp. 136-37.

35. Ibid., p. 138.

36. Ibid., p. 139.

37. Swarthmore College. Library. Annual Report of the Librarian. 1960/61, p. 1.

38. Ibid., 1961/62, p. 1.

39. Ibid., p. 2.

40. Findings of a Committee Appointed to Explore and Report on a Possible Program of Inter-Library Cooperation between Bryn Mawr, Haverford, and Swarthmore Colleges. [n.p.], November, 1945.

41. Swarthmore College. "Report of the Special Committee on Library Policy," in Critique of a College, p. 378.

42. Charles B. Shaw, "Special Collections in the College Library," College and Research Libraries, XVIII (November, 1957), 479-84, 517.

43. Swarthmore College. "Report of the Special Committee on Library Policy," in Critique of a College, p. 335.

44. Ibid., p. 337.

45. Ibid.

46. Ibid., p. 339.

47. Ibid., p. 341.

48. Ibid., pp. 459-61.

49. Interview with James F. Govan, Librarian, Swarthmore College, October 23, 1969.

50. Swarthmore College. "Report of the Special Committee on Library Policy," in Critique of a College, p. 356.

51. Interview with James F. Govan, Librarian, Swarthmore College, December 2, 1969.

52. Interview with James F. Govan, October 23, 1969.

53. Swarthmore College. Library. Annual Report of the Librarian. 1968/69, p. 1.

54. "McCabe Library," Swarthmore College Bulletin, Alumni Issue, LXV (March, 1968), 2.

55. Interview with James F. Govan, October 23, 1969.

56. The du Pont Science Library and other campus libraries have the main science collections.

57. Swarthmore College. Library. Annual Report of the Librarian. 1968/69, p. 9.

58. Ibid., p. 11.

59. Ibid., p. 9.

60. Swarthmore College. Library. "Circulation Department Statistics." November 30, 1969. (Handwritten.)

61. Swarthmore College. Library. Swarthmore College Library [A Guide], n.p., n.d., p. 4.

62. Swarthmore College. Friends Historical Library of Swarthmore College (Swarthmore: The College, 1969), p. 1.

63. Swarthmore College. Library. Annual Report of the Librarian. 1968/69, p. 10.

64. Interview with James F. Govan, October 23, 1969.

65. 51 student assistants worked in the Circulation Department and 19 in technical services in October, 1969.

66. U.S. Office of Education. "Higher Education General Information Survey, Library Collections, Staff, Expenditures, and Salaries." (Swarthmore College's Report for 1968/69.)

67. Swarthmore College. Library. Annual Report of the Librarian. 1968/69, p. 11.

68. "Selected Library Statistics for 1968/69" [Collected by Bowdoin College Library]. (Mimeographed.)

69. Interview with Martha A. Connor, Associate Librarian, Swarthmore College, October 23, 1969.

70. Interview with James F. Govan, October 23, 1969.

71. Swarthmore College. Library. Annual Report, Circulation Department. 1967/68, p. 2.

72. Ibid., 1968/69, p. 2.

73. Swarthmore College. "Report of the Special Committee on Library Policy," in Critique of a College, p. 358.

74. Swarthmore College. Library. Annual Report, Circulation Department. 1968/69, p. 4.

75. Interview with Catherine J. Smith, Head, Circulation Department, McCabe Library, Swarthmore College, December 2, 1969.

76. Swarthmore College. Library. Annual Report, Circulation Department. 1968/69, p. 6.

77. Ibid., p. 5.

78. Interview with George K. Huber, Special Collections Librarian, Swarthmore College, December 2, 1969.

79. Swarthmore College. Library. Annual Report of the Librarian. 1950/51, p. 11.

80. Swarthmore College. Library. Annual Report, Reference Department. 1968/69, p. 3.

81. Ibid.

82. Interview with James F. Govan, October 23, 1969.

83. Interview with Howard H. Williams, Reference Librarian, Swarthmore College, October 23, 1969.

84. Swarthmore College. Library. Annual Report, du Pont Science Library. 1962/63, pp. 3-4.

85. Ibid., 1966/67, p. 1.

86. Ibid., 1967/68, p. 3.

87. Letter from Eleanor A. Maass, Science Librarian, Swarthmore College, to Billy R. Wilkinson, May 5, 1970.

88. Interview with Howard H. Williams, October 23, 1969.

89. Interview with Blondine Regan, Order Department, McCabe Library, Swarthmore College, December 4, 1969.

90. Ellsworth Mason, "Back to the Cave or, Some Buildings I Have Known," Library Journal, LXXXXIV (December 1, 1969), 4357.

91. Letter from James F. Govan, Librarian, Swarthmore College, to Billy R. Wilkinson, June 17, 1969.

92. Swarthmore College. "Report of the Special Committee on Library Policy," in Critique of a College, pp. 347-48.

93. Ibid., p. 348.

94. Ibid., p. 355.

95. Swarthmore College. Library. Annual Report, Reference Department. 1967/68, p. 1.

96. Ibid., pp. 1-2.

97. Ibid.

98. Ibid., 1968/69, pp. 1-2.

99. Interview with Howard H. Williams, October 23, 1969.

100. Definitions of information, reference (R-1 through R-7), search, and problem questions are given in Chapter 1. Hereafter in this section, these definitions are used.

Chapter 6

CASE IV: EARLHAM COLLEGE

> Perhaps we have forgotten, but there are places of learning, places of the past, perhaps, as much as of the future. They exist, here among us, and they deserve a hearing for our sense of self-renewal as well as for their own. One such place is Earlham College....
>
> Thomas J. Cottle, "A Learning Place Called Earlham." Change, The Magazine of Higher Education, III (January-February, 1971), p. 52.

Historical Highlights of The College

In the early 1800's, Quakers from North Carolina settled in eastern Indiana along the Whitewater River. "They were a part of the great folk movement of members of the Society of Friends away from the slaveholding South where those farmers who rejected slavery were at a serious economic disadvantage."[1] They settled in or near the town of Richmond, which was incorporated in 1818. By 1847, it had a population of 2,500.

Members of the Indiana Yearly Meeting, concerned about the education of their children, founded the Friends Boarding School in 1847. This school, with both high school and college students, was the beginning of Earlham College. The name, officially changed in 1859 when it was agreed that degrees would be granted, was "for the ancestral home of the famous Quaker family of Gurney near Norwich, England...and the gathering place of liberal and forward-looking Friends who initiated so many of the reforms of the eighteenth and nineteenth centuries."[2]

The history of Earlham College has been summarized into three eras:

> From its founding until 1900, Earlham was primarily concerned with serving Midwestern Quakers and other residents of eastern Indiana. Enrollment increased to over three hundred; several buildings were built, and several hundred acres of land were acquired. In general, however, Earlham was a modest, regional, and somewhat parochial institution during the first period of its history.
>
> The second period can be regarded as extending from 1900 to 1946. Earlham drew more and more of its students from other regions, and the proportion of non-Quakers rose. When the enrollment reached about five hundred students, more than half of them were not Quakers. Furthermore, non-Quakers were appointed to the faculty. The years of the depression and of both world wars brought financial stringency and policies of caution to cope with the assorted difficulties. As a matter of conscience, the faculty decided not to seek a military unit during World War II, preferring to cut their own salaries substantially.
>
> The third era dates from 1946, when Thomas E. Jones, a Quaker and a graduate of Earlham, became President and undertook a major renovation of the college's plant, program, and staff. He communicated to the entire college a conviction that Earlham was on the threshold of an era of increasingly significant service to the world. When he retired in 1958, the college chose as his successor Landrum Bolling, another Quaker, not an alumnus but a member of Earlham's faculty in the Department of Political Science.
>
> In this postwar period, Earlham was at first flooded with students as war veterans returned, and then went through a period when it was difficult to find enough qualified applicants to fill the college. In recent years it has had to turn away three for each one accepted. It is hard to predict whether the college will choose to become highly intellectual and competitive, like Reed, Oberlin, and Swarthmore, for example, or decide that it

> has moved far enough in that direction and should place more emphasis on other aspects of the development of young people.[3]

Contemporary Scene

Located on the outskirts of Richmond, Indiana, the main Earlham campus of 120 acres and over 25 buildings is adjoined by another 600 acres of farm and wooded land. Earlham is coeducational and is primarily a residential college with 75% of the students living on campus in dormitories or college-owned houses.[4]

In 1968/69 the students numbered 1,149 (508 women and 641 men) from 44 states and 11 foreign countries.[5] There were 95 full-time faculty members and 19 part-time faculty (4.86 in full-time equivalents). Over 70% of the teaching faculty had doctorates. During the 1969 Fall term, 1,054 undergraduates were enrolled.

The liberal arts academic program consists of four divisions: Natural Science, Social Science, Humanities, and Physical Education. Pre-professional programs in dentistry, engineering, law, medicine, and the ministry are also offered. Seven foreign languages are available.[6] Earlham is accredited by the North Central Association of Colleges and Secondary Schools. It is certified by the American Chemical Society and also accredited by the National Council for Accreditation of Teacher Education for both elementary and secondary teachers.

Approximately 70% of the Earlham undergraduates participate in "an educational experience of a term or more off-campus, either abroad or in one of the American study centers."[7] Regularly scheduled are academic programs in England, Germany-Austria, and France. Less frequently, groups are arranged for study in Italy, Greece, Spain, and Scandinavia. Students may also study in Lebanon, Columbia, Mexico, and Japan. On campus, the Center for East Asian Language and Area Studies offers instruction in Japanese language and courses in East Asian history and culture. During the Winter term, students may go to Washington, D.C. for special studies in political science and other subjects; New York City for studies in the arts; the Hoover Institution at Stanford University for research in its collections; or St. Petersburg, Florida to study marine biology.

The College also has an arrangement with the Merrill-Palmer Institute of Human Development and Family Life in Detroit for Earlham students to study there for a term.[8]

The Earlham School of Religion, established in 1960, is affiliated with the College. The School offers two graduate programs: a two-year program leading to the M.A. degree in Religion and a three-year program culminating in the B.D. degree.[9]

The Eastern Indiana Center (EIC) of Earlham College was begun in 1946 by Earlham and Indiana University to provide late afternoon and evening classes for students in the Richmond area. In July, 1967, Ball State University and Purdue University joined in the cooperative effort. The Center offers college credit courses at the freshman and sophomore levels, some adult education courses, and a few upper class and graduate courses. Earlham classrooms, laboratories, and library are used by EIC students.[10]

Earlham was also instrumental in the creation of another cooperative venture in higher education. With the leadership of President Landrum R. Bolling, Earlham and eleven other colleges--Albion, Antioch, Denison, DePauw, Hope, Kalamazoo, Kenyon, Oberlin, Ohio Wesleyan, Wabash, and Wooster--formed the Great Lakes Colleges Association "for cooperative action aimed at strengthening and enriching the programs of member institutions."[11] There is an exchange of some students and faculty and a host of "projects, great and small, are undertaken by the group which would be impossible for one member college alone."[12] Five foreign languages, not usually found in small college curriculums, are available--Portuguese at Antioch, Arabic at Kenyon, Hindi at Wooster, Chinese at Oberlin and Wabash, and Japanese at Earlham.

A description of Earlham College is not complete without additional emphasis on its Quaker traditions. The Quaker belief in the supreme value of every individual permeates the campus.

> It seems to lead, at Earlham, to a concern for the individual student which the students certainly feel and which even a casual visitor could hardly overlook. Other aspects of life in the Earlham community probably stem from this principle--emphasis on freedom of thought and expression,

> concern for service to others, and a minimizing of hierarchical distinctions.[13]

A deep sense of community is the most important characteristic of Earlham.

The Earlham College Library

The Earlham College Library also had its beginnings with the Friends Boarding School. In a circular sent to parents in 1847, the boarding school committee of the Indiana Yearly Meeting prescribed the books: "It is thought best that no books, periodicals, or papers be brought into the school, except such kinds as are used in the school...."[14] By the second term, 1847, the library contained 500 volumes, purchased from a fund given by English Friends. By gift and purchase, the collection grew to approximately 1,000 volumes in 1859. In addition, the school had the Yearly Meeting's reference collection of 400 volumes. Now one of the treasures of the College Library, this collection of writings by Friends, including early seventeenth century editions, was also sent by English Friends.[15]

In 1866, books costing $500.00 were purchased. The collection, then 1,657 volumes, was moved from the superintendent's office to the lecture room. It was a reference collection and the libraries of the two literary societies--Phoenix Band for women and Ionian for men--furnished books for general reading. Also available to Earlham students since it opened in 1865 was the local public library, the Morrisson-Reeves Library.[16]

By 1888, about one-third of the College Library was composed of religious works, including books about Friends. Literature accounted for 17% of the collection; history, 12%; and science, 7%. Scientific works had previously held the predominant position.[17]

At the beginning of the twentieth century, two men, Harlow Lindley and Robert L. Kelly, greatly influenced the College Library. Lindley, upon his graduation from Earlham in 1898, began a thirty-year career as librarian and professor of history. He immediately introduced the Dewey Decimal system and "began to press toward more adequate quarters. As chairman of the curriculum committee, he was in a position to correlate changes in the program with library improvements."[18] Robert L. Kelly, who had "gained a keen appreciation of the library as the proper intellectual center of the college"[19] in his graduate study at the University of Chicago, became President of Earlham College in 1903. President Kelly, in his first annual report, called for more library and museum space.

Andrew Carnegie was busy at this time building libraries throughout the country. In 1905, it was announced that Carnegie would give Earlham $30,000 for a new library if the College would raise an equal amount for a library endowment. During the next year and a half, the money was subscribed with contributions from Trustees, faculty, alumni, and with proceeds from the 1906 May Day festivities.

After hiring an architect:

> Almost immediately it became apparent that by spending $10,000 more the book capacity could be almost doubled, providing for 70,000 volumes, but since no increase was available from Mr. Carnegie it must come from added subscriptions. The plan proceeded on this basis although a building debt of $7,713 resulted on the total cost of $38,329. By the end of 1907 the new brick building was ready for use.[20]

Now, with adequate quarters, the Library under Lindley's direction made an even greater contribution to the intellectual life of the College. A letter supporting Earlham's application in 1926 to the Carnegie Corporation for financial assistance gave this evaluation:

> The College Library has been an unusual one in many respects. It has been administered by a man who has instilled the love of books among the students and has stimulated a remarkable interest in library service among them over a long period of years. I doubt that there is another college in America of its size which has sent as many trained recruits into the library profession. Foremost among these is Chalmers Hadley ['96] of Cincinnati.
>
> The Library's collection of 30,000 volumes is superior in its selection to the average college library, particularly in the older books forming the

> library background.... Its great need has been that of an adequate supply of modern material... [and] special collections, such as art and music, for which no funds have ever been available.[21]

Librarians of Earlham College in the twentieth century were:

Harlow Lindley, 1898-1928
Ruth Ethel Cundiff, Acting Librarian, 1926-27
Eva May Hurst Fowler, Acting Librarian, 1927-28
Helen Sharpless, 1928-31
Joseph B. Rounds, 1931-36
Gladys Cosand Johanning, Acting Librarian, 1936-37
Sarah Geist, 1937-48
James H. Richards, Jr., 1948-50
Robert M. Agard, 1950-61
Philip D. Shore, Acting Librarian, 1961-62
Evan I. Farber, 1962-

The Lilly Library, 1963

By Robert Agard's tenure, the Library was crowded with books and students. Planning for a new building began in 1957 with the definition of space needs. The architectural firm of Baxter, Hodell, Donnelly, and Preston was hired and drawings were begun. Construction commenced in April, 1962 and the building opened on June 8, 1963.[22]

At a total cost of approximately $1,108,000, Earlham secured an attractive, inviting library of 48,000 square feet. The air-conditioned building has a book capacity of 180,000 volumes.[23] Study places number 387, with 194 additional seats in classrooms and other special facilities for a total seating capacity of 581. The seats range from individual carrels and lounge chairs to a Japanese alcove--Tokonoma--with straw mats and Oriental prints and sculpture.

The main floor houses the reference area, catalog, circulation desk, technical services room, an after-hours study room, faculty lounge, microform reading rooms, librarian's office, and seminars. The reference collection, current periodicals and newspapers, reserve books, pamphlet files, and the language and literature collections are shelved on this floor. The lower level includes quarters for the audio-visual area (language lab, self-instruction room, projection/classroom, and listening rooms) as well as the Tokonoma, smoking rooms, typing rooms, an exhibit area, faculty carrels, and seminars. Bound periodicals and the fine arts and science-technology collections are also shelved on the lower level. The upper level contains seminar rooms, the Friends Collection, and the Earlham Archives. Government documents and the history, biography, travel, philosophy, psychology, religion, and other social science collections are shelved on the upper level.

The new building was named "in honor of the families of Eli and J. K. Lilly whose foundation, Lilly Endowment, Incorporated, had been since World War I the major single benefactor of higher education in Indiana. Earlham's grants from this source totaled more than a million dollars."[24]

Book and Microform Collections

The total volumes in the Earlham collections numbered 158,967 in June, 1969. Table 41 shows the growth of the collections during the last four years.

Table 41.--Volumes, Microforms, and Current Periodicals, Earlham College Library, 1966-1969[a]

	Holdings on June 30 of:			
Type of Material	1966	1967	1968	1969
Volumes	134,769	141,434	149,245	158,967
Reels of Microfilm	4,187	4,776	5,071	5,233
Physical units of other forms of microtext (cards, prints, fiche)	5,019	6,121	6,183	11,363
Periodical titles being received (excluding duplicates)	810	920	1,000	1,082

[a]Data from Earlham's annual report to the U.S. Office of Education "Higher Education General Information Survey, Library Collections, Staff, Expenditures, and Salaries."

Materials in the humanities constituted the largest proportion of the collection, with the social sciences in second place (Table 42). In current acquisitions, unclassified materials (including periodicals) were the highest percentage, followed by the humanities and the social sciences. In 1969, the Library received 1, 082 periodicals and 18 foreign and domestic newspapers.

Table 42.--Holdings in Major Subject Areas of Earlham College Library, 1968/69[a]

Subject Area (Dewey and Library of Congress classification)	% of Total Collection	% of Current Acquisitions
Humanities and General Works (000, 100, 200, 400, 700, 800; or A, B, M, N, P, Z)	40	30
Social Sciences (300, 900; or C-L)	25	25
Physical Sciences, including Math (500-559; or Q-QE)	5	5
BioMedical Sciences (560-599, 610-619; or QH-QR, R, S)	5	5
Technology and Engineering (600-609, 620-699; or T, U, V)	2	1
Unclassified Materials (including unclassified bound periodicals)	23	34

[a]Approximations by measuring shelflist cards.

Earlham students also have available the periodical and newspaper files of other local collections: the Morrisson-Reeves Library, Richmond High School, Avco Corporation, and Reid Memorial Hospital. The holdings of Morrisson-Reeves and Reid are entered in the periodical records of the Lilly Library for convenient use.[25]

Expenditures for books and other library materials amounted to $60, 523. 21 in 1968/69. Binding costs were $8, 929. 39.[26]

The Lilly Library maintains a separate U.S. government documents collection, arranged by Superintendent of Documents numbers. Federal periodicals and some serials are shelved with the regular collection, but on May 31, 1969, the total holdings of documents were 15, 306.[27] Earlham has been a depository for selected U.S. publications since the summer of 1964.[28]

Only 688 books, pamphlets, and magazine articles were placed on closed reserve back of the Circulation Desk for the Fall term, 1969. An additional 85 volumes (dictionaries, Bibles, and Magill's masterplot series) are kept on permanent reserve. Approximately 240 phonograph recordings (both music and "spoken word") were also on closed reserve. No volumes are on open-shelf reserve. The total items on reserve for the term were 1, 015.

The Lilly Library has two special collections. The Friends Collection in 1969 numbered approximately 10, 000 books, bound periodicals, Yearly Meeting and other minutes, and pamphlets by or about Friends. The Earlham College Archives includes rare books, minute books, financial records, correspondence, student and alumni records, clippings, photographs, and the papers of individuals.[29] The furnishings in this area of the Library are antiques related to Earlham or to Quakers.

Earlham has extensive collections of microforms (Table 41). In addition to yearly acquisitions, a major program of conversion of periodicals to microform was undertaken in 1966/67. Back files of a number of periodicals were sold for approximately $25, 000. This amount was then re-invested in obtaining microform copies of those same titles with funds made available to purchase additional periodicals in microform.[30]

Other Campus Libraries

In addition to the Lilly Library, Earlham has a separate science library in Dennis Hall. The Ernest A. Wildman Science Library was moved into new quarters in an annex of the classroom building in 1969 with approximately 11, 000 monographs, 4, 000 bound volumes of periodicals,

650 reels of microfilm, 600 pieces of microfiche, and 160 periodicals currently received. Readers were provided with 44 seats.[31]

The Coate Library, a small collection of religious and philosophical works, is located in the Stout Memorial Meetinghouse. The Teague Library, which serves as a study for Professor Elton Trueblood and houses his personal collection, is also open for student reading.[32]

Librarianship of Evan I. Farber, 1962-

Robert Agard resigned as Earlham's Librarian in 1961. He has been credited with the basic planning of the Lilly Library.[33] During 1961/62, Philip D. Shore was Acting Librarian and carried forward the planning with the architects and the faculty committee. Evan I. Farber was selected as Librarian in 1962 and continues to serve in 1970. To Farber and Jack Hodell, the project architect, fell the responsibility of refining the interior lay-outs and selecting the furnishings.

The years in the new building under Farber's direction have been ones of extraordinary growth. When 1960/61 (in the old building) is compared with 1968/69, the advances are evident in many areas (Table 43).

Farber's greatest contributions have been in the reference services and library instruction program of the Lilly Library. They are described in detail later in this chapter. He has also contributed to the profession the *Classified List of Periodicals for the College Library* (with a new edition now in preparation) and various journal articles. During 1968/69, he served as Chairman of the College Libraries Section of the Association of College and Research Libraries. For several summers, he was Director of the Institute on the Acquisition of Non-Western Library Materials for College Libraries, held at Columbia University.

Library Staff and Budget

In addition to the Librarian, four other professional staff members are employed: the Associate Librarian, Reference Librarian, Documents Librarian, and Science Librarian. Five non-professional positions complete the full-time positions. The non-professional staff members each have a major responsibility--as head of the circulation desk, acquisi-

Table 43.--Percentage Changes in Seven Variables from 1960/61 to 1968/69, Earlham College Library[a]

Variable	1960/61	1968/69	% of Increase
Volumes in Collections	102, 843	158, 967	54. 5
Current Periodical Subscriptions	500	1, 082	116. 4
Total Library Expenditures	$57, 795	$166, 945	188. 1
Expenditure for Personnel	$33, 700	$ 90, 751	169. 3
Expenditures for Books, Periodicals, and Binding	$18, 867	$ 69, 452	268. 1
Library Expenditures as Percentage of Total College Budget	4. 9%	5. 74%	Increase in Share: . 84% Rate of Percentage Increase: 17. 1%
Library Expenditures Per Student	$68.	$147.	116. 2

[a]Data extracted from: Earlham College. Library. Annual Reports of the Librarian. 1963/64; and "Selected Library Statistics for 1968/69" [Collected by Bowdoin College Library].

tions, binding, the reclassification project, and secretary to the Librarian.

The Archivist and College Historian Emeritus now serves in a part-time capacity. Administratively under the Librarian, but working independently, is the full-time Director of Audio-Visual Services and a technical associate and a secretary who are both part-time.

During 1968/69, part-time student assistants worked a total of 14, 620 hours in the libraries. Another 5, 053 hours were worked by other part-time assistants.[34] A professional works about ten hours per week in cataloging. During the Fall term, 1969, there were 54 part-time assistants working in the Lilly Library.

Wages of $17, 514. 59 were paid to students and other hourly assistants during 1968/69. Salaries of the regular staff amounted to $73, 236. 45. The cost for personnel ($90, 751. 04) was 54. 1% of the total library expenditures ($167, 545. 63). A sum of $60, 523. 21 was spent on books and other library materials and $8, 929. 39 on binding for a total expenditure of $69, 452. 60 (41. 4% of the library budget). An additional $7, 241. 99 went to other operating expenses.[35]

Technical Services

The Associate Librarian is in charge of all technical processing. He is the only professional in technical services, with the exception of a librarian who catalogs ten hours per week. Three non-professional staff members and several part-time student assistants added 10, 986 volumes to the collections in 1968/69.

The decision to shift from the Dewey to the Library of Congress classification was made in 1965/66 and the first books were classified in the Library of Congress scheme in May, 1966. The reclassification of older material began that summer.[36] From July, 1966 through May, 1969, 39, 383 volumes have been reclassified.[37]

Another decision was made in 1965 to expedite technical processing. The adoption of a guide card system for subject headings in the card catalog eliminated the typing of subject headings on individual cards. The catalog is divided into two sections: author-title and subject. The Science Librarian succinctly summarized this area of the Lilly Library:

> Earlham has streamlined technical services so well that two or three professionals are not needed to do the technical processing.[38]

Lilly as Campus Study Hall and Social Center

No regular library attendance records have been kept at Earlham. During a one-day study in the old Carnegie building in May, 1961, 283 students, seven faculty members, and two other persons used the Library. They gave 445 reasons for using the library; 183 (41%) were there to study their own books. The Lilly Library continued to be used as a study hall, but with the completion in 1968 of the Runyan Campus Center--with a theatre, coffee shop, bookstore, and other facilities for music, art, and recreation--there was a marked change in the Library. Attendance figures taken in the Library before and after the opening of Runyan showed that "10 to 20% fewer students came into the Library after the opening of the Center."[39]

The Library also was no longer the social center of the campus. The coffee shop and other areas of Runyan attracted students. The Librarian reported that

> use of the library as a working facility increased. The difference is indicated by the reduced noise level--the students in the library now are here to work, whereas a substantial number in past years came because it was the campus social center.[40]

An after-hours study room, which has a separate outside door, is provided in the Lilly Library. During regular library hours, this room serves as a place for student-faculty conversations. Beginning in 1969, the entire Library was opened on Saturday nights as a study hall, with few library services. Attendance was over 130 students on most Saturday nights.

Lilly as Reserve Book Dispenser and Browsing Collection

The circulation of reserve material takes a secondary position to use of the main collection at Earlham. However, in two studies in the old Library, it was found that 40% of the books on reserve were charged out only once or not at all (Table 44). A campaign was undertaken to acquaint professors with the little-used items. In the design of the Lilly Library, shelving space for reserves was deliberately limited. In the Fall term, 1964, only 21.2% of the reserve items were used once or not at all.

During 1968/69, the total reserve circulation amounted to 21,193--a 20.9% drop from 26,460 during the previous year.[41] This was an average of 18.4 reserve loans to each Earlham student enrolled in 1968/69.

Table 44.--Use of Reserve Books, Earlham College Library, Fall Terms, 1962-1964[a]

Variable	Fall Term, 1962[b]	Winter Term, 1963[b]	Fall Term, 1964[c]
Total Books on Reserve	664	519	1, 075
Percentage of Total Which Were Checked Out:			
Once or not at all	40. 7%	40. 0%	21. 2%
2 to 5 times	16. 0	21. 8	23. 2
6 to 9 times	15. 5	10. 8	15. 4
10 to 25 times	20. 0	19. 7	40. 1 (10 to 25 times and more than 25 times combined)
More than 25 times	8. 5	7. 7	

[a]Earlham College. Library. Booklist, December 5, 1962, p. 1; May 27, 1963, p. 1; and January 8, 1965, p. 5.

[b]In old Carnegie building.

[c]In Lilly Library.

The main collection, which is freely accessible to all, accounted for 35, 865 loans to Earlham students during 1968/69, or an average of 31 loans to each student. This was an increase of 2. 7% over the 34, 931 loans to students during 1967/68.

During 1968/69, 2, 627 recordings were also charged out to Earlham students. Faculty members, College staff, students in the Eastern Indiana Center, and others borrowed a total of 14, 298 books and recordings. The total home loans of books and recordings (excluding reserve material) to all patrons in 1968/69 was 52, 790. This compares to a total use of 51, 490 in 1967/68.[42] No records are kept of the number of volumes used in the building and not charged out, but the number is substantial.[43]

Lilly as Audio-Visual Facility

The Library's audio-visual materials became "increasingly important in its program"[44] in the 1950's. Musical recordings were the most frequently used non-print medium. A modern language laboratory for instruction in foreign languages was also a part of the Library. The Carnegie Print Collection, a gift to the College, has been available since the 1930's.[45]

In the design of the new building, there was an opportunity to expand greatly the audio-visual collections and equipment. Non-print media are now substantial resources of Lilly Library. Phonograph recordings numbered 1,148 albums (993 musical albums; 155 spoken word albums) in 1969. An extensive collection of tape recordings of College convocations and other public meetings is maintained. The Library has approximately 75 filmstrips. The College's collection of art slides is housed in Lilly as well as several hundred mounted photographs of art and architecture. The Library also has a collection of 200 paintings and prints (originals, reproductions, and posters) which are displayed in the building and are available for rental by students at fifty cents per term.

An audio-visual area, consisting of a complex of rooms and equipment, occupies the south wing of the lower level. A projection/classroom provides for film and slide presentations. A series of small rooms has equipment for listening to recordings and viewing filmstrips and slides. The Language Laboratory consists of two large rooms--a classroom with 30 electronically equipped carrels plus control center and a self-instruction room with carrels for individual study of language tapes. Classes in French, German, Spanish, and Japanese meet in the classroom. Students may also study individually Greek, Russian, Finnish, Italian, and Chinese. The audio-visual staff also videotapes special classes, individual biology projects, musical groups, and sports events. A dark room for photography development completes this area of the Library.[46]

The circulation of recordings for home use amounted to 3,167 loans in 1968/69. This does not include the use of recordings placed on closed reserve. The Language Lab classroom is used 23 hours each week for class sessions. No record is kept of the number of students individually studying language tapes.

Although housed in the Lilly Library and administratively under the direction of the Librarian, the Director of Audio-Visual Services and his staff work independently. There is not a complete integration of the audio-visual services with other library programs. Films are the weakest area of the audio-visual program.

Reference Services for Undergraduate Students

Library Publications

As a basic introduction to the Lilly Library and the Science Library, the Library Handbook is available. Revised annually, the 1969/70 edition consisted of 21 pages in loose-leaf format which could be inserted into the student's personal notebook.

Booklist is issued several times each year as a means of communicating with the faculty. Several mimeograph pages contain informal notes of library news. "New Books in the Library" is regularly appended to Booklist. A separate listing of "Recent Gifts" is also frequently included.

The Library's most extensive series of publications has been over 130 annotated bibliographies on many subjects which are given to students in the Library's instruction program. They are described in a later section of this chapter.

Interlibrary Borrowing

The borrowing of items from other libraries has undergone a nine-fold increase in five years. Only 114 items were borrowed or photocopied from other libraries in 1963/64; by 1968/69 the number had increased to 1,010 items.[47] Students borrowed the most items (71) in 1963/64; faculty received 28 and other persons, 15. Student requests were mostly from those enrolled in English, history, biology, and psychology courses. Earlham borrowed most heavily from Indiana University, University of Illinois, and Miami University.[48] Having the Eastern Indiana Center at Earlham qualifies the Lilly Library for the special service provided by the Indiana University Library to regional campus libraries.

> Almost any book the library in Bloomington has can be borrowed...and almost any article will be duplicated and sent without charge. In effect, this puts at our disposal the entire resources of the IU Library, one of the major libraries in the nation.[49]

Communications with Faculty

In addition to the Booklist and the lists of recent purchases and gifts, there are many other methods used by Earlham librarians to communicate with faculty members. Candidates for faculty positions are all shown the Library and meet the Librarian during their campus interviews. In 1969, the Librarian was a member of the Faculty Affairs Committee which is responsible for the selection of new faculty, but even before this official committee membership, the Librarian took part in the interviewing process. After acceptance of an appointment, each new faculty member receives a welcoming letter from the Librarian in which an offer is made for the library staff to check bibliographies or to answer any questions about specific holdings. Later, during a general orientation period, the Librarian speaks to all new faculty members.

The five professional members on the library staff have faculty status. They serve on committees of the College and attend faculty meetings. (The Librarian attends the meetings of the Humanities Division; the Science Librarian, the Science Division; the Documents Librarian, the Social Science Division; and the Reference Librarian, the School of Religion faculty meetings).

The Librarian recently taught a section of the History of Civilization course. He and a small group of students explored periodicals and their social influence. He has offered to teach a section in 1970/71 on the Spanish Civil War. Several librarians either currently act as advisors to students or have done so in the past. Two librarians have served as coaches in the Earlham sports program.[50]

Greatly supplementing these formal contacts, the librarians have frequent informal associations with individual faculty members. The Lilly Library has an attractive faculty lounge (where coffee is available) which provides an opportunity for librarian-faculty conversations. An informal luncheon is held once a week for faculty members. College receptions, private dinner parties, and other social events contribute to an excellent rapport between librarians and faculty.

When asked: "Is the faculty (and the librarians' contact with the faculty) the key to successful reference services for undergraduates?" the Librarian of Earlham responded that:

> The key is contact with the faculty and with the students--making yourself known, making yourself part of the whole college so that people feel free to ask you for favors or service or anything.[51]

Earlham librarians have, to an extraordinary degree, become part of the whole college. This uncommon rapport with faculty has made possible the development of a highly successful library instruction program which in turn has greatly influenced the reference services for students.

Library Orientation and Instruction

There is a long history at Earlham of library orientation. In the 1890's, an attempt was made to "familiarize students with the use of the Library as an adjunct to the work in the various departments of the College, and to give them some knowledge of the bibliography of various subjects of study."[52] During the librarianship of Harlow Lindley (1898-1928), library instruction took various forms: voluntary lectures at the beginning of the year, a lecture as part of a required introductory course for freshmen, and finally lectures and tours as part of the freshman week. From 1932/33-1942/43, a one-hour bibliography course was given.[53]

More recently, a library instruction program unparalleled at any college or university in the country has been developed by Evan Farber. From orientation tours conducted for new students at the beginning of each term and two or three lectures given in college courses in 1963/64,[54] the program has expanded each year. By 1965/66, special bibliographies were prepared and lectures given in 38 Earlham and seven Eastern Indiana Center courses.[55] During 1968/69, the librarians gave approximately 90 lectures in 50 different courses.[56] "During the last five years, Earlham's four librarians who give instruction have prepared and updated some 130 annotated bibliographies and met more than 200 classes."[57]

There are currently four levels of instruction. The first step is taken during the summer when each entering freshman is sent a letter saying that he will be given a brief test covering twelve basic reference sources during Earlham's New Student Week. The test, simulating a search for material on Vietnam, singles out "students whose knowledge is so poor they need some special instruction."[58] No tours or general orientation lectures are given to all freshmen at this point "because of the frantic pace of New Student Week and the lack of motivation to use the sources."[59]

The next stage is integrated with the required two-term freshman Humanities course. During the first term, students write a short personal reaction paper each week. During Term II, a long paper is assigned and the librarians have an hour session to discuss search strategy and the basic reference works in the humanities and social sciences with classes of 20 students each. These classes are also divided into tutorials of four to six students. After the students have begun work on their papers, a librarian meets with each tutorial group for a discussion of specific problems which have been encountered. After class, students often accompany the librarian to the reference collection for additional individual guidance.[60]

The third level of the instruction program is tied to basic, introductory courses in various disciplines. The amount of instruction is usually from one to four hours for each course. Psychology students, for example, are introduced to Psychology Abstracts, Annual Review of Psychology, Mental Measurements Yearbook, and other sources basic to the discipline.[61] The General Biology course, taken by approximately two-thirds of the Earlham students, is closely related with the resources of the Science Library. Thomas Kirk, the Science Librarian, has developed and experimented with two methods of library instruction: lecture-demonstrations and guided exercises.[62] The guided exercise gives the student an introduction to the bibliographical tools in the biological sciences, acquaints him with the types of sources which may be used for specific information, and illustrates the techniques of searching biological literature.[63] In 1969/70, when the instructors of the biology course asked the Science Librarian to lecture on government documents, to prepare twelve sections of students for research on pollution control, a videotape was made of the lecture. Screenings were then scheduled for the students.[64]

The fourth level of instruction is related to the more advanced courses in various disciplines. For example, an English professor who had a seminar on morality plays of the fifteenth and sixteenth centuries met with the librarian to acquaint him with the subject of a long paper each student would be writing.[65] The librarian then prepared himself to meet with the seminar at the next week's session and lead a bibliographical discussion designed to assist in locating sources for the papers. This final level of the Earlham program usually involves specialized assistance with individual students.

For use at all levels of the library instruction, Earlham's librarians have prepared annotated bibliographies on subjects ranging from American government to fossil man, Spanish American literature, and Shakespeare. The bibliographies are kept up-to-date and are given individually to students when the librarian meets with a course.

James R. Kennedy, Earlham's Reference Librarian, has estimated that the entire library instruction program requires approximately one-third of the time of four librarians during the first half of each of the three academic terms.[66] What are the returns on this investment? In 1965, when the scores of Earlham seniors jumped an exceptional forty-one points in one year on the Graduate Record Examination, James V. McDowell, Director of Testing and Educational Research at Earlham, credited the "cumulative impact" of the Library as partly responsible for the increase.[67] This was the same year in which Evan Farber reported:

> For the first time in my three years as Librarian, I feel that we have been giving effective reference service.... The reference department is the crucial point of contact between student and book collection....
>
> The staff's contact is implemented in a number of ways, of varying degrees of immediacy. The most immediate is the reference service usually thought of when the term is used--that is, helping individuals find answers to questions they have on how to use reference tools (bibliographies, indexes, the card catalog), or for specific bits of information and more general questions on suggesting sources or even topics. Another major part of reference work is instructing classes in the use of

> the library and in the bibliography related to the individual courses.... This year we have done more of this than ever before with, I feel, gratifying results, but much more of it needs to be done.[68]

One of the professors in the General Biology course has commented upon the library instruction program in describing the course:

> Our examinations are designed to give an opportunity to develop knowledge in depth on a specific problem, as for example: Why most of the crimes of violence committed by women are committed in the pre-menstrual week. Students are asked to consider problems similar to this one and to prepare answers based on evidence documented from the literature following a thorough library search, a technique at which, thanks to the careful guidance of Tom Kirk, [the Science Librarian] they become quite proficient.[69]

Another dividend from the instruction program was an increase in activity at the reference desk. In 1964, when library instruction was just beginning, there were fewer questions asked of the reference librarians than are presently asked.[70] Having seen the librarian in class may make the student feel freer to ask for assistance later at the reference desk.

The Reference Collection

Approximately 5,000 volumes were in the reference collection of the Lilly Library in 1969. During 1968/69, the cost of additions to the collection was $2,474.23; in 1967/68, the expenditure was $2,809.98. Reference volumes added to the separate Science Library in 1968/69 cost $327.32.[71]

The general reference collection is housed on open shelves; a few titles, such as the *Interpreter's Bible*, are kept on permanent closed reserve behind the circulation desk. A small collection of heavily used reference volumes --approximately 125 items--is shelved on open shelves near the reference desk. There is also a small collection of bibliographical tools for U. S. documents which are separated from the main reference collection and shelved for convenience near the desk. A file containing several thousand pamphlets and other ephemeral material is part of the reference area. (The pamphlets may be charged out for home use.) Atlases and a collection of college catalogs complete the major resources in the main reference area. The national and trade bibliographies are shelved on the main floor adjacent to the Technical Services room, but not too distant from the reference desk.

Description of Reference Area and Desk

The program for the Lilly Library called for a reference area which would be "easily found as readers enter the building."[72] This requirement could not have been more perfectly met: the reference area and desk are immediately adjacent to the main entrance (Figure 5). In refining the interior lay-out, the Librarian asked the architect for a

> clearly defined reference area. The old fashioned reference room--rather sedate and formal, with much wall shelving--may not be aesthetically pleasing, but I believe that it really does contribute to an atmosphere conducive to serious reference work. It is this atmosphere which I should like to get into our reference area.[73]

The architect once again succeeded--the reference area is clearly defined, yet open and inviting. "The reference area is carpeted, not only for beauty and quiet, but also to give the reference service dignity and importance."[74]

The wood reference desk is exceptionally small (top measurements: 14" by 27") and there are chairs for the librarian on duty and the person seeking assistance if he wishes to sit down. It is the least formidable reference desk ever seen by this writer. The desk, located on the Library's first floor, is only a few feet from the main entrance, card catalog, reference collection, current periodicals and newspapers, and circulation desk. Immediately behind the reference desk are two offices with glass panels for the Reference Librarian and the Documents Librarian. During the first years, one of the offices was used for microform reading.

Staffing of Reference Desk

The hours of professional reference service during a regular week in the Fall term, 1969 were: Monday-Thurs-

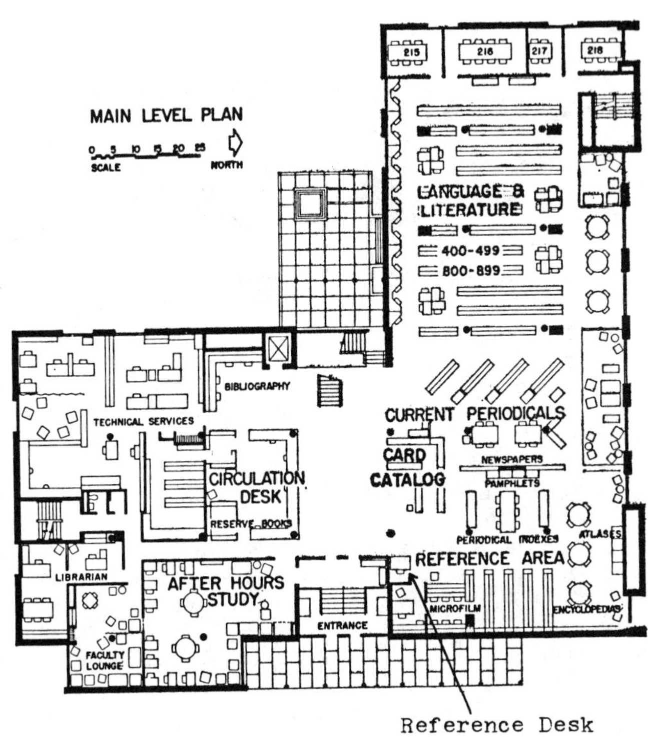

Figure 5.--Main Level, Lilly Library, Earlham College, 1964. Source: Evan I. Farber, "Attention to Details in Planning Makes a 'Most Considerate' Library," College and University Business, (March, 1964), p. 60.

day, 8 A.M.-12 Noon, 1-5 P.M., and 6:30-10 P.M.; Friday, 8 A.M.-12 Noon and 1-5 P.M.; Saturday, 1-5 P.M.; and Sunday, 1:45-5 P.M. and 6:30-10 P.M. This totalled 64 hours and 45 minutes (67.4%) of the 96 hours the Lilly Library was open for full service. The Library was also open from 5-11:15 P.M. on Saturday nights for study with limited service at the circulation desk. The separate after-hours room was open throughout the night.

An Earlham senior was on duty at the reference desk for an additional 6.5 hours each week (Friday, 6:30-10 P.M. and Saturday, 9 A.M.-12 Noon).

The Reference Librarian and the Documents Librarian cover most of the daytime hours, with the Librarian and the Associate Librarian occasionally taking some of them. These four professionals each work one week-night in the Lilly Library and the Science Librarian works one night in the Science Library. All five librarians alternate the weekend hours in the Lilly Library.

Only one librarian is usually needed at the reference desk; however, there are some busy times when two assist inquirers.

Qualifications of Staff in 1969/70

A profile of the reference librarians in the Lilly Library in October, 1969 would portray a man in his thirties or forties who had worked at Earlham for 5 or 6 years. He also had experience in other libraries after earning his library science degree. His undergraduate major was in the social sciences and he had done graduate work in a subject area.

Individually the five librarians have varying backgrounds. Two had Earlham as their undergraduate alma maters; Cornell, Duquesne, and the University of North Carolina were also represented. The library schools attended were varied (Carnegie Institute, Columbia, and Indiana University with one librarian each; two staff members from the University of North Carolina). Two have master's degrees in subject fields and two others have done substantial graduate study in a subject. Four of five had experience in other libraries before coming to Earlham. The number of years of service at Earlham ranged from 3 to 9 years. The total number of years of professional experience was from 4 to 16 years.

Scope of Reference Services

The Lilly Library offers assistance at the reference desk previously described. There is also telephone service for students as well as any other callers. The librarians, however, do not anchor themselves at the reference desk awaiting students to approach them. The staff members frequently go up to students using the catalog or a reference volume and ask if the students need assistance.

In addition to serving Earlham students, faculty, and staff, the reference librarians assist Eastern Indiana Center students, local residents, high school students, and others. The reference librarians also call other local libraries, particulary the Morrisson-Reeves Library, in order to assist readers.

Philosophy of Service

Before coming to Earlham, the Reference Librarian stated his personal philosophy:

> we are public servants. We serve not merely one boss but all the readers who make up our public. Our situation as everybody's servant is dramatized by the crowds and the ringing telephones at peak hours at the different service desks.[75]

After being at Earlham, he summarized the philosophy there:

> Earlham's librarians have the philosophy that in order to fulfill our library's role in the teaching program, we must help students learn to make use of the library's resources more effectively and efficiently. A good bit of this instruction, of course, comes with individual reference assistance, but we believe it can also be accomplished through a program of class instruction, and we've made such instruction one of the cornerstones of this library's service.[76]

In discussing the implementation of the primary purpose of a college library--bringing together the student and the books he needs or wants--the Librarian of Earlham College emphasized

> individualized and expert reference service, for no matter how good the collection, how efficiently it is arranged, or how comfortable the facilities, unless students know how to use the library effectively the entire program is virtually wasted.[77]

When the five Earlham librarians were asked in individual interviews "Do you consider reference services for undergraduates to be one of the most important functions of the library?", they all replied that this was the most important function of a college library.

Use of Reference Services

No statistical records have been kept of the number or types of questions asked at the Lilly Library reference desk. Each librarian on duty at the desk frequently records his impressions of the reference activity, but these are short phrases which usually note whether it was exceptionally slow or busy.

In interviews with the librarians, they agreed that Earlham undergraduates formed the largest number of inquirers, with the faculty being a much smaller number. They also had the impression that brief information and directional questions were a small percentage of the total questions asked, and that bibliographical assistance with the catalog and holdings of the library was the most frequent kind of help they gave students. They did not believe that requests for retrieval of specific data were as numerous.

Samples of Questions: October and November, 1969

All questions asked at the Lilly Library's reference desk were monitored during two weeks of the Fall term, 1969 (October 13-17 and November 17-21, 1969). The hours, methodology, and definitions used in recording the questions asked by undergraduate students are described in Chapter 1.

Undergraduates were the major users of the reference services. During the first week, they accounted for 71% of the total questions asked (188), with faculty, staff, and others asking 29%. During the second week, 83% of the total (195) were undergraduate questions; faculty, staff, and others asked 17%.

During the 36 hours of the first week's monitoring, 134 questions were asked by undergraduates, an average hourly rate of 3.7 questions. Questions by undergraduates during 38 hours of monitoring during the second week increased to 163, an hourly average of 4.3. Questions were asked in person and by telephone. There were no phone calls from undergraduates during the October week and only three questions via phone during the November week. Faculty and staff called in their questions in far greater numbers than did students.

The afternoon and evening hours were considerably busier than the morning hours. On Wednesday morning, October 15, 1969, no questions were asked because of a College Convocation on the war in Vietnam. Fridays were the slowest days and the other four weekdays were considerably more active and about equal in volume of questions asked.

Table 45 categorizes the questions[78] asked by undergraduates. Substantive reference questions (84.4% in the first week; 78.5%, the second week) overwhelmingly outnumbered the information questions (13.8% and 20.9%). There were no problem questions (over one hour), but there were four search questions (over 30 minutes) during the two weeks. Two search questions were also undertaken for faculty members.

Of the 241 reference questions asked by Earlham undergraduates in the two periods, librarians spent more than five minutes with 37 of the questions (15.3%). For many of the questions, they assisted students for 15-20 minutes. Earlham librarians also made certain that almost all students were successful in finding the material or the answer being sought. Students were not simply directed to possible sources with no additional assistance. If the librarian had not assisted throughout the entire search, he returned to check the student's progress.

Earlham librarians also approached students in the reference area or at the catalog, not waiting for students to gather courage to ask for help. The staff initiated 34 (11.4%) of the 297 questions asked by undergraduates. The fact the Earlham librarians know many students contributed to the success of this approach.

Table 45.--Questions Asked by Undergraduates at Reference Desk, Lilly Library, Earlham College, in Two One-Week Samples, 1969

	Oct. 13-17, 1969		Nov. 17-21, 1969	
Type of Question	No.	%	No.	%
Information	18	13.4	34	20.9
Reference				
R-1	68	50.8	75	46.1
R-2	. .	. .	. .	. .
R-3	4	3.0	11	6.7
R-4	25	18.7	32	19.6
R-5	9	6.7	2	1.2
R-6	6	4.5	8	4.9
R-7	1	0.7	. .	. .
Sub-total	113	84.4	128	78.5
Search	3	2.2	1	0.6
Problem	. .	. .	. .	. .
Total	134	100.0	163	100.0

A further analysis (Table 46) of the information questions, which accounted for only 13.4% and 20.9% of the total questions, reveals that about one-half of the questions in each week concerned locations for various materials or services in the Library. During November 17-21, questions about periodicals were the most numerous, indicating that more students were working on papers than during the earlier week of the term. Only one student asked the simplest of all questions ("Where is the pencil sharpener?").

A broad analysis of all questions asked by undergraduates (Table 45) shows that R-1 questions (bibliographical assistance with the catalog and holdings) accounted for 50.8% and 46.1% of the total questions. A more detailed analysis of the R-1 questions (Table 47) reveals that they comprised 60.2% and 58.6% of the total reference questions asked. When students requested general bibliographical assistance, librarians most often responded by using the reference collection. Assistance at the main catalog or serials catalog was a very close second. Earlham librarians also

Table 46.--Types of Information Questions Asked by Undergraduates at Reference Desk, Lilly Library, Earlham College, in Two One-Week Samples, 1969

Type of Information Question	Oct. 13-17, 1969		Nov. 17-21, 1969	
	No.	% of Total Information Questions Asked	No.	% of Total Information Questions Asked
Assistance with physical facilities of library:				
Location of pencil sharpener or request to borrow pen, stapler, etc.	. .	. .	1	2.9
Request for keys or unlocking of rooms	. .	. .	. .	. .
Location of areas in library	2	11.1	4	11.8
Sub-total	2	11.1	5	14.7
Requests for location of particular volume (librarian gave directions):				
Monographs in main collection (student had call number)	2	11.1	5	14.7
Reference books (student usually requested by title)	2	11.1	2	5.9
Sub-total	4	22.2	7	20.6

Table 46.--Continued.

Type of Information Question	Oct. 13-17, 1969		Nov. 17-21, 1969	
	No.	% of Total Information Questions Asked	No.	% of Total Information Questions Asked
Requests for information or publication (student did not have call number):				
Librarian knew answer without referring to any source	3	16.6	1	2.9
Librarian referred student to catalog or reference collection, giving no additional assistance	. .	. .	2	5.9
Librarian knew that question would be better answered in another library and referred student to it	. .	. .	. .	. .
Sub-total	3	16.6	3	8.8

Table 46.--Continued.

Type of Information Question	Oct. 13-17, 1969		Nov. 17-21, 1969	
	No.	% of Total Information Questions Asked	No.	% of Total Information Questions Asked
Questions concerning collection or services (librarian responded with brief directions or information):				
Periodicals	1	5.6	9	26.5
Newspapers	. .	. .	1	2.9
College catalogs	2	11.1	2	5.9
Main catalog or serials catalog	1	5.6	3	8.8
Reserve books	. .	. .	. .	. .
How and where to charge out books	2	11.1	2	5.9
Use of reference volume in another part of library	. .	. .	. .	. .
Photocopying machine	2	11.1	. .	. .
Exam file	. .	. .	. .	. .
Location of another library	. .	. .	. .	. .
Sub-total	8	44.5	17	50.0

Table 46. --Continued.

Type of Information Question	Oct. 13-17, 1969 No.	Oct. 13-17, 1969 % of Total Information Questions Asked	Nov. 17-21, 1969 No.	Nov. 17-21, 1969 % of Total Information Questions Asked
Miscellaneous information questions	1	5.6	2	5.9
Total information questions	18	100.0	34	100.0

used both the catalogs and the reference collection in a significant number of instances (11.5% and 8.6% of the total reference questions asked in the first and second weeks of monitoring).

There were no requests for bibliographical assistance with the holdings of other campus libraries (R-2).

During the first week, 3.5% of the undergraduate reference questions were for bibliographical verification of materials not on the campus (R-3). By November 17-21, these requests had grown to 8.6%, perhaps indicating that more students were actively engaged in writing papers at this point of the term.

During October 13-17, 1969, 22.1% of the reference questions were requests for retrieval of factual, non-bibliographical information (R-4). This category increased to 25% during November 17-21. These questions varied widely with no particular subject or type of material dominating the questions.

R-5 questions (counseling of students in a reader's advisory capacity) were 8% of the reference questions in the first week with a substantial decrease to only 1.5% during the later week. Perhaps this may again be explained by the writing of term papers: during October, students were be-

Table 47.--Bibliographical Assistance with Library's Own Catalogs and Holdings (R-1 Questions) Requested by Undergraduates at Reference Desk, Lilly Library, Earlham College, in Two One-Week Samples, 1969

	Oct. 13-17, 1969		Nov. 17-21, 1969	
Type of Response by Type of R-1 Question	No.	% of Total Reference Questions Asked	No.	% of Total Reference Questions Asked
Requests for particular volume or type of volume; librarian gave assistance by:				
Checking list of frequently used reference titles and giving student call number	..	..	..	..
Charging out heavily used item from drawer of desk	..	..	..	..
Going to reference shelves and producing particular volume for student who had usually given title or described type	11	9.7	7	5.5

Table 47. --Continued.

Type of Response by Type of R-1 Question	Oct. 13-17, 1969 No.	Oct. 13-17, 1969 % of Total Reference Questions Asked	Nov. 17-21, 1969 No.	Nov. 17-21, 1969 % of Total Reference Questions Asked
Going to main collection shelves and locating monograph, periodical or newspaper which student had been unable to find	3	2.7	4	3.1
Sub-total	14	12.4	11	8.6
Requests for general bibliographical assistance; librarian responded by:				
Using reference collection	21	18.6	27	21.1
Assisting student at main catalog or serials catalog	18	15.9	25	19.5
Assisting student at both the catalog and the reference collection	13	11.5	11	8.6
Using *Subject Headings Used in... the Library of Congress*	..	..	..	..

Table 47.--Continued.

Type of Response by Type of R-1 Question	Oct. 13-17, 1969 No.	Oct. 13-17, 1969 % of Total Reference Questions Asked	Nov. 17-21, 1969 No.	Nov. 17-21, 1969 % of Total Reference Questions Asked
Assisting in use of microforms	2	1.8	1	0.8
Assisting in use of circulation records	. .	. .	. .	. .
Sub-total	54	47.8	64	50.0
Total R-1 Questions	68	60.2	75	58.6
Other Reference Questions (R-2 through R-7)	45	39.8	53	41.4
Total Reference Questions	113	100.0	128	100.0

ginning to pick topics and asked the librarians for assistance in getting started; by November 17-21, the topics were already chosen by most students.

R-6 questions (informal, personal instruction in use of the library or any of its resources) constituted 5.3% of the reference questions during Week I and 6.2% during Week II. Most of the questions were instruction in the use of a particular reference volume. This category would probably be larger if Earlham did not have a comprehensive library instruction program.

One reference question was placed in the miscellaneous category (R-7).

Table 48.--Home Loans and Reserve Use During Two Weeks of Monitoring Questions at Reference Desk, Lilly Library, Earlham College in 1969[a]

Variable	Oct. 13-17, 1969[b]	Nov. 17-21, 1969[b]
Attendance in Library	No Record Kept	No Record Kept
Total Home Loans from Main Collection (Earlham Students Only)	542[c]	1,005[c]
Average Daily Home Loans (Earlham Students Only)	108	201
Total Home Loans	775[d]	1,332[d]
Average Daily Home Loans	155	266
Total Reserve Use	461	364
Average Daily Reserve Use	92	73

[a]Earlham College. Library. "Lilly Library Daily Circulation Count." October and November, 1969. (Handwritten.)

[b]15.5 hours each day (7:45 A.M.-11:15 P.M.).

[c]Does not include: 34 recordings loaned for home use (daily average of 6) during October 13-17; 37 recordings (daily average of 7) during November 17-21.

[d]Does not include: 60 recordings loaned for home use (daily average of 12) during October 13-17; 63 recordings (daily average of 13) during November 17-21.

Other Library Activities During Reference Monitoring

In order to place the two weeks of monitoring questions at the reference desk into the over-all context of the Lilly Library, Table 48 gives the appropriate data.

The number of home loans from the main collection to Earlham undergraduates greatly increased when October 13-17 is compared with November 17-21. The second week was almost double the first week. In contrast, the use of reserve material decreased by 21% in the second week when compared to the first week. Indication is again given that the October week was more a time of preparing daily class assignments while the November week was a period of writing term papers.

Notes

1. Opal Thornburg, Earlham, the Story of the College, 1847-1962 (Richmond, Indiana: Earlham College Press, 1963), p. 3.

2. Ibid.

3. This historical sketch is based on A Profile of Earlham College, prepared by the College in 1961 for the Ford Foundation and is quoted from a condensed version appearing in: William E. Cadbury, Jr. and Everett K. Wilson, "Earlham College" Struggle and Promise: A Future for Colleges, by Morris Keeton and Conrad Hilberry (New York: McGraw-Hill, 1969), pp. 284-85.

4. Earlham College ("Barron's Profiles of American Colleges"; Woodbury, N.Y.: Barron's Educational Series, Inc., 1969), p. 3.

5. Earlham College. Office of Admissions. The 1969 Report to Principals, Headmasters, and Guidance Counselors (Richmond, Indiana: Earlham College, 1969), p. 4.

6. Ibid.

7. Earlham College. *Earlham College Catalog, 1968-1970* (Richmond, Indiana: Earlham College, 1968), p. 15.

8. *Ibid.*, pp. 16-17.

9. *Ibid.*, p. 26.

10. Earlham College. Eastern Indiana Center. *The Eastern Indiana Center of Earlham College Bulletin of General Information* (Richmond, Indiana: Eastern Indiana Center, 1968), p. 4.

11. Thornburg, p. 423.

12. William E. Cadbury, Jr. and Everett K. Wilson, "Earlham College," *Struggle and Promise: A Future for Colleges*, by Morris Keeton and Conrad Hilberry, p. 298.

13. *Ibid.*, p. 286.

14. Circular, dated "Third Month, 22nd, 1847," over the name of Benjamin Fulghum, as quoted in Thornburg, p. 47.

15. Thornburg, p. 63.

16. *Ibid.*, p. 104.

17. Ellen L. Stanley, "The Earlham College Library: A History of Its Relationship to the College" (unpublished Master's thesis, Graduate School, University of Illinois, 1947), p. 26.

18. Thornburg, p. 240.

19. *Ibid.*

20. *Ibid.*, pp. 245-46.

21. Letter from Charles E. Rush, '05, then head of the Indianapolis Public Library, to the Carnegie Corporation, 1926, as quoted in Thornburg, p. 285.

22. Evan I. Farber, "Earlham's 'Considerate' Library," *Library Journal*, LXXXVIII (December 1, 1963), 4561.

23. *Ibid.*, p. 4564.

24. Thornburg, p. 429.

25. Earlham College. Library. *Booklist*, October 1, 1968, p. 1.

26. U.S. Office of Education. "Higher Education General Information Survey, Library Collections, Staff, Expenditures, and Salaries." (Earlham College's Report for 1968/69.)

27. Earlham College. Library. *Documents Librarian's Annual Report*. 1968/69, p. 1.

28. Interview with Leo Chang, Documents Librarian, Earlham College, October 16, 1969.

29. Opal Thornburg, "The Role of the Archives at Earlham," *Earlhamite*, XC (Spring, 1969), 10-12.

30. Interview with Evan I. Farber, Librarian, Earlham College, October 16, 1969.

31. Earlham College. Library. *Booklist*, January 10, 1969, p. 1.

32. Earlham College. *Earlham College Catalog, 1968-1970*, pp. 50-51.

33. Farber, "Earlham's 'Considerate' Library," p. 4561.

34. U.S. Office of Education. "Higher Education General Information Survey, Library Collections, Staff, Expenditures, and Salaries." (Earlham College's Report for 1968/69.)

35. *Ibid.*

36. Earlham College. Library. *Annual Report, Technical Services*. 1965/66, p. 1.

37. Earlham College. Library. *Booklist*, June 18, 1969, p. 1.

38. Interview with Thomas G. Kirk, Science Librarian, Earlham College, October 16, 1969.

39. Interview with Evan I. Farber, October 16, 1969.

40. Earlham College. Library. Annual Report of the Librarian. 1968/69, p. 2.

41. Earlham College. Library. "Lilly Library Circulation Statistics." 1967/68 and 1968/69. (Mimeographed.)

42. Ibid., 1968/69.

43. Earlham College. Library. Booklist, May 31, 1964, p. 3.

44. Robert M. Agard, "Earlham's A-V Program," Library Journal, LXXXV (February 15, 1960), 743.

45. Ibid.

46. Interview with John Schuerman, Director of Audio-Visual Services, Earlham College, November 19, 1969.

47. Earlham College. Library. Annual Report of the Librarian. 1964/65, p. 1; 1968/69, p. 1.

48. Earlham College. Library. Annual Report of the Reference Librarian. 1963/64, p. 3.

49. Earlham College. Library. Annual Report of the Librarian. 1964/65, p. 2.

50. Evan I. Farber, "Library Instruction Beyond the Orientation Level," Paper Read before the 55th Conference of Eastern College Librarians, Columbia University, New York, November 29, 1969.

51. Interview with Evan I. Farber, October 16, 1969.

52. Earlham College. Report of the President. 1892/93, pp. 4-5 as quoted in Stanley, p. 28.

53. Stanley, pp. 43-44.

54. Earlham College. Library. Annual Report of the Reference Librarian. 1963/64, p. 2.

55. Ibid., 1965/66, p. 1.

56. Earlham College. Library. Annual Report of the Librarian. 1968/69, p. 2.

57. James R. Kennedy, "Integrated Library Instruction," Library Journal, LXXXXV (April 15, 1970), 1453.

58. Ibid., p. 1451.

59. Ibid.

60. Ibid.

61. Ibid., pp. 1451-52.

62. Thomas G. Kirk, "A Comparison of Two Methods of Library Instruction for Students in Introductory Biology" (unpublished Master's thesis, Graduate School, Indiana University, 1969).

63. [Thomas G. Kirk], "Guided Exercises for Locating Biological Literature," [Earlham College General Biology Course, 1969.] (Mimeographed.)

64. Letter from Evan I. Farber, Librarian, Earlham College, to Billy R. Wilkinson, March 1, 1970.

65. This conference was attended by the author. Bibliographical lectures to both Earlham College and Eastern Indiana Center students were also attended.

66. Kennedy, p. 1453.

67. Earlham College. Library. Annual Report of the Librarian. 1964/65, p. 2.

68. Ibid., pp. 1-2.

69. Jerome Woolpy, "General Biology Seeks Relevance," Earlham Post, XXV (October 14, 1969), 5.

70. Interview with James R. Kennedy, Reference Librarian, Earlham College, October 17, 1969.

71. Interview with Philip D. Shore, Associate Librarian, Earlham College, October 16, 1969.

72. Earlham College. Library. "Program for a Library Building for Earlham College." [Richmond, Indiana] November, 1959, p. 3. (Mimeographed.)

73. Letter from Evan I. Farber to Jack Hodell, Baxter, Hodell, and Donnelly, Cincinnati, Ohio, July 16, 1962.

74. Farber, "Earlham's 'Considerate' Library," p. 4563.

75. James R. Kennedy, "Library Services in Perspective," *College and Research Libraries*, XXV (March, 1964), 91.

76. James R. Kennedy, "Library Instruction," *GLCA* [Great Lakes Colleges Association] *Librarians' Newsletter*, I (December, 1966), 1

77. Evan I. Farber, "Where Students Meet Books," *Earlhamite*, LXXXIX (Autumn, 1968), 7.

78. Definitions of information, reference (R-1 through R-7), search, and problem questions are given in Chapter 1. Hereafter in this section, these definitions are used.

Chapter 7

COMPARISONS AND CONCLUSIONS

> The problem with libraries as I see them is that they seem to allow only two categories of behavior. If you know what you want, you can go in and get some help. If you don't know what you want, but just about anything will do, you can go in and quietly browse. If you find yourself somewhere in the middle--in that noisy, confused, irascible, fitty, and starty stage when you think you've got an idea but you're not quite sure you can explain it and that's not it but maybe this sounds right I'm not sure though and WOW--then to go to a librarian for help is often to feel you've committed an anti-social act. That's the one that puts me--and I think my generation--in a bind.
>
> Rick Kean, "Finding People Who Feel Alienated and Alone in Their Best Impulses and Most Honest Perceptions and Telling Them They're Not Crazy," Wilson Library Bulletin, XLIV (September, 1969), 44.

Comparisons of Reference Services for Undergraduate Students

Limited Number of Cases

A caveat should be immediately given the reader: reference services for undergraduate students at only four institutions--the University of Michigan, Cornell University, Swarthmore College, and Earlham College--have been studied. Additional case studies should be made to test the major findings of the present study. Therefore, no generalizations concerning reference services for undergraduates can now be made. The following comparisons among the cases are presented, however, as a step toward documenting reference services for undergraduate students.

Reference Services in Two Undergraduate Libraries

There were many similarities between the reference services of the University of Michigan Undergraduate Library and the Uris Library at Cornell. Both had about the same size reference collection (3, 549 volumes at Michigan UGLI; 3, 294 volumes in Uris) on open shelves in a central location. Only a few volumes were shelved back of the reference desks permitting limited access. Other similarities of the two undergraduate libraries included: (1) all professional staff members alternately worked at the reference desks and had another major responsibility (i. e., in charge of reserve books, audio equipment and recordings, or other library service); (2) the reference desks were manned 76 hours each week during the Fall, 1969 semester; and (3) librarians were on duty most of the hours, although non-professional staff members worked a few hours each week at the reference desks.

If the undergraduates in the arts and sciences college at each university are taken as the primary group of students served by the reference librarians in the two undergraduate libraries, each undergraduate, on a per capita basis, asked only one substantive reference question during 1968/69 in both Michigan and Cornell undergraduate libraries.

Major differences may also be noted. The Michigan UGLI had many more potential users than Uris Library (undergraduates enrolled at the University of Michigan totalled 20, 299 in the Fall term, 1969, with 12, 442 undergraduates in the College of Literature, Science, and the Arts; 10, 042 undergraduates were enrolled at Cornell University, with only 3, 241 undergraduates in the College of Arts and Sciences). The librarians on the UGLI staff each had a large number of potential inquirers when computed on a per capita basis (2, 030 Michigan undergraduates for each librarian if the total campus enrollment is considered, or 1, 244 students if only the undergraduate enrollment of the College of Literature, Science, and the Arts is included). The per capita figures are not as staggering for the Uris librarians (1, 673 undergraduates over the entire campus for each Uris librarian, or 540 undergraduates if just the enrollment of the College of Arts and Sciences is considered).

Seven times as many questions were asked in 1968/69 in the Michigan UGLI as in the Uris Library: the total questions in UGLI numbered 36,520; only 5,385 questions were asked at the Uris reference desk. This was an average of 3,652 questions for each of the ten librarians on the UGLI staff during 1968/69, and 769 questions for each of the seven Uris librarians during that year.

While Michigan UGLI had ten professional positions allocated to its staff (nine were filled in September, 1969), Uris Library had but six librarians at the beginning of the Fall semester, 1969. Two librarians were on duty at the UGLI reference desks during 36 hours each week (47.8% of the hours of service); only one staff member was ever on duty at the Uris reference desk.

When the two groups of reference librarians are compared, there are both similarities and differences. Most members of each staff were young. Women held more of the professional positions in both undergraduate libraries (Michigan UGLI: 8 women, 1 man; Uris: 4 women, 2 men). In 11 of 15 cases, the librarians had done their undergraduate work at a college or university other than their present employer. However, in contrast to 6 of 9 librarians in UGLI who had majored in English, the Uris librarians collectively possessed a greater variety of majors (music, mathematics, medieval history, philosophy, and German literature). Science and social science backgrounds were lacking in both groups. While the University of Michigan School of Library Science had professionally trained 8 out of 9 librarians in the UGLI, 5 library schools were represented among the 6 Uris librarians. The Uris librarians also had wider and more varied professional experience than the Michigan undergraduate librarians. Only one Uris librarian began his professional career in the Uris Library (all others had worked in other libraries at Cornell or elsewhere). In UGLI, 5 of 9 librarians were in their first professional positions.

Other differences were: (1) the Michigan UGLI had an extensive vertical file (over 25,000 pamphlets and other items) as a part of its reference resources while Uris Library maintained only a small file devoted primarily to Cornell University; (2) Michigan undergraduates were unable to telephone the reference librarians for assistance, in contrast to the telephone reference service offered by the Uris Library; (3) librarians in UGLI rarely called another campus library in order to assist students, while Uris librarians used the phone in their reference service; and (4) the staff members in UGLI were not acquainted with the reference librarians in the Michigan General Library, but Uris librarians were familiar with the reference librarians in the Olin Library.

Reference Services for Undergraduates in Two University Libraries

Undergraduate students at Michigan and Cornell also had available for their use the reference departments of the main university libraries. How extensive were these reference collections and services? How did they compare to each other? And how many undergraduates used them?

The reference collections in the University of Michigan General Library and Cornell's John M. Olin Library were approximately the same size and were over four times larger than the reference collections in their undergraduate libraries (an estimated 15, 000 volumes in the Michigan General Library and 16, 222 volumes in Olin Library). The collections were, however, quite differently housed. Michigan's main reference collection was located on the second floor of the General Library in a large monumental reading room. Most of the collection was around the periphery of the room at great distances from the reference desk. As a partial solution to this problem, approximately 850 volumes were shelved back of the reference desk. The public catalog was also at a considerable distance from the reference librarians. An information desk staffed by graduate students was near the catalog and technical service staff members also answered questions at the catalog. In contrast, the Olin reference collection was compactly shelved in the center of the first floor. The reference librarians on duty were located in the center of the reference collection and the public catalogs and were visible from the Library's main entrance. It was unnecessary to keep a large number of reference books back of the desks or to maintain a separate information desk.

Reference assistance was available at all hours the two university libraries were open during the regular semester. Professional staff members were on duty three-quarters of the time (Michigan: 75 hours, or 74.2% of the 101 hours the General Library was open; Cornell: 81 hours, or 75.7% of the Olin Library's 107 hours). Graduate students manned the desk during the other 25% of the hours. Both university reference departments had two librarians on duty during the mornings and afternoons, Monday-Friday. Each reference librarian had duty at the desk as well as another area of responsibility (i.e., interlibrary borrowing, maintenance of reference collection, etc.).

There were additional differences between the Reference Departments of the Michigan General Library and the Olin Library: (1) the Olin librarians had a program of orientation lectures for graduate students at the beginning of the year, but the Michigan reference librarians did not; (2) the Michigan Reference Department maintained an extensive vertical file which included newspaper clippings while the Cornell Reference Department had none; (3) the map collection and room were administratively a part of the Reference Department at Michigan, but at Cornell maps were part of another public service department; (4) a periodical room with current issues of selected journals was administered by the Reference Department at Cornell, but in the Michigan General Library, it was a separate department; (5) Cornell undergraduate and graduate students could obtain reference assistance via telephone, while in the Michigan General Library's Reference Department only faculty members and university staff had this privilege; and (6) although both reference departments borrowed items from other libraries through interlibrary loan for graduate students, faculty, and staff, the Cornell department also loaned Cornell material to other libraries; at Michigan this service was provided by the Circulation Department.

There were nine professional staff members in each of the university reference departments in the Fall semester, 1969. Two of the Olin reference librarians, however, worked only one-half time. The Olin department had considerably more full-time non-professional assistance (7.5 clerical positions) than did the General Library department (3.5 positions).

Comparison of the two groups of reference librarians in the university libraries at Michigan and Cornell revealed that they had extensive experience. Five Michigan librarians had worked in the General Library Reference Department for periods ranging from 8 to 32 years; four had been on the staff from 1 to 4 years. The Cornell librarians had worked in the Olin Reference Department for fewer years: five had from 2 to 8 years, three had worked only one year in the Department, and one had just joined the staff. Six of the Cornell librarians had worked, however, in other academic or public libraries before coming to Cornell and only three persons had begun their careers at Cornell. At Michigan, not as many had experience in other libraries. Two of the Olin reference librarians had previously worked in the Uris Library; none of the librarians in the Michigan General Library had worked in the Undergraduate Library.

Six reference staff members in the General Library had received their professional training at the University of Michigan School of Library Science and three had attended other schools (Columbia, Drexel, and Illinois). At Cornell, three were graduates of Columbia's School of Library Service while six were from other schools (Carnegie, Michigan, North Carolina, Rutgers, Simmons, and Toronto). Two Michigan reference librarians had Master's degrees in a subject; three Cornell librarians had subject Master's degrees and one had done extensive graduate work not for credit toward a degree. The majority of both reference groups were women (Michigan: 8 women, 1 man; Cornell: 7 women, 2 men).

During 1968/69, the total number of questions asked at the main reference desk of the Michigan General Library was 54, 561. An additional 15, 308 questions were asked of the graduate student attendants at the separate information desk. The total number of questions asked at the reference desks of the Olin Library during the same year was 26, 610.

During the October 6-10 and November 10-14, 1969 monitoring of questions asked at the reference desk of the Michigan General Library, undergraduate students asked 21. 8% of the total questions (617) during the first week and 28. 4% of the questions (665) during the second week. At the reference desks of Cornell's Olin Library, undergraduates asked 23. 5% of the total questions (554) during the November 3-7, 1969 monitoring. During the second period of monitoring (December 8-12), the proportion of undergraduate inquirers had increased to 34. 3% of the total questions (548).

At Michigan during the October week, the Undergraduate Library reference librarians were serving almost seven times as many undergraduates as were assisted by the General Library reference staff. During the November week, the librarians in UGLI served over five times as many undergraduates as did the reference librarians in the General Library. Cornell presented a contrasting situation. The reference librarians in Olin Library answered 130 questions from undergraduates during November 3-7, 1969 while the Uris librarians were answering only 167 questions during the same hours. During December 8-12, Olin librarians almost pulled even with the Uris reference staff (188 questions by undergraduates in Olin; 196 questions in Uris).

Reference Services for Undergraduates in Two College Libraries

The reference services of the McCabe Library, Swarthmore College, and the Lilly Library, Earlham College, have approximately the same number of potential undergraduate users (1,149 students at Earlham in 1968/69; 1,062 students at Swarthmore). Although there were similarities between these two college reference services, there were major differences in the reference collections, staffing, philosophies of service, programs of library instruction, and the numbers of students who asked for reference assistance.

Earlham's reference collection numbered approximately 5,000 volumes. The Swarthmore collection was larger--an estimated 8,000 volumes in 1969. Earlham spent $2,474.23 on additions to the reference collection during 1968/69. Swarthmore's reference expenditures were $4,787.76 during the same year. An additional amount--approximately $8,000--had been spent during the past two years on large reference sets to fill gaps in the collection.

At Earlham's Lilly Library, all five professional members of the staff took turns at the public reference desk, giving service at nights and on weekends. In McCabe Library, only one staff member--the Reference Librarian--of the ten librarians at Swarthmore manned the reference desk during week days. Regular night and weekend reference hours were not scheduled.

Since 1962, when Evan I. Farber became Librarian of Earlham College, the philosophy of reference services has been to teach students how to use the library effectively for their course work. He and his staff have gradually implemented over the years an extensive program of library instruction. Using this program as a base, the assistance given to individual students at the reference desk has been expanded.

When James Govan was appointed Librarian of Swarthmore College, he found a long tradition of self-service on the part of Swarthmore students using the Library. Reference services were minimal. The Special Committee on Library Policy, in its year-long study of the Library in 1967, developed and recommended a new philosophy of service to replace this self-service tradition. The Committee recommended that Swarthmore develop a "teaching library" and that two additional staff members--known as Divisional Librarians (one for the humanities and the other for the social sciences)--be appointed to assist the Reference Librarian and the Science Librarian in teaching students to find and use library materials. Earlham and Swarthmore libraries in the Fall semester, 1969 were at two different stages in the development of their reference services: Earlham, after seven years of effort, had achieved an extensive program of instruction and reference assistance (and in the opinion of this observer, one of the most successful programs in American college libraries) while Swarthmore, using a different approach, was at an earlier interim stage of development after two years of effort.

Undergraduate students were the major inquirers at the reference desk of Lilly Library. During the October 13-17, 1969 monitoring of reference activity, they accounted for 71% of the total questions (188), with faculty, staff, and others asking 29%. During November 17-21, 83% of the questions (195) were asked by undergraduates while faculty, staff, and others accounted for 17%. Swarthmore undergraduates asked 64.8% of the questions (108) at the reference desk of McCabe Library during October 20-24, 1969, with faculty, staff, and others asking 35.2%. During the second period of monitoring (December 1-5), questions by undergraduates were 64% of the total (64); faculty, staff, and others asked 36%.

At Earlham during 36 hours of the first week's monitoring, 134 questions were asked by undergraduates, an average hourly rate of 3.7 questions. Questions by undergraduates during 38 hours of monitoring during the second week increased to 163, an hourly average of 4.3. At Swarthmore during 27.5 hours of the first week's monitoring, 70 questions were asked by undergraduates, an hourly rate of 2.5. Questions by undergraduates decreased to 41 during 27.5 hours of the second week's monitoring, for an average of 1.4 per hour.

Testing of Hypotheses

Before the case studies of the two undergraduate libraries were begun, it was hypothesized that separate undergraduate libraries have over-estimated the use[1] which will be made of professional reference services by undergraduate students. It was found that no formal studies had been undertaken at either Michigan or Cornell to gather data for estimating the number of questions which might be expected at the reference desks of the proposed undergraduate libraries. However, at Michigan a highly accurate forecast was made: that approximately 750 questions per week would be asked at the UGLI reference desks. During the first ten years of operation, the weekly averages have varied from a high of 900 questions per week during 1958/59 to a low of 695 questions per week in 1966/67, but when the weekly averages for the ten-year period are computed, 771 questions were asked.[2] In the case of the Michigan Undergraduate Library, the hypothesis was incorrect.

At Cornell there were no predictions of the number of questions which would be asked of the Uris reference librarians. It was estimated that a professional staff of ten librarians would be necessary to give reference assistance as well as carry on the other library services. Positions for nine librarians were then allocated in Uris Library's first budget. This proved to be an overly generous estimate of professional staff when the requests for reference assistance did not come up to expectations. It was found to be unnecessary to have two librarians on duty at the reference desks at nights, as first scheduled, and several Uris librarians also had time to work some hours each week at the reference desks of the Olin Library. Although this was excellent assistance for the Olin Reference Department and valuable experience for the individual Uris staff members, it was made possible by the prevailing philosophy of service that reference assistance was available to students but that they must take advantage of it themselves. In the case of Cornell's undergraduate library, the hypothesis was supported.

The <u>second hypothesis</u> stated that use of reference services in undergraduate libraries has decreased after the first years of operation. Detailed records of the number of questions asked at the reference desks have been kept in both the Michigan and Cornell undergraduate libraries. The Michigan UGLI documents show that during the first complete year of operation--1958/59--the total questions asked amounted to 46, 825 (32, 537 spot questions[3] and 14, 288 reference questions[4]). During the next five years, spot questions decreased until an all-time low of 11, 610 was reached in 1963/64. In the same period, reference questions increased in number each year until an all-time high of 31, 844 was attained in 1963/64. A reversal of this trend then began and has continued. The more substantive reference questions decreased in each of the next five years; spot questions increased in four of five years. During this later period, there was an overall decrease in the total number of questions asked. By 1968/69 reference questions had returned to slightly under the level set in 1958/59. But more startling is the 55% decrease from the high of 31, 844 reference questions in 1963/64 to only 14, 110 in 1968/69. While the UGLI reference services have suffered drops of 31. 1% in spot questions, 1. 2% in reference questions, and 22% in the total number of questions when 1958/59 is compared with 1968/69, undergraduates enrolled in the College of Literature, Science, and the Arts (the primary group of students served by UGLI) have increased by 69. 9%. During the same eleven years, home loans from UGLI have jumped by 117% and total book use has increased by 91%.

The situation has been basically the same at the Uris Library reference desk. During its first year, 1962/63, there were 6, 609 questions asked (3, 792 information questions,[5] 2, 800 reference questions,[6] and 17 search questions[7]). In five of the next six years, information questions decreased with the all-time low of 2, 130 occurring in 1968/69. Reference questions grew in number for two years reaching a high of 3, 951 in 1964/65. However, during three of the four most recent years, reference questions have declined. By 1968/69, reference questions numbered 3, 248; still above the level of 1962/63, but 17. 7% below the vintage year of 1964/65. With the Uris Library reference services declining by 18. 5% in total questions (but increasing by 16% in the number of reference questions), the undergraduates enrolled in the College of Arts and Sciences have increased by 10% in the seven years Uris Library has been open. During this same period, home loans from the main collection have more than doubled.

The second hypothesis that use of reference services in undergraduate libraries has decreased after the first years of operation was confirmed in both case studies of undergraduate libraries.

The third hypothesis stated that communications[8] between the staff in undergraduate libraries and the faculty concerning reference services for their students have been minimal when contrasted with communications between liberal arts college librarians and faculty members concerning available reference services for their students. In interviews with librarians in the two undergraduate libraries and through examination of documents in their files, it was found that communications with the faculty concerning reference services for their students were almost non-existent. The two areas in which undergraduate librarians were in contact with faculty were reserve books and the audio services. Only a few attempts have been made by the librarians to communicate with the faculty about reference services.

In contrast to the staffs in undergraduate libraries on university campuses, librarians of the two college libraries had extensive communications with faculty concerning reference services for their students. Earlham librarians, particularly, were in contact with faculty members through their program of library instruction and in many other ways. Although the Reference Librarian and the Science Librarian at Swarthmore had not yet achieved the degree of contact with faculty that their Earlham colleagues enjoyed, they had much greater contact than did librarians in the undergraduate libraries. At Earlham all professional staff members in the Library have faculty status; Swarthmore granted faculty status to the Reference Librarian, the Science Librarian, and the Associate Librarian in 1968. This official acceptance as peers by the faculty has made communications between librarians and faculty much easier. The situation was entirely different for librarians of the undergraduate libraries. Cornell librarians have "academic status" which is not faculty status. Of the professional staff in the Michigan Undergraduate Library, only the Head and the Assistant Head became members of the University Senate in November, 1968. The other eight librarians were ineligible.

The third hypothesis was proved in the limited cases under consideration here.

Hypothesis 4 stated that no effective means of stimulating use of reference services (such as integrating bibliographical lectures or discussions by library staff with courses at the exact time students have need of such assistance) have been developed by reference librarians in separate undergraduate libraries (there having been only a reliance on brief and general orientation lectures or tours at the beginning of the students' freshman year). The histories of library orientation at the Michigan UGLI and the Uris Library described in detail in Chapters 3 and 4, confirm the hypothesis. These two undergraduate libraries have not gone beyond brief lectures which are unconnected to specific undergraduate courses. An extensive program of library instruction integrated with courses, as illustrated by Earlham College, has never been attempted at Cornell or Michigan. Although at an earlier stage of development in their program of library instruction, librarians at Swarthmore--particularly the Science Librarian--have begun to integrate library instruction with college courses.

The fifth hypothesis conjectured that there is a difference in the types of questions asked by undergraduate students at reference desks of liberal arts college libraries and those asked by undergraduates at reference desks in undergraduate libraries on university campuses. A sub-hypothesis stated that the major difference is a greater proportion of reference questions[9] concerning bibliographical assistance at the library's catalog is asked of liberal arts college reference librarians than is asked of reference librarians in undergraduate libraries. At the University of Michigan Undergraduate Library, assistance at the catalog and the record of periodical holdings accounted for 23.8% of the reference questions in the first week of monitoring and 22.2% in the second week. In Cornell's Uris Library, assistance at the main and serials catalogs amounted to 19% and 18.3% of the total reference questions. When these undergraduate libraries are compared to the college libraries, the sub-hypothesis was confirmed at the Lilly Library of Earlham, but not at the McCabe Library of Swarthmore. Assistance at the catalog by Earlham librarians during the first week's monitoring was 27.4% of the reference questions (in 15.9% of the reference questions the librarian assisted only at the catalog and in 11.5% of the reference questions he assisted both at the catalog and with the reference collection). During the second week, assistance at the catalog was 28.1% of the reference questions (in 19.5% of the reference questions the librarian assisted only at the catalog; in 8.6% of the questions he assisted both at the catalog and with the reference collection). At Swarthmore, assistance at the catalog accounted for only 3.9% of the reference questions during the first week with a significant increase to 21.2% during the second week. However, during both weeks of monitoring, the largest proportion of reference assistance was bibliographical verification of materials not on the campus (R-3 questions). These R-3 questions constituted 34.6% and 54.5% of the reference questions. Swarthmore's strategic location near other excellent collections and the added advantage of the Reference Librarian having telephone access to the Union Library Catalogue of Pennsylvania were the factors which made bibliographical verification of materials not on the campus the most numerous kind of reference question. Thus, the fifth hypothesis and its sub-hypothesis were confirmed at Earlham College, but not at Swarthmore.

Hypothesis 6 and its sub-hypothesis predicted that there is also a difference in the types of questions asked by undergraduate students at the reference desk of a main university library and those asked by undergraduates at the reference desk of the undergraduate library on the same campus, and that the major difference is that a greater proportion of reference questions concerning bibliographical assistance at the catalog is asked of librarians at the main library reference department than is asked of reference librarians in the undergraduate library on the campus. The monitoring of questions at the Uris and Olin Libraries of Cornell University substantiated the hypothesis and its sub-section, but the data from the Undergraduate Library and the General Library at Michigan did not confirm the hypothesis and its sub-section. At the Uris Library, reference questions in which librarians assisted students with volumes in the reference collection constituted the largest number of substantive questions. The Olin librarians, in contrast, assisted students at the catalogs more frequently (38.7% of the reference questions during the first week; 33.4%, the second week). Uris librarians assisted students at the catalogs in a significantly smaller proportion of the reference questions (19%, first week; 18.3%, second week). At the University of Michigan, librarians in UGLI assisted students at the catalog in 23.8% and 22.2% of the total reference questions. Librarians at the General Library's reference desk only occasionally assisted undergraduates at the catalog or list of periodical titles (8.7% and 7.6% of the total reference questions asked by undergraduates). The great distance to the catalog from the reference desk accounted for this small proportion of catalog-assistance questions. The Information Desk near the catalog and technical service personnel working at the catalog performed this function in Michigan's General Library. Once again an hypothesis was confirmed by one case study and found not to be true in the other case of reference services on a university campus.

The seventh hypothesis concluded the conjectures made before the investigation was begun. It suggested that unassisted use by undergraduate students of the union catalog inreases use of main university libraries and decreases use of the undergraduate library on the same campus. Interviews with 474 undergraduates at the union catalog of the Michigan General Library revealed that 59% of the students had not used the catalog in the Undergraduate Library before coming to use the General Library's catalog. Among 427 Cornell undergraduates interviewed at the union catalogs of Olin Library, an even larger proportion (75.6%) had not used the Uris Library's catalog. Those who had not used the undergraduate library catalog (280 students at Michigan and 323 students at Cornell) were then asked if they usually by-passed the catalog in the undergraduate library and came to the main library's union catalog first. The affirmative responses were 65.8% at Michigan and 77.5% at Cornell. The final question posed to all undergraduates using the union catalog was: "If the Undergraduate Library had a catalog like this one which includes the holdings of all campus libraries, would you use it there or still come here?" The responses were: 41.8% of the Michigan students and 47.6% of the Cornellians would still come to the main university library's union catalog; 51.3% of the Michigan students and only 35.7% of the Cornell students would use a union catalog in the undergraduate library if that library had a duplicate copy.

The last hypothesis was confirmed at both Michigan and Cornell. There seemed to be no question that undergraduates, particularly upperclassmen, go in substantial numbers to use the union catalog in the main university library--entirely by-passing the undergraduate library's catalog in most cases. The major reason given by the undergraduates was the obvious and excellent one that holdings of all campus libraries are listed in the union catalog. It would not seem worth the high costs involved to duplicate a copy of the union catalog for the undergraduate library because only about one-half of the Michigan undergraduates and about one-third of the Cornell students would use such a catalog in the undergraduate library. The large number of volumes housed in the main university library is a magnet apparently too strong to be overcome even by the expensive duplication of the union catalog.

Other Findings and Personal Observations

Other major findings and personal observations during the monitoring of the six reference services would be beneficial to those planning new reference services for undergraduate students or to those evaluating existing reference services. These additional findings, backed by data; and the observations, more subjective in nature, were:

1. Even where telephone reference service was available (both libraries at Cornell; Earlham, and Swarthmore), students used it infrequently. Telephone questions from undergraduates accounted for only 16 (1.4%) of the 1,089 questions received from undergraduates.

2. A very brief time was spent by the librarian with each undergraduate student asking a question. There were only seven search questions (requiring from thirty minutes to one hour to answer) and only one problem question (over an hour) in the total of 3,352 undergraduate questions asked at the six reference desks included in the case studies. In 76 other instances, librarians spent five or more minutes with students. Combining these 76 questions with the eight search and problem questions reveals that in only 2.5% of the 3,352 questions did a librarian spend an extended period with the student's question. Earlham librarians spent five or more minutes assisting students with 41 questions; the other five reference department staffs combined helped individual students for five or more minutes on only 43 occasions. It is the personal opinion of the monitors in this study (backed by extensive periods of observation) that the questions were not simpler nor the staff members more able to answer questions in a shorter period of time at Cornell, Michigan, and Swarthmore, but that the Earlham librarians were more adept at and more interested in ascertaining the real needs of the student asking the question. These real needs were then answered, not the superficial question which the student may have asked when he first approached the reference librarian. Earlham librarians provided assistance to students in "that noisy, confused, iracible, fitty, and starty stage"[10] described by Rich Kean. In the subjective opinion of the monitors, the reference librarians at Cornell, Michigan, and Swarthmore were not providing as good service to students in this "fitty, starty stage" as were Earlham librarians.

3. Librarians in five of the reference departments rarely initiated the encounters with students. In only 10 (0.3%) of the 3,055 questions asked by undergraduates at the reference desks of Cornell's Uris and Olin Libraries, Michigan's Undergraduate and General Libraries, and Swarthmore's McCabe Library, did librarians approach students to offer assistance. In contrast, the reference librarians at Earlham's Lilly Library initiated 34 (11.4%) of the 297 dialogues with undergraduates, not waiting for students to gather courage to ask for assistance.

4. The reference librarians of the University of Michigan Undergraduate Library assisted more undergraduate students (1,939) during the hours of monitoring than the other five reference staffs combined (1,413 undergraduates). The 20,299 undergraduates enrolled in the Fall term, 1969 in the schools and colleges on the Ann Arbor campus were also the largest number of potential inquirers for any of the institutions studied. The undergraduates in the University of Michigan College of Literature, Science, and the Arts accounted for 12,442 of these students. The UGLI staff also assisted more inquirers (1,939) than either of the two reference departments of the main university libraries (total questions from undergraduate and graduate students, faculty, staff, and others at the Michigan General Library's reference desk during the monitoring: 1,282; Cornell's Olin Library; 1,002).

5. The hourly rate of questions by undergraduates during the monitoring was also much higher at the University of Michigan Undergraduate Library than at Cornell's Uris Library, Swarthmore's McCabe Library, or Earlham's Lilly Library. The later three had rates ranging from only 1.4 questions per hour (second week at McCabe Library) to 5.2 questions (second week at Uris Library) while the UGLI at Michigan was many times busier, with 24.7 questions per hour during the first week and 26.3 questions per hour the second week. The data place the activities at the Michigan UGLI in another magnitude of quantity when the reference services for undergraduates in these four institutions are compared.

6. Evening hours were busier at the reference desks of the two undergraduate libraries than were afternoon hours. Morning hours were least busy. This is significant for Swarthmore College, which has not instituted evening reference service, and for other libraries which wish to schedule their staff for the greatest convenience of students.

7. During the hours of monitoring, information questions (requiring only brief directional answer from reference librarian who uses no library resources) accounted for half of the total questions asked at the reference desks of the University of Michigan Undergraduate Library (53.4% during the first week; 47.8%, the second week). In contrast, information questions asked of Earlham librarians during the two weeks of monitoring amounted to 13.4% and 20.9% of the total questions. Based on only the personal observations of the monitors, two possible explanations of this significant difference are: (1) the small student body at Earlham seemed to be more familiar with the physical layout of the Lilly Library while at the University of Michigan, some of the students were unfamiliar with the Undergraduate Library, perhaps paying their first or an early visit, and (2) Earlham librarians, having fewer students to serve, had the time to receive what may have been a hesitant request for brief directions by the student, ascertain the real need of the student, and answer the more complicated question that often lay behind the original request.

8. The simplest of information questions, such as "Where is the pencil sharpener?" and "Where is the rest room?" were very infrequent during the monitoring of activity at five of six reference departments. The monitoring data clearly reveal that the calibre of questions begins at least one level higher than these simplest of directional questions. Cornell's Uris Library was the exception, with 20.9% and 26.7% of the total information questions falling in this category. This was caused by a number of requests by Cornell undergraduates to borrow a pencil or stapler and for scrap paper, which is kept at the Reference desk for distribution to students.

9. Undergraduates rarely requested bibliographical assistance with the holdings of other campus libraries (R-2 questions). The few questions concerning holdings of other campus libraries usually were for periodical holdings. Students will not know all campus resources, but reference librarians, particularly in universities, should refer students to other campus collections.

10. Bibliographical verification for undergraduates of material not on the campus (R-3) was rare in the two university library systems. However, at Swarthmore's McCabe Library, verification and interlibrary borrowing were significant parts of the reference work. This service of locating

and borrowing material lacking on the campus is usually extended to graduate students and faculty by university libraries but not to undergraduates. Swarthmore's more liberal policy treats undergraduate students as first-class library users.

11. Retrieval of factual, non-bibliographical information from any source (R-4) accounted for a substantial proportion of the total questions, particularly at the reference desks of Cornell's Olin Library (16.2% and 18.1% during the first and second weeks of monitoring), Michigan's General Library (13.4% and 18.5%), and Earlham's Lilly Library (18.7% and 19.6%). That these types of questions do not constitute an even higher proportion of the total questions may be a holdover from the tradition of librarians who were reluctant to furnish answers to factual questions, lest they be accused of spoon-feeding students instead of teaching students.

12. Counseling of students in a reader's advisory capacity (R-5) was a small proportion of the total questions --ranging from none during both weeks of monitoring at the Olin Library to 6.7% during the first week of monitoring the Earlham reference activity. In the personal opinion of the monitors, reference librarians, except at Earlham, were reluctant to assume this role and believed that it should be left to the faculty.

13. Informal personal instruction to students in the use of the library or any of its resources (R-6) constituted a small proportion of the total encounters at the six reference desks. (Naturally, some personal instruction takes place in almost all encounters between librarians and inquirers at a reference desk. The simple act of going to a particular reference source may teach the student that he might go there himself in the future when he has a similar question. However, questions were placed in the R-6 category only when more than this simple act was performed by the librarian. The R-6 questions are those instances in which the librarian overtly gave instruction to the student, spending at least some measurable amount of time in the process.) Swarthmore's Reference Librarian had the highest percentage for any one week of monitoring (8.7% during the first week), but no questions were categorized as informal instruction during the later week of the semester. The Earlham librarians gave instruction to students in 4.5% and 4.9% of the total questions during the two weeks. The reference staff in the Michigan UGLI gave instruction on

more occasions than any other reference staff (34 instances during the first week and 31 times during the second week), but these questions accounted for only 3.6% and 3.1% of the total questions.

Conclusions and Implications

One of the original justifications for the separate undergraduate library was to provide the same quality of library services for university undergraduates as was available for students in a good liberal arts college library. Keyes Metcalf stated the facts plainly:

> A student at Amherst, Williams, Dartmouth, Bowdoin, Oberlin, or one of the better women's colleges has at his or her disposal a much larger and better collection of books than has the Harvard undergraduate.[11]

Going beyond the mere provision of books, Harvie Branscomb, at the dedication of Harvard's Lamont Library in 1949, called for undergraduate library staff members who would give students "much reference direction and also [have] a better knowledge of the curriculum of study than librarians generally possess."[12] Branscomb suggested "that at last we shall have found a way to bridge the oft-discussed gap between class instruction and library service."[13]

The basic conclusion to be drawn from the limited number of case studies which have been presented is that full advantage has not been taken of the opportunities afforded by the creation of undergraduate libraries. The librarians in the Cornell and Michigan undergraduate libraries have not closed the "gap between class instruction and library service." Reference services are of low calibre. Too often the assistance given students is superficial and too brief. Although the reference services in both undergraduate libraries have been in a state of decline for several years, there have been almost no attempts to discover why or to make changes from traditional practices.

Undergraduate libraries have provided large numbers of study places for students. These seats have been heavily used. Undergraduate libraries have become one of the social centers of the campuses. They have been successful at dispensing required readings to students. The carefully selected basic book collections, which are freely accessible to all readers, have been another of the successes of undergraduate libraries. Recordings and audio equipment have been parts of most undergraduate libraries. However, there are major areas which need development: collections of visual materials (films, prints, slides, and other media); imaginative programs of library instruction; and reference assistance for individual inquirers.

Library services for undergraduate students in liberal arts colleges--particularly the programs of library instruction and individual reference assistance at Earlham College's Lilly Library--should serve as archetypes worthy of imitation by undergraduate libraries on university campuses. Although Earlham, in its highly developed library programs, may not be characteristic of even most liberal arts colleges, and although it may be more difficult for librarians at universities (with their larger numbers of students) to achieve the Earlham level of development, Evan Farber and the staff of the Lilly Library have shown ways in which other librarians could begin to improve reference services for undergraduate students. In contrast to the passive behavior of reference librarians in the undergraduate libraries--waiting for students who know little about libraries to request assistance--Earlham librarians initiated some of the reference questions by approaching students.

The undergraduate librarians also offered very limited and unimaginative instruction programs, spending relatively little time, talent, and funds on the programs. Where there was some kind of instruction for beginning students, advanced students and disadvantaged students were usually ignored. Few attempts had been made to integrate library instruction with courses taken by the students. Earlham librarians, however, had expended much time, talent, and funds in their instruction program integrated with courses. Swarthmore was beginning the development of a more extensive instruction program. There was a lack of communication between librarians and the faculty concerning reference services for students in the undergraduate libraries whereas at Earlham and Swarthmore, the librarians had initiated and achieved more extensive contact with the faculty.

On the national scene, there are hopeful signs. The Council on Library Resources and the National Endowment for the Humanities have made grants to several institutions for innovative library programs. Eastern Michigan University, for example, has received $50,000, to be matched by the university, for a five-year "Library Outreach" program. It will seek to "identify for the teaching faculty the contributions librarians are prepared to make to the students' learning, to encourage their working together to achieve this goal, and to demonstrate the role librarians can play in the motivation of students."[14] Several other colleges and universities have recently undertaken similar programs with the help of the Council on Library Resources and the National Endowment for the Humanities.

Another conclusion to be drawn from these studies is that the attitude of the individual librarian--his interest, desire to serve, willingness to help, dynamism, and imagination--may be the most important factor influencing the calibre of reference services. Whether reference services for undergraduate students are provided in a separate undergraduate library on a university campus, at the reference desk of the main university library, or in the library of a small liberal arts college, the attitude of each librarian may be the key variable. Separate undergraduate libraries exist on many university campuses. The buildings and collections have been achieved. The top priority should now become the selection of staff members who have the desire and the talent to develop library instruction programs and reference services of the highest order. Building a separate undergraduate library may still be a valid approach to the provision of library services for university undergraduates, but this is only the first step. The building will not automatically produce good service for undergraduates. In the personal opinion of this observer, only a totally service-oriented staff can begin to improve library service for undergraduates.

Research Needed

Additional case studies of reference services for undergraduate students, as well as graduate students, faculty, and other inquirers in academic libraries, are needed to continue the detailed documentation necessary for developing in the future standards for the measurement and evaluation of reference services. Samuel Rothstein has pointed out that in order to evaluate reference services, there

> would be no substitute for the knowledge and understanding that derive from detailed case studies....

> Such case studies would, in fact, seem to offer the most fruitful field for further investigation. Despite the existence of a voluminous literature on reference work, there are practically no studies offering full details in quantitative form on the reference operations of a library.... [15]

Several other useful studies have suggested themselves during the monitoring of questions and observations of reference librarians at work in four institutions. These areas were not studied in the cases here described and no data were gathered, but it is suspected that in addition to the personal attitudes of librarians, poor interview techniques by librarians of inquirers and the involvement of professionals in clerical work[16] have contributed, perhaps in large measure, to the lack of greater development of reference services. Future studies might attempt to answer these questions: Do reference librarians expect few requests for assistance from undergraduates, and with this low expectation, unconsciously help keep the requests few in number? Are questions asked by undergraduates so strongly assumed to be easy, unchallenging, and repetitive that this attitude is conveyed to students who oblige by keeping them easy and unchallenging or perhaps never returning in the future to ask for assistance? Do reference librarians answer only the tentative and very broad first question asked by a student and then dismiss him without detecting his real need? Do librarians have preconceived notions of how a question should be asked and when a student fails to frame the question in this "proper" form, is the librarian's answer brief and superficial instead of tentative and probing? Do librarians in undergraduate libraries consider themselves to be at the lowest level of reference work in a university library system, serving only third class citizens, while reference librarians in the main library and in subject libraries serve the first-class (faculty) and second-class (graduate students) citizens? How much clerical work are reference librarians performing as a conscious or unconscious escape from the more demanding professional tasks of teaching and giving reference assistance?

Accompanying these studies of librarians, there should be user studies: extensive interviews with a large number of users and non-users to ascertain who they are, what they need from reference librarians, why they do or do not return to reference librarians for assistance, and why many never ask for assistance?

Another kind of research is also needed. Anonymous questions should be asked of reference librarians in academic libraries as an unobtrusive and accurate measurement of the quality of assistance which is being received by inquirers. The studies of Lowell Martin[17] and Terence Crowley[18] of the reference and information services in public libraries provide a model for the investigations needed in academic libraries to determine the actual performance of librarians.

Summary Statement

Perhaps these case studies of reference services for undergraduate students can best be summarized by tracing the use of three prepositions--"to," "for," and "with"--in the literature of librarianship and in the minds of librarians. In the 1950's, university librarians held symposia entitled "Library Service to Undergraduates"[19] and "Library Service to Undergraduate College Students."[20] When librarians discussed reference services, they spoke of reference services to students. In the 1960's, articles began to appear with such titles as "Library Service for Undergraduates."[21] *For* undergraduates is a vast improvement over *to* undergraduates. It is not too much to read into these simple prepositions a change in attitude from paternalism to service. It is imperative that library services be carried one preposition further in the 1970's. It must be students *with* librarians. Academic librarians, and particularly the reference librarians in undergraduate libraries, must get in touch with students and truly work with them--librarians learning from students and students learning from librarians.

William M. Birenbaum wrote in his *Overlive: Power, Poverty, and the University* that

> *The most squandered, underutilized, misused, and abused educational resource in this country's colleges and universities is students*....
>
> Perhaps the most important consequence of the technological success and the new knowledge is the extent to which they have dramatically expanded everybody's ignorance. Given what there is to know and to do now, nobody can say that he knows or is doing very much. About the only significant comparisons to be made between today's college student and his teacher are these: usually the stu-

> dent is an adult somewhat younger than his teacher; each knows something the other doesn't; and both are in deep trouble. In each of these categories who holds the advantage is a moot point.
>
> ...There are an extraordinary number of campuses in this country where the faculties and the administrators in charge really think the students are a bother and a deterrent to the main business of the institution!
>
> At the same time, there is a persuasive body of evidence establishing the fact that the most bothersome students--the ones who upset the campus system the most--generally are the brightest, measuring brightness in the system's own terms. There is equally persuasive evidence indicating that in all of our formal learning systems students have a more penetrating and enduring educational impact on each other than their teachers have on them.
>
> <u>In the adult world of learning which a university should be, everybody is a teacher and everybody is a student. That's the ultimate meaning of a community of scholars.</u>[22]

Notes

1. "Use" is defined as the number of questions asked by undergraduate students at a reference desk where a professional is on duty.

2. Michigan. University. Library. Undergraduate Library. <u>Annual Report, Reference Collection and Service.</u> 1967/68, p. 2.

3. Spot questions are defined at Michigan as questions asking for information and directions which are "usually very simple, often answerable in a few words plus some directional motions."

4. Michigan defines reference questions as more substantial questions for which the librarian "explains in some detail the mechanics" of a reference volume, the catalog, the holdings records of periodicals, or other resources, perhaps going to the shelves or catalog to assist the student.

5. Information questions concern "library resources and/or their use. [They are] answered from the personal knowledge of the staff member without consulting any other library resource."

6. Reference questions are "answered through the use of library resources.... The source of information used is most frequently one which is obvious to the staff member at the time inquiry is made." Less than 15 minutes is required to answer this type of question.

7. Search questions require "more than 15 minutes to answer and, ordinarily, the use of three or more library resources."

8. "Communications" are defined as: conferences with chairmen of departments and with individual faculty members; informal discussions in any social situation; orientation sessions for new faculty; brochures, letters, memoranda or other written material sent to faculty members; and other similar methods.

9. In this section, "reference questions" refers to the more substantive questions; the brief information questions are not included in the discussion.

10. Rick Kean, "Finding People Who Feel Alienated and Alone in Their Best Impulses and Most Honest Perceptions and Telling Them They're Not Crazy," *Wilson Library Bulletin*, XLIV (September, 1969), 44.

11. Keyes D. Metcalf, "The Undergraduate and the Harvard Library, 1937-1947," *Harvard Library Bulletin*, I (Autumn, 1947), 289.

12. Harvie Branscomb, "The Future of Libraries in Academic Institutions, Part III," *Harvard Library Bulletin*, III (Autumn, 1949), 345.

13. *Ibid.*

14. "Miscellany," *College and Research Libraries News*, XXXI, No. 11 (December, 1970), 344.

15. Samuel Rothstein, "The Measurement and Evaluation of Reference Service," *Library Trends*, XII (January, 1964), 466.

16. A. Venable Lawson found that "Over 40% of the work time of the professional staff at both libraries was spent in other than professional activities" in his "Reference Service in University Libraries, Two Case Studies" (Unpublished D. L. S. dissertation, School of Library Service, Columbia University, 1970), p. 283.

17. Lowell A. Martin, Library Response to Urban Change, A Study of the Chicago Public Library (Chicago: American Library Association, 1969), pp. 27-28.

18. Terence Crowley, "The Effectiveness of Information Service in Medium Size Public Libraries" (Unpublished Ph. D. dissertation, Rutgers, The State University, 1968).

19. "Library Service to Undergraduates: A Symposium," College and Research Libraries, XIV (July, 1953), 266-75.

20. "Library Service to Undergraduate College Students, A Symposium," College and Research Libraries, XVII (March, 1956), 143-55.

21. M. W. Moss, "Library Service for Undergraduates," in The Provision and Use of Library and Documentation Services, ed. W. L. Saunders, International Series of Monographs in Library and Information Science, Vol. 4 (Oxford: Pergamon Press, 1966), 85-113.

22. William M. Birenbaum, Overlive: Power, Poverty, and the University (New York: Delacorte Press, 1969), pp. 182-84.

BIBLIOGRAPHY OF SOURCES CONSULTED

I. General Sources

A. Books

Bergen, Dan, and Duryea, E. D., eds. Libraries and the College Climate of Learning. Syracuse: Program in Higher Education of the School of Education and the School of Library Science, Syracuse University, 1964.

Birenbaum, William M. Overlive: Power, Poverty, and the University. New York: Delacorte Press, 1969.

Braden, Irene A. The Undergraduate Library. ACRL Monographs, No. 31. Chicago: American Library Association, 1970.

Branscomb, Harvie. Teaching With Books. Hamden, Connecticut: Shoe String Press, 1964. [Reprint of Chicago: Association of American Colleges and American Library Association, 1940.]

Farber, Evan I. Classified List of Periodicals for the College Library. 4th ed. rev. and enl. to July, 1957. Useful Reference Series, No. 86. Boston: F. W. Faxon, 1957. [New edition in preparation.]

Goldsen, Rose K.; Rosenberg, Morris; Williams, Robin M., Jr.; and Suchman, Edward A. What College Students Think. Princeton: Van Nostrand, 1960.

Harvard University. Library. Harvard University Library, 1638-1968. Cambridge, Mass.: Harvard University Library, 1969.

Indiana. University. Library. The Undergraduate and the Library. Bloomington: Indiana University Libraries, 1965.

Kerr, Clark. *The Uses of the University.* Cambridge: Harvard University Press, 1964.

Knapp, Patricia B. *College Teaching and the College Library.* ACRL Monographs, No. 23. Chicago: American Library Association, Association of College and Research Libraries, 1959.

________. *The Monteith College Library Experiment.* In Collaboration with Carol E. Ballingall and Gilbert E. Donahue, with the Assistance of Grace E. Dawson. New York: Scarecrow Press, 1966.

Lyle, Guy R. *The Administration of the College Library.* 3rd ed. New York: H. W. Wilson, 1961.

________. *The President, the Professor, and the College Library.* New York: H. W. Wilson, 1963.

Martin, Lowell A. *Library Response to Urban Change, A Study of the Chicago Public Library.* Chicago: American Library Association, 1969.

Metcalf, Keyes D. *Planning Academic and Research Library Buildings.* New York: McGraw-Hill, 1965.

Rowland, Arthur R., ed. *Reference Services.* Contributions to Library Literature, No. 5. Hamden, Connecticut: Shoe String Press, 1964.

Shaw, Charles B. *A List of Books for College Libraries.* 2nd prel. ed. Chicago: American Library Association, 1931.

________. *A List of Books for College Libraries, 1931-38.* Chicago: American Library Association, 1940. [A Supplement to, not a revision of, *A List of Books for College Libraries*...1931.]

Shores, Louis. *Origins of the American College Library, 1638-1800.* Contributions to Education, George Peabody College for Teachers, No. 134. Nashville: George Peabody College for Teachers, 1934.

________; Jordan, Robert; and Harvey, John, eds. *The Library-College: Contributions for American Higher Education at the Jamestown College Workshop, 1965.*

Drexel Library School Series, No. 16. Philadelphia: Drexel Press, 1966.

Stanford University. Stanford Study of Undergraduate Education, 1954-56. The Undergraduate in the University: A Report to the Faculty by the Executive Committee of the Stanford Study of Undergraduate Education, 1954-56. Written for the Executive Committee by Robert Hoopes and Hubert Marshall. Stanford: Stanford University, 1957.

United States of America Standards Institute. Sectional Committee Z39 in the Field of Library Work and Documentation. U.S.A. Standard for Library Statistics. New York: United States of America Standards Institute, 1969.

B. Periodical Articles and Essays in Monographs

Arragon, R. F. "The Relationship Between the Library and Collegiate Objectives." Library Quarterly, XXIV (October, 1954), 284-95.

Barnett, Abraham, "The University Student and the Reference Librarian." College and Research Libraries, XX (July, 1959), 321-24.

Blackburn, Robert T. "College Libraries--Indicated Failures: Some Reasons--and a Possible Remedy." College and Research Libraries, XXIV (May, 1968), 171-77.

Blake, Fay M. "The Library-College Movement Dying of Old Age at Thirty: A Personal View." Wilson Library Bulletin, XLIV (January, 1970), 557-60.

Braden, Irene A. "The Separately Housed Undergraduate Library." College and Research Libraries, XXIX (July, 1968), 281-84.

Branscomb, Harvie. "The Future of Libraries in Academic Institutions, Part III." Harvard Library Bulletin, III (Autumn, 1949), 338-46.

"Built for the Undergraduates: New Library Seats 1,905." Illinois Alumni News, XLVIII (October, 1969), 1, 3.

Burke, Redmond A. "The Separately Housed Undergraduate Library Versus the University Library." College and Research Libraries, XXXI (November, 1970), 399-402.

Carpenter, Charles A. "The Lamont Catalog as a Guide to Book Selection." College and Research Libraries, XVIII (July, 1957), 267-68.

Cassell, Jean. "The University of Texas Undergraduate Library Collection." Texas Library Journal, XXXIX (Winter, 1963), 123-26.

Coney, Donald. "The Future of Libraries in Academic Institutions, Part I." Harvard Library Bulletin, III (Autumn, 1949), 327-31.

"Conference on the Place of the Library in a University." Harvard Library Bulletin, III (Spring, 1949), 305.

Deale, H. Vail, ed. Trends in College Librarianship. Vol. 18, No. 1 of Library Trends. Urbana: University of Illinois Graduate School of Library Science, July, 1969.

"The Dedication of the Lamont Library." Harvard Library Bulletin, III (Spring, 1949), 304-5.

Dix, William S. "Library Service to Undergraduate College Students, A Symposium: Undergraduates Do Not Necessarily Require a Special Facility." College and Research Libraries, XVII (March, 1956), 148-50.

________. "Library Service to Undergraduates: A Symposium: Undergraduate Libraries." College and Research Libraries, XIV (July, 1953), 271-72.

Elkins, Kimball C. "Foreshadowings of Lamont: Student Proposals in the Nineteenth Century." Harvard Library Bulletin, VIII (Winter, 1954), 41-53.

Farber, Evan I. "But Yes! Mr. Dane." Wilson Library Bulletin, XXIX (September, 1954), 71-72.

________. "The College Library and Its Community." Alabama Librarian, V (July, 1954), 8-11.

Finzi, John C. "The University Libraries Section" [Report on Symposium entitled "The Undergraduate Library: A Time for Assessment"]. Library of Congress Information Bulletin, Appendix II, XXIX (Aug. 6, 1970), A83-85.

Freides, Thelma. "Will the Real Reference Problem Please Stand Up?" Library Journal, LXXXXI (April 15, 1966), 2008-12.

Gittelsohn, Marc. "Progress Report on the Moffitt Undergraduate Library, University of California at Berkeley." UGLI Newsletter, II (November, 1969), 1-4.

Golter, Robert. "The Afro-American Collection, Meyer Memorial Library, Stanford University." UGLI Newsletter, II (November, 1969), 4-5.

Gore, Daniel. "Anachronistic Wizard: The College Reference Librarian." Library Journal, LXXXIX (April 15, 1964), 1688-92.

________. "The Mismanagement of College Libraries: a View from the Inside." AAUP Bulletin, LII (March, 1966), 46-51.

Govan, James F. "Collegiate Education: Past and Present." Library Trends, XVIII (July, 1969), 13-28.

________. "This Is, Indeed, the Heart of the Matter." College and Research Libraries, XXIII (November, 1962), 467-72.

Gwynn, Stanley E. "The Liberal Arts Function of the University Library." Library Quarterly, XXIV (October, 1954), 311-21.

________. "Library Service to Undergraduates, A Symposium: The College Library at the University of Chicago." College and Research Libraries, XIV (July, 1953), 267-68.

Haak, John R. "Goal Determination." Library Journal, XCVI (May 1, 1971), 1573-78.

________. "Report on the Meeting of Undergraduate Librarians at A.L.A." UGLI Newsletter, I (July, 1969), 1-3.

[Haak, John R.] "A Listing of Documents Received Concerning Undergraduate Libraries." UGLI Newsletter, II (November, 1969), 10-16.

Haro, Robert P. "College Libraries for Students." Library Journal, XCIV (June 1, 1969), 2207-8.

Haviland, Morrison C. "The Reference Function of the Lamont Library." Harvard Library Bulletin, III (Spring, 1949), 297-99.

Henne, Frances. "Instruction in the Use of the Library and Library Use by Students." Conference on the Use of Printed and Audio-Visual Materials for Instructional Purposes, Columbia University, 1965. The Use of Printed and Audio-Visual Materials for Instructional Purposes. Papers Given at the Conference held at the School of Library Service, Columbia University, November 22-23, 1965, Supported by the U.S. Office of Education. Prepared by Maurice F. Tauber and Irlene R. Stephens. New York: Columbia University School of Library Service, 1966 (Reprinted 1968), 164-90.

Hinchliff, William. "Ivory Tower Ghettoes." Library Journal, XCIV (November 1, 1969), 3971-74.

Horney, Karen. "Building Northwestern's Core." Library Journal, XCVI (May 1, 1971), 1580-83.

Jestes, Edward C., and Laird, W. David. "A Time Study of General Reference Work in a University Library." Research in Librarianship, II (January, 1968), 9-16.

Jones, Frank N. "Libraries of the Harvard Houses." Harvard Library Bulletin, II (Autumn, 1948), 362-77.

Jones, Norah E. "The UCLA Experience: An Undergraduate Library--for Undergraduates!" Wilson Library Bulletin, XLV (February, 1971), 584-90.

Jordan, Robert T. "The 'Library-College,' a Merging of Library and Classroom." Libraries and the College Climate of Learning. Edited by Dan Bergen and E. D. Duryea. Syracuse: Program in Higher Education of the School of Education and the School of Library Science, Syracuse University, 1964.

Josey, E. J., and Blake, Fay M. "Educating the Academic Librarian." Library Journal, XCV (January 15, 1970), 125-30.

Kean, Rick. "Finding People Who Feel Alienated and Alone in their Best Impulses and Most Honest Perceptions and Telling Them They're Not Crazy." Wilson Library Bulletin, XLIV (September, 1969), 36-44.

Kells, H. R., and Stewart, C. T. "Summary of the Working Sessions; Conference on the Cluster College Concept." Journal of Higher Education, XXXVIII (October, 1967), 359-63.

Keniston, Kenneth. "The Sources of Student Dissent." Journal of Social Issues, XXIII (July, 1967), 108-37.

Kennedy, James R. "Library Service in Perspective." College and Research Libraries, XXV (March, 1964), 91-92.

Kuhn, Warren B. "The J. Henry Meyer Memorial Library, Stanford University." California Librarian, XXIX (April, 1968), 93-99.

________. "Princeton's New Julian Street Library." College and Research Libraries, XXIII (November, 1962), 504-8.

________. "Summary of the Responses to the Warren B. Kuhn Questionnaire [on Undergraduate Libraries]." UGLI Newsletter, II (November, 1969), 5-10.

________. "Undergraduate Libraries in a University." Library Trends, XVIII (October, 1969), 188-209.

"Lamont Library, Harvard University." Architectural Record, CV (June, 1949), 86-95.

"Library Service to Undergraduate College Students: A Symposium." College and Research Libraries, XVII (March, 1956), 143-55. Contains articles by Frank A. Lundy, William S. Dix, and Frederick H. Wagman.

"Library Service to Undergraduates: A Symposium." College and Research Libraries, XIV (July, 1953), 266-75. Contains articles by Arthur M. McAnally,

Stanley E. Gwynn, Philip J. McNiff, William S. Dix, and Wyman S. Parker.

Logan, Albert A., Jr. "College Libraries Called Inadequate in Meeting Students' Reference Needs." Chronicle of Higher Education, IV (August 3, 1970), 1.

Lovett, Robert W. "The Harvard Union Library, 1901 to 1948." Harvard Library Bulletin, II (Spring, 1948), 230-37.

________. "The Undergraduate and the Harvard Libraries, 1877-1937." Harvard Library Bulletin, I (Spring, 1947), 221-37.

Lundy, Frank A. "Library Service to Undergraduate College Students, A Symposium: The Divisional Plan Library." College and Research Libraries, XVII (March, 1956), 143-48.

McAnally, Arthur M. "Library Service to Undergraduates, A Symposium: Introductory Remarks." College and Research Libraries, XIV (July, 1953), 266.

McCarthy, Stephen A. "Library Provisions for Undergraduates in the United States." College and Research Libraries, XXVI (May, 1965), 222-24.

McKeon, Newton F. "The Future of Libraries in Academic Institutions, Part II." Harvard Library Bulletin, III (Autumn, 1949), 331-38.

McNiff, Philip J. "The Charging System of the Lamont Library." Harvard Library Bulletin, III (Autumn, 1949), 438-40.

________. "Library Service to Undergraduates, A Symposium: Lamont Library, Harvard College." College and Research Libraries, XIV (July, 1953), 269-70.

________, and Williams, Edwin E. "Lamont Library: the First Year." Harvard Library Bulletin, IV (Spring, 1950), 203-12.

Marchant, Maurice P. "Faculty-Librarian Conflict." Library Journal, XCIV (September 1, 1969), 2886-89.

Metcalf, Keyes D. "Harvard Faces Its Library Problems." Harvard Library Bulletin, III (Spring, 1949), 183-97.

________. "The Lamont Library, Part II: Function." Harvard Library Bulletin, III (Winter, 1949), 12-30.

________. "To What Extent Must We Segregate?" College and Research Libraries, VIII (October, 1957), 399-401.

________. "The Undergraduate and the Harvard Library, 1765-1877." Harvard Library Bulletin, I (Winter, 1947), 29-51.

________. "The Undergraduate and the Harvard Library, 1937-1947." Harvard Library Bulletin, I (Autumn, 1947), 288-305.

Miller, Robert A. "Indiana's Three-In-One." Library Journal, XCIV (December 1, 1969), 4399.

Mills, Elizabeth. "The Separate Undergraduate Library." College and Research Libraries, XXIX (March, 1968), 144-56.

Moss, M. W. "Library Service for Undergraduates." The Provision and Use of Library and Documentation Services. Edited by W. L. Saunders. International Series of Monographs in Library and Information Science, Vol. 4. Oxford: Pergamon Press, 1966, 85-113.

Mount, Ellis. "Communication Barriers and the Reference Question." Special Libraries, LVII (October, 1966), 575-78.

Muller, Robert H. "Master Planning for University Libraries." Library Trends, XVIII (October, 1969), 138-49.

________. "The Undergraduate Library Trend at Large Universities." Advances in Librarianship, Vol. 1. Edited by Melvin J. Voigt. New York: Academic Press, 1970, 113-32.

Orne, Jerrold. "The Undergraduate Library." Library Journal, XCV (June 15, 1970), 2230-33.

Packard, Frederick C. "The Harvard Vocarium Disc." Harvard Library Bulletin, III (Autumn, 1949), 441-45.

________. "Harvard's Vocarium Has Attained Full Stature." Library Journal, LXXV (January 15, 1950), 69-74.

Page, B. S. "Library Provision for Undergraduates in England." College and Research Libraries, XXVI (May, 1965), 219-22.

Parker, Wyman S. "Library Service to Undergraduates, A Symposium: The Vital Core." College and Research Libraries, XIV (July, 1953), 272-75.

Pautzsch, Richard O. "The Classification Scheme for the Lamont Library." Harvard Library Bulletin, IV (Winter, 1950), 126-27.

Powell, Lawrence Clark. "Shoe on the Other Foot: From Library Administration to User." Wilson Library Bulletin, XLV (December, 1970), 384-89.

"Preparations for the Lamont Library." Harvard Library Bulletin, II (Spring, 1948), 270-71.

Ransom, Harry H. "Academic Center: A Plan for an Undergraduate Library." Library Chronicle of the University of Texas, VI (Winter, 1960), 48-50.

________. "Arts and Sciences: The College Library." Texas Quarterly, II (Winter, 1959), 7-12.

Reames, J. Mitchell. "First in the South: Undergraduate Library, University of South Carolina." South Carolina Librarian, III (March, 1959), 22-23.

________. "Undergraduate Library, University of South Carolina." Southeastern Librarian, X (Fall, 1960), 130-36.

Rogers, Rutherford D. "Measurement and Evaluation." Library Trends, III (October, 1954), 177-87.

Rohlf, Robert H. "The Freshman-Sophomore Library at Minnesota." College and Research Libraries, XIV (April, 1953), 164-66.

Rothstein, Samuel. "The Measurement and Evaluation of Reference Service." Library Trends, XII (January, 1964), 456-72.

Shepley, Henry R. "The Lamont Library, Part I: Design." Harvard Library Bulletin, III (Winter, 1949), 5-11.

Shores, Louis. "The Measure of Reference." Southeastern Librarian, XI (Winter, 1961), 297-302.

________. "The Undergraduate and His Library." The Library in the University: The University of Tennessee Library Lectures, 1949-1966. Hamden, Connecticut: Shoe String Press, 1967, 199-207.

"Standards for College Libraries." College and Research Libraries, XX (July, 1959), 274-80.

Sweeney, John L. "A Place for Poetry: The Woodberry Poetry Room in Widener and Lamont." Harvard Library Bulletin, VIII (Winter, 1954), 65-73.

Tauber, Maurice F.; Cook, C. Donald; and Logsdon, Richard H. "The College Library" and "The Undergraduate Library Problem at Columbia." The Columbia University Libraries. New York: Columbia University Press, 1958, 152-62.

Taylor, Robert S. "The Process of Asking Questions." American Documentation, XIII (October, 1962), 391-96.

________. "Question-Negotiation and Information Seeking in Libraries." College and Research Libraries, XXIX (May, 1968), 178-94.

"There Are No Barriers Between Students and Books." University of North Carolina, Chapel Hill Alumni Review, LVII (October, 1968), 12-18.

UGLI Newsletter, No. 1, July, 1969- . (Edited by John R. Haak, University of California at San Diego, La Jolla, California.)

Vavrek, Bernard F. "Eliminate the Reference Department." RQ, IX (Fall, 1969), 33-34.

Weber, David C. "Stanford: Precision Instrument for Undergraduates." Library Journal, XCII (December 1, 1967), 4351-52.

White, Lucien W. "University of Illinois Award Winning Undergraduate Library." Illinois Libraries, L (December, 1968), 1042-46.

Wilkinson, Billy R. "A Screaming Success as Study Halls." Library Journal, XCVI (May 1, 1971), 1567-71.

Williams, Edwin E. "The Selection of Books for Lamont." Harvard Library Bulletin, III (Autumn, 1949), 386-94.

C. Reports, Proceedings, Unpublished Material, and Miscellany

Allen, Kenneth S. "Proposed Undergraduate Library--Food Service Building, University of Washington, Seattle." American Library Association, 1967 Library Buildings Institute, Buildings Committee for College and University Libraries, June 5, 1967. (Mimeographed.)

Association of Research Libraries. Academic Library Statistics, 1968/69. Washington, D.C.: Association of Research Libraries, 1969.

Braden, Irene A. "The Undergraduate Library--The First 20 Years." Paper presented at the Institute on Training for Service in Undergraduate Libraries, University of California, San Diego, August 17-21, 1970.

________. "The Undergraduate Library on the University Campus." Unpublished Ph.D. dissertation, Department of Library Science, University of Michigan, 1967.

California. University. San Diego. Library. "Proposal [to the U.S. Office of Education] for an Institute Entitled Training for Service in Undergraduate Libraries, August 17-21, 1970." Director: Melvin J. Voigt. La Jolla: University Library, University of California at San Diego, 1969. (Mimeographed.)

Conference on the Present Status and Future Prospects of Reference/Information Service, Columbia University,

1966. The Present Status and Future Prospects of Reference/Information Service. Proceedings of the Conference held at the School of Library Service, Columbia University, March 30-April 1, 1966, under the Sponsorship of Columbia University School of Library Service and the American Library Association Reference Services Division. Edited by Winifred B. Linderman. Chicago: American Library Association, 1967.

Conference on Use, Mis-Use, and Non-Use of Academic Libraries, 1970. Use, Mis-Use, and Non-Use of Academic Libraries. Proceedings of the New York Library Association College and University Libraries Section Spring Conference held at Jefferson Community College, Watertown, May 1-2, 1970. Edited by the Committee on the Requirements of the Academic Library Users, John Lubans, Jr., Chairman. [Troy, New York: Rensselaer Polytechnic Institute, 1970.]

Crowley, Terence. "The Effectiveness of Information Service in Medium Size Public Libraries." Unpublished Ph.D. dissertation, Rutgers, The State University, 1968.

Gore, Daniel. "On Teaching Bibliography; Or Why I Am, and Choose to Remain, a Librarian." Paper read before Missouri Association of College and Research Libraries, St. Louis, April 29, 1969.

Haak, John R. "Goal Determination and the Undergraduate Library." Paper presented at the Institute on Training for Service in Undergraduate Libraries, University of California, San Diego, August 17-21, 1970.

Hieber, Caroline E. An Analysis of Questions and Answers in Libraries. Studies in the Man-System Interface in Libraries, Report No. 1. Bethlehem, Pennsylvania: Center for Information Sciences, Lehigh University, 1966.

Jones, Norah E. "The College Library at UCLA." Paper read before the University Libraries Section, Association of College and Research Libraries, American Library Association, Detroit, June 29, 1970.

Knapp, Patricia B. "The Library, the Undergraduate and the Teaching Faculty." Paper presented at the Institute on Training for Service in Undergraduate Libraries, University of California, San Diego, August 17-21, 1970.

Kuhn, Warren B. "Planning the Undergraduate Library." Paper presented at the Institute on Training for Service in Undergraduate Libraries, University of California, San Diego, August 17-21, 1970.

Lawson, A. Venable. "Reference Service in University Libraries, Two Case Studies." Unpublished D. L. S. dissertation, School of Library Service, Columbia University, 1970.

Lundy, Frank A. "The Undergraduate Library at the University of Nebraska: the Nebraska Hall Project, 1969." February, 1969. (Mimeographed.)

Lynch, Mary Jo, and Menges, Gary L. "A Proposal for Undergraduate Library Service, 1970-1980." University of Massachusetts/Amherst Library, February 2, 1970. (Mimeographed.)

Metcalf, Keyes D. Report on the Harvard University Library: A Study of Present and Prospective Problems. Cambridge: Harvard University Library, 1955.

Nelson Associates, Inc. Undergraduate and Junior College Libraries in the United States, A Report Prepared for the National Advisory Commission on Libraries. New York: Nelson Associates, Inc., 1968.

Saidel, Cynthia A. "A Survey of the Lamont Library of Harvard College." Unpublished Master's thesis, School of Library Service, Columbia University, 1952.

"Selected Library Statistics." 1965/66-1968/69. [Collected and Distributed by Bowdoin College Library.] (Mimeographed.)

Taylor, Constance M. "Meeting the Needs of Undergraduates in Large University Libraries." Unpublished Master's thesis, Graduate School of Library Science, University of Texas, 1956.

Toombs, Kenneth E. "The Undergraduate Library at South Carolina." Paper read before the University Libraries Section, Association of College and Research Libraries, American Library Association, June 29, 1970.

Voigt, Melvin J. "The Undergraduate Library; The Collection and Its Selection." Paper presented at the Institute on Training for Service in Undergraduate Libraries, University of California, San Diego, August 17-21, 1970.

Wilkinson, Billy R. "Are We Fooling Ourselves About Undergraduate Libraries?" Paper read before the University Libraries Section, Association of College and Research Libraries, American Library Association, June 29, 1970.

________. "The Undergraduate Library's Public Service Record: Reference Services." Paper presented at the Institute on Training for Service in Undergraduate Libraries, University of California, San Diego, August 17-21, 1970.

II. Sources for the Study of the University of Michigan Libraries

A. The University

1. Books, Essays, and Periodical Articles

"The College of Literature, Science, and the Arts." Michigan. University. The University of Michigan, An Encyclopedic Survey. Edited by Wilfred B. Shaw. 9 Vols. Ann Arbor: University of Michigan Press, 1941-58, III and IV.

Krause, Edward H., and Woodburne, Lloyd S. "The Administration and Curriculums of the College of Literature, Science, and the Arts." Michigan. University. The University of Michigan, An Encyclopedic Survey. Edited by Wilfred B. Shaw. 9 Vols. Ann Arbor: University of Michigan Press, 1941-58, III, 425-37.

Michigan. University. The University of Michigan, An Encyclopedic Survey. Edited by Wilfred B. Shaw. 9 Vols. Ann Arbor: University of Michigan Press, 1941-58.

Peckham, Howard H. The Making of the University of Michigan, 1817-1967. Ann Arbor: University of Michigan Press, 1967.

Shaw, Wilfred B., and Robbins, Frank E. "The Early History of the University of Michigan." Michigan. University. The University of Michigan, An Encyclopedic Survey. Edited by Wilfred B. Shaw. 9 Vols. Ann Arbor: University of Michigan Press, 1941-58, I, 26-38.

"University Enrollment Increases...." Michigan Daily (Ann Arbor). October 6, 1969.

2. Annual Reports

Michigan. University. President's Reports. 1956/57-1958/59. [By Harlan Hatcher.]

________. President's Report. January, 1969. [By R. W. Fleming.]

________. Office of University Housing. Residence Halls Libraries. Annual Report. 1968/69. [Contains annual reports of all twelve residence halls libraries.]

3. Catalogs, Bulletins, Announcements, Special Reports, and Miscellany

Michigan. University. College of Literature, Science, and the Arts, 1969-70, Official Publications, Vol. LXX, No. 112. Ann Arbor: University of Michigan, 1969.

________. College of Literature, Science, and the Arts, Residential College, 1969/70. Ann Arbor: University of Michigan, 1969.

________. General Information, 1970-71, Official Publications, Vol. LXX, No. 146. Ann Arbor: University of Michigan, 1969.

________. Office of University Housing. "Manual of Policies for Residence Halls Libraries at the University of Michigan." Prepared by Charlene A. Coady and Onva K. Boshears, Jr. Revised June, 1969 by Virginia J. Reese. Ann Arbor, 1969. (Mimeographed.)

________. Monthly Reports of Residence Halls Libraries. September, 1968-December, 1969.

B. The University Libraries

1. Books, Essays, and Periodical Articles

Bishop, William W. "The Library Service to the University." Michigan Alumnus, XXXV (May 18, 1929), 611-14.

________. "The University Library to 1941." Michigan. University. The University of Michigan, An Encyclopedic Survey. Edited by Wilfred B. Shaw. 9 Vols. Ann Arbor: University of Michigan Press, 1941-58, VIII, 1369-84.

"The Clements Library." Research News [University of Michigan Office of Research Administration], XV (June, 1965), 1-16.

Davis, Raymond C. "The Growth of the Library." Michigan. University. Public Exercises on the Completion of the Library Building of the University of Michigan, December 12, 1883. Ann Arbor: University of Michigan, 1884, 13-17.

"The General Library." Research News [University of Michigan Office of Research Administration], XV (April, 1965), 1-12.

Michigan. University. Public Exercises on the Completion of the Library Building of the University of Michigan, December 12, 1883. Ann Arbor: University of Michigan, 1884.

Rice, Warner G. "The University Library, 1941-1953." Michigan. University. The University of Michigan, An Encyclopedic Survey. Edited by Wilfred B. Shaw. 9 Vols. Ann Arbor: University of Michigan Press, 1941-58, VIII, 1384-97.

Shaw, Wilfred B. "General Library Building." Michigan. University. The University of Michigan, An Encyclopedic Survey. Edited by Wilfred B. Shaw. 9 Vols. Ann Arbor: University of Michigan Press, 1941-58, VIII, 1633-35.

________. "The Old Library Building." Michigan. University. The University of Michigan, An Encyclopedic Survey. Edited by Wilfred B. Shaw. 9 Vols. Ann Arbor: University of Michigan Press, 1941-58, VIII, 1674-75.

2. Handbooks, Guides, and Manuals

Koch, Theodore W. Handbook of the Libraries of the University of Michigan. Ann Arbor: George Wahr, 1910.

Michigan. University. Library. "How to Use the General Library Card Catalog." [Ann Arbor, n. d.] (Mimeographed.)

________. The University of Michigan General Library Building. [Ann Arbor: University of Michigan Library, n. d.]

________. The University of Michigan Library Handbook for the Faculty. Preliminary Ed. Ann Arbor: University of Michigan Library, 1963.

3. Annual Reports

Michigan. University. Library. Annual Reports of the Director. 1953/54-1968/69. [By Frederick H. Wagman.]

4. Statistical Reports

Michigan. University. Library. Circulation Department. "Daily Attendance, General Library." September 29-October 3, 1969; October 6-10, 1969; and November 10-14, 1969. (Typewritten.)

________. "Monthly Statistical Sheets." September, October, and November, 1969. (Typewritten.)

________. Graduate Reserve Service. "Monthly Statistics." October and November, 1969. (Typewritten.)

________. Technical Services Department. "Weekly Reports, Catalog Information Desk." September 29-October 3, 1969; October 6-10, 1969; and November 10-14, 1969. (Typewritten.)

5. Special Reports, Scripts, Minutes, Unpublished Papers, and Miscellany

Michigan. University. Library. Organization Charts, University Library of the University of Michigan. Ann Arbor: University of Michigan Library, 1968.

________. University of Michigan Library Plant Expansion. Ann Arbor: University of Michigan Library, [1957].

________. Operations Research Unit. General Library Utilization Survey. [A Preliminary Report of a Survey of 2,764 Library Patrons, Winter Term, 1968. Prepared by Pat Fulford and D. Carr.] (Typewritten.)

________. General Library Utilization Survey. [Final Report of a Survey of 2,705 Library Patrons, Winter Term, 1968. Prepared by Pat Fulford and Noel M. Ernst. November 13, 1969.] (Typewritten.)

________. Survey Research Center. Faculty Appraisal of a University Library. A Report of the Responses of the University of Michigan Faculty to a Mail Questionnaire Concerning the University Library's Collections, Services, and Facilities as of April, 1961. Prepared for the Library Council under the Direction of Charles F. Cannell and Jack M. McLeod, in Collaboration with a University Library Committee Consisting of Fred L. Dimock [and Others] Robert H. Muller, Chairman. Ann Arbor: University of Michigan Library, 1961.

Wagman, Frederick H. "The Library Situation and the Program of Plant Expansion." Paper presented to the Library Committee of the College of Literature, Science, and the Arts, University of Michigan, Ann Arbor, [October] 1954.

C. The Undergraduate Library

1. Books, Essays, and Periodical Articles

Braden, Irene A. "The Undergraduate Library, The University of Michigan." The Undergraduate Library. By Irene A. Braden. ACRL Monographs, No. 31. Chicago: American Library Association, 1970, 29-62.

Cook, J. J. "Increased Seating in the Undergraduate Library: A Study in Effective Space Utilization." Case Studies in Systems Analysis in a University Library. Edited by Barton R. Burkhalter. Metuchen, New Jersey: Scarecrow Press, 1968.

Eiker, Meredith. "Ten Years in Circulation." Michigan Daily (Ann Arbor). January 12, 1968.

Keniston, Roberta. "Circulation Gains at Michigan." Library Journal, LXXXIII (December 1, 1958), 3357-59.

________. "The University of Michigan Undergraduate Library." Michigan Librarian, XXV (June, 1959), 24-25.

Meier, Richard L. Social Change in Communications-Oriented Institutions. University of Michigan Mental Health Research Institute Reports, No. 10. Ann Arbor: University of Michigan, 1961.

"A New Intellectual Center." Michigan Alumnus, LXIV (December 14, 1957), 151-53.

[Packard, James]. "The Undergraduate Library." Research News [University of Michigan Office of Research Administration], XV (May, 1965), 1-12.

"The 'Ugli' Routine: Student Subculture." Michigan Daily (Ann Arbor). February 16, 1969.

"The University of Michigan Undergraduate Library, Ann Arbor, Michigan." News of the Lite-Weight Concrete Products Industry, XXI (October, 1958), 1-13.

Wagman, Frederick H. "Library Service to Undergraduate College Students, A Symposium: The Case for the

Separate Undergraduate Library." College and Research Libraries, XVII (March, 1956), 150-55.

________. "The Undergraduate Library of the University of Michigan." College and Research Libraries, XX (May, 1959), 179-88.

2. Handbooks, Guides, and Manuals

Michigan. University. Library. Undergraduate Library. "Fact Sheet on the Undergraduate Library." Ann Arbor, n. d. (Mimeographed.)

________. "Fact Sheet, The University of Michigan Undergraduate Library." Ann Arbor, September, 1961. (Mimeographed.)

________. UGL: Guide to the University of Michigan Undergraduate Library. Ann Arbor: University of Michigan, 1969.

________. "UGLI's Automated Reserve System." Ann Arbor, n. d. (Mimeographed.)

________. The Undergraduate Library Building of the University of Michigan. Ann Arbor: University of Michigan Library, 1960.

________. "The University of Michigan Undergraduate Library Audio Room." Ann Arbor, n. d. (Mimeographed.)

________. "The University of Michigan Undergraduate Library Reserve Information." Ann Arbor, n. d. (Mimeographed.)

3. Annual Reports

Michigan. University. Library. Undergraduate Library. Annual Reports. 1957/58-1962/63. [By Roberta Keniston.]

________. Annual Reports. 1963/64-1968/69. [By Rose-Grace Faucher.]

________. Annual Reports, Undergraduate Library Reference Collection and Reference Service. 1958/59-1968/69.

4. Statistical Reports

Michigan. University. Library. Undergraduate Library. "Charging Desk Monthly Reports." October and November, 1969. (Typewritten.)

________. "Reference Desk Statistics, Desk No. 1 and Desk No. 2." October 6-12, 1969 and November 10-16, 1969. (Typewritten.)

________. "Reserve Collection: Monthly Reports." October and November, 1969. (Typewritten.)

________. "Reserve Collection: Weekly Circulation Statistics." October 5-11, 1969 and November 9-15, 1969. (Typewritten.)

________. "Stacks--Monthly Reports." October and November, 1969. (Typewritten.)

________. "Weekly Attendance and Stack Statistics." October 5-11, 1969 and November 9-15, 1969. (Typewritten.)

________. "Weekly Circulation Statistics." October 5-11, 1969 and November 9-15, 1969. (Typewritten.)

5. Special Reports, Scripts, Minutes, Unpublished Papers, and Miscellany

Michigan. University. Library. Advisory Committee on the Undergraduate Library. Minutes of Meetings. 1954-56. (Typewritten.)

________. "Preliminary Program for the Undergraduate Library." Ann Arbor, August 18, 1954. (Mimeographed.)

________. "Program for an Undergraduate Library." Submitted by Frederick H. Wagman, Director of the University Library, for the Advisory Committee on the

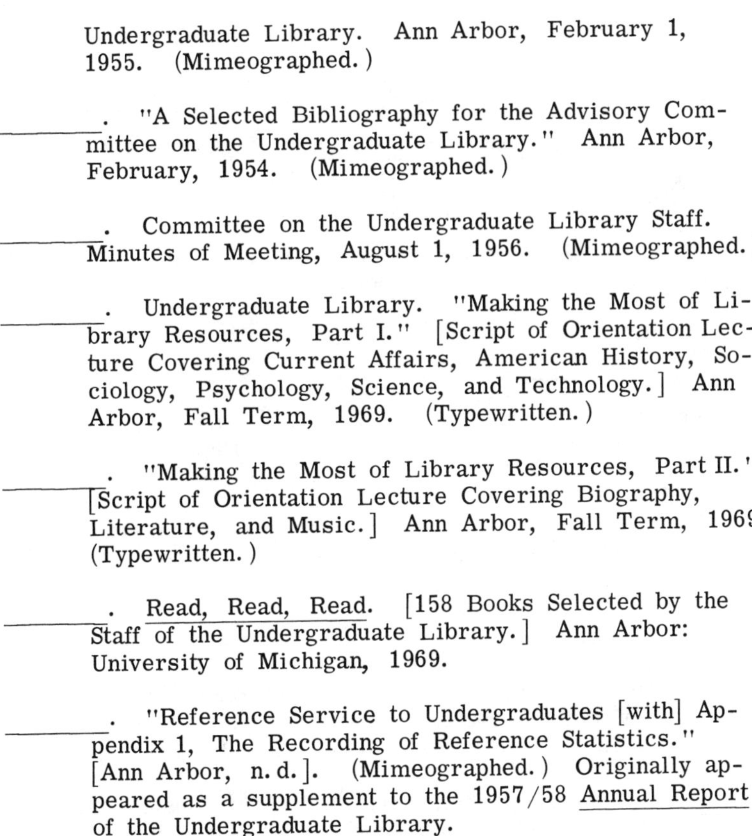

Undergraduate Library. Ann Arbor, February 1, 1955. (Mimeographed.)

________. "A Selected Bibliography for the Advisory Committee on the Undergraduate Library." Ann Arbor, February, 1954. (Mimeographed.)

________. Committee on the Undergraduate Library Staff. Minutes of Meeting, August 1, 1956. (Mimeographed.)

________. Undergraduate Library. "Making the Most of Library Resources, Part I." [Script of Orientation Lecture Covering Current Affairs, American History, Sociology, Psychology, Science, and Technology.] Ann Arbor, Fall Term, 1969. (Typewritten.)

________. "Making the Most of Library Resources, Part II." [Script of Orientation Lecture Covering Biography, Literature, and Music.] Ann Arbor, Fall Term, 1969. (Typewritten.)

________. *Read, Read, Read.* [158 Books Selected by the Staff of the Undergraduate Library.] Ann Arbor: University of Michigan, 1969.

________. "Reference Service to Undergraduates [with] Appendix 1, The Recording of Reference Statistics." [Ann Arbor, n.d.]. (Mimeographed.) Originally appeared as a supplement to the 1957/58 *Annual Report* of the Undergraduate Library.

________. [Script of Orientation Lecture With Slides.] Ann Arbor, Fall, 1969. (Typewritten.)

________. [Untitled Paper Describing the Orientation Program of the Undergraduate Library.] Ann Arbor, n.d. (Typewritten.)

Stewart, Rolland C. "The Undergraduate Library Collection." Paper presented at the Institute on Book Selection and Acquisitions, University of California, San Diego, August 25-September 5, 1969.

Wilkinson, Billy R. "Visit to the University of Michigan Undergraduate Library, Memorandum to Stephen A. McCarthy, Felix Reichmann, and G. F. Shepherd, Jr.

[Cornell University Libraries]." Ithaca, [1961]. (Typewritten.)

D. Reference Department, General Library

1. Handbooks, Guides, and Manuals

Material on the Reference Department is included in the items listed under II. B. 2 above.

2. Annual Reports

Michigan. University. Library. Reference Department. Annual Reports of the Reference Department. 1956/57 and 1957/58. [By Margaret I. Smith.]

________. Annual Reports of the Reference Department. 1958/59-1968/69. [By Agnes N. Tysse.]

3. Statistical Reports

Michigan. University. Library. Reference Department. "Monthly Reports." September, 1968-November, 1969. (Typewritten.) [By Agnes N. Tysse.]

________. "Weekly Statistics, Information Desk, Reference Department." October 6-10, 1969 and November 10-14, 1969. (Typewritten.)

4. Special Reports, Scripts, Minutes, Unpublished Papers and Miscellany

Michigan. University. Library. Reference Department. "Examples of Letter Inquiries Received in Reference [Department, General Library] During October, 1968." (Typewritten.)

________. "Samples of In-Person Inquiries at the Reference Desk [General Library] During March 1969 and Samples of Telephone Questions Received in Reference Department During March, 1969." (Typewritten.)

III. Sources for the Study of the Cornell University Libraries

A. The University

1. Books, Essays, and Periodical Articles

"Abolition Asked for Frosh English." *Cornell Daily Sun* (Ithaca), December 1, 1965.

Becker, Carl L. *Cornell University: Founders and the Founding.* Ithaca: Cornell University Press, 1943.

Bishop, Morris. *A History of Cornell.* Ithaca: Cornell University Press, 1962.

Cornell University. *Aspects of a University.* Ithaca: Cornell University, 1970.

________. *Cornell University: "In Excellence and Diversity."* Ithaca: Cornell University, [1961].

Guerlac, Rita. *An Introduction to Cornell.* Ithaca: Cornell University, 1962.

White, Andrew Dickson. *Autobiography of Andrew Dickson White.* 2 Vols. New York: Century, 1905.

2. Annual Reports

Cornell University. *Reports of the President.* 1966/67 and 1967/68. [By James A. Perkins.]

3. Catalogs, Bulletins, Announcements, Special Reports, and Miscellany

Cornell University. *College of Arts and Sciences, 1969-70, Announcements,* Vol. LX, No. 18. Ithaca: Cornell University, 1969.

________. *General Information, 1969-70, Announcements,* Vol. LXI, No. 1. Ithaca: Cornell University, 1969.

________. Office of the Vice-President for Academic Affairs. "Report on Undergraduate Education." *Cornell Chronicle,* I (October 30, 1969), 5-11.

________. Registrar. "Registration--Fall Term, 1968." Ithaca, October 4, 1968. (Mimeographed.)

________. "Registration--Fall Term, 1969." Ithaca, October 17, 1969. (Mimeographed.)

________. "Undergraduate Enrollment by Class--Fall Term, 1969." Ithaca, October 17, 1969. (Mimeographed.)

Rosenberg, Edgar. *The Freshman Humanities Courses.* [Ithaca: Cornell University, 1966.]

B. The University Libraries

1. Books, Essays, and Periodical Articles

Cantor, Enid A. "The Cornell Library Complex." *Cornell Daily Sun* (Ithaca), October 10, 1962.

Cornell University. *Exercises at the Opening of the Library Building, October 7, 1891.* Ithaca: Cornell University, 1891.

Cornell University Libraries Bulletin. No. 1, August 4, 1959-
(Title from 1959-October 7, 1963: *Information Bulletin.*)

Cornell University. Library. *The Cornell Library Conference. Papers Read at the Dedication of the Central Libraries, October, 1962.* Ithaca: Cornell University Library, 1964.

________. *The Laying of the Cornerstone, The John M. Olin Library at Cornell University.* Ithaca: Cornell University, 1960.

________. *Program of the Conference and Dedication of the John M. Olin Library and the Uris Library, October 9 and 10, 1962.* Ithaca: Cornell University, 1962.

Einaudi, Mario. "Our Biggest Day." Cornell Alumni News, LXIII (April 15, 1961), 500-9.

Ex Libris, Notes from Cornell University Libraries, Vol. 1, April, 1969- . (Newsletter sent to Cornell faculty.)

Guerlac, Rita. "Cornell's Library." Cornell Library Journal, No. 2 (Spring, 1967), 1-33.

"The John M. Olin Library." Cornell Daily Sun (Ithaca), February 10, 1961. [Entire Issue Devoted to the New Library.]

Keast, William Rea. "The True University of These Days Is a Collection of Books." Cornell University. Library. The Cornell Library Conference, Papers Read at the Dedication of the Central Libraries, October, 1962. Ithaca: Cornell University Library, 1964, 41-50.

McCarthy, Stephen A. "The Cornell Library System." Cornell University. Library. The Cornell Library Conference, Papers Read at the Dedication of the Central Libraries, October, 1962. Ithaca: Cornell University Library, 1964, 25-32.

________. "The Cornell Library System: Present and Future." Cornell Daily Sun (Ithaca), October 10, 1962.

________. "Olin: Apex of the System." Cornell Alumni News, LXIII (April 15, 1961), 510.

McQuade, Walter. "Cornell Rediscovers Architecture." Architectural Forum, (February, 1962), 64-69.

Potter, John M. A Library Is a High Place. Ithaca: Cornell University, n.d.

"Study Group Analyzes Libraries' Future Needs." Cornell Chronicle, I (November 6, 1969), 1.

Towne, Jackson E. "Building the Cornell Library." Cornell Alumni News, LV (June 15, 1953), 533.

"Video Center," The CUL Weekly Gazette, I (August 17, 1970), 3.

Warner, Charles H., Jr. "The Central Library Buildings." Cornell University. Library. The Cornell Library Conference, Papers Read at the Dedication of the Central Libraries, October, 1962. Ithaca: Cornell University Library, 1964, 33-40.

2. Handbooks, Guides, and Manuals

Cornell University. Library. The Central Libraries. Ithaca: Cornell University, [1962].

________. Cornell University Library Service. Ithaca: Cornell University Library, 1965.

________. The Cornell University Library: Some Highlights. Ithaca: Cornell University Library, 1965.

________. Directory of Locations, Hours, Services, Cornell University Libraries. Ithaca: Cornell University Library, 1969.

________. Handbook of the Libraries for Graduate Students and Faculty. 6th ed. Ithaca: Cornell University Library, 1967.

________. John M. Olin Library Handbook. Ithaca: Cornell University Library, 1969.

________. Mann Library. Albert R. Mann Library. Ithaca: Albert R. Mann Library, n. d.

________. An Introduction to Albert R. Mann Library, New York State Colleges of Agriculture and Human Ecology. Ithaca: Albert R. Mann Library, 1969.

3. Annual Reports

Cornell University. Library. Annual Reports of the Director of the University Libraries. 1960/61-1966/67. [By Stephen A. McCarthy.]

________. Annual Report of the Director of the University Libraries. 1967/68. [By G. F. Shepherd, Jr.]

________. *Annual Reports of the Director of the University Libraries.* 1968/69 and 1969/70. [By David Kaser.]

4. Statistical Reports

Cornell University. Library. "Library Use Surveys; May 17-20, 1965; December 6-9, 1965; and January 10-13, 1967." Ithaca, 1965 and 1967. (Typewritten.)

________. Olin Library. Circulation Department. "Daily Attendance." October 27-31, 1969; November 3-7, 1969; and December 8-12, 1969. (Typewritten.)

________. "Daily Statistics." October 27-31, 1969; November 3-7, 1969; and December 8-12, 1969. (Typewritten.)

________. "Monthly Reports." October, 1969-December, 1969. (Typewritten.)

U.S. Office of Education. "Higher Education General Information Survey, Library Collections, Staff, Expenditures, and Salaries." (Cornell University's Report for 1968/69.)

5. Special Reports, Scripts, Minutes, Unpublished Papers, and Miscellany

Cornell University. Library. "Central Library Facilities." [Draft of a Statement Outlining History of Various Library Building Plans.] Ithaca, n.d. (Typewritten.)

________. "Library Building Proposals." [Charts Giving Costs and Other Details of Eight Different Approaches to Expansion of Library Facilities.] Ithaca, n.d. (Mimeographed.)

________. Committee on Reference Statistics Terminology. "Definitions of Reference Statistics Terminology." Ithaca, July 1, 1962. (Mimeographed.)

[McCarthy, Stephen A. "Introduction" to the] "Central Library Facilities: the Wood Report; the Metcalf Report." Ithaca, 1955. (Typewritten.)

Wilson, Louis Round; Downs, Robert B.; and Tauber, Maurice F. Report of a Survey of the Libraries of Cornell University for the Library Board of Cornell University, October 1947-February 1948. Ithaca: Cornell University, 1948.

Wood, Frederic C. "The Expansion of the Cornell Library." [Report of Frederic C. Wood, Consulting Engineer, to Cornell University, July 8, 1955.] Greenwich, Connecticut, 1955. (Typewritten.)

C. The Uris Library

1. Books, Essays, and Periodical Articles

Barnes, Christopher R. "Classification and Cataloging of Spoken Records in Academic Libraries." College and Research Libraries, XXVIII (January, 1967), 49-52.

Braden, Irene A. "Uris Library, Cornell University." The Undergraduate Library. By Irene A. Braden. ACRL Monographs, No. 31. Chicago: American Library Association, 1970, 93-115.

Cantor, Enid A. "The Old Becoming the New Undergraduate Library." Cornell Daily Sun (Ithaca), March 14, 1962.

"A Second Youth for Main Library." Cornell Alumni News, LXV (January, 1963), 4-17, 20.

"Staff Transfers [to Undergraduate Library] Announced." Cornell University Libraries Information Bulletin, No. 55 (April 4, 1962), 1.

"Undergraduate Library." Cornell University Libraries Information Bulletin, No. 42 (July 25, 1961), 1.

Whitten, Benjamin G., and Wilkinson, Billy R. "A Day of Books and Students." Cornell Alumni News, LXIX (July, 1966), 7-11.

Wilkinson, Billy R. "The Arthur H. Dean Book Collection Contest." Cornell Library Journal, No. 3 (Autumn, 1967), 55-56.

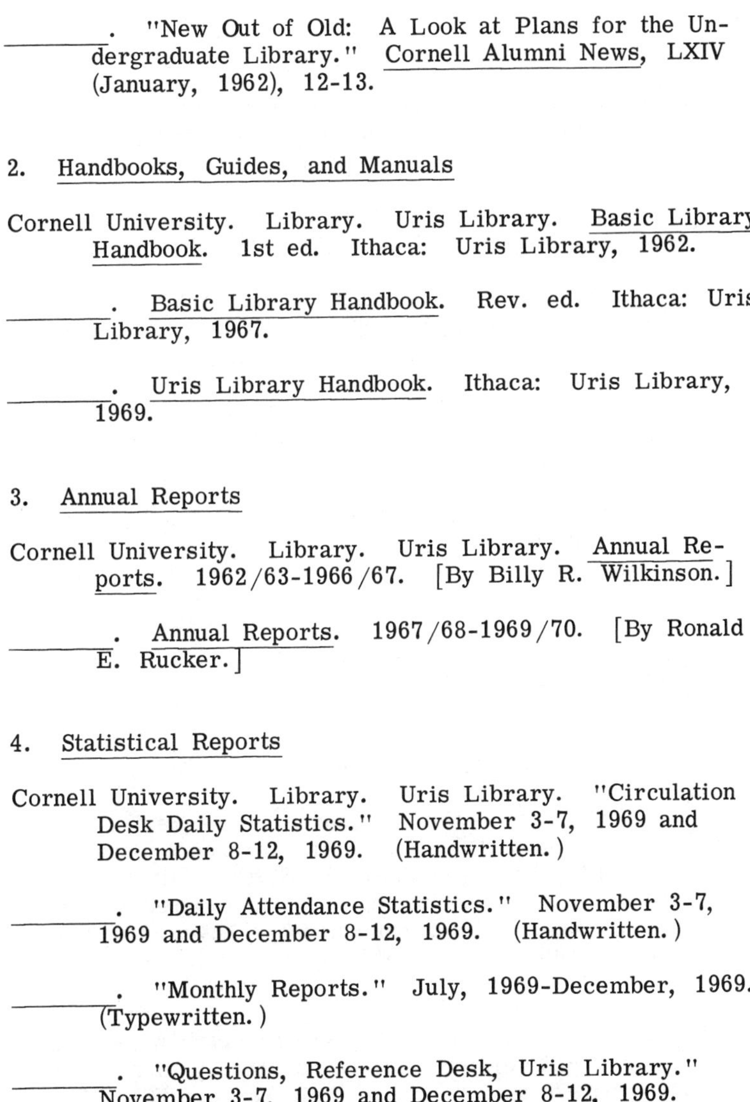

________. "New Out of Old: A Look at Plans for the Undergraduate Library." Cornell Alumni News, LXIV (January, 1962), 12-13.

2. Handbooks, Guides, and Manuals

Cornell University. Library. Uris Library. Basic Library Handbook. 1st ed. Ithaca: Uris Library, 1962.

________. Basic Library Handbook. Rev. ed. Ithaca: Uris Library, 1967.

________. Uris Library Handbook. Ithaca: Uris Library, 1969.

3. Annual Reports

Cornell University. Library. Uris Library. Annual Reports. 1962/63-1966/67. [By Billy R. Wilkinson.]

________. Annual Reports. 1967/68-1969/70. [By Ronald E. Rucker.]

4. Statistical Reports

Cornell University. Library. Uris Library. "Circulation Desk Daily Statistics." November 3-7, 1969 and December 8-12, 1969. (Handwritten.)

________. "Daily Attendance Statistics." November 3-7, 1969 and December 8-12, 1969. (Handwritten.)

________. "Monthly Reports." July, 1969-December, 1969. (Typewritten.)

________. "Questions, Reference Desk, Uris Library." November 3-7, 1969 and December 8-12, 1969. (Handwritten.)

________. "Reserve Desk Statistics." November 3-7, 1969 and December 8-12, 1969. (Handwritten.)

5. Special Reports, Scripts, Minutes, Unpublished Papers, and Miscellany

Cornell University. Library. "Program for the Undergraduate Library." Draft Program, March 26, 1956. Ithaca, 1956. (Mimeographed.)

________. "Program for the Undergraduate Library." July 13, 1959. Ithaca, 1959. (Mimeographed.)

________. Committee on Undergraduate Library Service. Minutes of Meetings, 1966/67. (Typewritten.)

________. Subcommittee on the Undergraduate Library. "First Report of Subcommittee on the Undergraduate Library to the Library Committee." Ithaca, [1959]. (Mimeographed.)

________. Uris Library. "Costs of Remodeling the Building, 1961." [Statement prepared by Harold B. Schell, Assistant to the Director of University Libraries, July 3, 1964.] Ithaca, 1964. (Typewritten.)

________. "Periodical Titles in the Uris Library, September 18, 1963." Ithaca, 1963. (Mimeographed.)

________. "Seating Count, Uris Library, April, 1966." Ithaca, 1966. (Typewritten.)

________. "Selected Reference Sources." [A Series of Bibliographies Prepared by the Reference Department, Uris Library. The Following Seven Bibliographies Have Appeared: "Selected General Reference Sources," "Psychology," "Political Science," "Literature," "History," "Sociology and Anthropology," and "Economics."] Ithaca, 1969. (Mimeographed.)

________. [Script of Untitled Library Orientation Lecture Given by Reference Staff, Uris Library to Freshman English Classes.] Ithaca, Fall Term, 1963. (Typewritten.)

"It's All Happening at the Zoo." [Anonymous Poem Distributed in Uris Library, April, 1968.] (Mimeographed.)

McCarthy, Stephen A. "The Cornell Undergraduate Library." [Proposed Draft of Statement for the Use of Arthur

H. Dean, Chairman, Cornell Board of Trustees.] Ithaca, December 2, 1959. (Typewritten.)

Wilkinson, Billy R. [Text of Untitled Talk to First Meeting of Freshman Class, College of Arts and Sciences, Cornell University, September, 1964, and September, 1965.] Ithaca, 1964. (Typewritten.)

________. "William Henry Miller and the Cornell University Library." Paper read before Cornell Campus Club, Ithaca, November 17, 1964.

D. Reference Department, John M. Olin Library

1. Handbooks, Guides, and Manuals

Material on the Reference Department is included in the items listed under III. B. 2 above.

2. Annual Reports

Cornell University. Library. Olin Library. Reference Department. Annual Reports. 1959/60-1961/62. [By Josephine M. Tharpe.]

________. Annual Reports. 1962/63-1968/69. [By Caroline T. Spicer.]

3. Statistical Reports

Cornell University. Library. Olin Library. Reference Department. "Monthly Reports of the Reference Department, John M. Olin Library." July, 1969-December, 1969. (Typewritten.) [By Caroline T. Spicer.]

________. "Questions Received at Reference Desk, John M. Olin Library." November 3-7, 1969 and December 8-12, 1969. (Handwritten.)

Jebb, Marcia. "Reference Desk Questions, July, 1969, Memorandum to Caroline T. Spicer," [November 5, 1969]. (Typewritten.)

4. Special Reports, Scripts, Minutes, Unpublished Papers, and Miscellany

Cornell University. Library. Olin Library. Reference Department. "A Bibliography of Selected Reference Sources." Ithaca, September, 1967. (Mimeographed.)

________. "Presidential Elections." [Example of a "Library Problem" used by the Reference Department during 1960 Orientation Lectures to Freshman English Classes.] Ithaca, 1960. (Mimeographed.)

________. "Racism and Restructuring, A Selective, Annotated Bibliography of Periodical Articles, 1966-September, 1969." Compiled by Marcia Jebb. Cornell University Libraries Bibliography Series, No. 3. Ithaca, 1969. (Mimeographed.)

________. [Script of Untitled Library Orientation Tour Conducted by Reference Department for Freshman English Classes, Fall Term, 1960.] Ithaca, 1960. (Typewritten.)

IV. Sources for the Study of the Swarthmore College Library

A. The College

1. Books, Essays, and Periodical Articles

Bekavac, Nancy. "Superweek: the Rest of the Year is Nothing Compared to this." Swarthmore College Bulletin, LXV (March, 1968), 23-24.

Boroff, David. "Swarthmore: Use Thy Gumption!" in his Campus U.S.A., Portraits of American Colleges in Action. New York: Harper, 1961.

Lafore, Lawrence D. "Honors at Swarthmore: A Setting in Which Things May Go Well." Swarthmore College Bulletin, LXI (May, 1965), 1-10.

Magill, Edward Hicks. Sixty-five Years in the Life of a Teacher, 1841-1906. Boston: Houghton Mifflin, 1907.

Swarthmore College. Critique of a College, Reports of the Commission on Educational Policy, the Special Committee on Library Policy, and the Special Committee on Student Life. Swarthmore: Swarthmore College, 1967.

________. Faculty. An Adventure in Education: Swarthmore College Under Frank Aydelotte. By the Swarthmore College Faculty. New York: Macmillan, 1941.

Van Til, Jon. "Superweek: Swarthmore at Its Strongest." Swarthmore College Bulletin, LXV (March, 1968), 24-25.

2. Annual Reports

Swarthmore College. President's Report. 1967/68. [By Courtney Smith.]

________. President's Report. 1968/69. [By Edward K. Cratsley, Acting President.]

3. Catalogs, Bulletins, Announcements, Special Reports, and Miscellany

Babbidge, Homer D., Jr. "Swarthmore College in the Nineteenth Century, A Quaker Experience in Education." Unpublished Ph.D. dissertation, Graduate School, Yale University, 1953.

Swarthmore College. Catalogue Issue, 1968-1969, Swarthmore College Bulletin, Vol. LXVI, No. 1, Swarthmore: Swarthmore College, 1968.

________. Catalogue Issue, 1969-1970, Swarthmore College Bulletin, Vol. LXVII, No. 1. Swarthmore: Swarthmore College, 1969.

________. Swarthmore, Swarthmore College Bulletin, Vol. LXII, No. 2. Swarthmore: Swarthmore College, 1965.

________. Swarthmore: Guide to the Campus. Swarthmore: Swarthmore College, 1968.

________. Task Force on Government. "Governance at Swarthmore, Memorandum to the Swarthmore Community." Swarthmore, November 21, 1969. (Mimeographed.)

B. The Library

1. Books, Essays, and Periodical Articles

Blanshard, Brand. "Rules for Readers." Swarthmore College Bulletin, LXV (March, 1968), 12-19.

"Building a College Library--Swarthmore Style." American School and University, XLI (May, 1969), 56-57, 72.

Govan, James F. "The Teaching Library." Paper read before the 55th Conference of Eastern College Librarians, Columbia University, New York, November 29, 1969.

McCabe, Thomas B. "A Diary of the Human Race." Swarthmore College Bulletin, LXV (March, 1968), 11.

"McCabe Library." Swarthmore College Bulletin, LXV (March, 1968), 1-7.

Mason, Ellsworth. "Back to the Cave or, Some Buildings I Have Known." Library Journal, XCIV (December 1, 1969), 4353-57.

"Not Only Magnificent but Enabling...." Swarthmore College Bulletin, LXV (March, 1968), 8-10.

Shaw, Charles B. "Special Collections in the College Library." College and Research Libraries, XVIII (November, 1957), 479-84, 517.

2. Handbooks, Guides, and Manuals

Swarthmore College. Library. Friends Historical Library of Swarthmore College. Swarthmore: Swarthmore College Library, 1969.

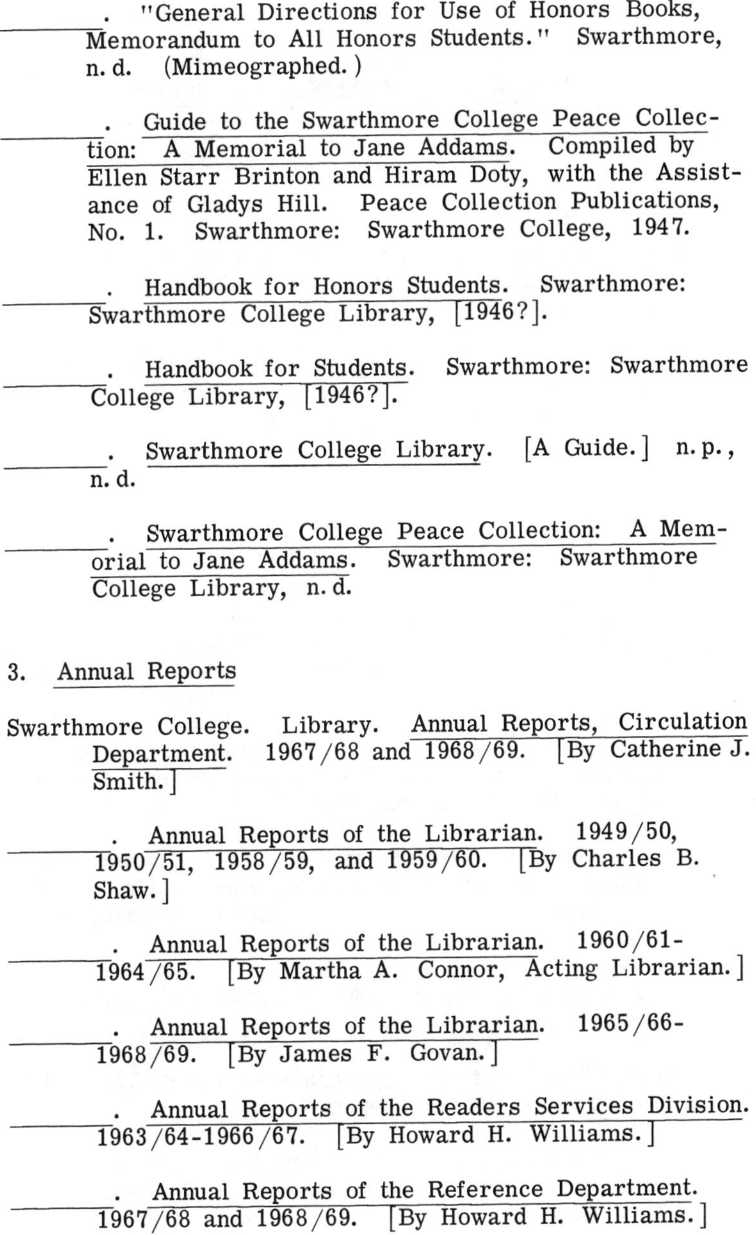

______. "General Directions for Use of Honors Books, Memorandum to All Honors Students." Swarthmore, n. d. (Mimeographed.)

______. Guide to the Swarthmore College Peace Collection: A Memorial to Jane Addams. Compiled by Ellen Starr Brinton and Hiram Doty, with the Assistance of Gladys Hill. Peace Collection Publications, No. 1. Swarthmore: Swarthmore College, 1947.

______. Handbook for Honors Students. Swarthmore: Swarthmore College Library, [1946?].

______. Handbook for Students. Swarthmore: Swarthmore College Library, [1946?].

______. Swarthmore College Library. [A Guide.] n. p., n. d.

______. Swarthmore College Peace Collection: A Memorial to Jane Addams. Swarthmore: Swarthmore College Library, n. d.

3. Annual Reports

Swarthmore College. Library. Annual Reports, Circulation Department. 1967/68 and 1968/69. [By Catherine J. Smith.]

______. Annual Reports of the Librarian. 1949/50, 1950/51, 1958/59, and 1959/60. [By Charles B. Shaw.]

______. Annual Reports of the Librarian. 1960/61-1964/65. [By Martha A. Connor, Acting Librarian.]

______. Annual Reports of the Librarian. 1965/66-1968/69. [By James F. Govan.]

______. Annual Reports of the Readers Services Division. 1963/64-1966/67. [By Howard H. Williams.]

______. Annual Reports of the Reference Department. 1967/68 and 1968/69. [By Howard H. Williams.]

________. Annual Reports, du Pont Science Library. 1961/62 and 1962/63. [By John G. Daly.]

________. Annual Reports of the Science Librarian. 1964/65-1968/69. [By Eleanor A. Maass.]

4. Statistical Reports

Swarthmore College. Library. "Circulation Department Daily Statistics." October 20-24, 1969; November 30, 1969; and December 1-5, 1969. (Handwritten.)

U.S. Office of Education. "Higher Education General Information Survey, Library Collections, Staff, Expenditures, and Salaries." (Swarthmore College's Reports for 1967/68 and 1968/69.)

5. Special Reports, Scripts, Minutes, Unpublished Papers, and Miscellany

Findings of a Committee Appointed to Explore and Report on a Possible Program of Inter-Library Cooperation between Bryn Mawr, Haverford, and Swarthmore Colleges. n.p., 1945. [Members of Committee: Henry B. Van Hoesen, Brown University Library; Fremont Rider, Wesleyan University Library; and Rudolph H. Gjelsness, University of Michigan Library. Known as the "Van Hoesen Report."]

Swarthmore College. "Report of the Special Committee on Library Policy." Swarthmore College. Critique of a College. Swarthmore: Swarthmore College, 1967, 333-461.

________. Library. "New Books." 1969- . (Mimeographed.)

________. "Swarthmore College Library Budget, 1969/70." Swarthmore, 1969. (Typewritten.)

________. News Office. "Swarthmore College to Dedicate McCabe Library." [News Release.] Swarthmore, November 27, 1967. (Mimeographed.)

V. Sources for the Study of the Earlham College Library

A. The College

1. Books, Essays, and Periodical Articles

Cadbury, William E., Jr., and Wilson, Everett K. "Earlham College." Struggle and Promise: A Future for Colleges. By Morris Keeton and Conrad Hilberry. New York: McGraw-Hill, 1969, 282-302.

Cottle, Thomas J. "A Learning Place Called Earlham." Change, The Magazine of Higher Education, III (Jan.-Feb., 1971), 52-59.

Earlham College. Barron's Profiles of American Colleges. Woodbury, N. Y.: Barron's Educational Series, Inc., 1969.

"Freshman Humanities Discussion: Where Opinions Really Matter." Earlhamite, XC (Winter, 1969), 13-20.

"Freshman Humanities: An Explanation." Earlhamite, XC (Winter, 1969), 13.

Jenkins, Wendy. "A Day in the Life of a Student." Earlhamite, XC (Winter, 1969), 34-35.

Thornburg, Opal. Earlham, The Story of the College, 1847-1962. Richmond, Indiana: Earlham College Press, 1963.

Wanner, Susan. "A Day in the Life of a Faculty Member." Earlhamite, XC (Winter, 1969), 33-34.

Woolpy, Jerome. "General Biology Seeks Relevance." Earlham Post, XXV (October 14, 1969), 5.

2. Annual Reports

Earlham College. President's Annual Report. 1968-1969. [By Landrum R. Bolling.]

________. Office of Admissions. The 1969 Report to Principals, Headmasters, and Guidance Counselors. Richmond, Indiana: Earlham College, 1969.

3. Catalogs, Bulletins, Announcements, Special Reports, and Miscellany

Earlham College. Earlham, A Campus Guide. Richmond, Indiana: Earlham College, n. d.

________. Earlham College Catalogue, 1968-1970. Richmond, Indiana: Earlham College, 1968.

________. "Earlham's Values and Standards." [Sixth Draft.] Richmond, Indiana, October 14, 1969. (Mimeographed.)

________. Biology Department. "Class Assignment for General Biology Course." Richmond, Indiana, 1969. (Mimeographed.)

________. [Objectives of General Biology Course.] Richmond, Indiana, 1969. (Typewritten.)

________. Eastern Indiana Center. Bulletin of General Information. Richmond, Indiana: Eastern Indiana Center, [1968].

B. The Library

1. Books, Essays, and Periodical Articles

Agard, Robert M. "Earlham's A-V Program." Library Journal, LXXXV (February 15, 1960), 743.

Bolling, Landrum R. [The New Lilly Library.] Earlhamite, LXXXIV (July, 1963), 2.

"Construction Underway on New Library; Million Dollar Building to Be Center of the Entire Educational Program." Earlhamite, LXXXIII (April, 1962), 3.

"Earlham College Board of Trustees Approve Site and Plans for Million Dollar Library." Earlhamite, LXXXI (October, 1960), 3.

Farber, Evan I. "Attention to Details in Planning Makes a 'Most Considerate' Library." College and University Business, (March, 1964), 58-61.

________. "Earlham's 'Considerate' Library." Library Journal, LXXXVIII (December 1, 1963), 4561-64.

________. "Reference Service." Earlham College Library Booklist, (June 10, 1965), 2.

________. "Where Students Meet Books." Earlhamite, LXXXIX (Autumn, 1968), 6-8.

________, and Shore, Philip. "High School Students and the College Library." Library Occurrent, XXI (September, 1964), 164-66.

"The Lilly Library." Earlhamite, LXXXIV (July, 1963), 13.

"Lilly Library Dedication." Earlhamite, LXXXIV (October, 1963), 4-5, 22.

Kennedy, James R. "Integrated Library Instruction." Library Journal, XCV (April 15, 1970), 1450-53.

________. "Library Instruction." GLCA [Great Lakes Colleges Association] Librarians' Newsletter, I (December, 1966), 1-2.

Sweitzer, John H. "Lilly Library Built with Tender Loving Care." Earlhamite, LXXXIV (April, 1963), 4.

Thornburg, Opal. "The Role of the Archives at Earlham." Earlhamite, XC (Spring, 1969), 10-12.

2. Handbooks, Guides, and Manuals

Earlham College. Library. Library Handbook, Lilly Library, 1969/70. Richmond, Indiana: Earlham College Library, 1969.

3. Annual Reports

Earlham College. Library. *Annual Report of the Archivist and Historian of Earlham College.* 1968/69. [By Opal Thornburg.]

________. *Annual Reports of the Documents Librarian.* 1966/67 and 1968/69. [By Leo Chang.]

________. *Annual Reports of the Librarian.* 1963/64, 1964/65, and 1968/69. [By Evan I. Farber.]

________. *Annual Reports of the Reference Librarian.* 1962/63 and 1963/64. [By Donald L. Siefker.]

________. *Annual Reports of the Reference Librarian.* 1964/65 and 1965/66. [By James R. Kennedy.]

________. *Annual Reports, Technical Services.* 1965/66. [By Philip D. Shore.]

4. Statistical Reports

Earlham College. Library. [Attendance in Library Before and After the Opening of the Runyan Center, 1967/68 and 1968/69.] Richmond, Indiana, 1969. (Typewritten.)

________. "Lilly Library Daily Circulation Count." October 13-17, 1969 and November 17-21, 1969. (Handwritten.)

________. "Lilly Library Circulation Statistics." 1967/68 and 1968/69. (Mimeographed.)

________. "Resume of One-Day (May 9, 1961) Study of Library Use." Richmond, Indiana, 1961. (Typewritten.)

________. [Seven-Day Survey of Reference Questions, November 13-19, 1964.] Richmond, Indiana, 1964. (Handwritten.)

U.S. Office of Education. "Higher Education General Information Survey, Library Collections, Staff, Expenditures, and Salaries." (Earlham College's Reports for 1965/66-1968/69.)

5. <u>Special Reports, Scripts, Minutes, Unpublished Papers, and Miscellany</u>

Earlham College. Library. "Basic Reference Sources in Lilly Library for Papers on the Amarna Revolution, Hammurabi's Code, the Rosetta Stone, and Stonehenge." [Annotated Bibliography Given to Eastern Indiana Center's Course in Western Civilization.] Richmond, Indiana, October, 1969. (Mimeographed.)

_______. "History of Science, Basic Reference Sources in the Lilly Library." [Annotated Bibliography Given to Interdepartment Course 60: History of Science.] Richmond, Indiana, October, 1969. (Mimeographed.)

[The two bibliographies noted above are examples to represent over 130 bibliographies which have been prepared by Earlham librarians.]

Earlham College. Library. <u>Booklist</u>. 1962-1969. [A Newsletter distributed to Faculty and Others at the College.] "New Books in the Library" is regularly appended to <u>Booklist</u>; "Recent Gifts" is occasionally appended.

_______. "Important Information about Library Instruction." [Material Sent to Each Freshman Entering Earlham College.] Richmond, Indiana, 1969. (Mimeographed.)

_______. "Library Knowledge Test." [Test Given to All Freshmen.] Richmond, Indiana, September, 1968. (Mimeographed.)

_______. "Program for a Library Building for Earlham College." [Richmond, Indiana,] November, 1959. (Mimeographed.)

_______. "Report of Departmental Allocations, November 18, 1969." Richmond, Indiana, 1969. (Typewritten.)

_______. Science Library Notes. Nos. 1-4 (1968-69). [Newsletter distributed to Science faculty.]

________. "Tentative Program for a Library Building for Earlham College." Richmond, Indiana, March 12, 1957. (Mimeographed.)

Farber, Evan I. "Library Instruction Beyond the Orientation Level." Paper read before the 55th Conference of Eastern College Librarians, Columbia University, New York, November 29, 1969.

________. "Library Instruction for the Undergraduate Beyond the Orientation Level: Earlham College Program." Paper read before College Library Section Meeting, American Library Association, Atlantic City, New Jersey, June 26, 1969.

________. [Untitled Draft of a Paper Concerning the Interior and Furnishings of Lilly Library.] Richmond, Indiana, n. d.

Kennedy, James R. "Outline of Earlham's Program of Library Instruction." [Distributed at Meeting of College Library Section, American Library Association, Atlantic City, New Jersey, June 26, 1969.] Richmond, Indiana, June 1969. (Mimeographed.)

Kirk, Thomas G. "A Comparison of Two Methods of Library Instruction for Students in Introductory Biology." Unpublished Master's thesis, Graduate School, Indiana University, 1969.

________. "Guided Exercise for Locating Biological Literature." [Earlham College General Biology Course.] Richmond, Indiana, 1969. (Mimeographed.)

________. "Techniques for Locating Biological Literature." [Earlham College General Biology Course.] Richmond, Indiana, 1969. (Mimeographed.)

Schuerman, John. "The Use of the Language Laboratory, Term 1, 1967." Richmond, Indiana, 1967. (Typewritten.)

Stanley, Ellen L. "The Earlham College Library: A History of Its Relation to the College, 1847-1947." Unpublished Master's thesis, Graduate School, University of Illinois, 1947.

INDEX